HOUSING

CALIFORNIA STUDIES IN
URBANIZATION AND ENVIRONMENTAL DESIGN

HOUSING

THE SOCIAL AND ECONOMIC ELEMENTS

Wallace F. Smith

UNIVERSITY OF CALIFORNIA PRESS

BERKELEY, LOS ANGELES, LONDON · 1971

UNIVERSITY OF CALIFORNIA PRESS
BERKELEY AND LOS ANGELES, CALIFORNIA

UNIVERSITY OF CALIFORNIA PRESS, LTD.
LONDON, ENGLAND

COPYRIGHT © 1970, BY
THE REGENTS OF THE UNIVERSITY OF CALIFORNIA

LIBRARY OF CONGRESS CATALOG CARD NUMBER: 71-86372

FIRST PRINTING 1970
SECOND PRINTING 1971

ISBN: 0-520-01561-4

DESIGNED BY JAMES MENNICK
PRINTED IN THE UNITED STATES OF AMERICA

Respectfully dedicated to the memory of
CATHERINE BAUER WURSTER

CONTENTS

PREFACE

This book is an introduction to economic reasoning for people who are concerned about housing, and it is an introduction to housing issues for people who are trained in economics. Its double premise is that economics is too narrowly understood by most of those who think and argue and write about housing today, and that housing is a more complex commodity than most economists realize. The purpose of the book, therefore, is to provide a meeting ground for the several disciplines which explain and, increasingly, influence the conditions in which urban populations live.

The frame of reference is very large. There is no area of the world nor segment of the population which does not expend some of its limited resources on dwellings. Just as the "economic problem" of resource allocation exists in every culture and in every political system, there exists always a "housing problem" concerning the share of the housing sector in the overall allocation of resources and the shares of individuals in the use of housing resources. This book describes the essential elements of these resource allocation systems, in a manner which is sufficiently general to be of some practical significance anywhere. This search for generality is at the expense of particular applications. It is not an econometric undertaking. If there is a set of useful parameters which emerges from this study, they concern functional elements in the operation of a housing economy rather than quantitative relationships. The "housing problem" does not arise from difficulty in measuring supply or demand, but from the manner in which these forces interact.

The last chapter of the book is about housing problems in urban areas of the United States today. It presents a minimum of statistical information plus commentary to describe both physical and intangible problems that confront the makers of housing policy. The purpose of the chapter is not to suggest that American housing problems and policies can serve as a model for study and action around the world; quite the contrary. This brief review of America's problems sustains the view that each society has its own unique housing issues. The only common element is the purpose of the inquiry.

Housing is a composite, social good. It is not produced or consumed piecemeal. Substantial improvement in housing standards requires extensive restructuring of economic decision-making systems. A housing stock, once created, is a community resource of great importance and, in one way or another, is managed as a whole by the community. The use of one dwelling unit affects the usefulness of others in very material ways. The structure of social, moral, legal, and business relationships in the community is relentlessly relevant to the economics of its housing sector.

The nature of the housing commodity makes this true. The basic resources of which housing is made are land and capital. Land, particularly urban land, is not only limited and indispensable, but it ties people together spatially. Capital is the hard-won foothold in the swamp of subsistence living, which any community is loathe to squander and which only a community can create. Because he must share in the land which defines the community and in the capital which is jointly created by that community, the individual does not have the opportunity to determine his own housing standard. The standards for one and all are determined by a system or set of systems which cross the frontiers of several disciplines and which, in consequence, are too readily unappreciated. The real root of any housing problem is a misunderstanding of its cause.

This book tries to look at those roots.

ACKNOWLEDGMENTS

The argument of this book developed out of rich experiences in the classroom and in research at the University of California over the past decade. Assistance and encouragement from many colleagues in several departments and colleges and the stimulus of concerned, open-minded students played a large role in defining and selecting the issues which are discussed in this book. I am indebted especially to the continuing counsel of Professor Paul F. Wendt, Professor Albert H. Schaaf, Sherman J. Maisel, and Dean William L. C. Wheaton.

The deeper origins of the book involve the perception of housing as an object of important and complex human need. This perception was strengthened and magnified by a distinguished and very kind friend who is now sorely missed by all those who must struggle with vital and difficult problems of housing. So, in a very special way, this book owes its beginnings to the late Catherine Bauer Wurster.

My early concept for the book was limited to the methodology of housing-market analysis, with the intention of providing a tool for market forecasting and for predicting the performance of specific governmental programs related to housing. Professor Chester Rapkin encouraged me to move in the direction of evaluation of both public and private activities and to produce policy guidelines rather than a predictive methodology. His advice enriched the sense of purpose behind the book and increased its meaningfulness.

Perhaps because much of the work on the book was done in Japan, the text reveals a strong interest in comparative business institutions. The great abundance of information on Japanese housing which was provided by many very helpful people in Japan serves to improve the validity of the comparisons made. However, it also suggested that a separate book on housing problems in Japan be undertaken, material for which is now being prepared. Hence the acknowledgment of help from people in Japan will be deferred, pending that later book. One exception, however, must be Professor Genpachiro Konno of Tokyo University and Waseda University, who has been most generous with his help and concern in a much wider sense over many years.

Financial assistance during the sabbatical leave, in addition to that provided by the University of California, came from Resources for the Future, Inc. That organization and the people in it showed the greatest consideration in coping with obstacles which arose, and provided sympathetic criticism of early proposals. Travel funds were provided for me by the Institute for International Studies at the University of California in Berkeley.

The library resources of the Center for Real Estate and Urban Economics have been of great use in relation to the writing of this book. The manuscript was typed by Mrs. Ellen McGibbon, whose careful and interested work helped to straighten out many inconsistencies and sources of confusion.

My wife, Masuko, knows a great deal about how this book got written, but she might disclaim making any contribution to it. People in the book business know better, though.

I think I have produced an objective and factual work. Actually, there may well be substantial errors of fact, and there is undoubtedly room for the reader to believe that the views expressed are biased. For either flaw I assume complete responsibility. No one should take pride in factual errors, and I do not, but no one ought to shy away from defensible positions on some pressing human, social, and economic problems. Ideas, controversy, and candor are very much needed in dealing with urban housing problems today; I do not think that agreement with my expressed point of view will necessarily confirm the usefulness of the book.

HOUSING

1 · ▞

THE NATURE

OF HOUSING

What Is Housing?

There is probably not a single major city in the world without some form of "housing problem." In Los Angeles and Tokyo, in New York and Moscow, in Hong Kong and Paris, in Stockholm and in Brazilia housing is a serious public issue.[1] Novelists have set pessimistic tales in the slums of Victorian England and Czarist Russia. Architects, planners, social reformers, and ordinary city dwellers have raised protests against housing conditions. Governments in every historical epoch have adopted a bewildering variety of measures to cope with widespread dissatisfaction about housing. The problem is durable and well-nigh universal. But what is the problem? What is housing and how much of it does a community need?

SHELTER

Housing is often called "shelter," particularly in textbooks on economics. In some societies this is literally all that housing provides. People in arctic winds and tropical downpours need protection from the elements. Cliff-dwelling Indians in the American southwest sought shelter from their enemies. Shelter itself is certainly a part of what is meant by "housing." Just as certainly it is not all that is meant; and it appears that the simple function

3

of shelter from the elements or from enemies is a relatively minor aspect of housing needs.

Shelter is provided by some primitive societies in the form of a large roof under which all the male members of the community may gather (there is a separate roof for the ladies). Shelter for soldiers is provided in the form of large barracks buildings; and for victims of floods or earthquakes, shelter often takes the form of schoolrooms and gymnasiums. During World War II subway stations played an unexpected role as shelter from bombs and fires.

PRIVACY

These illustrations would probably convince most of us that we mean by "housing" something much more complex than merely "shelter." Privacy is also bound up with the concept of housing, perhaps even as a matter of definition. People desire *separate* shelter, and the separation is probably just as important as protection from the elements. Privacy is a rather difficult concept to define, however, and a suitable interpretation of housing needs and housing problems requires knowledge of the manner in which people define privacy.

Privacy is clearly a social rather than a physical concept. The primitive community with one big roof might conceivably saw the roof into separate pieces. Apart from the effort or expense of providing additional posts on which to set the individual roofs, the housing issue would be one of deciding how many pieces to make out of the one large roof. Here is where social custom enters the picture. Every society has some set of notions about groupings of people who ought to share the same roof. The descriptive term "household" is used to describe such a group, but the normal composition of households varies significantly among cultures.* A man and his wife (or wives) and

---

* The United States Census defines a household as a group of persons, or a single individual, occupying a separate dwelling unit. The unit, in turn, is defined as living space which contains cooking and sanitary facilities for the exclusive use of its occupants. Though the census reports data for families and other sociological groupings, the concept of household in the United States is very elastic, without the presumption that people having certain bonds of kinship will share the same dwelling.

their young children are generally expected to share the same roof. In some societies certain of the married children are expected to remain with their own new families in the parental home, but this is a practice which seems to break down as the community grows affluent. In many cultures widowed or retired parents give up their own dwellings to share those of married children, but this practice, too, seems to give way to general economic progress. In every culture there may be some circumstances under which an unmarried adult leaves the home of his parents to establish his own household or to join a different type of grouping such as a monastery, a convent, an army, or an industrial dormitory. It appears to be increasingly acceptable in prosperous nations for young adults to enjoy the maximum privacy of single-person dwelling units.

Along with the number of persons which constitutes a separate household there is the question of the kinds of living activities or functions which may be carried on within the privacy of the dwelling. Perhaps it is obvious that the "shelter" should be used for sleeping, but many other functions are bound up with the traditional definition of a dwelling or house. The concept of "housekeeping" adds food preparation space and facilities to the house. Actual requirements vary considerably. Housewives in Aztec Mexico spent most of their waking hours preparing food. Housewives in contemporary Japan can telephone to order a prepared meal (complete with dishes and utensils) after their husbands have returned from work or after their dinner guests have arrived.

The dwelling may serve as a workplace for some or all of the family members, but the "seriousness" of the labor seems to diminish with rising economic affluence. In poorer nations the husband often works in a store or primitive factory which is part of the family dwelling. In industrialized countries the executive may bring work home in a briefcase, but the "working man" is more likely to have a "do-it-yourself" workshop at home for pleasure more than for earning family income.

Recreation is a very unstandardized element of housing need. In subsistence economies there is little, if any, recreation to be concerned about, since all the waking hours must be given over to labor. As societies advance economically, recreation outside the home seems to become customary and there appear to be such substantial "economies of scale" (i.e. the efficiency of providing entertainment to large groups of customers at once) that group or communal recreation has become one of the principal hallmarks of urban civilization. Nevertheless, events in the present century seem to suggest that a significant fraction of recreation activities are being brought into the home. Television and recorded music are added to book-reading as home-based recreation in prosperous nations, to the dismay of some but to the pleasure of most.

Private sanitary facilities—toilets, washbasins, baths, laundry equipment, and kitchen running water—migrate very quickly into individual dwelling units as a society's economic standard rises. Though most of the world's population today does not enjoy the private use of all facilities, and while some people in the wealthiest societies may not consider these things personally necessary, there seems to be a nearly universal opinion that every separate household should have a full complement of sanitary facilities for its exclusive use.

We could make a longer list than this of living activities which are commonly thought of as part of the concept of "housing privacy." This subject is the architect's realm, however, and we can leave the further study of these functions to him. For our purposes it suffices to note that a "housing unit" is generally thought of as a collection of facilities for the exclusive use of a separate social group called a household, and that the set of facilities involved in this concept seems to change in fairly predictable ways as general living standards rise.

There is an additional dimension of housing privacy which is of vast importance in the way in which cities are built. Privacy for the household may be achieved by surrounding each household with open space or by separating households with walls, or by some combination of these two methods. As urban populations multiply, it becomes more and more difficult to provide each household with a shield of open space, so walls are substituted. Walls are not perfect substitutes for open space, however, for a number of reasons. A yard is a place for recreation as well as a buffer against the activities of neighbors. Open space around individual dwelling units is generally considered to be the most desirable method of providing light and air for those units. Walled-off apartments are more difficult to buy and sell than are plots of ground (for legalistic but very practical reasons). Human beings whose ancestry is based in rural areas often simply "feel" the need for an individual bit of ground which they need not share with other households.

LOCATION

If privacy were the only important attribute which a unit of shelter had to possess, we might solve the problem by dispersing households over the entire landscape. This would be an expensive way to learn another major attribute of housing, which is its relative *location*. Urban households usually derive their incomes from employment which requires daily trips between home and workplace. There is a practical limit to the length of such trips so that the dispersal of households is held in check by the desire to economize on the time and cost of transportation. Urban households must make regular trips to other urban locations as well—for school, shopping, recreation, and general household management. Despite their separateness, urban households also usually like to visit one another. The location of the dwelling unit relative to the place of employment and to "everything else" is thus one of its most significant features. A household not only requires housing which is private, but which is also reasonably close to places of employment and other urban activities, requirements which can seem contradictory.

The quality of location depends very much upon the availability and cost of transportation to other urban locations. Fortunately, transportation is "improved" by increases in purchasing power (permitting families to own automobiles and to pay for fast highways) and by technological progress. A city can expand, providing the same amount of privacy to each of an increasing number of households without imposing unacceptable transportation costs if transport systems are improved and/or incomes rise so that more can be spent for transportation. "Housing" does not mean much to an urban family unless it knows where that housing is located and what transportation systems are available. Location is part of the urban housing commodity.

ENVIRONMENTAL AMENITIES

A third major dimension of the housing commodity can be given the long but descriptive name of "environmental amenities." These are the characteristics of the surrounding area which affect the desirability of the residence. Families are concerned not only with the distance to a school for their children, but also with the quality and prestige of that school. Since the quality of schools varies widely in most American cities, American families tend to consider this factor most carefully when searching for a home. To a lesser degree, perhaps, the quality of local fire and police protection are also considered. Other urban services such as parks, playgrounds, and hospitals influence the relative desirability of housing. The physical appearance of the neighborhood—trees and grass belonging to prospective neighbors, the view obtained from the house in question, and the peculiarities of the neighborhood's climate (temperature, wind, fog, etc.) are also part of the housing "package."

One very subjective kind of "environmental amenity" which can nevertheless play a most important role in housing is the social character of people in the neighborhood. Absolute privacy is neither desirable nor possible for most city dwellers. Association with neighbors will be a necessary and perhaps valuable part of living in a particular dwelling unit. Sometimes the social desirability of a neighborhood is significantly influenced by the past history of the area; some locations acquire "fashionable" reputations and others suffer from a relatively bad name. For better or worse, the real and the traditional social status of the area will rub off on families moving into it.

Environmental amenity can be influenced to an important degree by community programs of land-use control. If small factories and eating places are mixed in with residential uses, the resulting noise, congestion, and visual appearance may make housing in the area less attractive and enjoyable. The placement of utility lines and traffic control devices may be beneficial or harmful, depending upon the skill and authority exercised by public officials. Local laws governing the passage of pedestrians or vehicles across otherwise private land have substantial meaning for the would-be residents of the area.

INVESTMENT

For a small but influential fraction of the world's urban population housing is an investment as well as a place to live. The fact that a family owns its home gives that family a degree of security in a psychological and financial sense. Psychologically, ownership is an extension of the attribute of privacy, for the home-owning household can be confident that its dwelling will not be entered by others except by invitation and that the family will not be required to surrender the dwelling to others. Financially, ownership is not only a symbol of wealth, but as a practical matter, the most important actual wealth which most families ever manage to accumulate.

Home-ownership, like other forms of property rights, is greatly dependent upon the laws and business practices of the community. In some societies tenants enjoy security against eviction to such an extent that they are virtually owners. (Indeed, such "property rights" are frequently bought and sold.) In certain societies, legal ownership is subject to occasional public expropriation so that its security attributes are seriously diluted. The value of financial investment in a home may increase due to a sudden rise in demand for property in the area, or it may fall as the neighborhood becomes less desirable or as the community as a whole suffers an economic decline. Homes which are likely to rise in value and which are relatively secure from various types of expropriation are more desirable than other physically comparable homes. The investment quality of a home, then, is very complex, and each home has to be studied from this point of view.

Sheer physical shelter—a roof over one's head—is certainly an element of housing and it may require no more in terms of economic resources to build an attractive, secure, private dwelling than it costs to provide an exposed, insecure, uncomfortable eyesore. Sometimes the resource cost for the better house may even be less. From the standpoint of the general economist, then, housing is just a lump of resources which might as well be called "shelter." As far as the rest of us are concerned, particularly those of us who want to understand the "economics of housing," the attributes of privacy, location, environmental amenity, and investment are at least as important as the resource bulk of the housing commodity—the wood and plaster, pipes and wires. Housing economics involves an investigation of many physical, social, and psychological dimensions which the housing commodity assumes in the eyes of the consuming public. It is deceptive to attempt to reduce problems of housing economics to a single scale of input costs because the real efficiency of the housing sector depends on a complex balancing of personal requirements, community institutions, and spatial linkages, in addition to considerations of resource costs.

The Dual Nature of the Housing Sector

In most nations the housing sector—the portion of the economic system which is concerned with the production, management, and distribution of housing—is a blend of private enterprise and government activity. The nature of the mix varies greatly from nation to nation, but the role of government is substantial even in those countries which generally allow the marketplace the greatest freedom in making economic decisions. Public and private components of the housing sector are generally so closely interdependent that the housing sector may be said to have a dual decision-making system. It is important to understand why this is so. The dual nature of the housing sector makes economic analysis of housing both more difficult and more necessary.

INSTITUTIONS

The private component of the housing sector—that is, the whole range of business activities associated with housing—is heavily dependent for efficient operation upon the existence of a set of laws, institutions, and public agencies. It cannot function effectively unless the community has recognized and clarified the concept of real-property ownership. A builder will not build, a lender will not finance, and a family will not buy a dwelling unless the legal system of the community assures each party that the rights thus acquired will be respected. The builder can then expect payment from the purchaser, the lender can expect some security of his investment, and the family can expect relatively undisturbed occupancy of the home. The first necessity for the operation of a housing market is a system which defines rights pertaining to property and establishes a set of procedures for the transfer of these rights.[2] The private housing entrepreneur cannot create these legal institutions. He is dependent upon the community to do so.

In a similar way the large financial aspects of housing development and purchase require the existence of financial institutions which accumulate the savings of some households and business firms and advance these funds to other households and firms. Financial institutions are thus middlemen in a commodity of such vast importance that governments in all countries either operate these financial institutions directly or regulate them extensively. Housing requires special kinds of financial institutions because the product involved is so durable and heterogeneous. Housing finance involves very long-term investment in a form of wealth which is not very liquid—which is not readily salable. Housing is so unstandardized that investors' interests in housing loans or equity are also relatively difficult to sell. There are many technical aspects of housing and the housing market which suggests that a certain degree of specialization in housing by some financial institutions will improve the efficiency of the sector.

The ability of the housing stock to provide good housing services to its occupants depends in part, as we have earlier noted, on the transportation system, the schools, other public facilities, and upon the manner in which nearby land uses are controlled. In most cases the private housing entrepreneur is not able to provide these elements of the housing product or to improve them. He is dependent upon the community's public agencies to assist him in making housing available to the market.

The housing product is so complex that it is difficult to build and difficult to sell. Through incompetence, indifference, or greed, builders might use materials which would ultimately be hazardous or inadequate for the occupant. Occupants and purchasers seldom have the knowledge about housing which is needed to detect all such flaws. It is common for public agencies to assume some of the burden of inspection, either at the time of construction by imposing limitations upon builders or at the time of sale by requiring ethical behavior on the part of housing brokers.

Despite a generous assortment of public agencies and activities to provide good background conditions, the private housing market may be inefficiently organized. Too few entrepreneurs may be willing to enter the various complementary parts of this industry and those who do might lack knowledge about conditions of demand or of cost which they should have in order to serve themselves and the public well. Even an ideal set of supportive institutions will not guarantee the effective performance of the private housing industry. The housing "chain" is as strong as its weakest link.

PUBLIC WELFARE

Given the best possible set of supporting institutions and well-informed and motivated entrepreneurs, the private component of the housing sector ordinarily does not serve all the housing needs which the public, as a community, may feel should be served. Low-income families are an obvious case in point. The most effective and efficient private housing industry will not meet a housing need which is not backed up with purchasing power. Here, and in similar situations involving public concern about unmet housing needs, the public component of the housing sector acquires an additional function. It must change the nature of demand by means of subsidy or of supply by means of public investment (also involving subsidy) so that these nonmarket needs are satisfied.

Thus, the private component of the housing sector is unable to provide certain legal and financial institutions which are necessary for its own efficient functioning, and it is unable to provide for some housing requirements which communities—because housing is a necessity of physical and social life—feel must be met. The public component of the housing sector has a twofold function; it must act to facilitate the efficient operation of the private component and it must subsidize the housing sector as a whole in some fashion to overcome problems of socially inadequate market demands for housing.

INTERACTIONS

It follows that the development of public policy with respect to housing requires a particular type of economic analysis. The establishment of legal and financial institutions will stimulate private housing activity, while public subsidies will change the direction of that activity as well as stimulating it further. In formulating a public program for housing, it is necessary to know not only the current limitations or faults of the private housing-market equilibrium, but also the manner in which that equilibrium would be changed by particular proposals for government activity in connection with housing. The private portion of the sector will respond to changes in institutions or in purchasing power available for housing. The responses may or may not produce the overall changes in the supply and use of housing which is contemplated by the public program. The manner in which a set of institutions is created may freeze a portion of the nation's capital market into a structure which is not best suited to the nation's long-term needs. Housing activities may, at one time or another, be overstimulated or depressed by the very institutions and systems which were intended to make it perform efficiently. The form of a subsidy to needy families or to accomplish other social purposes may produce private housing-market responses which aggravate those needs still further. Public policy does not simply amend what has taken place in the market. It acts as a catalytic agency to alter the very character of that market.

Public programs cannot be designed merely by noting the inadequacies in the present housing situation. This is necessary information, but between this information and the set of housing conditions which public policy intends to create, a large, complicated process intervenes which must be taken into account in the design of effective public programs. The process is the restoration of market equilibrium after the initial equilibrium has been invalidated by a public activity or set of activities.

The housing economist's task is to discover and describe

this process of reaching a new equilibrium. He must be able to anticipate the various significant alterations in the total housing sector which will result from some publicly inspired changes. If possible, the economic analysis should be expressed in a manner which conveniently indicates the one among various alternative public policies that will achieve a particular result most successfully.

The dual nature of the housing sector results from qualities inherent in the housing commodity and in social attitudes about this commodity. The housing sector will not behave efficiently or satisfactorily without a variety of vital and substantial public activities. Housing-market economic analysis requires an understanding of the interaction between private activities and public activities so that public activities will be able to accomplish their purpose. The public purpose in connection with housing is to secure for that sector as much of the nation's economic resources as the well-being of the whole community requires and to encourage the efficient use and appropriate distribution of these resources. In this complex, large, and dualistic sector the housing economist has a great responsibility. He must create and explain flexible, broad-gauged, analytical methods which will facilitate the formulation of business plans and public programs associated with housing.

Some Concepts of Special Importance

There are some relatively obscure terms which occur often in the discussion of housing economics. It is desirable to clarify the more important of these terms at an early stage, since a clear understanding of them will often be critical to the thread of the argument in the following chapters.

ECONOMIC LIFE

"Economic life" is one of these concepts. Housing is a durable capital good, and its durability raises a host of difficult economic and business questions. Unlike an apple or a gallon of gasoline, ordinarily consumed within a short space of time, a housing unit continues to perform valuable economic services to consumers over an extended period. Some housing structures in Europe have been in use for many centuries, and we can say at a minimum that housing is one of the most long-lived things produced by an economic system. Dams, bridges, and office buildings are among the forms of capital wealth which, on the average, are expected to be useful longer than a typical residential structure, but machines, transportation equipment, and some types of nonresidential buildings are expected to be used up in a shorter period of time. Among the commodities which ordinary consumers use, housing is certainly the most durable.

We might want to ask at once how the economic life of a house is determined, and why—as a matter of common practice—housing is made in such a durable way. Some thoughtful critics, indeed, have said that housing structures are much *too* durable for the good of the community; this is an argument which can be taken up at a later point.[3]

One consequence of durability is that when the commodity is created or sold, its value must be estimated by forecasting its earning capacity over an extended future period. Houses will be rented on a monthly or yearly basis or, if they are owner-occupied, the occupants will receive "housing services" in each time period. The present value of a dwelling is not the simple sum of such future rents or the sum of future housing services, but rather an amount derived by the process of capitalization from these expected future receipts. The theory and techniques of capitalization are involved and they sometimes prove confusing to even the most experienced housing entrepreneurs. A short description of some capitalization methods will be presented in a later chapter.

Of course, when a builder or investor estimates the present value of a structure, he must make some assumptions about how long into the future the building will be useful and productive of housing services. This is the question of "economic life" in its narrowest sense. The entrepreneur must make a relatively exact prediction of how long the building will be useful. This is only in part dependent upon the physical durability of the structure, for a sound building may not be in demand, a dilapidated building may have a ready market, and the land which the dwelling occupies may suddenly become so valuable for some other use that a useful structure will be demolished.

The economic life of a house thus differs in a significant way from that of, say, an electric light bulb. There is not a simple physical event which determines that the house should be replaced, but rather a combination of conditions related to the market for the house and for the land under it.

A durable dwelling can serve a succession of households during its economic life—households which can afford or are willing to pay different amounts of money for that dwelling. This is an additional dimension of the forecast which is necessary to establish the present value of a housing unit. The builder or investor must foresee changes in the relative desirability of the housing unit as time goes by and as market conditions—the number, income, and housing preferences of households, and the quantity and quality of competitive housing supply—undergo change.

Another difficulty inherent in the durability of dwellings is that they may be at various times susceptible to different types or degrees of repair, remodeling, or neglect. Under some circumstances it may be good sense for both business and economic or social reasons to stop spending money on physical maintenance of the structure, while there may be other circumstances which call for major increases in expenditures for upkeep or substantial capital improvements to the building. Each such possibility requires forecasts of the future earning capacity of the property under hypothetical new conditions and the reduction of these forecasts to present capital values.

The concept of economic life which applies to housing is quite different from the concept which is frequently applied to industrial equipment. A particular machine is sometimes said to be "obsolete"—i.e. at the end of its economic life—when a new machine can do the same job in a more efficient way, sufficiently more efficient to justify scrapping the old machine. The focus of the replacement question for industrial equipment is on the *product,* the manufactured good, which is assumed to be constant through a succession of machines. In housing, on the other hand, the focus is on the capital good which produces over its lifetime a succession of different "products" as different types of households make use of it. The industrial entrepreneur keeps the product unchanged while he replaces his capital equipment. The housing entrepreneur, in essence, keeps the capital equipment while he changes his "product" by selling the housing services in a succession of different markets. Definitions of economic life derived from industrial plant-management practices are not appropriate in the study of housing.

One reason for this is the locational fixity of a housing structure. A machine which is to be replaced can be hauled away from the factory and a new one installed. A house or apartment building which is changing its use does not move. The users move. It is natural, then, to focus our attention on that immobile capital good, particularly since the locational pattern of housing structures is an important determinant of the physical form of the city, and we have particular interest in this overall urban form.

Durability results in one form of differentiation of the housing stock. Older dwellings will generally be less desirable than new dwellings of the same type. The passage of time will make the older buildings relatively obsolete and years of use will cause the older buildings to become less sturdy and less attractive. If some houses are constructed each year, then the housing stock of the community will necessarily include dwellings with different degrees of desirability. (Of course, the stock may be further differentiated by differences in the design of new structures.) An interesting and important question about the operation of the housing market arises from this differentiation. Which households will live in the more desirable dwellings? Since the least desirable dwellings—the oldest and least well maintained—may be considered by the community as "inadequate" housing for any household, what is the appropriate way to narrow the range of housing differentiation? Will a law prohibiting the use of dwellings below a certain minimum standard have the desired effect? There is a wide variety of issues and proposals related to the qualitative differentiation of the housing stock, and this differentiation arises in part from the durability of the housing commodity.

The fact that housing is a durable commodity means, furthermore, that it is an investment good. It represents capital wealth in the same sense that a factory and its machinery are capital. Capital must be created and "paid for" before it can be put to use and so it cannot come into existence unless "savings" have been accumulated. To create or improve a stock of housing requires that sufficient saving must occur in the society and that this saving must be diverted from other investment opportunities. Housing cannot be paid for as it is consumed. Someone must pay for it and then make it available for use. That someone is an "investor" of one sort or another, a person or agency with savings to be used and with the knowledge to comprehend investment opportunities in housing. The housing sector of the economy is indissolubly linked with the financial sector, and the study of housing economics requires a study of the structure and capacities of financial institutions.

RENT

The term *rent* has already been used in this discussion of housing. It is, of course, a very familiar word and it has been used thus far in its ordinary sense—the payment made by a tenant for the right to live in a dwelling which belongs to another. To the economist, however, the word "rent" conveys something more than this, and difficult misunderstandings may arise in the following discussions unless this deeper significance of the concept of "rent" is appreciated by the reader.

To begin with, economists have traditionally given the name "rent" to the price of a commodity which is fixed in supply.[4] Land, whether agricultural or urban, fits in this category. Housing or other buildings are relatively fixed in supply, because they are so durable that the size of the stock changes very slowly. Sometimes labor also receives a "rent" if it is so specialized that good substitutes are not available. A movie star's high income is a "rent" in the language of the economist.

The problem with rent is to understand why it should be paid at all. The equilibrium price of something which is absolutely fixed in supply is determined entirely by demand. If I own an acre of land in the wilderness, the demand for it will be very limited and my rental income will be very modest. If this acre

of land is located at the center of a large, prosperous city, however, the demand will be so great that rent from this land will
provide me with a handsome income. The land is a free gift of
nature, however, wherever it is located. It cost nothing to produce and the supply cannot be expanded at any price. If nothing
at all is paid as rent for the land, this acre continues to exist
and to be useful. Why should I receive a handsome income from
rent-payers if I happen to own some city land? Why should the
city landowner receive more than the owner of wilderness land?
The existence of rent raises questions of equity or fairness. Why
should one owner receive more rent than another owner receives?
Why should tenants pay for something which is essentially "cost-
less?"

The issue of equity is obscured somewhat by two notions
about "cost." The owner of a building may feel that the rents he
collects are only a fair return on the price he paid for the building, that is, on his cost of acquiring the property. This investment
cost, however, did not represent a use of physical resources and
so it is not a "cost" in the economist's sense. The price of an
existing building may be said to represent the capitalized value
of the rents expected from that building, using "rents" in our
specialized sense of a payment in excess of resource cost. The
present owner of a building has simply paid the previous owner
in advance much or all of the expected future economic rent
from the property. A transfer in ownership seems to disguise,
but does not really change, the "unnecessary" nature of rental
payments because financial investment costs are transfers of
wealth rather than sacrifices of physical resources.

Suppose, however, that the present owner of a building was
responsible for having it constructed in the first place. Certainly,
buildings, unlike land, can be created out of other resources and
these resources have real economic cost. Are not rent payments
necessary to recover these real costs? The property owner would
certainly argue that they are.

Unfortunately for his argument, the real costs incurred in
constructing a building must be considered "sunk" for business
and economic purposes. If the building does not earn rent, the
costs cannot be withdrawn. There is no alternative, once the

building has been completed, but to let it be used for whatever rent it will bring. The level of rents has no necessary relation to the historical costs incurred. An extravagantly constructed building may represent costs far greater than the capitalized value of market-determined rents, and a building constructed just before an inflation may produce rents greatly in excess of its historical cost. Rent is not dependent on historic building costs, and historic costs thus do not require that tenants pay rent to occupy the building. Again we must ask, why should rents be paid?

The answer lies in the word "rationing." If some useful commodity is fixed in supply, then it becomes important in both an economic and a business sense to use that commodity as fully and effectively as possible. If no rents were charged for the use of land or buildings, these commodities might be used by people who derive relatively little advantage from them to the exclusion of people who can use them most beneficially. The high rent asked for land near the center of a city prices it out of the agricultural market and limits that land to business use, for which it is best suited. Without the rent payment, it might be used as a farm, greatly disrupting the business activities of the city. Economic rent rations a fixed resource by excluding all potential users except the one who derives maximum benefit from that resource. Very broadly, all market prices are rationing devices and economic rent is an important special type. Most prices are also related to resource costs, but there are no resource costs in rents to obscure the rationing function.

It does not follow, of course, that market-determined rents will ration a fixed supply of housing or other goods in a manner which conforms to the community's idea of "fairness." Property owners simply hold out for the best price they can get and the best price for housing usually comes from those families with the highest incomes to spend. Poor families might value the house as much in a psychological sense as a rich family, but the rationing function of the market will award it to the family which offers the most money. A public agency might decide to ration housing on some other basis than market-determined rents and ability to pay, and this often happens. In the absence of a public rationing scheme, however, market-determined economic rents will plan the disposition of the housing stock. For a number of reasons, public rationing programs often tend to approximate the results of market rent rationing in any case. Rents, then, provide some type of indication as to how a fixed supply of dwellings "should" be allocated among households. The market, of course, actually carries out this allocation program as well as planning it.

The payment of economic rent often results in "unearned" incomes to property owners, and this inspires some people to urge the abolition of rents. Property incomes can, however, be taxed away without disturbing the rationing function of rent, as in Henry George's well-known discussion, so long as rents continue to be charged.[5] Even if the property is expropriated by a public agency, its use must be rationed in some manner and such programs usually result in the reinstitution of a rent system in some form. Rent's rationing function does not depend on the creation of property incomes. Rent is a useful rationing device whether or not property incomes are permitted.

EXTERNALITY

The third term on our list is "externality." This refers to the fact that some of the benefits or inconveniences associated with certain types of goods escape the consideration of people engaged in buying or selling those goods. Such costs or benefits are external to the market transaction though they may very significantly affect the efficiency of economic life as a whole. For example, a music store sells a trumpet to a budding soloist. The price covers the cost of the instrument to the store and represents the value of the instrument to the purchaser, but it does not reflect the inconvenience which will be caused to neighbors if the purchaser practices his trumpet playing late at night or early in the morning. If these inconveniences were reflected in the price, that price might be so high that the aspiring musician would be discouraged. On the other hand, the price does not reflect the enjoyment which many people may eventually receive if the purchaser becomes an outstanding artist. The market transaction is between two people. The interests of other people in the community are external to the transaction and are, therefore, ignored even though these other people may derive great discomfort or great pleasure as a result of the transaction. The "audience" is unable to discourage the transaction or to encourage it through the market system. The general public may sometimes act outside the market to prevent private activities from creating external costs or act to encourage private activities which would create external benefits.

Many kinds of private economic activities give rise to such significant external costs and benefits that public control or encouragement of these activities is an established tradition. The use of trucks and automobiles is basically of great benefit to the economy as a whole, so public agencies furnish roads and bridges and sometimes parking space. Misuse or uncoordinated use of motor vehicles, however, can cause damage to property, injury or death to people, and disruption to the flow of traffic; thus, the manner in which private owners of these vehicles can use them is restricted in a great variety of ways. The careless manufacture or sale of food and drugs involves serious risk of external costs, and the use of a stream for the disposal of industrial wastes causes definite external losses. Whenever such situations are brought to the public attention, some form of public regulation or encouragement is likely to be inaugurated. It is probably correct to say that every market transaction involves some kind of external costs and benefits, but public interest is necessarily limited to the more prominent problems.

The private use of urban real estate in general and housing in particular creates unusually important external effects. Many of the things which can be done on or with a piece of urban property will affect neighbors noticeably. A noisy party, burning of rubbish, parking cars on the lawn, a well-kept garden, the color of exterior paint, and the very shape of the dwelling will affect the neighbors' feeling of well-being and very likely their property values. An increase in the number of residential units on a given piece of land will create additional street traffic, possibly worsen parking problems in the area, create demands for additional schools, and, in some degree, affect the opportunities for retail store operation in the neighborhood. This is only a slight sprinkling from the vast pepper-shaker of external effects associated with the use of residential urban land.

There is another side of the coin. Just as the use of one piece of residential land affects the usefulness of the nearby area, the development of the nearby area helps mightily to determine the usefulness of a given piece of residential land (or of an existing dwelling). Individual property owners are gravely concerned about this type of external effect while they may be complacent about the external effects produced by their own actions. This sets the stage for many of the problems of developing and conducting local government.

The significance of externalities in housing activities—indeed, in all urban real estate activities—requires the economist to give attention to factors other than market events in judging the performance of the housing market.

Housing Status

Both the community and the individual household are interested in the housing status of that household. By "housing status" we mean the whole complex of activities, satisfactions, rights, obligations, conveniences, and expectations surrounding the use of a particular dwelling unit by a particular household. In turn, both the community and the individual household participate in determining what this housing status will be.

The accompanying diagram suggests in broad outline what it is that makes up housing status and what the effects of this status are. From the preceding discussion we can identify at least four major components in the housing status of a household. One of these is the structure itself, which in an earlier epoch might be regarded as "shelter" but which in reality provides far more than mere protection from the elements. In the present context, *Structure* means all the physical attributes of the dwelling itself, including the land upon which that dwelling rests. By inference, it includes the natural environment such as the climate; the threat of earthquakes, landslides, or flooding; and the intangible aspects of the building such as the danger of fire, or the practical necessity of performing certain tasks such as removal of snow in the wintertime and fallen leaves in the autumn.

Accessibility and utilities are tangible services rendered to a particular dwelling by the community or businesses operating within the community. To be useful, an urban dwelling must be joined by some form of transportation system to the remainder of the urban area, and the more adequate is the accessibility, the more useful is the dwelling, generally speaking. Some degree of seclusion is admired by most households so that the transporta-

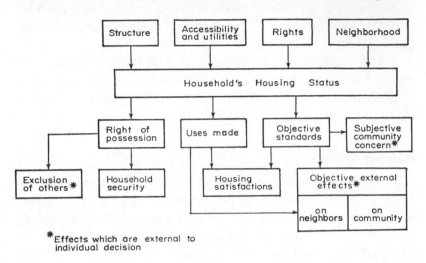

Figure 1
Components and Effects of Housing Status

tion network usually grades off from heavily traveled trunk routes to feeder roads or conveyances, to paths or corridors. Accessibility is also very much a matter of distance in time, space, or expense from points within the urban area which are meaningful to the household. Utilities, such as the provision of water, electric power, gas, sewerage service, telephone connections, and so on must always be provided in some form for each household and the expense of securing them is properly part of the cost of housing. Fire protection, which is ordinarily a public service, might be added to the list of "utilities" without straining the concept, for it is another physical service which adds to the usefulness of the dwelling. Accessibility and utilities are usually provided in return for charges of various kinds—taxes for streets and fire protection, prices for gasoline, fares for public transit, rates for water and electricity, premiums for fire insurance, and so on, though the relationship between expense and benefit is often obscured. From the individual's point of view, however, there is often little choice about whether the services are provided or not. They either exist or they do not, and the schedule of charges for them is relatively inflexible. Accessibility and utilities thus constitute a package of services related to housing and tied rather closely to the particular dwelling.

The next bundle of components is labeled *Rights*. The privilege of enjoying a particular segment of real property is established by the laws of the community and transferred from one individual or household to another in a manner prescribed by law. These rights are almost always subject to restrictions of two broad types, public and private. The community itself limits the uses which may be made of a particular dwelling, for example, the number of persons who may inhabit it or the way in which refuse can be disposed of, and usually reserves the right to appropriate the property for a public use. The community offers occupants of dwelling units the enjoyment of certain public facilities such as schools, streets, fire protection, and the right to participate in community government. Taxes are imposed upon occupants, directly or indirectly, which become inescapable parts of housing cost.

Private individuals are free to varying degrees to surrender rights which they have previously enjoyed to others in exchange for money payments or the promise of money payments, or for reciprocal concessions. The seller or landlord may expect a settlement in cash; a mortgage lender awaits future repayment at which time he will relinquish his rights to the property. A neighboring owner may grant an easement or the household in question may itself grant an easement to some other party. Sellers or landlords may place exact restrictions upon the use or disposition of the dwelling place which is given to the household, such as the prohibition of major architectural changes, the keeping of certain types of animals, or the sub-leasing of an apartment unit. Thus, a whole complex of rights and obligations surrounds the enjoyment of a dwelling by a household, matters which do not affect the physical usefulness of the dwelling or its location, but which do constitute real and important attributes of housing.

The fourth block at the top of Figure 1 is labeled *Neighbor-*

hood. It is in the nature of housing, as pointed out in this chapter, that the immediate physical environment and the society about the household qualifies the kind of enjoyment which the household can expect from its dwelling. The appearance of neighboring houses, the activities of neighbors, and the reputation of the neighborhood within the larger community may add to or detract from the ultimate housing satisfactions to be enjoyed by the occupant household. The expectation of change in any of these factors must also be significant for the household's own evaluation of the dwelling.

To enlarge upon this point we might say that the community as a whole, with its employment opportunities, its commercial facilities, and its complement of cultural and recreational establishments, also gives a particular dwelling characteristics which affect its usefulness. This is so fundamental a fact that it may seem self-evident in any discussion of urban dwellings, but it is a point not to be forgotten. The broad community effects bear upon every dwelling in the community, though not in exactly equal ways, for a shift in employment opportunities, for example, may intensify the demand for one neighborhood or type of dwelling while diminishing the demand for others.

Neighbors and the broader community affect the usefulness of a particular dwelling in a relatively inflexible way. There is very little which the individual householder can do to change the effects of the neighborhood or of the community upon the housing welfare of his family. Whatever their characteristics, benefits, or inconveniences, these things must be taken as they are. The fact that they cannot be changed does not make them unimportant as components of a household's housing situation for they are among the most real and direct elements of housing.

The aggregate of these components is the *Household's housing status*. This status is an assemblage of physical, financial, legal, and social elements of considerable complexity and, therefore, existing in great variety. The whole is called "housing" and it would be a poor housing economist, builder, real estate agent, or city planner who imagined that "housing" is anything simpler. When it becomes known that a community has a "housing problem," we can expect soon to see an entrepreneur or inventor proffering a revolutionary kind of building material, an architect with a tidy sketch, a civil engineer with a new type of public transit vehicle, a city planner with new multicolored maps, a sociologist with a regression equation, a politician with a bill to change property rights, and a housing economist with a financial scheme (probably involving "debentures"). The kind of housing problem which is afflicting a particular city may yield readily to one or the other of these nostrums, but the chances are that by the time that housing has become a problem to the community, it has become a complicated problem. It has to be examined in all its elements and it will probably call for a set of measures subtly integrated and balanced to repair the problem without creating something worse.

Housing status is not inert. The fact that a particular household occupies a certain dwelling does not end the matter, either for that household or for the community. Our diagram shows three first-level effects of housing status, each of which produces a complex of other effects. The first-level effects are the creation of the *Right of possession,* the *Uses* (actually) *made* by the household of the dwelling, and the *Objective* (or largely physical) *standards* of housing enjoyed by the household.

The right of possession is much more than the legal right conferred in the transaction between buyer and seller or between tenant and landlord, for it means that the occupant household comes into a pattern of relationships with its total environment. It enjoys access from that location to other parts of the city, it has the opportunity to call upon community services and to use utilities, and, of course, it becomes a member of a neighborhood. By virtue of the relatively durable nature of housing, this multi-dimensional privilege can be projected into the future. Indeed, it must be, for it is seldom practical for households to consider themselves completely mobile in their housing arrangements. The trouble and expense of moving again will encourage them to put up with any unforeseen or underestimated disadvantages.

In general, these rights and circumstances create a beneficial sense of permanence or household security. A tenant with an unwritten month-to-month lease has less security in his housing arrangements, obviously, than a family with free and clear ownership of its home, but almost any housing status means some kind of predictability.

The right of possession which accrues to one household creates effects upon other households. Those others are excluded so long as the possession by the occupant continues. The significance of this exclusion is most vivid in a period of severe housing shortage, but it is always present. The fact that household A occupies dwelling X means that household B must occupy some other dweling, or none at all. Even in a community with an absolute surplus of dwellings, dwelling X might be more suitable for household B, but the normally prevailing concepts of possession would require that household to get some other accommodation. In turn, household B must enter into a competition for other dwellings, perhaps contributing to an increase in value to be enjoyed by sellers of housing and ultimately excluding still another household from the dwelling which B does obtain. In widening circles these external effects of one act in the housing market spread out across the community, perhaps seeming trivial or not susceptible to improvement. Sometimes, however, it may be of real importance to the community that certain households are not able to occupy particular dwellings. For example, if elderly couples continue to reside in large, family-sized houses after their children have grown up and left, then new child-raising households in the community may have to make do with inconvenient apartments or create a demand for the construction of new family-sized homes in excess of the "real" needs of the community.

The basic point is that the effects of exclusion are borne by people other than the household itself. It is of little moment to the household, when deciding whether to accept an offer of a dwelling, that some other household will be discomfited or some other segments of the housing market will be stimulated. The individual household can ignore such external effects, and, indeed, may be quite unaware of them. The community as a whole cannot ignore them, for the agglomeration of individual decisions influences the community's housing welfare.

By *Uses made* of housing, we mean to suggest the activities carried on by the household once in possession. Members of the family will spend certain amounts of time in the dwelling and near it, engaging in certain house-related functions. Ordinary housekeeping, recreational or avocational pursuits, social behavior, and sometimes gainful employment will occur there. Each household has some unique pattern of activities which it brings into its dwelling, depending upon its own membership, their inclinations, and the nature of the dwelling itself. A solitary bachelor may seem to derive little use from a family-sized house, and a family group of cousins and grandparents may seem to make too much use of their dwelling, but some pattern of activities will emerge in every case. One of the more interesting uses of a dwelling appears during periods of absence of the occupants, for it is a safekeeping place for possessions, a proxy for community participation, and a refuge when the journey is done.

These uses combine with the *Objective standards* of the dwelling—its physical dimensions and characteristics—to define the household's current housing satisfactions. This is to be understood in a sense more psychological than material, much as the economist's concept of "utility." The enjoyment which some middle-aged men derive from an old felt hat, or which some ladies get from a collection of flimsy materials in the form of a hat, is a source of wonder to objective observers, but the impartial economist concedes that if the person says he likes something, then he does; or, if the person is not happy with something of great quality and value, then that thing is not a great source of satisfaction to that person. Individuals are the judges of what they themselves enjoy, and that is the meaning of our phrase about "housing satisfactions."

The community is wont to make its own judgment, however, about the desirability of a particular dwelling for a particular household. In general, the community conscience aims to evaluate dwelling standards just as occupants themselves do, feeling quite certain that the absence of running water is an inconvenience, for example, or that infestation by rodents is a condition which the family itself would like to see corrected. So the community develops a subjective concern for the housing welfare of its members—to varying degrees—but it does so on the basis of objective standards. The modal concept of what "good" housing should be tends to become the prescription for what all housing should be. The elderly widow who weeps at the thought of leaving a firetrap room in a dismal slum is sometimes thought to be shortsighted. In reality, she may fear losing her friends by being helped to move, or she may simply have an emotional attachment to the room in which her husband died. This is a dilemma in the development of community housing standards, for we let our sympathies become aroused by tangible factors when, in truth, sympathy is of an intangible world.

A family's housing and the uses made of it provide objective effects upon the community and neighborhood in addition to any evocation of sympathy. Let the head of the household neglect his front lawn and he will find that he has offended his neighbors. When a youthful apartment-dweller takes up the drum, or a family accumulates refuse in such a way that pests breed, the neighborhood becomes conscious of these things. It may acquiesce or not, but the fact is that most dwellings are too small and too close together to be regarded as the proverbial "castle." Proximity can be a source of pleasure, as in the case of tasteful gardens facing the street, but whether comforting or discomforting, it means that housed families are to some extent living with one another. The rules for sharing neighborhoods are never spelled out exactly, and this only adds the further burden of uncertainty to the inhibitions or constraints of being neighbors. "What would the neighbors think?" the family members ask themselves, and part of the problem is that none of us really knows. The timid person may magnify his neighbors' irritability, and the casual person may dismiss it much too lightly.

One does impart some burden or some joy to those around him, however. This is part of life and as the home is a focus of much living, much of this interpersonal influence originates with the dwelling. The nature of the dwelling and of its surroundings creates a scheme in which behavior by the individual has effects external to him. As with all external effects, those arising from sights, sounds, hazards, or morality in connection with one's use of his residence can be ignored by the individual. It is not reasonable to suppose that members of households can be completely aware of or sensitive to all the direct influences of their housing status upon others. The neighborhood or the community which feels these effects and is significantly disturbed by them may take measures to regulate them.

Objective external effects upon the community rather than the neighborhood are illustrated by the problem of commuter traffic. When an apartment complex is created in a suburban area, a new burden is placed upon the roads or transit facilities linking that area to central districts of commerce and employment. Each householder contributes to the inconvenience of every other when these transportation facilities become overloaded. Families also place differential burdens upon the school system of the community and upon the fire, police, and welfare agencies. Many of the latter costs may not be related to housing status, though a number of social scientists have tried to establish the association (of slum housing to crime and delinquency, for example). The household's choice of residential density affects the gross burden of transportation and communication costs for the community and the scale and incidence of location rents.

Housing is as diverse in its effects as in its components. We can suppose that within the range of its information and choices the household tries to select that dwelling which provides the best combination of current housing satisfactions, long-term housing security, and the enjoyment of other goods. Such choice under the most favorable circumstances may not always produce results which the community at large prefers, and the community has always the power, if not the inclination, to enforce some aspects of its own preference.

This multiplicity of effects makes the housing sector something more than just a means to provide jobs and enlarge the gross national product. It is not the only product which influences by its form and use the quality of community life, but it is a principal example of such products.

2 · ▚

THE HOUSING SECTOR

The first chapter described the housing commodity—the physical object, with its several dimensions and attributes, which is the object of consumer or household demand. The present chapter is concerned with housing in a larger context. We now look at the set of activities and issues in which a community is involved because of the demand by individuals for housing. Thus, we focus not upon the product, but upon the process of providing it. Because housing as a commodity is rather complex and, in essence, a necessity of life, the system which provides it is also complex and large in scale. This system, the collection of activities and interactions which evolves out of the elementary need for places to live, can be called the "housing sector." It is one slice, and a rather large one at that, in the pie chart of aggregate economic production and consumption.

Economics in general is concerned with the allocation of resources. Material resources—land, labor and capital—which can be used to satisfy human desires for consumption, are limited. Desires to consume things which can be created from these resources, on the other hand, are virtually unlimited. Thus, a problem arises of allocating resources among potential uses, and also among potential users in some acceptable fashion. The study of economics, as usually understood, can point to some ways in which a community can avoid wasting scarce resources through illogical systems of allocation, but it does not render any independent judgment about which allocation of resources is "best" for that community. Economics is, in effect, a language which has been developed for discussing the problem of resource allocation. The discussion occurs among the people of the community—the decision-makers of households, business, and government—rather than economists, per se. The economist plays a role not unlike that of an interpreter, helping people to communicate about the use of resources effectively and without destructive misunderstanding. A basic purpose of this book is to develop and present some economic language which is especially suited to discussions about housing.

The allocation of resources occurs at several levels of magnitude. The major distribution is among sectors—food, manufactured goods, machinery, buildings, etc. Even so gross a cataloguing of economic activities can be interesting and useful. We note, for example, that the proportion of total resources devoted to the production of food tends to diminish as a nation or region advances economically. In the postwar reconstruction of Europe, machinery, and then buildings, commanded exceptionally large shares of total available resources. Though housing

1 THE HOUSING SECTOR IN THE UNITED STATES ECONOMY— SELECTED DATA

Gross National Product, 1968	$860.7 *
Gross Private Domestic Investment	127.5
Structures	87.1
New Construction	84.2
Private	56.6
Nonfarm residential	28.4
New housing units	22.4
Personal Consumption Expenditures, 1968	$533.7
Housing services, including imputed value of owner-occupied dwellings	76.2
New Housing Starts, 1968 (000's of units)	1,542.9
Private housing	1,502.9
One-family homes	897.0
Two or more family dwellings	605.9

Sources: *Economic Report of the President* (Washington, D.C., 1969), various tables.
U.S. Department of Commerce, *Construction Reports,* C 20-68-12, Housing Starts, 1969.
Note: Most data are preliminary; figures do not add because only selected entries are shown.
* dollar amounts in billions

is a "necessity," the production of dwellings seems to involve more of a nation's resources as that nation grows in affluence.

The housing "sector" is, in reality, a subsector within the usual major category of "private investment" or "construction" which appears in national and international publications of economic statistics. Housing is of such widespread interest, however, that the share of current output devoted to it is often segregated from other types of construction such as factories, office buildings, and public works. Table 1 presents illustrative data for the United States.

Much that can and will be said about the activities of the housing sector apply to other kinds of investment or construction. Much that is understood by the term "real estate"—the development of land, construction of buildings, exchanging of properties, etc.—applies to offices, stores, and factories as well as to housing, so that in describing the housing sector we inevitably get involved in matters of wider interest.

A Macroeconomic View

The position of the housing sector in the economy as a whole, and some of the important activities within the housing sector are represented in Figure 2. The starting point is *Total current output,* the aggregate volume of valuable goods and services which the national (or local) economy produces in a period of time such as one year. Gross National Product is another term used to described the aggregate. A portion of this current output consists of goods and services which are destined for the housing sector, such as the new houses which are constructed during the period; the land which is prepared for housing; renovation or maintenance of older housing units; personal services in managing existing dwellings, and in facilitating transfers of dwellings both new and old (such as brokerage, appraising, and the processing of loan applications). An important part of the housing sector's share in total output consists of housing services performed by previously constructed dwellings ($76.2 billion worth in 1968), although we may question whether this is really a "resource-consuming" activity. The long, branching arrow on

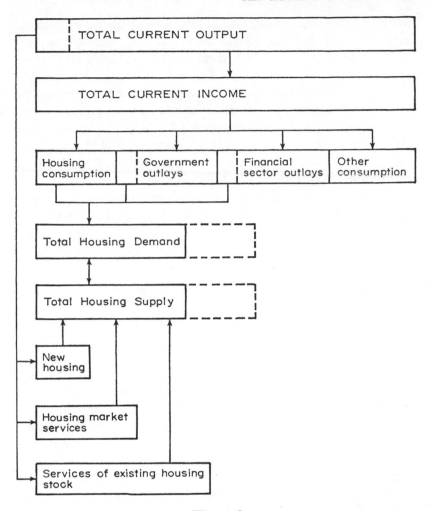

Figure 2
The Housing Sector—a Macroeconomic View

the left side of the diagram shows that these several parts of the community's current economic output become elements of supply in the current housing market.

The production of total current output gives rise to incomes in the form of wages, rents, interest, and profits. These incomes are disposed of for consumption, for saving and investment, and for taxes. A portion of the household consumption expenditure is for housing, but we must be careful to distinguish current expenditures for housing services—that is, for "shelter" enjoyed during the current period—from capital expenditures which reflect changes in ownership of dwellings which will produce services during future periods. *Housing consumption* in the diagram represents only the purchase of current services.

A portion of the income which goes to government is spent on housing. Directly or indirectly government may provide housing for some needy persons in the community or, through tax exemptions, may allow many people in the community to enjoy more housing than their own current incomes would permit. Since the "housing sector" can be thought of as including those community facilities which are important to housing though not part of dwelling structures, we can think of government outlays in the housing sector as including the construction and maintenance of utility systems, streets, and perhaps even schools and firehouses. The concept of the "housing sector" is rather elastic on this point, but whatever we include or exclude in the definition of expenditures on housing, we must reflect in the definition of housing sector output. If we include the expenditure on streets in the total of housing demand, for example, we must include the services provided by streets in the measure of housing sector output.

The block labeled *Financial sector outlays* represents the net investment activities of financial institutions and individuals. Since dwellings are durable goods, a large portion of their value or cost when first produced is investment rather than consumption of current services. Buildings are constructed mostly with funds earmarked as savings rather than with current household budgets for shelter. Thus, the financial sector, which is a pool of the community's current savings, plays a very important role in determining the rate of growth or improvement of the housing stock.

Total housing demand is the sum of housing consumption expenditures, government outlays for housing, and housing investments by the financial sector. *Total housing supply,* as already mentioned, brings together the increment in the housing stock, services related to the functioning of the housing market, and the intangible services derived from the older housing stock by virtue of the fact that it is occupied and enjoyed. Demand and supply meet in an allocation process which we usually think of as a "market." The outcome of the market decisions can be expected to influence the scale and composition of the housing sector's share in total current output of a subsequent period, so that the large process which we are describing is a dynamic one, constantly adjusting itself over time.

The dotted extensions of the *Total housing demand* and *supply* blocks signify that the significant market process in the housing sector is not limited to current output or current income. Exchanges of previously constructed dwellings also occur within any housing sector, and these exchanges may be important to secure the maximum economic advantage from what is, in effect, "sunk capital." These exchanges require the use of current resources (already represented in the diagram) and, in the long run at least, may exert an important influence upon the character and the scale of current housing sector outputs, helping to determine, for example, whether the new houses to be built are for low-income or for high-income families. The housing sector thus deals with the administration of previously accumulated capital as well as with decisions about the creation and use of new capital. It also deals with a variety of current services.

The figure is described as a *Macroeconomic View* of the housing sector. Macroeconomics is concerned primarily with the aggregate size of current production. It is a study of the size of the "forest" rather than the fate of individual "trees." Total current production, or GNP, is made up of output for the housing sector, the nondurable consumption goods sector, the balance of the government sector, the sectors for consumer services and other nondurable goods, and so on, so that macroeconomics is concerned to some extent with the composition of total output as well as its aggregate value. Exactly what types of houses are produced, or what type of bread is baked by bakeries, is a matter beyond the realm of macroeconomics. We may say that macroeconomics is also concerned with the origin of total housing demand, so that it recognizes the divisions among housing consumption expenditures, government outlays for housing, and financial sector outlays for housing which are shown in the diagram. Macroeconomics does not deal with the output of an individual firm, however.

Microeconomics, on the other hand, is concerned with the manner in which equilibrium is reached when total housing demand confronts total housing supply. Each individual in the marketplace must be considered, at least in principle, by microeconomics. In an important sense, microeconomics is likely to involve optimizing concepts such as the maximization of utility by individual consumers or of profit by individual producers, while macroeconomics seeks only to simulate or forecast the overall outcome without attempting to show that what is produced is either rational or optimal. Microeconomics explicitly deals with individual transactions and, in particular, with transactions involving the previously acquired stock of dwellings, while the role of the older stock in macroeconomics is limited, indirect, and obscure.

With this diagram before us, we can list the main types of resource allocation questions which arise in the housing sector, under the two headings of "macro" and "micro."

Macro

What proportion of the *Total current output* (GNP) is for the housing sector?

How much of this housing sector share of total current output is accounted for by new dwellings (or related facilities), by services related to the operation of the housing sector, and by the utilization of the previously accumulated stock of dwellings, respectively?

How much of *Total current income* is to be used for the consumption of current housing services?

How much of total *Government outlay* is to be for housing (or housing-related) facilities?

How much of total net savings and investment activities by the financial sector will be directed to the housing sector?

Micro

Which households will occupy which dwelling units in the enlarged and altered housing stock?

What prices will each of these households pay for current housing services yielded by the dwellings they occupy?

Which households will benefit from government outlays on housing and in what way?

What transactions will occur within the housing sector, between which individuals, involving which kinds of business services and what manner of investment transactions?

What kinds of new dwellings will be created?

What capital values will accrue to each unit of the housing stock?

What alterations or repairs will be made on each unit of the previously existing housing stock?

A Microeconomic View

The macroeconomic scale of housing sector activities is a summation of the effects of individual transactions. We are able to make macroeconomic *forecasts* for the housing sector only if broad patterns of individual behavior in this sector persist long enough. Only then can we make useful statements about the total without delving into the probable outcome of each prospective transaction.

The same is true of macroeconomic *planning* for the housing sector. A plan can be implemented only by consummating a multitude of individual transactions, so that a realistic plan for the housing sector includes at least implicitly a practical routine for arriving at each individual transaction involving housing resources and for affecting the outcome of each transaction so that it advances, or at least does not retard, the achievement of the housing plan.

To understand how the housing sector "works," we need to see how individual transactions are usually made. In a market economy this means becoming familiar with the manner in which significant business decisions are made by persons involved in a transaction. Thus, our study of the housing sector involves a description of, and an evaluation of, business practices in this sector. This inquiry differs materially in kind and method from macroeconomic analysis. It includes an examination of the way an individual bit of housing business is ordinarily done (given an existing set of business institutions), and the development of normative decision rules which would tell us how the business ought to be done, given some set of criteria.

The macroeconomist and the housing planner (such as the head of a government housing agency) do not concern themselves with individual transactions as a rule, so they might be inclined to overlook the microeconomic aspects of the housing sector. They can do this safely only if two conditions exist in the structure of microeconomic behavior. That behavior must be stable, so that parameters representing private transactions can be employed in forecasts and plans. This behavior must also be optimal, in the sense of making efficient use of housing sector resources.

When we take a look at microeconomic behavior in the real world of the housing sector, however, we are likely to find that its structure is not stable. The conduct and outcome of individual transactions in the housing sector tend to change over time as the economic world (technology, urbanization) becomes more complex, economic preferences change, and business practitioners become more sophisticated. An important source of instability in microeconomic behavior is the economic planner himself, for his tax and subsidy programs and various regulatory innovations are likely to affect the way in which individual decisions are made. It then becomes necessary for the housing planner (at the governmental level) to formulate his plans on the basis of anticipated changes in the business sector, but he cannot anticipate those changes until he understands the why and wherefore of existing business practices.

If the structure of microeconomic decisions is not optimal at present, then the planner who wishes to improve the performance of the housing sector has an important alternative to crude macroeconomic tools. Housing welfare may sometimes be improved more significantly by changes in the pattern of business practices than by efforts to pump up the level of housing construction. For example, if there are many large families living in small houses and a similar number of small families living in large houses, it may be possible to relieve a "housing shortage" (among the large families) by encouraging exchanges of existing dwellings rather than by striking out to construct many additional large homes. There are practical reasons for believing that housing-market behavior is far from an optimal pattern in most parts of the world, so that microeconomics of the housing sector is a most promising approach to housing problems which seem at first like matters of macroeconomics (net new investment, etc.), pure and simple.

Figure 3 is a *Microeconomic View* of the housing sector. Its central element is the individual housing-market transaction. This might be the purchase of a home by a family, or the renting of an apartment. It might be the granting of a mortgage loan, or the acquisition of a residential property for investment. It might be the construction of a new residential structure, or the improvement of an existing one. Whatever its nature, it is an individual event involving one item of real property and two principals (at least). These principals "meet" in the market and the conduct of their meeting is affected by a set of institutions such as those mentioned along the right-hand side of the figure. The outcome of the transaction is a set of effects such as those along the bottom of the figure. Much of the subsequent discussion in this book concerns the nature of principals, institutions, and effects in housing sector transactions. A brief commentary is in order at this point, however.

The transaction can involve any interest in residential property. The right to occupy a dwelling unit is perhaps the most important object in housing sector transactions, but there are many other steps in the process of turning economic resources into housing services. Lenders secure certain rights to property used as collateral in addition to their expectation of repayment at interest. Equity investors engaged in constructing new dwellings acquire materials and services from construction firms and, probably, funds from lenders. One person may wear more than one hat in a given transaction, as one when one household sells a home to another, for each will be to some extent a user, landowner, and equity investor and, possibly, a lender as well. Government agencies may act as principals in lending money, for example, or in making publicly owned housing available to low-income families. The transaction itself may be the creation of new rights or simply a transfer of existing rights.

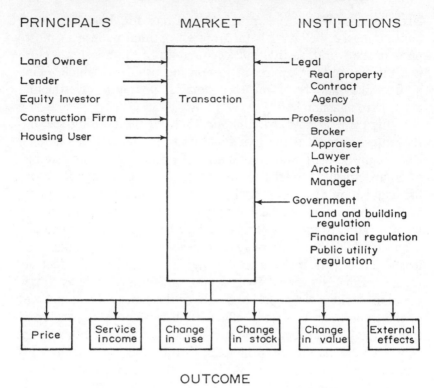

Figure 3
The Housing Sector—a Microeconomic View

The category of *Institutions* is broad indeed. The conduct and significance of any market transaction is very much affected by laws governing the ownership and transfer of real property; the pledging of residential interests as security for loans; the rights of the public with respect to "private" residential property; and the obligations of buyers, sellers, and their agents. These legal institutions are in the nature of "facts" or "data" which the principals must consider. For example, if there are tenants with leasehold rights who are not party to a sale of the dwelling structure, it is the legal system of the community which determines whether the new owner will be able to occupy the dwelling.

The other "institutions" are not facts, but people. Various professional services may be employed when housing market transactions are concluded and, of course, any one of these professionals may be a principal in the transaction. The list of such professionals seems to be expanding as economic consultants take over where appraisers leave off. Tax advisors may be brokers, appraisers, lawyers, or specialists in their own right. Subdivision planners and traffic engineers provide advice to housing developers which goes beyond the customary concepts of architecture. Financial counselors manage some of the intangible aspects of property ownership and development.

The legal institutions are created by government, of course, but the direct role of government in private housing transactions may be much more extensive. Regulations governing the use of urban land—such as zoning, and the construction and use of residential buildings—are found in most of the urbanized areas of the world, varying enormously in purpose, detail, and effectiveness. Governments exercise varying kinds of control over financial institutions which facilitate housing transactions. Governments impose taxes of various kinds which affect the cost and profitability of acquiring interests in particular kinds of housing property, some of these being intended to achieve specific housing sector results, while others are simply by-products of the community's fiscal philosophy. Governments often supervise or take direct responsibility for the provision of water, power, sewerage, and transportation facilities as well as education, police and fire services, etc., which influence the usefulness of particular dwellings.

Any transaction in this sector produces several distinguishable effects, each of which has its own significance to the individuals involved and to the community at large. Prices are established and paid, and tax burdens are assumed. Professional participants receive income. The use or ownership of the property in question is changed. The stock of housing in the community may be changed physically if the transaction was, in effect, a decision to build, demolish, or remodel dwellings. Price, adjusted for costs of various kinds, will be capitalized into value.

Residential transactions affect people other than direct participants, as we have already noted. If a new family moves into the neighborhood, the neighbors' lives will be influenced in a variety of ways. Local schools may find a change in their responsibilities and resources. Nearby transportation or utility systems may be used differently. The widening circles of external effects never quite end, but they are matters which the principals in a transaction may be unaware of or unconcerned about.

The housing sector is portrayed in this microeconomic view as a process of business decision-making. We might also like to think of microeconomics as a series of more or less physical actions—the arrival of new households in the community, the clearing of land, installation of utility systems, construction and management of dwellings, etc. These tangible aspects of the housing sector's performance may, however, simply be thought of as implied by, or following necessarily from, a business transaction. If a landowner secures financing, and contracts with a home-building firm, houses will be built. The physical aspects do not disclose their origin; we must look into the decision-making process if we are to understand why tangible aspects of the housing sector come into being.

It may be convenient to divide housing sector transactions into four categories: use or occupancy, ownership, finance, and development. The last of these does not mean a physical process directly, but only the intention to engage in the physical production (or demolition) of dwellings. A single transaction may combine several of these categories.

Housing Statistics

Housing has so many quantitative dimensions that a book on housing economics might seem an appropriate place to look for some interesting statistics. The reader will see quickly by glancing through this book that very little in the way of statistical information is provided. There are two main reasons for this—one being that this book is concerned primarily with "why" rather than with "what"—that is, with explanation rather than description. The second reason, which is really a corollary, is that we must direct our attention to the general nature of housing economics rather than to the situation in any one country. A veritable mass of numbers would be needed to suggest the situations which exist in major areas of the world. The qualification necessary for these numbers would tend to overwhelm their significance.

Statistics and descriptions of housing do exist in abundance, and the reader who wishes to explore the relevance of concepts presented in most of the remaining chapters of this book can probably find much pertinent information near at hand. Government agencies, such as the U. S. Census Bureau, produce the broadest and perhaps the most reliable statistical information about housing. Sometimes this information has to be inferred from reports dealing with other things, such as population growth or movement, or the components of total investment. Local governments, especially through their planning agencies, are likely to keep somewhat closer watch on certain aspects of their immediate housing situation, such as the volume and kinds of building activity. Banks and real estate businesses may have systematic measures of vacancies, prices, and the volume of transactions.*

This "raw" information is supplemented in some places by parametric relationships which have been identified by analysis of that information. For example, if we have data on interest rates and the volume of new housing construction for several time periods, we can calculate the interest-elasticity of residential construction; there are various examples illustrating this concept.[1] By operations on data we can develop many interesting and useful constants which help to characterize the housing economy we are studying, such as a variety of elasticities (income, cost, price, and the above-mentioned interest-elasticity); age-specific household formation and home-ownership rates; and the ratio of

---

* In the United States the decennial Census of Housing provides detailed information of high quality concerning the nature of housing stock, its occupancy, prices, and financing. The Federal Housing Administration conducts vacancy surveys in a large number of communities and publishes housing market analyses for individual metropolitan areas. The annual report of the Department of Housing and Urban Development contains information about the many housing programs in which the Federal government is involved. The Department of Commerce and the Bureau of Labor Statistics collect and publish current data on construction activity and housing costs. Data collection is also undertaken in many communities by business organizations; The Northern California Real Estate Report, for example, is published by the Bay Area Council and contains statistics on the volume of real estate transactions and loans, estimates of construction costs and trends in the value of homes.

housing expenses to total household income, the number of persons per household, and so on. By recognizing more than two dimensions in a relationship, such as a study of home-ownership rates by different age groups and by different income classes within the age groups, we have an almost inexhaustible opportunity to derive what may be significant relationships from the statistical information already at hand.

The problem of definition happens to be particularly troublesome in statistical housing studies. To take a well-known example, the amount of money which a family spends for its housing in a period of time (say one year) may or may not include any or all of the following items, depending on the perspicacity of the investigator or the comprehension of the respondent:

>   utilities (electricity, water, scavenging, etc.)
>   property taxes
>   ground rents
>   depreciation
>   mortgage amortization
>   mortgage interest
>   imputed interest on equity
>   unrealized capital gain or loss
>   brokerage and loan fees
>   do-it-yourself repair and landscaping
>   transportation costs

Studies of housing construction may deal variously in terms of number of housing units, the amount of floor space, or the aggregate cost of construction of new dwellings (which itself may or may not include the price of land or land preparation costs, and the selling expenses incurred by the builder). "Density" may mean persons (or households) per housing unit, housing units per unit of land, the proportion of land covered by buildings, or the number of floors per building.

The business side of housing seems to be covered quite inadequately by even very ambitious statistical programs. The "profitability" of owning, buying, renovating, selling, leasing, refinancing, or demolishing a particular type of dwelling in a given city or neighborhood is seldom, if ever, to be discovered in any other fashion than by hearsay or experience, both of which are unreliable and may be expensive. Trends in selling prices or terms, in rents and vacancy rates and in opportunities for financing or refinancing, and other data which the housing entrepreneur really needs are rarely available in quality and useful form.

The social side of housing is usually neglected by producers of raw data but is sometimes worked over to good effect by students of particular problems. In some communities the housing standards of racial, age, or occupational groups are of particular interest and, in most communities, the nature of neighborhood interaction is significant as an aspect of housing amenity and cultural development. The characteristics of households moving into an area are important to school, welfare, and other public officials, and to merchants and property owners.

The physical environment of housing is seldom reduced to statistics; a notable exception to this has been the effort of the American Public Health Association.[2] Whether there are street trees, traffic signals, sources of air pollution, fire hazards, or noise in the neighborhood can be quite important to the quality of housing but will seldom be apparent in housing data. If you want to know about them, you have to look or, if possible, live there for a while, forming impressions which are valid, perhaps, but not transmissible.

There is a great body of literature on housing which is descriptive but not basically statistical. Dwellings do make up a large part of the community, both spatially and spiritually, and it is no surprise to find that their characteristics have provided dramatic effects for novelists (such as for Charles Dickens in *Oliver Twist*), for political agitation (about various kinds of ghettos, for example), and for deliberate observers of housing's role in national economic development. This seems entirely proper and, perhaps, indispensable. Despite the bias, exaggeration, scapegoat-seeking, or myopia which must enter any fervent description of so vital and persistent an artifact, pristine statistics and analyses about housing would have little purpose or meaning without a background of literate alarums.

Someday, perhaps, the study of housing economics will benefit from standard definitions of its most important terms and the extension of measurement to some of the business, social, and environmental aspects of the housing sector. For the moment we may do well to indicate two main kinds of housing data which usually exist in some form and around which other information tends to cluster. One of these is information about present user standards, the amount of floor space or number of rooms per family, the kinds of facilities available (e.g. private plumbing), the age and state of repair of the structures. These facts have to do with the existing stock of dwellings. The other major category is the rate of improvement in this stock, measured first of all by the share of GNP going into new dwellings. The distribution of this increment by type and location, and its availability to particular segments of the population are refinements of the basic information.

Thus, if we were to build a statistical description of a housing sector, we would probably begin by thinking of these two major categories. Both relate to an actual state of affairs. To develop a statistical program further, for purposes of business forecasting or for identifying desirable public policies, we should want to look into how and why user standards are likely to change—perhaps because of population increase or movement, deterioration of dwellings, changes in housing preferences and purchasing power—and into how and why the rate of gross addition to the stock of housing capital is likely to change—perhaps because of events in the capital market, or because of new incentives provided to businessmen. The format of the statistical effort should be tailored to the kinds of issues which seem relevant to the compiler of these statistics—whether he is interested in "equity," "amenity," or "efficiency" and what these things mean to him in measurable terms.

The subject of housing is so large that no digest of statistical information can be offered in lieu of a (perhaps prolix) discourse on the nature of the housing sector. This does not mean that numerical information is of minor value in this field, but only that it is another story.

Limitations of Traditional Economic Analysis

In its broader sense, economics is the study of choosing among limited alternatives. If we wish to have more of X, we must give up some of Y. Traditional economic analysis expresses the relationship between the quantity of X we might obtain and the sacrifice of other things which would be necessary to obtain that quantity, the sacrifice being called "price" or "cost." If the price of X is greater than X is worth to us, we do not produce it or consume it. Thus, the quantity of X to be produced is decided in such a manner that scarce resources are used to produce only the most necessary or desirable things. Economic analysis is based upon relationships between quantities of specific things and the prices which could or would be paid for those quantities.

In principle, housing market questions ought to lend themselves to analysis by these traditional methods. Housing is a product which can be produced in various quantities; for each quantity of output, a particular price would be paid, and a particular level of costs would be incurred. In fact, however, housing market questions seem to require quite different methods of analysis. The traditional concept of "supply-and-demand equilibrium" is not very relevant to most of the problems or issues which are associated with the housing sector of the economy.

Traditional types of economic analysis can, of course, tell us something about the housing market.[3] An increase in population can be represented by a shift of the *Demand* schedule in Figure 4 to the right, resulting in some combinations of increased production of houses and increased market price. An increase in the cost of housing can be represented by an upward shift in the *Supply* schedule, resulting in some combination of reduced output and higher price. To apply this reasoning in a practical situation, however, requires some knowledge of the slopes of the *Demand* and *Supply* schedules and this is where we begin to encounter difficulties. The slope of either of these schedules is a quantitative relationship between a change in price and a change in quantity, but a change in quantity cannot be measured unless the units involved in that quantity are uniform. If these units are not uniform, then the relationship between a price change and a change in output quantity may not be expressible at all. Of several different kinds of houses, which kind is produced when the general price is high? If the general price falls, which additional types of houses will be built and purchased? The relationship between price and any measurable index of house "quality" may not be smooth and continuous. We must also be concerned about the nature of the *quantity;* it may represent either the volume of transactions including existing dwellings, or the number of new units to be built.

Even if these problems were overcome, we would have some difficulty in defining *Price.* If a city's population rises and the demand for housing shifts to the right, the traditional method of analysis suggests that the "price" will probably rise (unless the

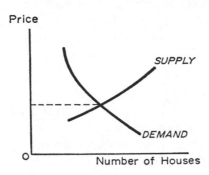

Figure 4
Microeconomic Equilibrium—a Traditional View

Supply curve is horizontal). Since the supply consists of different kinds of houses, however, will all their prices increase by the same amount? Or in the same proportion?

The individual home owner or home builder thus finds traditional economic analysis of very little use. He wants to know how much the price or rent of his particular dwelling will change if there is a general increase in community housing demand. What happens to the price of the "average" house is of little interest unless he knows the market relationship between his property and the average property. Traditional economic analysis will not help him to discover that relationship because it assumes, in the first place, that all the units of commodity X are homogeneous—that is, identical and perfectly substitutable. In our discussion of the nature of "housing," we have explored some of the many dimensions of housing which, taken together, mean that individual units of supply are almost certain to be imperfect substitutes for one another. Differences in location, in neighborhood characteristics, in aspects of privacy and security, as well as simple physical differences in size, equipment, and condition, cause individual dwellings within the community housing supply to differ significantly from one another. The differences are quite as important as the "average" house value in determining the value of a single property. For ordinary business decisions concerning the housing market, the elementary concept of demand-and-supply equilibrium is of very limited value, primarily because of the heterogeneity which is inherent in housing.

Ordinary business decisions, of course, are concerned with individual houses or with a small number of dwellings within a large, differentiated supply. If we took the macroeconomic point of view, perhaps traditional methods would be more useful. The "quantity" could be defined as homogeneous dollars of housing investment or as square meters of floor space.[4] Additions to the supply could be assumed to be of certain standardized types. Under some circumstances, such assumptions would be reasonable and useful; such quantities could be measured and their relationships with price or cost could be observed. Macroeconomic forecasting can be reliable and useful, assuming, as we have noted, that microeconomic behavior patterns are relatively stable. An example of this methodology is the following regression equation which, in a statistician's sense, "explains" the volume of U. S. housing construction.*

$$C = a_1 + a_2 \Delta HH + a_3 D - a_4 V + a_5 R - a_6 i + a_7 C_{-1} - a_8 C_{-3}$$

$C =$ number of new housing units started during a three-month period

$\Delta HH =$ net household formation

$D =$ number of net removals from the stock

$V =$ number of vacant available units

$R =$ index of rents

$i =$ index of interest rates

$C_{-1, -3} =$ number of starts in the first and third previous quarters

$a =$ parameters which were quantified by statistical research.

$R^2 = 0.85$

---

* This is a simplified form of the equation which appears in Maisel's "Nonbusiness Construction," in *Brookings Econometric Method*, p. 180.

As a policy tool, however, macroeconomic methods have an important weakness. The composition of increments to the housing stock is not described. It is of great importance for economic planning that additional dollars of housing investment be spent in the right places for the right kinds of structures. The assumption that certain "standardized" types of houses will be added to the supply begs the question of whether these particular kinds of dwellings—with their assumed locations, assumed environmental amenities, assumed investment characteristics, etc.—are needed more than other types which might be constructed. There is, in addition, the troublesome question of distribution. Who shall occupy the new dwellings? What changes in the pattern of occupancy of old dwellings will accompany the construction of new dwellings? National or regional economic analysis of housing issues requires attention to the qualitative differences within the housing supply, to the differences in effective demand among households, and to the precise nature of equilibrium. It is also noteworthy that econometric studies of housing in the United States often assume implicitly that factors of input—land, materials, labor, etc.—are in perfectly elastic supply. Regression equations developed for one nation obviously cannot be employed in countries with different economic characteristics.

Finally, effective demand for housing, as this might be identified in a traditional economic approach, is generally considered to be an inadequate measure of the social value of housing.[5] The benefits to society as a whole of an improvement in housing standards will not be reflected in equilibrium levels of output and prices which result solely from private considerations of demand and supply.

Economic theory does not have to be "applicable" to business or government planning in order to be of value. If the theory shows, under reasonably realistic assumptions, that equilibrium outputs could be predicted and interpreted in terms of the welfare of the community, then the abstract theory represents a helpful set of ideas. In the area of housing, the assumptions necessary to create an abstract equilibrium are not realistic and the information necessary to interpret this equilibrium is not provided by the analysis. Traditional economic analysis is not a particularly useful tool for the study of housing market issues, either private or public.

Market Institutions in the Housing Sector

In a market economy allocation-decisions are made one-by-one as individuals confront opportunities to buy or to sell, to produce or consume. The overall result, in terms of a consistent set of answers to the allocation questions posed earlier in this chapter, emerges from the complex of individual actions and bargains involving very small numbers of individuals. There is no conscious direction of individual actions toward a preconceived pattern of housing sector relationships. We might say that a market economy lets the overall pattern of resource use be simply the result of a great mass of individual decisions, while the opposite concept, perhaps to be called a "planned economy" determines the large outcome first and then takes a number of small decisions to achieve this large outcome.

There is a long, indeed historic, debate whether the end result of many individual decisions will conform to what the community, as a political body, wants to do with its resources and, from the other point of view, whether planned economy can devise an internally consistent plan for very complicated economic realities, plus administrative machinery which will assure that the multitude of small actions necessary to realize the plan can be identified and carried out.

The housing sector brings this set of issues into rather sharp focus, for housing is an imperative, human requirement and the aggregation of dwellings in an urban settlement plays upon a variety of strong social forces. A study of housing economics cannot help giving much attention to the question of "market vs. planned economy," and this book is oriented toward that issue.

One point to be made at the outset is that a market economy does not literally leave resource allocation entirely to individual decision-makers. Many of the decisions made by a market-oriented housing sector are made at a level between the individual and the entire community, by groups of people who consciously coordinate their activity. These social aspects of a market system are often called "institutions" and certain types of institutions are indispensable for the effective behavior of a market economy in the housing sector. We have mentioned institutions before, in connection with Figure 2, and now want to inquire into their origins.

To begin with, housing and urban land, as commodities in the marketplace, depend for their existence and quality upon the community's set of laws. Mr. X does not own a certain house just because he paid Mr. Y the price that was asked; the laws of the community establish whether the house was Mr. Y's to sell, whether Mr. X is a competent buyer, and whether the transaction is to be regarded as binding. Even beyond that, the community's laws impose some limits on what Mr. X can do with "his" house —whether he can sell it, rent out rooms, conduct a mail-order business from it, or paint it black. There are many possible divisions of interest in urban real property, usually of substantial economic value, so that the structure of community legal institutions related to property assumes major economic significance. It is a framework in which individual market decisions can be made.

Housing and urban land are durable commodities, giving up their valuable economic services over a long period of time. Thus, the creation of housing or the acquisition of housing or land must be "financed." Funds must be provided today which will be returned over many years. For this reason, financial institutions such as banks play a very important role in deciding who can acquire or develop which properties. Credit institutions are pools of funds, garnered from members of the community in one way or another, to be used according to conscious institutional decision. Credit institutions themselves are tied together by the community's or nation's monetary institutions—the national treasury and national bank or its equivalent—which impose broad limits on the activities of individual credit institutions. At the other end, financing of urban land development is influenced by the legal relationship between borrowers and lenders and by the legal implications of using real property as security for mortgage loans.

Builders of houses know that the success of their efforts

depends very much on what kinds of transportation, schools, shopping facilities, and other necessary adjuncts to housing are available in the area where they build. Usually these things are not provided by the builder himself, but depend on decisions of highway agencies, public transportation authorities, school boards, and other private firms whose decisions are, in turn, similarly dependent on the behavior of community institutions. One point of great importance to builders and to those who buy dwellings from them is some assurance that the pattern of land uses in the neighborhood of the new building will not change in a detrimental way. Thus, builders and property owners have long endorsed or anticipated the practice of zoning.

Users of housing, that is households, and the suppliers of either rental or sales housing urgently need a system of communication, so that dwellings and households may be matched in ways that are appropriate. Housing brokers, in various forms, and the media they employ such as local newspapers, perform this essential communication function. So scattered and diverse is a community's population and housing stock that a coordinated system of information is needed. So complex is the need for housing, and the housing commodity itself, that the brokerage function is technically difficult and morally demanding. To perform his function efficiently and without discredit, the housing broker needs to merge some of his activities with those of other brokers and to implement a system of regulations aimed at protecting those who use the broker's services.

Thus, if the "market" allocates resources, it must do so largely through its institutions. Individuals do make joint decisions on limited, specific aspects of the operation of the local housing economy. Their institutional coordination differs in a fundamental respect, however, from the type of coordination imposed from "above" in a planned economy. Market institutions, particularly those which are spontaneous groupings of individuals and businesses, serve individual interests. Builders and property owners subscribe to formal or informal zoning because the results of controlling land use are good for them as individuals, not for the sake of producing a pretty and orderly appearing town which will impress visitors, and not directly for the sake of cutting down traffic accidents or other urban hazards and inconveniences. That is, coordinating institutions arising in a market economy are not guided by a concern for all the external effects of private and business behavior. Parks consume both taxes and land, so it is hard for a property owner or business man as an individual or as the member of a market institution to understand why he should pay for them.

The "planned economy," at least in an ideal sense, starts with an awareness of all the externalities of individual economic behavior. It sees as criteria for the allocation of resources not only the gratification of household needs for good dwellings and pleasant neighborhoods, but also the desirability of communal facilities such as parks which are not to be sold through the marketplace, the esthetic value of an attractive city, and perhaps also the moral value of egalitarian housing standards or of social integration.

The objectives of this idealized, planned urban land economy are not substitutes for the goals of a market economy, but rather supplemental to it. Though it is possible for a community to dispense with the role of the market altogether, there are important arguments against doing that, and it is feasible to have an urban economy which is a blend of the two systems. This blend involves a division of labor—providing various levels of institutions, some private and some public—to look after the various external economies and diseconomies inherent in urban land use. This concept would assign to the "planning" agencies of the community two basic functions—to encourage the development of market institutions which most efficiently serve the narrow interests of individual decision-makers, and to establish public institutions which offset those external effects of market behavior which are held to be of substantial importance. Thus, to illustrate, in such a community the public agency would produce a clear, flexible, legal code regarding property so that individuals can buy or sell what they want to exchange without uncertainty, misunderstanding, or frustration, and the community would directly augment the purchasing power of low-income households so that their housing standards would not fall below a desirable minimum. Within this pattern, private exchanges could take place, flexibly using and developing the housing stock, with each individual making the decision which was in his own best interest at the moment, given the community-imposed "rules of the game."

Resource Allocation Through Prices

Allocation means deciding to use certain resources for the production of A rather than B, houses rather than office buildings, for example, or television sets rather than refrigerators. From the consumer's point of view, it is money income which is to be allocated rather than fixed resources, but the essence of the problem is the same. Is it better to buy, or produce A rather than B, an apartment in town or a home in the suburbs, a new car or a year in graduate school? Resources are limited and their possible uses are many, so choices have to be made. The end result of all the economic choices made by a community during a period of time is the resource allocation pattern which is evident in material living standards and accumulation of capital.

Actual economic decisions seldom involve a choice between two equally available, tangible commodities like a loaf of bread and a quart of milk. There are many, many types of useful commodities and services which might be fashioned out of the resources available, each type requiring a different combination of resource inputs and each exchangeable for another on something other than a one-for-one basis. Thus, the economic decision process as carried out by individuals is ordinarily a weighing of the desirability of one particular commodity or service, such as a new car, against a measure of the decrease in opportunity to consume all other types of goods which will result if the commodity in question is selected. The "cost" of the new car, or the new house, or whatever, is usually thought of in terms of a generalized resource unit—money—rather than as another specific commodity. Money can be exchanged in turn for any combination of goods which the recipient desires. Thus, money simplifies the buyer's task of persuading the present owner of a resource or commodity to part with it. A successful author may desire to build a new house, but it would be inconvenient and perhaps futile for him to ask those who wish to enjoy his book to perform labor on that house. Resources and commodities are what we all desire, but money is a very useful social tool for converting resources into commodities. Hence, the "opportunity cost" of a resource or commodity is usually expressed as a money price.

Prices actually originate through exchanges of goods and services, that is, through a market. The market may be free and competitive or it may be quite restricted through laws, customs, or collusive agreements. The price of labor is usually determined by competitive demand and supply, plus a variety of laws such as minimum-wage rates and child-labor restrictions, plus some noncompetitive organizations among workers, employers, or both. The toll on a bridge is set by law. The formation of prices is an activity in which the whole community constantly engages. The set of prices thus developed tells producers and consumers what they must give up in order to obtain one unit of any of the various commodities and services which figure in economic life.

The set of prices actually prevailing in a community may fail to indicate the real sacrifice of resources occasioned by the consumption of a particular commodity or resource. The institutional manner in which prices are actually established may distort the relative scarcity of various resources and goods. A very high bridge toll may discourage people from using it, resulting in the waste of other resources as people go around that bridge. A low price for land may keep farming profitable, while cities expand into unsafe swamps. Too low a price for the use of recreation areas may lead to their despoliation.

Since the concept of price really means a measure of resource sacrifice, it is easy to imagine that a set of prices is really implicit in the supply of various resources which exists, given the nature of desires for the ultimate product of those resources on the part of consumers. The implicit toll for a bridge is the price which would maximize its overall usefulness to the community. The same can be said for the price of land and other resources, probably including even labor. Since economic decision-makers in the community respond to prices of inputs and outputs, there must be some set of prices which would encourage all of them to make such decisions that the available resources are used to produce the most useful complex of products and services for which these resources suffice. These implicit prices are "ideal" in a sense both practical and impractical. They represent the realities of our resources and of our economic desires, but at the same time they do not appear spontaneously in our economic behavior. We know that there is some ideal toll for a bridge, but we would have to know very much about the activities of the community and the preferences of the people within it and their complex interdependence to form a judgment about what that ideal toll should be.

What we can do about the bridge toll and about the prices of land, houses, and other valuable things is to look carefully at the process in which these prices actually do arise, to see whether the underlying realities of resources and consumption desires are represented and reasonably combined in these decision processes. The "ideal" or implicit set of prices is thus a goal, and the actual price-creating mechanism—the ways in which resources are actually being allocated—is a means of approaching that goal. How good the approximation is and how the existing allocation process might be improved to bring that goal closer is the subject of this study, as it is of virtually any economic inquiry.

However they may be established, prices become information which guides people in their economic decisions. If the price of automobile X is $2,500 and the price of automobile Y is $2,700, then X will be preferred unless Y has some qualitative advantage worth at least $200. A house priced at $60,000 may be impossible to buy for a family with an income of $7,500. When the price of adding a swimming pool falls, more families will have one; and when the market value of a family's present house rises, that family has greater opportunity to purchase a better house. When the price of land, labor, and materials for a new house is less than the price which will be paid for such a house, builders will get busy adding to the housing stock. When the rent for her apartment goes up, the elderly widow may have to move to some other section of town.

By encouraging response in the use of resources, prices serve to ration those resources. The higher the price of land or a house, the fewer the people who can justify acquiring it. City land is priced out of the reach of wheat farmers or cattle raisers, and much of it is priced out of the reach of house builders as well. The price of borrowed money helps to determine the form and the timing of new investment or capital-creating activities and the rate of addition to the stock of consumer durables such as automobiles. Allocation and pricing are virtually inseparable activities, so that any system of prices tends to result in a particular allocation of resources and any selected pattern of resource use carries with it an implicit set of prices. It is not true, however, that an economic community which can identify a desirable allocation of its resources automatically produces a set of prices which will achieve that allocation.

A system of prices—which we must take to include such things as taxes, tolls, subsidies, and outright prohibitions—is thus a means to achieve resource allocation. Since most communities are constantly revising their demands for the way resources should be used, the economic institutions of the community tend to be devices for establishing prices rather than "planning boards" which allocate resources directly. Even in rigidly planned economies, the choices of planners are usually governed in various ways by "price tags" attached to particular resources and commodities—perhaps just for internal planning purposes. The economist is more interested, consequently, in the system which determines how resources are to be allocated than with the actual allocation scheme. In the housing sector, the economist would be more interested in the fact, for example, that mortgage loans are available to would-be housing purchasers than he would be in knowing that 54 percent of the families are homeowners.

Price-creating institutions such as markets, laws of contract, and taxing or fee-setting public institutions are established or sanctioned by the community. The community's approach to determining the allocation of resources is usually indirect and a generalized scheme is shown in Figure 5. First, the community establishes a system for determining prices (and other parameters of economic decisions such as taxes, subsidies, and prohibitions). This system creates and constantly revises prices. Prices, in turn, influence individuals, business firms, and government agencies in making economic decisions. The collection of economic decisions by members of a community results in the

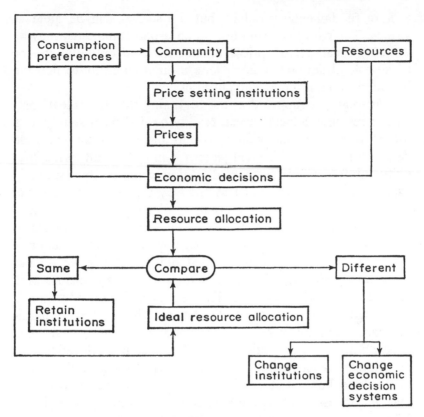

Figure 5
Resource-Allocation System

allocation of resources. The actual allocation of resources may differ from that which seems desirable to the community; if so, there are two possible reasons. Either the prices arising out of the established system are not the prices which are implicit in the community's resource and consumption desire pattern, or the individuals within the community are not responding consistently to the prices which are produced. The first circumstance is a reflection on the nature of the basic price-setting institutions, while the second is evidence of a problem in the administration of those institutions. An insurance company, for example, may fail because it employs a seriously erroneous mortality table or because its salesmen don't understand the rate book. The first is a more fundamental problem, but the second can be quite as serious. The pattern of land uses in an urban community may be wasteful because land prices do not indicate optimum use or because land developers don't look around carefully to find the best land for their immediate purposes.

It might be supposed at the beginning that the "ideal" pattern of resource allocation can readily be described simply as a list of what everyone would like to have or what everyone deserves. In reality, this ideal pattern is most difficult to identify. Criticisms of actual resource allocation come easily, especially from those who feel slighted by the way things are being done. To show that there is an alternative allocation of the community's limited resources which actually represents an improvement for the community as a whole, however, is a very difficult thing. Until we have actually tried out something we do not know how very intricately all the resource-using decisions of a community are tied together. The unexpected by-products of a step to remedy one apparent deficiency may be much more harmful than the initial problem. The economist's main social value is his ability to direct criticism of actual resource-allocation patterns into productive and logical channels of inquiry. To do this he needs to know quite a bit about the nature of the decision-making process all along the line, both as it is and as it might be. When we study housing economics, we don't want merely to forecast the number of houses which will be built next year, or to lament the fact that some families don't have running water. We want to know why certain aspects of an existing situation have emerged, what methods might be used to amend this situation, and what kinds of side effects each corrective action would have. The study of the housing sector is thus an examination of decision-making processes in the context of particular resource endowments and special requirements on the part of consumers.

Unique Aspects of Housing Prices

We have said that prices are instruments for guiding the allocation of resources. Where the system of prices seems to represent underlying realities of resources, technology, and needs, the community can give substantial respect to the prices that emerge. We should be hesitant under such circumstances to change the allocation of resources which the price system tends to produce.

In the housing sector there are several kinds of allocation tasks to be done, and for each task, different sorts of market institutions come into existence. There is a market for the ownership of land and existing buildings, with its own set of institutions including legal processes for recording ownership, linkages to the money market to secure "leverage" in individual transactions, and means of market communication so that buyers and sellers can find each other.

There is a market for the management of the housing stock, which includes demolishing old buildings, constructing new ones, and establishing physical and financial policies for making the housing stock available to users. This market has institutions which are visibly connected with the process of production—a complex of building firms with auxiliary services such as architecture, short-term credit, subcontractors, and a chain of materials suppliers. Institutions at this level also include property maintenance and management activities, whether formalized into business firms or carried out by individual proprietors.

There is also the basic market for housing services. The need for housing and the system of preference are rooted in the social and cultural origins of the community. The prevailing distribution of real purchasing power also reflects institutions which become significant to the housing sector at this point. There are, to be sure, market institutions of the business type at work in this market, such as the system of communication which lets households in the community know what kinds of housing exist, plus legal practices which surround the consumer transaction itself, say the renting of an apartment.

Figure 6 shows, in very broad outline, how these three markets are related to one another and to other parts of the economic system. We start with the sum total of our economic resources and end with *Current value output,* that is, with the intangible enjoyments and satisfactions derived currently from our resources.

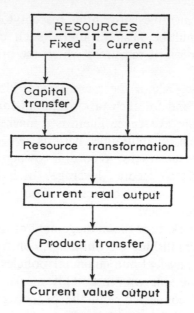

Figure 6
Levels of Resource Allocation

The resources include some which are *fixed*—such as land and buildings—whose existence and availability are not contingent upon current output. *Current* resources, primarily activities lumped together under the heading of "labor," vary in availability with the level of current output and the way in which it is distributed. In a very short period, say one day, the economic community might regard all its resources as *fixed* and in a period of ten or twenty years, perhaps all its resources would be *current* in the sense employed here. But for the usual state of affairs, we can assume that some resources are ready to be used while others will be available if we pay for them.

A more interesting distinction for our purposes is that fixed resources are durable and thus exchangeable on the basis of future contributions to output, while current resources seldom fall in this category. Thus, for fixed resources, there is a market process called *Capital transfer* on the diagram, in which the ownership of these fixed resources can be changed without necessarily altering any other aspect of economic life. Land and houses can be bought and sold. The ownership of a rental dwelling may change without any impact upon the tenant. The basis for the exchange is future rather than current "productivity" where the latter term means the economic value which can be derived from ownership under the prevailing legal and market conditions.

To become productive in a more literal sense, these fixed resources must usually be combined with current resources and "transformed" into things of practical usefulness. Farm land is combined with farm labor, and the two are transformed into wheat or cabbages. Urban land is combined with labor and building materials to be transformed into a dwelling. The dwelling becomes part of the stock of fixed capital for the future, but is still a component of current output. Previously existing urban dwellings are combined with some amount of management to provide what is usually the bulk of current housing-sector output in the form of intangible "services." *Resource transformation* requires that various types of inputs be brought together and combined in various ways so the goods and services can be produced. This is an allocation process inherently depending upon, and giving rise to, a set of resource prices. The function of these prices is to pull units of a specific type of resource from the production of one product to that of another if the latter product is more desirable. ("Desirability" is judged by the decision-makers at the level of production, much influenced, perhaps, by the opinions of ultimate consumers.)

Current real output, resulting from the transformation of resources, consists of goods and services. They become available for consumption, but a further process of distribution must occur before these goods and services are used. This process is called *Product transfer* in the diagram. We usually think of it as a competition among consumers, for things which are available, with a set of prices to restrict effective demand to the quantities actually available and to decide who gets what. These issues may be resolved by some combination of conscious rationing, rationing by price and "first come, first served," or other means, but in an abstract sense, the process of product transfer ought to see to it that the person who derives most satisfaction from the enjoyment of a particular good or service should receive it. *Product transfer* is often a multiphase process, for the distribution of spendable income or other "tickets of eligibility" to consume resources must first be distributed among households, the households must then select combinations of goods in competition with each other, and distribution within the household has to be accomplished so that each individual finally consumes some portion of the community's current economic product, deriving value or satisfactions or "utility" from so doing. Thus, a man's paycheck may be determined in part by his union contract, entrusted (in part, perhaps) to the housewife who allocates it among available types of consumption goods and who, bringing these goods into the home, decides which member of the family receives what. The household has to secure its dwelling in this process and then determine what use is to be made of its space and facilities by each member of the household. Product prices which accomplish the restriction of total demand and determine the household distribution of goods and services appear in this process as the result of income-determining forces, on the one hand, and perceived individual needs and desires on the other, given the quantity and types of goods and services currently available.

Thus, there are three distinguishable levels of resource allocation, each with particular institutions and each with some role for prices. The sets of prices which emerge and function at each level have some interrelationship, but the nature of their linkage is not obvious. Certainly, it cannot be said that all three kinds of transactions—capital, production, and distribution—occur within the same market.

Within any one of these markets, the commodities to be allocated are fixed in quantity and characteristics. Exchanges of capital goods do not increase or decrease the amount, or change the kinds of such goods. Allocations of labor, raw materials, and the current services of capital goods within the production process do not in themselves change the total quantities to be allocated. And in the final or product market, the level and structure of prices does not affect the supplies of goods and services currently available. Basically, transactions or exchange decisions within each of the three markets are simply transfers, putting something in this pocket rather than in that pocket.

As resources move vertically through this diagram, however, the prices paid in one market may affect the availability of resources. Resource owners want to share in current output. They can do this by requiring that prices paid in the process of allocating products be paid to them, the resource owners. Resources may then be allocated and reallocated in the production phase until some equilibrium-sharing of aggregate purchasing power for final goods comes to light, as among lines of products and types of resources. There is a circular or reciprocal relationship between the resource transformation process and the product transfer process; prices in one become purchasing power in the other.

The reciprocal relationship between the capital market and either of the other two markets is incomplete. Those who purchase capital goods from others, purchase it with the coin of future times, with the promise of participation in the distribution of current product of future periods. In this respect, the structure of prices within the capital market is independent of the role which fixed resources play in current production.

On the other hand, ownership of capital often is requisite to its use for current production. It is the owner of land who can permit it to be changed from one use to another. It is the ownership of a dwelling which provides those current satisfactions of secure tenure for a household. To make present use of elements of fixed capital, frequently it is necessary, simply from the form of legal and business institutions, to acquire that capital in a market where prices are not based upon current use. We can say that the best current use of all resources is not possible unless certain participants in the process of resource transformation are able to compete effectively in the noncurrent market for capital goods such as land and buildings.

In practical terms this means that a family should be able to acquire a home for its current use, including the incident of ownership, without regard to the level of prices prevailing for such ownership in the capital market.

This is too strong a statement because some types of current use—such as the construction of a building upon land acquired in the capital market—make the subsequent use of that acquired capital less flexible. The ideal set of prices for fixed capital goods (such as land and buildings) is the set which encourages the pattern and ownership of those goods which, in turn, best balances the desires for current output and for future output. It happens, however, that such functional prices are sometimes suppressed by institutions within the market for capital goods, most particularly in the types of fixed capital which are of greatest importance to the housing sector. To secure the right of occupying a particular dwelling, a household is often required to make a substantial equity investment in that property.

The "housing market" is thus, in reality, three markets, analytically distinct, but often in practice linked together in particular ways.

The Urban Land Ratchet

To say that capital goods such as land and buildings are bought with the "coin of the future" implies that there is a different monetary system for capital goods than for current production. There is substantial truth to this, for those goods which are not reproducible out of current resources have no direct linkage with current production through the price mechanism. Some of the community's money supply which is not being used to sustain the level of current output and transactions in current goods is drawn into the market for durable and essentially "free" assets such as land, to sustain a volume of transactions in these goods. The price level which prevails for land and buildings and similar assets in fixed supply depends on the balance between that fixed supply and the volume of spending power.

The familiar "equation of exchange," $MV = PQ$, in which M stands for the quantity of money, V for the velocity or number of times the money is spent in a given period of time, P for the average level of prices, and Q for the quantity of goods produced, must be modified somewhat in the case of durable assets such as land and buildings. Usually this equation is employed in discussion of the relationship between monetary events and the *general* price level, with interest primarily on goods being currently produced. The fact that we are interested in the prices of goods being exchanged but not being produced means that a slightly different formulation would be appropriate.

First, we can distinguish between money used for transactions in the market for current goods and money used for transactions involving fixed goods by using the subscript "f" to denote the latter. We could write:

$$M_f V_f = P_f Q_f$$

meaning that each aspect of the common equation of exchange has its counterpart in the submarket for fixed assets. We are interested in P_f as the dependent variable in our problem, we might at first regard Q_f as literally fixed, we realize that M_f is necessarily bound up with events in the market for current goods, and in the monetary system as a whole; and we may suppose that V_f is the result of custom, convenience, and liquidity preference, all as related to the particular market for fixed assets.

The problem with this expression is that it will account for the price level of the goods in question only if we assume that all these goods change hands once during the time period which is relevant for V_f. Such is the reasonable but implicit assumption in the usual equation of exchange, the context for which is GNP— i.e. current output. Fixed goods are not being produced, by definition, since they already exist, and there is a question whether they will be sold at all during the period or perhaps sold many times. We therefore need to understand Q_f as the volume of transactions in fixed goods or, perhaps preferably, to treat the volume of exchanges in the fixed assets market as the product of a truly fixed quantity of physical goods and a turnover rate, t, which varies with the inclination of the marketplace. Thus, we might write, after getting the dependent variable in its proper place:

$$P_f = \frac{M_f V_f}{Q_f \cdot t}.$$

This leaves the level of prices in this particular market quite free to vary, since M_f may ebb and flow from the larger monetary system, and V_f, as well as t, must reflect the changing views of a changing population of traders in this market.

We might suppose that there is a mechanism linking the price being paid for a fixed asset to its current productivity such as the rental income for land or buildings (though this would be a tenuous linkage if we were talking about the market for Rembrandt paintings). If the price level of fixed assets has risen while the income they promise to produce does not also rise, then potential buyers might back off, the effect of which would be to lower V_f or perhaps M_f. P_f might then fall, assuming no offsetting decline in t. If the price of fixed assets seemed too low in relation to prospective productivity, on the other hand, a rise in V_f or M_f might be induced and we might even suppose that t might fall as present holders begin to expect some speculative gains.

The demand for urban land is such, however, that productivity or rent is more likely to be determined by the price levels at which land and buildings are exchanging than vice versa. This follows from a combination of circumstances related to urban development. Demand for the use of fixed urban assets is very inelastic, so that users are inclined to spend what they can afford without regard to the quality of what they get. It is essential that they have something—some place to operate their businesses, some place to house their families. There is the further fact that additions to the supply of urban fixed assets—for additional land can be developed and more or better buildings built—are subject to lags which are more or less technological and, occasionally, to lags which are artificially imposed such as wartime limitations on the use of scarce resources for urban building.

There is also a peculiar relationship between urban land and the buildings upon it.[6] Once constructed, a building becomes part of the "land" in the terminology of the real estate trades (and often of the law) and in an important economic respect. The developed area of a city consists of "land" which can be put to new uses at any time, but the economic cost and the market price of doing so includes the acquisition and destruction of the existing building. In times when buildings become scarce, as in a period of housing shortage, "land" values rise. Since the increase in demand must be met initially from the existing supply of buildings, the price of such buildings and their rents must rise, often taking the form of decreased space per user and falling physical standards. (Net rents can rise without substantial increases in rent per user or even consistent with a decrease in the latter. Thus, the market opportunity for increasing or improving the supply of dwellings may be obscured.)

Households wishing to continue in their role as home owners and housing developers wishing to satisfy the intensified demand for housing can only acquire "land"—with or without buildings—by paying the inflated prices for property in this market. This can be done only by expanding the components of money demand for these assets, $M_f V_f$. This expansion tends to be irreversible for, in the investment sense, it is justified. Rents are high per unit of "land" throughout the area. Equities are high. The community comes to accept such conditions as normal.

Only large-scale construction can threaten such escalation of price levels, but the escalation itself discourages such construction. The original supply of dwellings, now inadequate, has a monopoly over the "land" which is best suited to more intensive rebuilding. This land cannot be acquired from willing sellers save by paying the escalated price. Once that price is paid, the capital structure of the new building demands a rent level which is no improvement upon the escalated level.

Thus, a ratchet effect may come into existence, with prices going up in periods of scarcity but not falling when the increase in demand levels off. This effect is represented in Figure 7. It describes the equilibrium level of replacement or improvement construction and the associated value of land, in an otherwise static community. It abstracts from site rent or other land value factors. The supply of building sites consists of some land which is vacant and other land which is improved. The supply price of the vacant land is its opportunity cost which might be for some agricultural use. The supply price of the improved land is the market value of an improved parcel. We can start with the assumption that this latter price is the sum of the opportunity cost of the land and the cost of construction; in other words, a competitive equilibrium price for a building plus land.

The horizontal position of the demand curve is a function of time. That is, if we are talking about a period of one year, then OR is the volume of replacement activity per year. The figure is so drawn that there is enough vacant land to meet the period's building needs, so the price of land remains at OA.

The effect of replacement construction must be to diminish

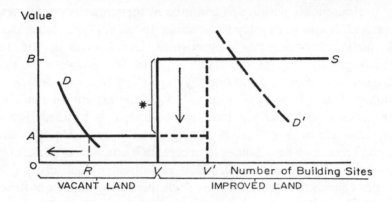

*Construction cost of first-generation buildings

Figure 7
The Urban Land Ratchet

the value of some portion of the stock of existing structures. If the activities of builders is successful in this period, then OR new buildings will cause the same number of old buildings to become vacant. As a result, VV' building sites will become available for the next replacement construction period. The supply of vacant land is thus replenished, and the price of building sites remains at the original opportunity cost of vacant land. The arrows indicate that the supply schedule shifts to the left for the next period, while a portion of the supply schedule for improved land collapses to the price level of vacant land.

This is the situation which should characterize a competitive replacement process. A certain amount of "excess" land is in use while replacement buildings are being created. When this land is occupied, some previously existing structures become redundant; and, the replacement process can continue smoothly into the future without having any effect on the price of land.

Suppose, however, that the development of vacant land is prevented or that the expression of replacement demand is deferred for a long period of time. Either problem can be represented by shifting the demand curve to the right so that it intersects the higher segment of the supply curve at price OB. This price now becomes the permanent minimum supply price for building sites. The household which desires now to replace its home must pay OB for land (either implicitly or explicitly), plus the cost of construction, AB (or whatever these costs have become in the interval). The supply schedule for building sites jumps up one more step with the creation of "second generation" buildings.

There is no necessary tendency for the price of land to fall below OB once it has reached that level. Urban land is an investment which enjoys general liquidity, and which can be used to secure debts. Whatever the price of land to the user, if the user has the resources to make a "tied-in" investment, he can buy the land.

A large amount of "new" land made available by new means of transportation, perhaps, plus public investment, might bring the equilibrium price of improved building sites down. The required scale of this is likely to be very great, however. Higher land prices resulting from postponement of replacement construction may discourage replacement construction still further, so that more and more of the stock of structures is in need of replacement. At the extreme, it would be necessary to recreate the entire stock on new land outside the city in order to drain away replacement demand from the old stock and thus lower the price of improved land. The original land would then be cheap, but probably it would not be useful, the city having moved outward.

This ratchet-like movement of urban land prices seems likely to produce two kinds of adverse effects on welfare. One is the projection of replacement demand into land more and more remote from the center of the city, causing aggregate transportation costs for the community to rise. Urban density is inadvertently reduced, as high-transport, distant land becomes the market equivalent of improved, high-opportunity cost land at the center, so individuals seeking land for replacement construction may be indifferent about its location. It is not a matter of indifference to the community, of course, and represents a type of external diseconomy which may result from market behavior under certain circumstances.

The other adverse effect is that the deteriorating conditions of the initial stock of structures gradually transforms the utility of building services into economic rent. That is, income is transferred from households (or other building users) to building and land owners so long as the progressive deterioration of the original stock is not matched by a decline in user payments. Since the demand for urban facilities is generally quality-inelastic in the short run, this transfer may eventually reach substantial proportions. Users are then paying for more than they get in terms of actual building services, but it is not profitable to enter this monopolistically exploited market because the value of a necessary ingredient—land—is based upon that monopoly transfer. There is no self-correcting tendency.

It is clear that this ratchet in land prices comes into effect only if the inherently continuous demand for housing replacement (or replacement of other urban structures) is somehow suspended. If national economic policy drains funds away from urban construction, then there is a danger that land prices will sooner or later leap from the level associated with raw land to that associated with improved land.

Inflation in urban land prices seems to invite some public remedies. Whether the inflation is understood to be the ratcheting just described or not, the community is likely to become acutely aware of the fact that prices have risen and the market for land and buildings is "tight." Often the outcry is against "speculation," so that measures to curtail speculation, such as high transfer taxes, are proposed. Another common response is to initiate some public programs to make up for the slowdown in private land development, and particularly redevelopment. These approaches attack the symptoms rather than the basic cause and may well produce new difficulties for the land economy of the city without substantially correcting even the symptoms.

Two courses of public action with respect to the ratcheting of urban land prices can be suggested. One is not to let it happen —that is, to assure that urban housing supply is so responsive to increases in demand that inflationary situations do not arise. The other is to supply the community which has undergone this kind of price rise with increased credit—M_f. Unless the buyers and developers of housing in the community receive access to enlarged amounts of funds, the level of transactions necessary to adjust the use of the housing and land supply to changing patterns of use will not be realized, and the hardships occasioned by inflation will be compounded. This is saying, in effect, that the higher price structure should be "lived with." Since there appears to be no easy way to bring the price structure down in just one segment of a community's economy, this advice is pragmatic. It is more important to have the urban land economy function than to paralyze its functions while trying to revert to some historic price level.

Housing and the Sense of "Community"

It has often been argued or assumed that the physical nature of family dwellings helps to mold the attitudes of people in a community toward one another, so that by changing the style of residential behavior new social outlooks can be instilled. Thus, in the United States, great importance has been attached to ownership of single-family homes in the belief, often consciously and explicitly put forward, that this type of living arrangement fosters the kind of citizenship which corresponds to traditional American values. Government agencies, such as the Federal Housing Administration and the Veterans Administration, have helped home ownership to become the dominant housing style in American life. Particular types of financial institutions, such as savings and loan associations, have, with the encouragement and direction of state and federal government, concentrated their substantial resources in the same direction. It can be said that society looks with moral approbation upon the single-family, owner-occupied dwelling.*

SOCIALIZING EFFECTS OF HOUSING

Of course, it is not fascination with an architectural form which underlies such public attitudes, but rather an awareness of how people who live in their own individual dwellings conduct themselves toward others. To be the legal owner of a piece of land and a dwelling means to have a direct and tangible share in the economic destiny of the community. The value of the equity depends very much upon whether the community is prosperous, whether the schools are desirable, whether the police are honest and capable, whether the local taxes are moderate and stable, and so on. Many people believe that property-owning families will develop serious interest in the management of community affairs, participate intelligently and prudently in elections and public meetings, and perform public services with genuine concern for community rather than simply individual benefit.

The assumption behind this support for homeownership is that local government is actually in the hands of local people, and this may be more characteristic of American political institutions than it is elsewhere. Further, it seems to be assumed that the proper management of community affairs is that which has the effect of supporting the economic value of "land" (which must be taken to include existing buildings). Since the value of urban land does reflect, in one way or another, most of the economic and even cultural aspects of community existence,

---

* See Beyer, *Housing and Society*, Ch. 7. Beyer presents quotations from three U.S. Presidents to make the point. Calvin Coolidge: "No greater contribution could be made to the stability of the Nation and the advancement of its ideals, than to make it a nation of home-owning families." Herbert Hoover: "The present large proportion of families that own their own homes is both the foundation of a sound economic and social system and a guarantee that our society will continue to develop rationally as changing conditions demand." Franklin D. Roosevelt: ". . . a nation of homeowners, of people who own a real share in their own land, is unconquerable." Beyer, *ibid.*, p. 249.

For extended discussion of the larger issue, see Robert K. Merton et al., eds., "Social Policy and Social Research in Housing," *The Journal of Social Issues*, VII, Nos. 1 and 2 (1951).

such a rationale for public decision-making has much to be said for it.

Home owners know that the value of their dwellings to themselves or to prospective future purchasers depends upon the condition of the property itself, and of the neighborhood, as well as upon general economic factors affecting the entire community (such as the level of employment). Hence, the home owner is thought to be diligent in caring for his home and land, not abusing it but, instead, protecting and improving it by his own labor. Gardening, painting, and timely repairs are responsibilities which it is usually in the owner's interest not to neglect.

It is important for one family that its neighbors not neglect their own properties, for if that happened, the appearance of the neighborhood would detract from the value of even a meticulously cared-for dwelling. At this point the "socializing" nature of home-ownership as an institution becomes particularly clear. The situation in which each neighbor has a stake in how the other cares for his own property gives all the members of the neighborhood an interest in the "morale" of the group. What each one does on his Saturday afternoons is important, not only to himself but to specific other people as well. A certain amount of social pressure can build up against someone who seems to be neglecting his own property, for if this neglect is not contained, it can demoralize the entire group. When demoralization has passed a certain point, spontaneous interaction within the neighborhood cannot restore the harmonious pursuit of joint interests. The quality of residential neighborhood has an almost natural tendency to decline, for moral efforts can ordinarily resist decline but not reverse it.

"Socializing" means, in this context, not much more than the maintenance of friendly contacts, letting each other know that work done upon one property is enjoyed and appreciated by all. We can easily imagine a more formal system of neighborhood discipline in which the efforts of each person are judged publicly, perhaps with concrete rewards for some and sanctions for others. The introduction of external compulsion in place of spontaneous response to the sensed feelings of others is rather critical in the evolution of any society. It appears to be largely irreversible, for internal "guidance systems" (to borrow the astronaut's phrase) which are in disuse while the environment changes soon lose their capability, at least in the sphere of interpersonal relationships with which we are concerned at the moment. Residential environment, for the individual and the community as a whole, is rather dynamic, so that when we have relied upon external instructions for some time, then we are likely always to need external controls.

External compulsion has the further characteristics of accretion and inflexibility. If we have a neighborhood government which rules that all houses must have front lawns, then we shall soon have regulations regarding how high the grass should be. Every regulation of residential behavior is vague enough to be abused and every abuse can only be deterred by supplementary regulations. As the body of formal regulation becomes more comprehensive and exact, the initial purpose of the system of control may come close to realization. The appearance of the neighborhood may be defended in a very effective way. In the process, however, cooperation which began in self-interest becomes nothing more than a "corvée," feudal forced labor. Each one has a "right" to the labor of others, and this is very different from having occasion to seek the effect of that labor by personal courtesies.

The ultimate courtesy between neighbors is not visible collaboration, but a respect for privacy, for the right of each person to make up his own mind about "going along" with neighborhood customs. People who can refuse to cooperate with one another have human rather than legal relationships.

Now we many consider briefly the interpersonal relationships in a very different residential environment.[7] In Japan, the single-family dwelling has perhaps even more cultural significance than in the United States. The interpersonal relationships of residential communities in Japan take remarkably different form, however. Where the American suburban dwelling is directly visible to neighbors and to passersby, the Japanese house is traditionally enclosed within a high, dense wall which lies on the property line, so that there is no lawn or garden to grace the appearance of the street. Within the fence, however, there is a garden, often in refined and elegant form and representing conscious effort and substantial expense (for land prices are high) on the part of the owner. The garden is for the family, not for the neighborhood.

There is a neighborhood organization (called *cho-kai*) which was an organ of government during the war, charged particularly with air raid measures and some aspects of rationing. Nowadays, these organizations have functions such as street maintenance and lobbying for local public improvements such as paving, extension of sewers, and other problems of public hazards or convenience. A tax is collected, more or less voluntarily, and residents are expected to take turns serving as officers of the organization.

The element of compulsion is there, but neighborhood organization in Japan does not involve itself very much with the way in which individual properties in the area are used or maintained. Indeed, there is relatively little sense that one must consider the convenience and happiness of others in a residential neighborhood, in contrast to characteristic attitudes in the United States. Japanese residential districts, for one thing, tolerate intermixture of land uses which would seem flagrant and distasteful in most American communities. It has been historic practice in Japanese cities for families to keep shops, offices, and even small workshops in their homes, and this practice has remained very common. Today, however, these businesses are served by noisy, hazardous, and obstructive motor vehicles, and they also employ equipment which produces noise, odors, sparks, electrical disturbances, and sometimes ground tremors. Dwellings themselves attract noise- and hazard-producing equipment such as TV, phonographs, and portable gas heaters (since central heating is very rare), and a collection of motorcycles and private cars in districts where housing lots have never provided parking space. Single-family dwellings themselves give way to crowded apartment buildings which immediately increase the congestion of the area in this period of rising urban population.

The neighborhood organization does little, if anything, to control the disturbing influence of these changes. For one thing, it has very little power. More fundamentally, though, the people who make up this essentially democratic association do not perceive the need for restrictive action as such need might be seen in an American community. In point of fact, the value of urban property is not clearly related to the quality of local land uses in Japanese cities. The present explosive growth of major urban centers has helped to produce a land inflation without precedent. Urban property needs only to exist to benefit from this inflation. A controlled neighborhood environment does not seem to add to the value of individual property under these circumstances and, perhaps, by diminishing the flexibility of uses within that neighborhood might even be a negative factor.

Another factor is the traditional rather than businesslike organization of the urban land market. Residential population in Japan has been relatively stable, in the sense that individual households do not move about very much. It is difficult to exchange dwellings, for transactions involving real estate are complex, uncertain, and costly. Thus, the owner of a home is not much aware of the "market value" of his particular property since his concept of the market is not so particular or refined. He may know that land values are rising but may not imagine that a new welding shop in the neighboring lot could adversely affect his own share of this general inflation.

Finally, it must be noted that the Japanese home owner or tenant family is much less demanding with regard to his neighbors' behavior than American families are wont to be. The walls which surround the Japanese dwelling are walls of the mind as well. What a person does within his own walls is to be tolerated and ignored, to a much greater degree than we might find in American society. Greater latitude is provided for doing things which in fact may be disturbing to others. A little wine shop may stay open well into the night, filling the dark alleys with boisterous sounds, or worse. A metalworker with an urgent subcontract may start his lathe in the wee hours and continue far into the night. Rubbish may spill out into the narrow road and so may household chores such as cooking and washing. Being a good neighbor in Japan usually means looking the other way. Community criticism which is forestalled in American life by active efforts and self-control is withheld in Japan. Yet both forms of behavior are evidence of "socialization," traditional systems of relationships among people who cannot avoid being interdependent.

The nature of the socializing system is evident in the physical attributes of the neighborhood, if we know what to look for. The walls around the Japanese dwelling and the lawn in front of the American home are valuable clues to the network of responsibilities in which the individuals are enmeshed. It occurs to some people, who may be social scientists or political philosophers, that the physical forms are the cause of the interpersonal behavior and feelings. If we take away the walls from Japanese house lots, we might soon see spontaneous and unofficial cooperation for the betterment of the district, in the American style, according to this point of view. Or, by requiring that high walls be built around American housing lots, we might diminish the voluntary aspects of community behavior, installing a formal neighborhood organization in its place.

The practical extreme of such reasoning is the design of residential facilities and districts in Soviet Russia (at least in terms of intentions and policies). Large apartment buildings are considered conducive to collective ways of thinking.[8] By limiting the facilities within the individual unit, families are brought together in community kitchens, dining halls, child-care centers, and recreation rooms. In this way the family is supposed to become less and less important as a social phenomenon, with the individual being guided instead by responsibilities to the larger society. A system of community decision-making is formalized, so that the individual's latitude for his behavior is continuously restricted. Eventually, this system and other aspects of daily life in that country are supposed to produce the "collective mentality," the substitution of group accomplishments for personal or family desires as motivations for action.

It is appropriate to question whether the causal relationship underlying the use of housing as an instrument of social reform really exists. Sciences seem to begin with observations of concurrent phenomena, but mature only when naïve assumptions about the direction of causality are discarded. It may be quite true, for example, that automobiles in motion usually have people seated on the front seat, but this will not keep an empty automobile from rolling downhill. The nature of the relationship can be rather complex, but if we study it honestly, we may eventually arrive at fairly sophisticated yet useful information.

We can ask, about housing, whether the form of dwellings and the physical appearance of neighborhoods result from, rather than cause, a set of social values. Perhaps Americans built their homes and their cities in a manner intrinsically consistent with interpersonal attitudes historically rooted in their society. The FHA may simply carry out inclinations that existed in the bosom of culture before the bureaucracy took its first breath. By this view, the Japanese built high walls around their homes because they already knew they wanted to give or to receive little interference in residential behavior. The same social fabric which produces the physical neighborhood can, in time, produce the formal, civic structure which makes it legitimate. That is, the inherent system of "socialization" may produce the public polity rather than vice versa.

The inquiry into this relationship has hardly begun. We know very little about any aspects of residential socialization, particularly those involving some economic factors. The larger science of which housing economics is a part is surely in its earliest stage. So we have to be careful about assuming directions of causality, of believing that we can make over the human conscience with architecture or subdivision ordinances, or, on the contrary, of reading immutable destiny in the accumulation of artifacts which make up a city. In fact, when we have learned very much about urban behavior, we may find ourselves without either a self-evident goal or a predictable tool. But it is a penalty of knowledge that we have to think harder when we have it.

The ultimate question about the interrelationship of housing and neighborhood form with the matrix of personal associations is this: how would the behavior and viewpoints of a given set of people react if their residential environment were changed in a particular way? That is no more than the situation already discussed when we have removed the assumption of causality. Perhaps we would find conditions under which intensely collective planning on the Russian style would produce stridently antisocial behavior and profound individualism. Again, it might develop that residential neighborhoods on the American style evoke petty dictatorships or cold hostility when installed in other cultures. Perhaps the mental walls around the homes in Japan are so impervious that demolishing the physical walls would mean nothing in terms of social organization or feeling. The point at which to begin our study of urban life is the admission that we do not know what would be the effects of certain concrete actions. Rationality withers under dogma, and urban existence is now too grave a matter for irrational exhortation.

MUTUALITY AND COLLECTIVISM

The housing sector is the scene of many kinds of interactions and much interdependence. Individuals within it are dependent upon legal systems of property, upon the organization of monetary and investment institutions, upon devices and agencies of communication, upon the technical knowledge of a variety of skilled practitioners (e.g. developers), and, ultimately, as we have suggested above, upon the condescension of neighbors. This means that people who live in cities have many problems in common, problems which necessarily require some kind of cooperation to solve. It is false, though, to think that the mutuality of urban existence leads necessarily to the development of fully collective institutions. Instead, there is a spectrum of cooperation, along which we may place any particular community. At one extreme is the community in which the disadvantages or difficulties of cooperative behavior outweigh any possible advantages. This is the dispersed community of traditional rural America, for example. Each family is virtually an island, not necessarily hostile, but satisfied with effective isolation. It is represented also by the community of tenants of a large apartment structure who may—if it is a well constructed building—ignore just about everything and everyone outside of their own family walls. It may be some deteriorated single-family district in which the lapse of neighborhood collaboration is so pronounced that there is no virtue in, and no incentive for, diligent housekeeping or gardening. Instead, it is a set of individuals who tolerate each other's disorderliness.

At the opposite extreme we have the collective mentality. The household ceases to exist as a decision-making unit and the individual derives his significance only from his ability to carry out social objectives. These objectives, moreover, cannot be cast in the mold of individual desire. The collective community is a monument to its designer, a monument which consists of intricate movements within a physical frame. The communes of Communist China represent the principle, with the ideas of Russian planners not too different, but the main elements of this are common to almost all city planners or urban welfare agencies. When a structure—whether physical or institutional—has been created in the image of the "good life," it becomes heresy not to conform to it. Individualism is thus "reaction," and antisocial under such a regime.

Between these poles lies a vast expanse of limited and flexible cooperation. Most communities in the world have a complex scheme of agencies, institutions, and "understandings," each of which has a specific, limited, and seldom obligatory function. Water is often supplied to a community by a semipublic enterprise which seldom tells people what to do with the water. The system of land title registration permits people to make transactions which are essential to the coordinated development of the city, but the legal system does not dictate specific transfers of land nor the set of prices. Zoning plans offer some degree of coordination in land uses, primarily the separation of mutually disadvantageous activities, but zoning commissions do not assume responsibility for the economic effects upon individuals. Neighbors concur on appropriate colors for exterior painting, but they respect each other's taste in TV programs—so long as the audio is not too loud. Common problems do lead to common action, but the integrity of the person and his family is secured. There is no absolute involvement, no total responsibility to the welfare of the community as opposed to the interests of the person. Individuals may initiate transactions or programs of limited collaboration. They may also withdraw from most of those to which they might have been drawn by prior circumstances. The form of the city, and its pattern of movement, conforms to no single design; it can be explained only in terms of an equilibrium of many individuals' motivations and means, achieved through a flux of institutions. Most communities live this way, so that their life looks disorderly and futile at first glance.

Housing and the Redistribution of Income

The individual's attitude toward the community may be related in some way to the kind of housing which he has, as we have suggested. The community's attitude toward the housing of specific individuals is another very different issue, though, which happens to be of practical importance in most parts of the world. If a particular family or segment of the community is poorly housed, then questions arise about the responsibility for correcting this situation and about the means of doing so.

Low income is a principal correlative of poor housing, though it is certainly not the only one. Members of the community may be poorly housed because they are deprived of access to the entire housing market for reasons of prejudice or for lack of self-respect and motivation, though these factors themselves tend to correlate with low income. Thus, the community is likely to become aware of a "welfare" issue within areas of poor-quality housing. People in these areas evoke varying amounts of sympathy, and the community sets out in some way to help them.

It is remarkable that this assistance often takes the form of a benefit in kind. New and better dwellings are constructed with public assistance and are made available to these underhoused families. This occurs despite the existence of at least two alternative routes for dispensing welfare and correcting housing deficiencies, routes which are directed to a more fundamental problem of which poor housing is a symptom.

One of these alternatives to assistance in kind is to improve, through welfare programs, the income position of disadvantaged families, leaving them in a position to acquire better housing on their own initiative from the market. Low-income families usually have health care, education, and other problems, and deficient diets, as well as poor housing, so a rehousing program meets only part of the admitted need. An "income" program works to relieve all aspects of the need in a balance tailored to the preferences of the individual.

The other alternative is to provide better housing indirectly by encouraging housing replacement activities throughout the community. The Federal Housing Administration in the United States undoubtedly had the effect of general upgrading of the housing stock, with some benefit to lowest-income families who could not participate directly in FHA programs. This concept (often called "filtering" for it suggests that as other families acquire new homes, they will allow good but older dwellings to filter down to low-income households) has been the subject of partisan controversy and academic debate in the past. In general, it is an approach which is distrusted by those who initiate welfare programs, perhaps because other people than the needy are assisted in the process.

The income approach to welfare needs is apparently free of partisan overtones, yet we find that housing problems usually elicit welfare benefits in kind. There can be several reasons for this, each of which stems from the attitudes and information of political prime movers who design and introduce welfare measures. One is the view of very early welfare workers that if poor people were given money, they would waste it on drink, gambling, etc., rather than using it to correct deficiencies in their standard of living. Thus, they had to be given the thing they required—housing—rather than money to buy it. A related point of view is that welfare recipients would spend at least a part of money grants on things, however worthy, other than housing. A program arising out of perception of housing need, then, could suffer substantially from leakage if the income approach were taken.

This suggests that some communities are more sensitive to housing deprivation than to other kinds of deprivation endured by segments of the population. In fact, this is often so. The desire to raise housing standards in a community is not exactly the same thing as a desire to raise living standards. The nature of the housing stock does things to the physical image of the community. Bad housing is more visible than bad health or poor nutrition. It may produce health and fire hazards for the community at large. It may, as many have argued, produce moral hazards such as delinquency, though thinking on this subject today is less confident than it was a generation ago. Housing, in short, is sometimes seen as a priority problem affecting not only the people who live in it, but the rest of the community as well. It would follow that a welfare program could aim to be more helpful with regard to the housing of disadvantaged people than toward their other problems.

We might imagine also that community leaders are sometimes influenced by the durable nature of housing. A housing project serves as a monument of civic "enlightenment" much more effectively than does a program of vocational training or social casework. A saving aspect of this viewpoint is that better housing often improves a family's social "status," its perception of its own relative worth, and so may constitute a form of therapy. Thus, housing's durability and visibility can produce psychic satisfactions for its inhabitants and its civic-minded sponsors simultaneously.

When housing is employed as a means of redistributing real income in the community, the absolute definition of "standard" or "adequate" housing is irrelevant. What is perceived is a gap between modal housing conditions and the low end of their distribution, and it is really the inequality rather than the conditions themselves which the community aims to correct. Most of the dwellings in Tokyo, for example, probably are structurally substandard by definitions employed in the United States, yet only a tiny fraction are classified as "dilapidated" in the Japanese census of housing.* Most of the housing regarded as substandard in the United States would be considered rather elegant in other areas of the world. Hong Kong's last word in humanitarian rehousing efforts would be considered scandalous in New York.†

---

* Approximately 0.2 percent of the dwellings in Tokyo were classified as dilapidated in the survey of 1963. Those in need of substantial repairs made up another 3 percent, while about 15 percent were classified as in need of slight repair. *Report on the Housing Survey of 1963*, Vol. 3, Part 13, Bureau of Statistics, Office of the Prime Minister of Japan, p. 37.

† Dwelling units in Hong Kong's massive new housing projects consist essentially of one room and are intended for occupancy by an entire family.

The housing sector attracts humanitarian concern in ways which can seem slightly irrational. Welfare programs in housing tend to be shaped more by the quality and structure of social organization than by "housing economics." Yet any study of the economics of the housing sector must consider the impact of various types of programs and the persistent interest of urban communities throughout the world in defining and then solving their "housing problems." In the housing sector, economics must be, in truth, a "social science."

Housing, Urban Economics, and Ecology

The economic life of the city can be studied in a much broader context than just "housing." There is ebb and flow in the level of employment. There are complex interrelationships among different kinds of employment which can be expressed as an "input-output" matrix.[9] The metropolitan community is also a small-scale macroeconomy, so that many of the elements of Keynesian economics have their counterparts in urban studies.[10] Investment, "imports," consumption propensities, and their derivative concepts are useful in the study of urban economics.

Fiscal problems of urban areas are different in kind from fiscal issues at the national level, for the tax base of the urban community is usually different from that of the nation (relying on property rather than income taxes, for example), and there may be many competitive local jurisdictions within a single metropolis.[11] Public functions of urban governments (usually including education, street building, police and fire protection) present relatively inflexible demands for local government expenditures and have highly specific impacts upon the wealth and well-being of individuals in the community.

Patterns of land use within a community and their determinants are also the objects of specialized study which might be encompassed by the term "urban economics." * While residential

* It is unnecessary to distinguish between urban economics and the institutionalized discipline of "Regional Science," for the latter has broadened substantially since its appearance as a study of industry location economics and now embraces most land-related issues of urban development. See, for example, W. L. Garrison, "Values of Regional Science," *Regional Science Association Papers,* Vol. XIII, 1964, pp. 7–11.

uses ordinarily account for the largest portion of an urban area, the land used for public facilities (particularly streets) and for retail, commercial, and industrial activities are often more strategic in determining whether the city functions well.*

All of these matters are certainly relevant to the study of housing economics. Most of them are introduced explicitly or implicitly in our discussion of housing. In order to keep our subject from mushrooming into a total analysis of urban economics, we must take the point of view that employment, fiscal activities, nonresidential land uses, and so on are "background" for the study of housing. The variables which we shall consider will be those most closely related to housing itself, and other factors will be "held constant" despite their great practical importance.

A city is an artifact which bears the imprint of humanistic institutions as well as economic forces. Thus, the "ecology" of the city is perhaps an even broader field of investigation than urban economics and, again, the study of housing is a subcategory.[12] The form and function of urban housing must be consistent with the entire range of human and natural constraints and impulses which we understand by the term "ecology." Let us take a very brief look at what this implies, for it will be useful throughout the study of housing economics to have in mind an idea of how physical structures in cities are related to human desires and activities.

A city is an aggregation of human beings. It brings them into closer contact with each other than dispersed living patterns would allow because of the cost in time and resources of transportation and communication. Some of these contacts are desirable, while some are undesirable, as judged from ordinary points of view. The city exists because the desirable aspects of these contacts outweigh the undesirable aspects. The physical form of the city, however, plays a significant role in determining the degree to which the net effect of these contacts is beneficial. Hence, the physical nature of the city—its houses, streets,

---

* The Bay Area Simulation Study, undertaken by the Center for Real Estate and Urban Economics, University of California, Berkeley, adopts this concept of strategic land uses. See *Jobs, People, and Land* (Berkeley: Center for Real Estate and Urban Economics, University of California, Special Report No. 6, 1968).

factories, and the like—is a variable which both reflects human attitudes toward each other and helps to determine the extent of urbanization.

Let us distinguish two categories of interpersonal contacts, those which are occasioned by productive activities or "work," and those which occur in other parts of life, or "nonwork." Within each of these categories, some contacts are desirable to the individual and others are undesirable. The following box diagram, Figure 8, identifies some of each.

	DESIRABLE	UNDESIRABLE
WORK	Complementarity	Competition
NONWORK	Culture	Responsibility

Figure 8
Interpersonal Contacts

In a person's working life he finds it very useful to associate himself with others who have complementary resources, skills, or needs.[13] An accountant benefits from contacts with nonaccountants, for only thus can he practice his skill. A baker needs contacts with flour merchants and retailers of bread. A lathe operator needs contact with a lathe maker, with people who perform previous operations upon the metal, and with those who develop the product of the lathe further. To avail ourselves of those complementary contacts which are greatly inhibited by distance, we tend to group ourselves in cities.[14]

On the other hand, contacts in the working world may provide us with competition for our skills or resources, and these we tend to avoid if we can. An accountant or a baker would be better off, up to a point, if he were the only person with such skill in the community. The merchant seldom relishes competition. The scholar or artist whose position is unique is immune from criticism.

In our nonworking lives we usually enjoy those contacts which intensify our understanding and pleasure. These are given the polite term of *culture* in the diagram. It is interesting to note that these are relatively anonymous or impersonal contacts. We can sit alone in a darkened theater or concert hall, enjoying the play or the music but shutting out concern for the artists as human beings. We can walk along the street or in the shops, seeing other people and conversing with them when and to the extent that we wish, but always with the option of breaking off our contact.

So the last box identifies *responsibility* as the kind of non-work association which is undesirable. Certainly it is human nature to seek some kinds of responsibilities—as parents, as citizens, as colleagues. But these are selective and limited. Community life can drown a person in his own conscience, for it heightens contrasts and perpetuates anguish. Most of what the sentient urban citizen might be impelled to do, he simply must refuse to do, since the human capacity for compassion is limited. Young adults weaken the contact with their parents when they are in the process of establishing different contacts.

The remarkable thing about urbanization, in this respect, is that it greatly increases the opportunity for desirable nonwork contacts—for *culture*—and seems also to diminish those which are undesirable—*responsibility*. Rural life and rural communities tend to present the individual with a network of "family" relationships and responsibilities. Personal freedom is inhibited by watchful, concerned eyes, and the call for self-sacrifice is almost uninterrupted. The history of urbanization seems to show that the personal liberty and anonymity of the city is a powerful magnet which entices people born and bred in rural areas. Quite apart from the economic opportunities in the city, when such are present, the flight to the city is often a flight from oppressive responsibility.

Thus far the advantages of the city seem greatly to outweigh the disadvantages to the individual. The edge of competition is dulled by general economic progress and loses its negative potential. But the city which grows and grows, which becomes a physical maze in which each of a myriad of individuals seeks to make those contacts he wants and to avoid those he does not want, begins ultimately to generate negative elements of its own. We pay a price to live in a city, and the kind of price depends on the kind of city—its physical attributes. Inadvertent contacts occur with people we neither like nor fear for their own sakes but who are there just as we are. We share the streets and the trains, the air and the water supply. We become innocent but not immune bystanders at every form of human conflict. We are exposed to theft and disgust, and so are those for whom we truly care. We look to community government for things which are increasingly necessary and find this government increasingly difficult to see.

Many of the discomforts which arise may be unnecessary. The form of the city as it is may aggravate them when it could relieve them. It may function poorly because the technology of urbanism is a weak infant in this age of rampant technology. It may not accord with the elementary disposition of the people who come to live in the city.

The physical city is a set of "streets" and "walls"—streets to bring people together, and walls to keep them apart. The people's instincts and their economic environment specify an implicit optimal pattern of "streets" and "walls," but the physical city may emerge in some other pattern.

Houses and neighborhoods are part of this broadly painted issue. The way they are fashioned imposes some set of contacts upon people who live in them and inhibits other contacts. Part of our concern with the development and management of urban housing resources must be couched in these terms of ultimate purpose.

Decision-Making in the Housing Sector

The next five chapters of this book are concerned with the way in which resource allocation decisions in the housing sector are made. There are two central themes. One is the distinction between "macroeconomic" and "microeconomic" aspects of the housing sector. There are some questions which relate to the overall dimensions of the housing economy—what fraction of current output to devote to it, how large particular cities should be geographically, what the overall housing replacement rate should be, and so on. These macroeconomic issues are intertwined in various ways with, and certainly are not independent of, the "microeconomic" or detailed decision-making processes within the housing sector. Nevertheless, both economic forecasting and the delineation of public policy for the housing sector generally call for aggregate economic measures and macroeconomic theory. It is possible in housing economics that theories at the aggregate level may be useful even though their microeconomic implications are unclear.

In the context of the housing sector, "microeconomics" means the problem of deciding what the composition and distribution of the total "output" should be. "Output" means not only the current period's volume of residential construction, but also the services produced currently by the preexisting stock of dwellings. The latter, in fact, typically outweighs the former in terms of human welfare and effect on the economic life of the city. Microeconomics means the process or technique of deciding what to do with a particular piece of urban property or with a particular household's housing budget. By extension it refers to the questions of investment, for there is little in the field of housing economics which cannot be considered at least in some respects as investment of personal wealth.

At the present stage of the study of housing it is necessary to offer a collection of theories covering macro- and microeconomic questions about the housing sector rather than one, integrated, general theory. There is no microeconomic event in this sector which does not have some implication for the sum total of housing resource use and productivity. Nor is there any significant macroeconomic question in this sector which does not have at its roots the welfare of particular individuals and the use of particular parcels of urban wealth. The integrating theory is not at hand, however. It seems destined to appear out of the computer-oriented "model-building" activity which now characterizes research into questions about the urban economy.[15] This book represents a relatively primitive approach in that sense, for we seek to answer only particular, qualitative questions about the housing sector—whether we can expect or recommend "more" or "less" of one type of housing resource activity under a given set of circumstances. Quantitative and disaggregated models depend for their development upon good qualitative concepts, so it is far from fruitless to dwell upon the simpler forms of theory.

We need a vocabulary before we can make sentences. The qualitative concepts, explored piecemeal and with only tentative integration in this book, will probably not be less meaningful when a composite macro–micro theory of the housing sector emerges.

The other central theme is a distinction between "equilibrium" and "optimum" patterns of housing sector behavior. Given a set of resources, consumption preferences, and housing sector institutions, we can predict or explain what the housing sector *will* do, and this is what we mean by "equilibrium." By "optimum" we mean our concepts of what the housing sector *should* do. The latter problem involves to some extent personal or social judgments, such as the desirability of assuring a minimum housing standard for all families in the community. Resources are scarce, however, and desirable objectives are linked together in a complex way, so that the search for an optimum is more an attempt to discover the best that can be done under the circumstances which exist. It is not an architectural rendering of paradise.

The gap between equilibrium and optimum is, of course, quite interesting, for it represents a wastage of actually available resources. Some of the problems associated with urban housing may have readily available solutions, and it is almost the central task of the economist to help identify such situations.

These two themes provide a four-way classication of urban housing theory. Macroeconomics has its equilibrium issues— what will be the total share of the housing sector in current output, for example—and its optimization issue—what should this share be? Microeconomics asks, for example, what kinds of new dwellings will be constructed this year and what kinds are in the best overall interest of the community.. The four chapters following take up the components of this four-way classification. Macroequilibrium, macrooptimization, microequilibrium, and microoptimization are taken up in turn.

Each of these chapters deals with specific economic inquiries which often appear in the real world. Other relevant questions may occur to the reader. It is in the nature of most economic methodology that tools and concepts are used in the illustration of central or prominent resource-allocation problems in the belief that such concepts and tools have application to other issues as well. Thus, there is a philosophy of resource allocation implicit in each system of economics, a philosophy which embraces the whole universe of relevant issues. Our succeeding chapters attempt to convey this philosophy or method both explicitly and by example. The usefulness of the economics in these chapters will best be seen if the reader knows there is an underlying philosophy and looks for it. We do not mean anything so crass as a "political" philosophy—an argument for more or less government intervention or for greater or less concern for problems of individual rights or welfare. These are issues which we discuss with our concepts; they are not the language of economics.

The central element in this philosophy may best be stated in the following way. Every decision concerning the use of resources produces many consequences both material and moral, some of which influence the decision while others are ignored. A community's institutions determine which potential consequences enter into economic decision making and, to some extent, the manner in which they are to be considered. Our economic investigation looks into several decision-making situations to identify the nature of the inputs, the logic of the decision, and the range of consequences.

Following these four chapters is one which explicitly considers the role of government in the housing sector. In a market economy we expect that private entrepreneurship enjoys considerable latitude in making decisions about the allocation of housing—and other resources. In most countries of the world the housing sector is in part a sphere for "public entrepreneurship" —direct administration of housing resources by a government agency. In socialized economies entrepreneurship is exclusively public, but even in nonsocialized nations, the housing sector often contains significant amounts of public resource allocation. Chapter 7 describes the spectrum of centralized–decentralized responsibility for the administration of housing resources.

3 · ▞

THE EQUILIBRIUM SIZE

OF THE HOUSING SECTOR

Measuring Stock Increment

From the consumer's point of view, "housing" is a group of services—shelter, amenities, accessibility, etc.—to be used daily and, often, to be paid for periodically. Consumers are thus concerned with the stock of housing available to them. From the viewpoint of the national economy, "housing" is a new capital good representing an important use of savings in competition with industrial investment and other forms of business or government capital needs. Questions about the "housing sector" are, therefore, usually concerned with increments in the stock, that is, with the level of investment in expanding or improving the stock. To use an old expression, it might be said that housing consumers are looking at the doughnut of total available housing, while economists concerned with housing are usually looking at the hole of new construction needs. In this chapter we shall adopt the essential point of view of the macroeconomist and define the housing sector as the level of new investment in housing or as the increment in the stock (measured in money or in numbers of housing units).

The level of new investment in housing is of interest for two basic reasons. The rate at which housing is actually constructed informs us about the progress we are making toward the solution of the various types of "housing problems" of which our community might be aware. Our ability to forecast the level of housing investment as a component of total national investment, also improves upon our management of the nation's economic life as a whole, anticipating the need for measures to sustain employment, stabilize prices, balance our international trade, or, perhaps, to adjust the basic structure of our economic system. The present chapter is concerned with the latter problem—that is, with the task of forecasting housing-investment levels as an element in macroeconomic understanding. We will be concerned with factors which explain why housing investment reaches the levels which it does, in fact, reach. Questions about housing problems— i.e. what the level of housing investment "should be"—are taken up in the following chapter.

Prediction about the level of output is the objective of most economic analysis and the methodology of economics is very much oriented to quantitative questions. This methodology looks upon the output of a specific commodity, or of all commodities taken together, as a compromise between Demand, or the expressed desire for the commodity, and Supply, or the availability of that commodity from a limited stock of resources. The economist answers the quantitative question "How much of X will be produced?" by identifying the conditions of supply of X and the strength of demand for X, and then by reconciling these opposing forces. If his concepts of demand and supply are realistic, and if his technique for deducing an equilibrium relationship between them is sound, his quantitative prediction will be good.[1]

A complex product or complex conditions of supply make the economist's task of prediction quite difficult. Housing is a sector of the economy which is characterized by a number of complexities on both demand and supply sides. Consider the problem of location, for example. A surplus of housing in City A is not available to meet a shortage in City B (except as families move from B to A). The same can be said concerning housing in two neighborhoods within the same city, except that here additional transportation costs might serve as a substitute for housing investment in the shortage area. Housing demand is quite heterogeneous, not only as to location, but also as to the size and quality of the units which are needed, their density, tenure, etc. The supply of available dwellings is likewise heterogeneous. To varying degrees, housing units which differ from one another can be substituted for one another and sometimes this substitution involves the use of resources for transportation or public facilities. It is very difficult even to envisage the range of alternative ways in which the housing sector may respond to a change in conditions of supply or demand. To select the precise form of response as our prediction about the behavior of the housing sector would require a most complex system of analysis.

Economic analysis of the housing sector is, in fact, not highly developed. Very simple methodology is used as a basis for macroeconomic planning, largely because the very complexity of the sector has discouraged economists from studying it. We shall examine this methodology in its basic form and attempt to improve upon it very modestly. It will remain true, however, that the use of simple analytical methods for a complex sector will result in a poor or unreliable prediction, and it is to be hoped that the student will develop a desire to see methods of housing analysis further improved.

Sources of Demand

Methods for predicting the level of new housing construction (i.e. of investment in housing) necessarily overlook much of the heterogeneity of housing demand and supply. We will find it convenient to make some drastic simplifications at first, later indicating how more complex problems can be handled. Let us begin the analysis of housing demand by calling each of the social groups which desire separate housing a "Family" and pay no attention to the number of people making up that household, the household's income, or its preferences regarding location, architecture, financing terms, etc. Similarly, let us consider every element of the dwelling supply to be a homogeneous "House," disregarding its size, quality, location, etc. With these simple terms, some elementary and hypothetical arithmetic of housing demand is possible—arithmetic which is, nevertheless, quite informative and useful.

The simplest concept of housing demand which we could state would be that each Family demands one House and there is no other source of housing demand. Symbolically,

$$H_d = f(F) \tag{1}$$

where H_d means the number of houses demanded, F is the number of families which exist, and f denotes a functional relationship. Simplifying H_d to H and noting that we have assumed a very specific type of functional relationship, we can rewrite this as:

$$H = F \tag{2}$$

It will help to carry a simple numerical example along with the development of a symbolic expression of housing demand, so let us imagine a community with exactly 1,000 families and write the above equation:

$$\begin{aligned} H &= F \\ 1{,}000 &= 1{,}000 \end{aligned} \tag{3}$$

This statement of demand will not satisfy even the most lethargic housing analyst. It is physically possible for the number of houses in the *supply* to exceed the number of families since some houses may be vacant and indeed, under almost any set of economic conditions, one expects to find housing vacancy.* Vacancy is usually thought to be a principal determinant of the level of housing construction. Using V to stand for the number— e.g. 100—of vacant houses, we can describe the size and use of the housing inventory as follows:

$$\begin{aligned} H &= F + V \\ 1{,}100 &= 1{,}000 + 100 \end{aligned} \tag{4}$$

This description of the inventory is a type of market information which is found to be of great practical importance, for excess present vacancy levels can cut into future demand for new houses. We must observe that Equation (4) is also an expression of housing *stock demand*. Vacant housing units are "inventory"

---

* "Households" are defined in the U.S. Census and related studies as persons or groups of persons occupying separate "housing units." Following this concept, it is not possible for the number of "families" (in our simplified terminology) to exceed the number of "houses."

in much the same sense that canned goods on a grocer's shelf are his inventory, and there is an economic demand for inventory. A grocer without an inventory may not stay in business very long; the inventory is costly but necessary. In a similar way, unoccupied houses represent an investment on the part of housing entrepreneurs. The grocer's demand for inventory is a net increase over total consumer demand for canned goods, and the owner of an unoccupied housing unit represents a "non-Family" source of demand for housing.

There are many reasons why an investor may hold vacant dwellings.[2] If the buildings are newly constructed, some "rent-up" or marketing period is inevitable and the entrepreneur must consider this in his financial calculations. New housing may also be built in anticipation of future need in order to preempt the market from competitiors or to take advantage of present favorable financing.[3]

Existing (i.e. older) rental units may remain vacant because owners may, under some circumstances, enjoy higher net income from high rents with some units vacant than from low rents with no vacancy.[4] Builders of tract housing may prefer to hold out for higher prices than to sell their homes quickly at lower prices. Owners wishing to sell older homes may similarly decide to wait for an improvement in market conditions, meanwhile paying mortgage installments and taxes on an empty dwelling but expecting to be more than compensated by the ultimate sale price. Owners of houses or apartments which are destined to be demolished for some more attractive land use may choose to keep the unmarketable structure on hand, pending the most favorable reuse opportunity. Some investors, interested primarily in the tax consequences of their ownership, may be relatively indifferent to variations in vacancy rates.

All of these reasons (and others) could lie behind the decision to "invest in vacancy." In the aggregate, such "intended vacancy" is probably a significant element in most local housing markets and properly belongs in the category of "demand for housing units."

Other residential vacancy represents involuntary or unintentional investment. Older homes may stand idle for months while the owner makes mortgage and tax payments which he has no hope of recovering. A decrease in local employment may cause vacancy rates in apartments to rise well beyond the level which owners find acceptable. Overoptimism on the part of builders may result in a number of new homes well in excess of the number of families seeking new homes.

Intentional or not, the ownership of vacant dwellings is an investment. Someone other than a household seeking "shelter" is responsible for the existence of each vacant dwelling unit. Undoubtedly, some of the unintended investment in vacancy today may cause investors to behave differently tomorrow—i.e. to try to reduce their unwanted inventory. Just as we cannot readily determine which investment is "wise" and which is "unwise," we cannot easily divide vacancy into that which is the result of a "true" investment demand and that which is a "false" demand. Vacancy always represents investment, and investment always represents demand. Equation (4), then, is an expression of demand.

It is an expression of the demand for the housing *stock,* however. Our real interest at this point is in the demand for a change in the stock of housing. The incremental form of Equation (4) is the following:

$$\Delta H = \Delta F + \Delta V$$
$$220 = 200 + 20 \tag{5}$$

The symbol Δ (delta) means the change in the number being measured over some specific period of time such as a year. (The changes will be assumed to be increases unless otherwise indicated.)

Equation (5) is to be interpreted as follows: the demand for houses has increased by 220 because the number of families has grown by 200 and investors are willing to increase their inventory of empty houses by 20. This might represent normal population growth or the movement of workers to a community following the construction of a new factory. It is common to suppose that an enlarged housing stock will include a greater number of vacant units simply because the scale of the housing sector has expanded. Of course, there might be periods of lower absolute vacancy in a community if population growth precedes housing construction, but that is getting ahead of the story. For the moment, we are considering only the components of demand, not of supply. We can expect that investors will want to hold more vacant units in a large community than in a small one, and this is an element of demand.

Perhaps, however, the number of vacant units previously held—100, as we assumed in Equation (4)—was greater or less than investors at that time desired. In that case the increment in vacant inventory, ΔV, would reflect efforts to adjust the previous inventory, as well as to provide for the enlarged scale of the housing sector. That is, ΔV depends on the previous state of the housing sector as well as on the increment in what might be called "user demand" (i.e. the number of families). There could be an adjustment in the number of vacant units without a change in user demand (subject to limitations described below). The change in V (or in F, for that matter) could be negative rather than positive. Total incremental demand is the algebraic sum of the increments in F and V.

It is time now to add a third component of demand to our incremental equation. New houses may be in demand by a community even if the number of families (or the number of desired vacant units) does not increase, because housing does need to be replaced eventually. Some level of replacement demand is probably present in every housing market. We can let R stand for the number of houses desired for replacement purposes, assuming this number to be 30 in our hypothetical housing market, and amend our previous equation into the following form:

$$\Delta H = \Delta F + \Delta V + R$$
$$250 = 200 + 20 + 30 \tag{6}$$

Note that the replacement component of demand is not incremental. There are no houses in the initial stock which can be labeled as "replacement inventory." Consequently, there is no such thing as a net change in replacement inventory. The effect of replacement construction, presumably, is to transform the stock into one better suited to the needs of users. Since we lack a convenient way of measuring "suitability," however, it is difficult to define the stock in such terms and, therefore, it is not feasible to portray replacement demand as incremental. Later we can shed a little light on this question of "incremental suitability," but for the moment, R can be treated simply as a net increase in the number of new housing units above those required by population increase and investor demand for additional vacant units.

There are several very practical observations which must be made concerning Equation (6), for this equation has extensive practical use. In the first place, ΔH, which is the number of houses which would be built if demand were to be exactly satisfied by supply, cannot be negative. The macroeconomic interest in housing investment is a concern for the quantity of new construction which will occur and that quantity cannot be a minus number. That is:

$$\Delta H \geq 0 \qquad (7)$$

The change in the number of families in a community may be negative, but it cannot be so negative that original total number of families is reduced to a negative number. That is:

$$F \geq 0, \quad \text{or} \quad \Delta F \geq -F \qquad (8)$$

In our example the number of families initially was 1,000, so the change in the number of families cannot be more negative than —1,000.

Vacancies follow the same rule as the number of families. Desired vacancies may conceivably rise to any positive number, but the reduction in vacancies cannot exceed the original number of vacant units. We can state:

$$V \geq 0, \quad \text{or} \quad \Delta V \geq -V \qquad (9)$$

The number of units to be built for replacement must obviously be positive. Thus:

$$R \geq 0 \qquad (10)$$

These nearly self-evident side conditions on Equation (6) prove to be quite important in the further development of our statement of housing demand.

Consider next the following question: does the volume of

housing demand in the economy depend on the movement of population from place to place within that economy? The answer is that it does, and in illustrating the independent effect of population mobility upon total housing demand, we improve the usefulness and significance of the simple expression of demand in Equation (6).

Mobility can be represented by breaking the hypothetical aggregate-demand situation of Equation (6) into two subsectors. Let us call these subsectors "urban" and "rural" (adopting the subscripts "u" and "r," respectively) and assume that in the same time period as that which produced the incremental demand of Equation (6) 100 families migrate from the rural area to the urban area. There is an incremental demand equation for each subsector and these can be written as follows:

$$\Delta H_u = \Delta F_u + \Delta V_u + R_u$$
$$\Delta H_r = \Delta F_r + \Delta V_r + R_r \tag{11}$$

We must add all the side conditions corresponding to Equations (7) through (10). In each subsector the possible values which the several components of its demand equation can take are limited and the limitations are defined simply by adding subscripts to the expressions (7) through (10). (These eight equations are omitted for brevity.)

With the side conditions, Equation (11) is a consistent disaggregation of the total housing sector. The important effect of the side conditions is not obvious, however. The numerical example, if carried further, will show what mobility and disaggregation do to aggregate housing demand.

First, assume some consistent data regarding the initial stock in the urban and rural areas. Table 2 presents these assumptions in compact form, with F representing the number of occupied dwellings.

Now we must assume a pattern of incremental demand in the subsectors which is consistent with the aggregate pattern in the example of Equation (6). A first attempt is Table 3.

The assumptions within the body of the table are consistent and the total row contains the same numbers as the earlier aggregated example. The movement of 100 families from the rural area to the urban area, and the net increase of 200 families over-all, are indicated by the ΔF column. The level of desired vacancy falls in the urban area because, we could assume, the situation of Table 1 included more urban vacancies than investors wanted to retain. In the rural area the demand for vacant units rises because owners of housing there, perhaps including some who

2

Initial Stock	H	$=$	F	$+$	V
Urban	550		500		50
Rural	550		500		50
Total	1,100		1,000		100

have migrated to the urban area, believe that the loss in population and user demand in the rural area may soon be made up in part. There is no replacement demand in the rural area, we also assume, so it is assigned entirely to the urban subsector.

3

Incremental Demand	ΔH	$=$	ΔF	$+$	ΔV	$+$	R
Urban	300		300		−30		30
Rural	−50		−100		50		0
Total	250		200		20		30

The convenient assumptions of Table 3 contain a glaring error. There cannot be an effective demand for a negative number of new houses, yet −50 appears in the ΔH column. Two things must happen if this minus quantity is to disappear. The total ΔH must increase from 250 to 300, and some change must be made in the "rural" row of numbers to the right of the equality sign. In fact, we must add 50 to each side of the "rural" equation and correct the total row accordingly.

Which element to the right of the equality sign in the rural row shall we adjust? If ΔF is altered, we would contradict an earlier assumption about the scale of population movement from rural to urban subsectors. The number of vacancies which investors in the rural area desire will not rise just to accommodate our arithmetic, and replacement damage in the rural subsector is discouraged rather than encouraged by the loss of population from that area. The adjustment must be made by the addition of a new term to the demand equation which represents the effect of mobility and which suffices to eliminate minus signs wherever they might appear in the ΔH column (for we certainly might be considering more than just two subsectors).

Table 4 is a corrected version of incremental demand as it appeared in Table 3, with a new column for demand resulting from mobility.

4

Incremental Demand	ΔH =	ΔF +	ΔV +	R +	M
Urban	300	300	−30	30	0
Rural	0	−100	50	0	50
Total	300	200	20	30	50

The M column of Table 4 must be interpreted with care. It adds a positive level of housing demand to an area which is losing population and has the effect of boosting overall demand for housing construction. In the urban area the pressure for new housing construction comes obviously from increasing population, but in the rural area housing construction is kept above a negative level by the realistic consideration which underlies an arithmetical side condition.

In fact, of course, the fifty houses which are no longer desired by rural families and not wanted as investments may continue to exist. "Mobility" demand is not going to pay the rent on these houses, but they do embody economic resources which in some sense are "used up" when families move. The economic cost will be paid by additional construction in the urban area.

If we say that these fifty rural houses are "abandoned," then the resource implications of Table 4 become clearer. The desire of families to migrate from the rural area to the urban area is, in effect, a desire to abandon a portion of the housing stock, a portion which must be recreated in the urban area if the actual requirements of housing users and investors are to be met.

Houses which are abandoned in this sense may remain under

the control of their owners. They may be held vacant or they may be demolished to make the land available for some other use. Their ultimate disposition is a supply response. The act of abandonment, however, is an element of housing demand.

This demand element, whether we call it mobility or abandonment, is very close to the ordinary concept of replacement. So close, in fact, that there is merit in consolidating these aspects of housing demand. The origin and meaning of "replacement" demand become far clearer if this is done. Replacement in any sense is attributable to mobility of households and their collective willingness to abandon portions of the existing housing stock. Whether they move from rural areas to urban areas, from neighborhood X to neighborhood Y, or from houses of poor quality to houses of better quality (or vice versa), the move is at the price of abandoning usable portions of the housing stock and so results in a net addition to the demand for new houses to be built—i.e. for new housing investment.

Replacement demand, in this enlarged sense, is a response by housing users to a change in the form or location of their housing requirements. If the tenure composition among households shifts—with fewer renter households and more owner households, for example—a replacement demand is created which may (depending on the supply response) lead to new housing construction in excess of actual population growth. Any change in the age distribution, size distribution, income distribution, or the pattern of housing tastes among households sets in motion some forces which may lead to net increases in the level of housing construction.

The lesson is that an aggregative statement of housing demand such as Equation (6) is likely to understate actual housing demand. The simple aggregate estimate cannot overstate the actual demand, so that the factor of correction is always a positive quantity. Giving the term "replacement" this enlarged meaning, we can correct the aggregate incremental housing demand of Equation (6) to the following:

$$\Delta H = \Delta F + \Delta V + R^*$$
$$300 = 200 + 20 + 80 \tag{12}$$

Using R^* to represent all forms of abandonment.

The econometrician who wants to forecast the level of housing construction sometimes writes an expression for housing demand which obscures the role or source of replacement demand, though the expression may serve the econometrician's purpose adequately.[5] For example, we may see expressions such as the following:

$$\Delta H = f(\Delta F, \Delta V, p, i, Y, \text{etc.}) \tag{13}$$

in which p refers to the price of labor, materials, etc. for the construction of homes, i refers to the interest rate for mortgage loans and Y refers to the level of family income. The implication is that the demand for housing, like the demand for beefsteak, is elastic with respect to its price, the price of borrowed money, the income of would-be purchasers, and other traditional determinants of commodity demand. From the preceding discussion it is clear that housing demand can be influenced by a factor which is not explicitly described by these conventional independent variables—that is, by movement of households resulting in the potential abandonment of portions of the stock. Implicitly, a change in the price of housing, the rate of mortgage interest, the level of family income, etc. may stimulate housing replacement and in this sense Equation (13) may be virtually the equivalent of Equation (12). One major flaw in the ambiguous econometric expression, however, is the absence of a variable recognizing sheer geographic mobility or demographic shifts within the population.

The multifaceted nature of "replacement demand" is an aspect of housing sector equilibrium which deserves close study. The traditional concept of replacement as an offset to depreciation of the stock cannot be overlooked. Deterioration of the inventory can be, and almost certainly is, one source of housing users' desire for mobility—along with geographic and demographic shifts, and changes in construction costs, mortgage rates, and family income levels. Microeconomic problems associated with replacement (to be discussed in a later chapter) are additional reasons for extensive consideration of this "catchall" component of the demand for new housing construction. Planning writers often select a level of replacement building which will permit their plans to be realized, without regard to the spontaneous nature and exacting characteristics of replacement demand. Econometricians are prone to attribute replacement demand implicitly to causes which may be relatively incidental (such as changes in construction costs) or to make replacement explicitly a function of time or of the condition of the initial inventory. In the broad sense which we have developed above, replacement demand is the sum of many specific dynamic forces affecting the housing sector.

The identification of aggregate housing demand requires an examination of movements or transfers of demand from one subsector of the housing market to another. This is close to saying that aggregate demand cannot be forecast except by the process of summing up disaggregated demands, the demands in each locality, in each qualitative category of housing in each income level, in each family size category, in the several categories of housing tenure and density preferences, etc. Such a highly disaggregated model of housing demand would be unfeasible if not quite impossible to construct. Some level of oversimplified aggregation is a practical necessity in the study of housing demand. There is a difference, though, between a simplification which merely omits an element of demand, and a simplification which roughly estimates that less precisely measurable element. Our discussion of demand suggests that careful efforts be made to estimate the level of replacement demand, in its large sense, by examining the pattern of demand shifts within the aggregate.

This comment applies to estimates of local housing demand as well as to the study of national aggregate housing demand. Geographic shifts are less likely to be overlooked in local studies, but other aspects of replacement—changes in the age or income structure, for example—might not seem immediately to be sources of additional demand for new residential building activity.

Before moving on to the supply aspects of housing market behavior, we must acknowledge that "housing demand" includes, in principle, a set of demands for the great complex of urban facilities which make housing useful—local transportation and utilities, schools and other public facilities, and private business services oriented to housing areas. This important fact is often obscured by the terminology in which housing demand is measured and discussed, but the society will think poorly of the macroeconomist who forgets what these other capital goods mean to the quality of urban life.

Economic Base

There is very little ambiguity about the principal component of the demand equation, the change in the number of households. We have referred to these households as "families," but it is clear that separate housing units are needed by many individuals and social groupings which may not be families (e.g. groups of single girls sharing apartments). The numbers and characteristics of households are readily determined from analysis of the population—its age distribution, marital status distribution, etc.[6] The change in numbers of households over a period of time is a reflection of changes in the size and characteristics of the adult population. Forecasts of the number of households at some future point in time (and, hence, in the change in the number between the present time and that future time) can be made primarily from forecasts of population and its characteristics. Demography, the study of population, is a well developed science, and social behavior concerning household formation (e.g. the likelihood that a person of a given age will be married) is relatively stable. With two important exceptions, information and predictions about the number of households can be relatively reliable as economic market data go.

One of the exceptions has to do with the influence of income—perhaps representing employment status—upon household formation.[7] In general, the higher the income of a potential household head, the more likely is that person to be a household head in actuality. The difficulty comes in forecasting changes in average income—that is, in correcting demographic forecasts for future fluctuations in the level of general business activity. As macroeconomic policies to reduce fluctuations in business activity enjoy increasing success, this problem for housing market forecasters diminishes.

The larger and more difficult exception to the relative ease with which a change in the number of households can be forecast, results from population movement, i.e. from migration into and out of the region for which the housing demand forecast is to be made. For an entire nation the amount of the net in- or out-migration may be relatively small and stable, but for a portion of the nation—and particularly for an individual urban area —the influence of population movement upon total housing demand can be very significant.

Changes in small-area population are usually closely related to changes in employment opportunities in that area. Hence, the study of housing demand for a particular urban area involves analysis of local employment-creating activities. This type of study is often called "economic base analysis" and has its own developing methodology.[8]

The underlying concept of economic base analysis is that certain types of employment, such as manufacturing, produce products which are sold outside the area while other types of employment, such as retail trade, exist in proportion to the population of the area itself. Knowing the volume of employment which will be supported by demand outside the area, we can infer the total level of employment in the area. For example, if one half of the employment in urban areas generally is of the "internal demand" type (such as retail trade) and city X has 50,000 jobs resulting from "external demand," total employment in city X will be approximately 100,000. An increase of 1,000 external demand jobs will result in an increase of total employment in this city of about 2,000 jobs. The task of forecasting total employment (and, hence, the total number of households) is reduced to the problem of forecasting the number of external demand jobs, only a fraction of the total.

This relationship between total employment and external demand employment can be demonstrated algebraically. Let T stand for the total number of jobs in the community, including L

jobs which serve local demand and E jobs which serve external demand. Then:

$$T = L + E$$

Dividing through by T:

$$1 = L/T + E/T, \text{ or } E/T = 1 - L/T.$$

Inverting and transposing E:

$$T = E \left(\frac{1}{1 - L/T} \right).$$

Since the ratio L/T is fixed by assumption (equal to one-half in the above illustration), the expression $\left(\frac{1}{1 - L/T} \right)$ is a constant (and would be equal to two in the illustration). This constant acts as a "multiplier" to determine total employment if external demand employment is known, and to forecast a change in total employment (and, hence, a change in the number of households) if we are able to forecast a change in external demand employment.

This "economic-base multiplier" must be estimated for the community in question before it can be used to forecast total employment. It is very similar to the macroeconomic "investment multiplier" which is commonly used to forecast changes in gross national product from changes in investment or in government spending. There is one interesting difference between the two multipliers. The macroeconomic investment multiplier is derived from the marginal (i.e. incremental) relationship between consumption and income, while the economic base multiplier is derived from the *average* relationship. The significance of this difference is clearer in Figure 9.

The A portion of Figure 9 shows the relationship between local demand employment (L) and total employment in a community (T), reflecting the theory of economic base. The B portion of the diagram represents the macroeconomic relationship between total consumption spending and total national income. In A the local employment function is a straight line from the origin, while in B the consumption function does not begin at the origin. In B a certain level of consumption expenditure (*a*) will occur even if national income is zero, so that the equilibrium level of national income will not be less than the amount at which the consumption function intersects the 45° dashed line. Below that level of income, total spending exceeds total income. Thus, a positive level of income will exist in the B portion of the figure even if there is no other source of income than consumption spending.

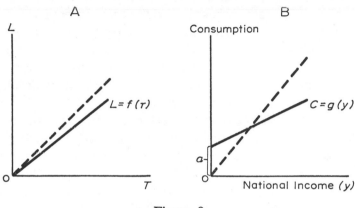

Figure 9

In the economic base example the equilibrium level of total local employment is zero if the locality has no external demand employment. In principle, this says that a community without a product or service to sell beyond its borders will not come into existence. An urban settlement can arise and live without local "service" types of business activity as long as it has products or services to be exported, but a community cannot exist on local demand employment only. A city in which the whole labor force simply sells groceries to each other cannot exist, according to the simple formulation of the economic base concept.

While this inference about local and external demand employment seems reasonable, it raises an interesting question about the nature of recent urban growth. In the past half century, as total urban population has grown very rapidly, few, if any, new urban settlements have appeared spontaneously in previously unurbanized locations. Previously existing urban areas have absorbed virtually all of the increase in "city-creating" external demand types of employment. One of the reasons most often given is that these existing cities offered local service facilities—grocery stores, schools, hospitals, etc.—which the employees of the new external demand industries could enjoy. If such an industry were to settle down in a nonurbanized place, its labor force would be difficult to recruit and to hold. This almost contradicts the usual formulation of the economic base theory as represented in Figure 9A, for it says that local demand employment attracts external demand employment rather than vice versa. In earlier periods, say before 1900, new urban centers did spring up when external demand industries located themselves in areas of relative wilderness. Perhaps the labor force of the period was less particular about urban services or was content to wait until they developed around the new export-type activity.

This is a subject of considerable current interest, for the principles governing the equilibrium size and equilibrium growth rates of urban areas appear to be less mechanical than the concept of the economic base implies. At the same time, more complex tools of analysis are being developed to refine the simple economic base idea, taking into account different employment multipliers for different types of external demand industries.[9]

Nevertheless, the economic base concept is widely used and seems to have a reasonable amount of predictive value. If a town's largest factory closes down, experience seems to confirm what the economic base theory would say: the grocery stores, department stores, real estate offices, and movie theaters are forced to reduce their employment levels also.

Perhaps the greatest usefulness of the economic base theory lies in the fact that it tells a community what to do if its service industries want to grow; it must look for and attract additional external-demand type industries. From another point of view, an area which seems likely to attract a new type of external-demand employment can be expected to produce a market for an even greater number of new dwellings, for local-demand type employment is apt to grow. The issue of starting a new city from scratch is of theoretical interest, and of some real interest to government planners (as the following chapter will indicate), but most local population-forecasting problems are concerned with moderate changes in established urban areas.

The equilibrium geographical distribution of external-demand type industries is obviously central to the determination of equilibrium new-housing demand in a particular locality. To give this matter its due, however, would take us far afield from the question of housing market equilibrium per se.* At this point we can observe only that a major component of new housing demand in a locality, population change, rests in large part upon changes in employment and, specifically, upon changes in external demand employment.

Supply Constraints

On the demand side, housing is most characteristically a "necessity"; it can be assumed quite reasonably that each family or other type of social household wishes to have a separate housing unit. On the supply side, housing's most significant characteristic is its heavy capital cost. To provide one family with housing often requires resources equal in value to substantially more than the family's total annual income. It is the most expensive single commodity which the ordinary family ever uses and, if the family owns its dwelling, the house usually represents by far the most important asset which the family can accumulate.

It is interesting to ponder why housing has this important supply characteristic. Many people suppose that it is the result of technological facts or of technological lags in the home building industry. Research and technological advances, it is argued, may someday bring the cost of housing units down to a very much lower level. From time to time there is substantial public interest in prefabrication or in the use of new materials (including aluminum, plastics, and even paper) which promise to make housing cheaper.

Technology is only part of the explanation for the costly nature of the housing product, however. Another aspect is the enduring demand for housing in urban areas, that is, in areas of large-scale human settlement. A family can usually look forward

---

* This large class of problems is the primary concern of "Regional Science" as that term is usually understood.

to occupying the same dwelling in the same location for several years. When that family's needs change, the house will be transferred to another family with needs like the original requirements of the first occupants. In this way, the usefulness of the dwelling in a fixed location is perpetuated. If we know we are going to find something necessary for a long period of time, it makes practical sense to buy a more elaborate product. The extra cost of extra comforts can be spread over a long period of time. Thus, there is a strong inducement to make the urban dwelling both durable and elaborate. Heavy materials are assembled into rigid forms, things regularly useful are incorporated within the structure itself (plumbing, for example), and luxurious embellishments are made nearly as permanent as the structure itself (carpeting and venetian blinds, for instance). Not least of the adaptations of human shelter to the enduring nature of urban housing demand is its attachment to and dependence upon facilities such as water, power, sewer, and telephone systems which are created as the result of joint demands by a large number of immobile, long-lived dwellings. Technological progress which greatly reduced the materials cost of urban dwellings would probably not bring equal reductions in the expensiveness of the individual housing product, as it would become both possible and practical to make that product more useful and more elaborate than before. It would be foolish to deny that a massive technological breakthrough could alter housing behavior in a significant way (leading, perhaps, to the adoption of "disposable" dwellings), but there is a force on the demand side which tends to counteract technological price-lowering developments on the supply side. Housing is a costly thing and is likely to remain so.

Economists in different parts of the world tend to stress either demand or supply as principal determinants of the volume of housing investment per year, depending upon circumstances with which they are most familiar. In the United States, for example, the business of forecasting residential construction revolves mainly around studies of population trends, or, locally, employment. The implicit assumption is that supply is nearly perfectly elastic, so that someone will finance and build a dwelling for each additional family which can pay the going price. The volume of house building is assumed to be limited primarily by the number of buyers or renters.* It does not usually occur to housing economists in the United States to wonder if there are enough carpenters or bankers or entrepreneurs to respond to an increase in effective demand. This oversight, or the implicit assumptions which it reflects, is perhaps quite appropriate to the business setting. Labor, entrepreneurship, and, to a considerable extent, capital are abundant and mobile in the United States.

In underdeveloped countries, or in a relatively well developed economy such as Japan, on the other hand, the basic assumption of housing economists is that *supply* factors limit housing construction.[10] Demand is perceived as virtually infinite, not because the population is unlimited, but because the situation in which an adequate amount of housing has been produced is unthinkable or at least quite remote. An increase in the supply of resources available to the housing sector in the current planning period is equated with an increase in the volume of housing which will be produced. This attitude, too, makes sense within its setting. Not only are resources generally scarce in such economies and allocated to what are regarded as "growth industries" (emphatically excluding housing), but the housing sector itself is typically quite unprepared to meet existing market demands for housing in a systematic fashion. In most of the world there never has been a "housing market" in the western sense of the term, and the idea that the business system might become involved in the solution of the housing problem tends to encounter ridicule or alarm.

We want to make our discussion of housing economics as nearly universal as possible. This means looking at both sides of the equilibrium (and later of the policy) situation, considering the relevance of each statement in a multitude of contexts, some of which the individual reader may not be aware of. It can be very valuable for one's understanding of housing markets to con-

---

* The popular presumption that demand, not supply factors, limit housing output in the United States is revealed by the construction industry's concern with marketing. See, for example, William R. Smolkin, *A Marketing Plan for Apartment Builders* (National Association of Home Builders, 1964).

sider what might occur in the absence of certain sets of conditions which are usually taken for granted.

Having said that housing is a large bundle of resources, we must now examine the principal types of resources within that bundle, noting some of their important characteristics and the conditions under which they are available for the construction of housing. We will consider in turn: finance, land, building materials, labor force, builder's equipment, and entrepreneurship. It is clear that this cataloging of economic resources—or what may properly be called "inputs" of the housing sector—is tailored to the characteristics and problems of our subject.

FINANCE

It might seem at first that a list of inputs which includes money as well as physical resources which will be purchased with that money involves "double counting." It is important to understand that this is not true and why, in fact, what we can call "finance" is a factor of production quite distinct from labor and materials—and even from "risk taking." The truth is that a home purchaser, under common United States market conditions, for instance, will eventually pay approximately as many dollars for financing his home as will be paid for all the other inputs—labor, materials, land, entrepreneurship, etc.—together. The cost of financing is added to the cost of other inputs.

The word "eventually" in the preceding sentence is the key to the puzzle. Supposing that land, labor, materials, etc. for the production of a house exists, their prices need to be paid at the time that these resources are used. Workers must be paid by the time the building is ready for occupancy, as a rule. (In fact, there are special laws in the United States to assure that this will be the case.) The previous landowner usually wants money so that he can acquire some new investment good. Materials are supplied by firms which have to keep up to date on their own production costs, and the entrepreneur must have current income to feed his family. The physical house must be paid for as it is created but the user of the house will derive valuable housing services from it only over a period of many years. Someone must be willing and able to foot the bill immediately for the physical

house and to wait for this bill to be repaid during the long lifetime of the dwelling. For this waiting, and for the risk which it
may entail, the supplier of financing ordinarily wants to be
compensated.

The word "financing," however, should not be translated
into "waiting." The supplier of financing does not supply merely
his patience; he provides a sum of money which he has accumulated. Without this financial accumulation, plus the willingness
to wait for its return at interest, labor and the other resources
necessary for the production of houses would lack a current
market in the housing sector and would look elsewhere for
employment. Housing demand would not be met. To build a
house we need land, labor, materials, certain skills and equipment—*and* a stack of today's money to pay for these things.
Financing is an independent and separate input required by the
housing sector.

Another semantic problem of substantially less importance
—but troublesome, nonetheless—is the question of whether housing "credit" is an element of demand or of supply. More (mortgage) credit, it is sometimes said, will increase the demand for
housing, and there is no doubt that a quantitative relationship
usually exists between the rate of mortgage interest (for example)
and the level of home building, other things being equal. This is
like saying that a decrease in the price of television sets will result
in more units being sold. This is not what the economist means
by an "increase in demand," but it is not worth arguing about.[11]
Another aspect of credit raises a different issue, however. If "an
increase in mortgage credit" means that a home buyer can borrow 90 percent of the price of his home rather than 60 percent,
then what has happened is that a new *source* of the necessary
financing input has been created. Down-payment requirements
mean that the home user must finance a portion of the dwelling.
Since home users (or apartment owners) as a group are not
primary elements of financial accumulation, the down-payment
requirement implies that a certain portion of the inputs required
for housing must be supplied by people with relatively little
capacity to provide that form of input. A parallel limitation
would stipulate that people who wish to live in a convalescent

home perform most of the labor involved in building it. Rapid amortization requirements have essentially the same effect, saying that the user must take over the financing task at some specified rate. There are sound reasons for down-payment and amortization requirements in the process of residential development and sale, as we shall discuss later, but they do have the effect of specifying that part of the resources needed for housing must be supplied by people whose capacity in this respect is relatively limited. It is helpful to consider that credit is always an element of supply, and that the entire direct physical cost of new housing must be financed from one source or another.

Housing finance is "investment" in the most practical sense of the term. All those who commit funds to new housing have other investment or consumption alternatives and a process of searching, examination, and weighing is presumably involved before the decision to invest in housing is made. For the economy as a whole, and for many individual or business investors, the choice between housing and other investments is not an "all or nothing" matter. The macroeconomic problem is to allocate available investment funds among the several sectors of the economy which require new financing. In the "ideal" capital market of a business economy, the competitive allocation of savings would first draw all savings into a common marketplace and the aggregate would be divided among sectors strictly on the basis of marginal rates of return. That is, dollars would be awarded first to the sector which could use them most productively, and then to less productive sectors until the pool of funds was exhausted. Each additional dollar going to Sector X would have to be capable of increasing the productivity of that sector by at least as much as that dollar would add to the productivity of Sector Y or Sector Z. When all funds have been allocated, the marginal returns—the productivity of the last dollar—would be the same in all sectors. The amount of new housing investment in each year, in an economic system with such a competitive capital market, would be that share of total new investment which was most advantageous to the economy as a whole. All other elements of housing demand and supply would be reflected in rates of return and, hence, in housing's share.

There are several reasons why such a capital market—at least with respect to the housing sector—has never been even roughly approximated in the United States (where it might seem most likely to emerge), and is not to be detected even in outline in any major nation. Not the least of these reasons is the fact that the supply of financial capital for housing is often seen as a "social" rather than a business matter, and the rate of return offered by housing to investors through the marketplace is widely believed to be an inaccurate indicator of housing's true worth to the economy. Very often public agencies contrive to discourage investment funds from going into housing. Under other circumstances, public agencies try to enlarge the flow of funds into new housing beyond that which the capital market seems willing to provide. Arguments on this point will be examined in the following chapter. We can note at this point that the conviction is widespread in almost all societies that the capital market *should not* allocate savings to the housing sector on the equimarginal principle described above.

In the absence of public policies restricting or encouraging investment in housing, it would still be very difficult to create a capital market which applied the equimarginal principle to the housing sector. The ownership of housing is customarily intertwined with the objective of occupancy. Demand for *equity* investment in a particular home is thus heavily biased in favor of the family which will live in it. Various amenities beyond the mere right of occupancy arise from the ownership of one's home, and so raise the "price" which a particular family is willing to pay for the investment. The equity investor in rental housing is often seeking employment for his managerial skills as well as a return on his investment. He is in a position comparable to that of a small businessman whose capital will facilitate his basic activities rather than establish him in the position of a "rentier." Where these considerations exist, a complex market for housing equities will serve little purpose as the highest bidder is known before the auction begins.

A competitive market for housing *debt* investments (i.e. a mortgage market) would require facilities of a very special and elaborate nature to overcome the investment peculiarities of the housing sector. Housing is highly heterogeneous and perfectly immobile. Various properties which are to serve as security for mortgage loans are difficult to compare. The risk involved in each property is unique; methods of risk evaluation are theoretically involved and, in practice, are not highly developed. The practical difficulties confronting the operation of a market for debt investment in housing are summed up in the term "imperfect information." The facts surrounding the investment potential of an individual property are difficult to convey in adequate detail to prospective investors and, when conveyed, are difficult to evaluate. Little wonder that mortgage investment tends to be a specialized activity which the general purchaser of financial investments approaches with caution. Mortgage investors are likely to concentrate on particular segments of the residential market, overlooking superior alternatives in other segments. Mortgage markets in the United States tend to be divided on the basis of geography, type of property, priority of the lien (first mortgages versus second, third, etc. mortgages), and even by the racial characteristics of residential neighborhoods. The supply of new funds for the housing sector, both in the aggregate and in terms of its composition, is determined in a manner little resembling a competitive capital market.[12] For this reason, the supply of funds for housing investment in an economy such as the United States cannot be forecast without expert, specialized analysis of the principal categories of mortgage lending institutions.

If housing investment is compared very generally with alternative types of investment, two characteristics stand out which tend to influence the scale and form of new housing investment. Housing investments are typically illiquid; they are also relatively secure in the long run. Illiquidity means that an investment cannot readily be converted into cash without unreasonable sacrifice. This characteristic results from the heterogeneity and immobility of the housing commodity which serves as security for a mortgage or as the vehicle for equity investment. The effect of illiquidity, other things being equal, is to discourage some potential housing investment and diminish the scale of the housing sector as we are discussing it. Devices which offset illiquidity, such as the Federal National Mortgage Association in the United

States or multiple listing services operated by local real estate brokers, have the effect of enlarging the flow of funds into the housing sector.

The relative security of housing investment results from several factors among which are the position of housing as a basic consumption necessity, a tendency for the demand to intensify for particular properties as population increases, and the fact that the housing inventory usually grows only slowly—the increment being but a small fraction of the stock. Housing investments are likely to retain their value over long periods, particularly if they are diversified. A dramatic example of the basic security of housing investment was the experience of the Home Owners' Loan Corporation in the United States.[13] Though established in the depths of the nation's worst economic depression with the intention of relieving banks of their least desirable mortgage investments, the agency ultimately produced a surplus for the U.S. Treasury. Economic recovery, wartime prosperity, rapid household formation, and a modest general inflation combined to turn nearly worthless mortgage paper into reasonably sound investments, much to the surprise of the agency itself. Housing is not a fad; the demand for it is virtually discouragement-proof.

The consequence of this characteristic for housing investment is that a relatively large proportion of the financing supplied in connection with housing may be obtained in the form of debt (i.e. mortgage) capital. Equity ratios are low compared to many other sectors of the capital market, providing equity investors with "leverage," that is, the ability to control large assets with small ownership capital. Since equity capital for housing tends to be limited by the traditional association between ownership and use, high debt-equity ratios tend in one respect to foster greater rates of total investment in housing than might otherwise obtain. Thin equities, on the other hand, magnify the risks for housing owners of short-term or random fluctuations in user demand, and might partly offset the encouragement provided by generous debt capital.[14]

The aggregate supply of capital for housing is often thought to fluctuate inversely to general business conditions, to be

"counter-cyclical" in the macroeconomist's language. The data
on this subject are not entirely conclusive, and the manner in
which mortgage capital availability responds to changes in overall
business conditions must be explained ultimately in terms of the
behavior of principal types of mortgage investors. There is an
obvious, if superficial, reason why this counter-cyclical tendency
should be present. When employment and aggregate consumer
demand are rising, business optimism leads to expansion of manufacturing plant capacity which, in turn, puts heavy demands
upon the capital market. Funds are drained away from other sectors to facilitate industrial expansion, and the housing sector is
obliged to retrench. The link may be indirect and subject to lags,
since the housing sector, as we have noted, is not on an equal foot-
ing with other sectors in the general market for investible
savings. Nevertheless—the pool of total savings being fixed—
when industry takes more, housing receives less. Contrariwise,
when general business conditions are pessimistic and industrial
plants are not being used to capacity, the desire to increase industrial equipment is weakened. Less funds are absorbed by
the industrial sectors and more is available for housing. Given
underlying housing demand and a supply of labor, materials, etc.
for residential construction, the pace of housing investment
accelerates.

This complementarity of housing and industrial investment
over the business cycle should tend to reduce the amplitude of
aggregate economic fluctuations. Slack demand for industrial
output is made up, at least in part, by greater residential construction, and vice versa. (It may be reasonable to think in terms
of *real estate* investment as a counter to industrial investment
rather than residential investment alone, though this involves
issues which are beyond the purpose of this book.)

The counter-cyclical tendency rests, however, on the manner
in which the capital market is organized or, more specifically,
the position of housing in that capital market. If the pool of
savings upon which industry and housing both draw is derived
from sources essentially independent of either sector—e.g. from
savings of "typical" households—then savings flows to the various sectors can be adjusted after a fashion to the investment
requirements of the several sectors. Suppose, however, that the

principal source of savings—i.e. investible funds—is the profit of industrial firms. Then the pool of savings itself will expand or contract with general business conditions. Housing investment will be undertaken directly or indirectly by industry and may well be intensified when business profitably is greatest. (Japanese cities have recently witnessed surges of luxurious office building construction by highly profitable industrial firms. In general, the capital market in Japan is very nearly a subsidiary of the industrial sector.) Waves of business optimism and pessimism—as well as the availability of funds—carry over from the industrial to the housing sectors under these circumstances. The cycle would then be aggravated by housing investment.

Whether counter-cyclical or cycle-aggravating, housing (or real estate) investment shares the available pool of savings with industrial development opportunities. A special set of circumstances has often been observed in which luxurious housing developments enjoy a persistently favored position in the capital market. These "pathological" situations have been noted in inflation-prone underdeveloped nations in which a small propertied class enjoys a living standard far above that of the large peasant population. The issue, with respect to investment in housing, is not so much its variation over time as a chronic "distortion" in type. Equity investment, particularly the ownership of urban land, is greatly favored over investment in fixed money terms because of the tendency for the monetary unit to lose value rapidly. Mortgage- or bond-interest rates would have to be extremely high to compensate investors for the depreciation of their fixed-sum investment. Much saving, in such circumstances, seems to take the form of hoarding—of gold, precious stones, etc.—which, though unproductive in the ordinary sense, is a sound hedge against inflation. Savings also migrate abroad, seeking investments in more stable currencies and in broader capital markets (where investments may also be more nearly "revolution-proof" than those at home). Savings capital which remains at home is strongly pulled to speculative (i.e. ownership) investment in luxury urban apartments, a tendency often criticized for overlooking the more pressing capital investment requirements of the nation.

This "pathological" investment behavior may, nevertheless, represent prudence on the part of the investor, given the set of circumstances in the market for capital. With most of the population near the subsistence level of income, broadly based consumer-goods industries (including nonluxury housing) lack even the prospect of a market, and investment in those industries is not promising (even apart from the problem of inflation). A peasant farmer is not likely to buy new shoes when he cannot even obtain food enough for his family, so shoe factories are not built. Investment in new types of export goods industries is not attractive unless undertaken on a scale sufficient to make the new form of industry viable and efficient, usually requiring substantial public investment in transportation and other facilities. In the absence of strong economic development planning and control, the stimulus to the growth of new export industries is lacking. Luxury housing is the one major form of equity investment commodity for which user demand is actually present. The problem in such a case is not with the investor's rationality, but rather in the set of conditions affecting the market for capital. A ban on luxury housing will not necessarily increase industrial investment.

LAND

For early economists such as Thomas Malthus and David Ricardo, the peculiar characteristics of land—as an economic resource—were the source of pessimistic prophecies about human society. Since land was both an indispensable input for the production of food, and virtually fixed in supply, growing population would cause the average output of food per capita to fall, keeping humanity close to the subsistence level. Since land of poorer and poorer fertility would be placed in cultivation as human demand for food increased, the owners of better land would receive an increasing share of society's total economic product, compounding general poverty with the grossest form of economic inequality.[15]

For one reason or another, at least for industrializing western nations, these fears proved to be exaggerated. In the midst of their emerging affluence, societies have found many things more serious and more interesting to worry about than a shortage of agricultural land. One of these modern specters is the shortage of urban land.

The surface aspects of the modern land problem are all too

apparent. Housing, which occupies the largest part of urban land, is everywhere regarded as insufficient or inadequate to some degree. The creation of more or better housing requires land, but such land is hard to find and harder to acquire. Its price is high, and the continuing increase in its price, in many of the world's urban areas, makes its present owners anxious to keep it as long as possible. Government agencies in Japan, for example, have resorted to very distant areas as the only practical means of acquiring land for public housing projects.[16] In desperation, squatters have seized land in defiance of all existing authority in many of the principal cities of the less developed nations.[17] The gap between the demand for housing land and the supply of available urban land in much of the world seems hopelessly vast.

A closer look at the urban land problem, however, raises doubts about some of these superficial observations. The amount of land within existing urban areas seems sufficient to accommodate greatly increased populations with space and comfort.[18] Measures and estimates for various metropolitan areas bear out this more optimistic observation. Simple arithmetic makes it easy to believe those scholars who feel that the shortage of urban land, if it does exist, is not due to the physical limitation of land. For example, a circular city with a radius of ten miles has some 200,000 acres within that circumference. Supposing half of this area to be in nonresidential use or unusable, the remaining 100,000 acres will accommodate one million persons at the very low average density of 10 persons (about 3 families) per acre. With an average density of 100 persons (about 30 families) per residential acre, the population of the present world's largest city could be housed within the ten-mile radius. Such numerical exercises lead us to wonder where the "urban land shortage" (which is offered as the reason for widespread housing inadequacies) can arise.

The factors which convert a physical abundance into a practical dearth include transportation and land-use inflexibility. To be usable for residential development, a parcel of urban land must conveniently adjoin an efficient intraurban network of public transportation or roads for the use of private cars. Heavy public expenditures are required, plus large private expenditures, to the extent that the system is automobile-oriented. The technology of blanketing a circular area with such a transportation system is complex, for efficient "trunk lines" must be essentially linear, while "feeder systems" fill in the spaces between major routes. Interchanges of various kinds must be created. For lack of adequate feeder facilities, urban development in many areas has shown a tendency to string out along trunk lines, greatly increasing the geometric radius of the area beyond that of the theoretical circular plane.

Utilities must also be provided in order for land to be residentially useful. The technology of water, gas, and electric power distribution, and of sewage disposal, is perhaps simpler or less ambiguous than that of human transportation, but the aggregate cost of such facilities is substantial. These are capital costs, in large measure, and usually represent assets which a metropolitan government must acquire. Their adequate provision rests upon the ability and willingness of local governmental bodies (sometimes with assistance from larger units of government) to commit the community to a large burden of fixed charges, and upon the position of communities as borrowers in the market for capital. All of these matters are highly specialized subjects in themselves, but we must observe at least that limitations upon community action in this respect result in a limitation upon the supply of residential land and hence, in principle, in a limitation upon the possible supply of housing.

With the most adequate financial resources and the most advantageous technology for the provision of transportation, utility, and other services to residential areas, a metropolitan area can, in principle, reach out so far that the supply of usable land is exhausted (when mountains or bodies of water block further expansion, for example); when the length of the typical intracity journey interferes with productive employment; or when the congestion of human and vehicle movement at transportation nodes becomes too difficult to manage. Then the question arises whether the growth of the city will, or should, cease. The "should" part of this question involves arguments about the creation of "new cities" and will be taken up in the following chapter. The "will" or market-equilibrium aspect seems to lack meaningful empirical background. There does not seem to be a historical or current example of a city whose further population increase has been blocked by the inadequacy of its supply of residential land. One might say that the effective barrier to further urban growth in some cities is the reluctance of public agencies (and the people for whom they speak) to make further efforts at unsnarling existing congestion or stretching out the already tiresome commuting trip, instead preferring to start afresh somewhere else. This is a confusion of the equilibrium issue with the notion of optimality, however, and is beyond the range of this study.

"Land-use inflexibility," which was mentioned above as the second principal reason for a virtual shortage of residential land, refers to the fact that residential development or redevelopment (with or without changes in density) is sometimes hampered by business, legal, and financial factors. Land which appears from a helicopter to be ideally suited to new types of residential uses turns out to be unavailable for that use when we look into it on the ground.

In the first place, we must observe that much of the land suitable for housing is occupied already by residential structures. A city which aims to *improve* the housing supply available to its inhabitants does not necessarily require any more land. Indeed, rebuilding of residential areas at higher densities means that ultimately less land in total will be used for housing. Thus, additional housing investment in the macroeconomic sense is not land consuming unless population is rising or densities are falling. Investments to upgrade the housing stock (except where this involves lowering density or abandoning less desirable areas) cannot be checked by physical limitations of the supply of land, for the land under existing housing is physically available.

This is akin to saying, for example, that the total of current *savings* is physically available to the housing sector. Under normal circumstances, the housing sector will command only a portion of available savings, as has been discussed in the preceding section, the fraction depending on the competitive strength of other capital-using sectors such as industry and government. This competition is decided on the basis of prices offered (i.e. yields or interest rates) by the several sectors and on institutional restrictions (government policies and specialized channels of capital distribution, for example) which affect or supersede the price mechanism itself. Exactly similar observations can be made about the extent to which the total of urban land is available as a complement to current new housing investment. There is price competition for this land and there is also a set of institutional circumstances which influences the distribution of this land among competing uses, including its use by existing residential structures.

Many observers have called attention to the high price of land for redevelopment in principal metropolitan areas of the world, and the barrier which this represents to effective housing-improvement measures. Urban land prices have risen in spectacular fashion in many areas of the world and it is presumably true that the inability of the housing sector—i.e. new housing construction—to command such land has inhibited the expansion of that sector.[19] It is the "improvement" and not the "growth" segment of local housing demand which is discouraged by the land price problem, however, and the severity of the restraint in any particular community depends on the mix of its desired new housing investment.

In part, the high price of urban land for redevelopment reflects institutional limitations upon its availability. That is, the total quantity which is offered on the local market is limited by considerations other than price with the result that the price of the remainder is driven up. Many specific kinds of limitations can be observed. In some nations the owner of developed land has very limited rights to recover the property from tenants. Though the landowner might be quite ready to sell the land or redevelop it himself, he cannot terminate the occupancy of tenants without heavy penalties. The knowledge that the same sort of limitations would afflict a new house or apartment on the same land can also make redevelopment of the land a less attractive proposition. Public redevelopment agencies often find themselves even more constrained by the legal and moral rights of tenants in the present dwellings which are to make room for better types of construction.

Imperfect legal titles to land can hinder its sale or re-use. Undeveloped market practices may make the search for suitable land within a complex metropolis both difficult and expensive. Heavy brokerage fees may reflect this condition and it is not uncommon to find that prospective buyers and sellers of urban properties distrust the established middlemen in the field to the extent of preferring a "do-it-yourself" effort. Transfer taxes of various sorts and, of course, some zoning restrictions deter potential changes in land use. Whether any or all of these restraints upon the availability of urban land for reuse are desirable is an "optimization" issue with which the following chapter is concerned. In equilibrium terms, the effect is undoubtedly to check a portion of new-housing investment which would otherwise take place through the activities of the housing market.

It might be noted that the practice of leasing land rather than selling it, common in areas of traditional land shortage, is not necessarily an impediment to the reuse of land. The practice might facilitate reuse since the redeveloper can avoid a lump-sum payment for land. Unfavorable lease terms may make the net effect unfavorable, however.

There is a persistent belief that urban land scarcity can be attributed, in part, to speculators who hold land off the market hoping that its price will rise and produce a gain exceeding the accumulated carrying costs of their investment (the market rate of interest on their funds invested in land, plus property taxes and other current out-of-pocket costs of ownership). The remedy prescribed is an increase in taxation, making it unprofitable to delay the sale of the land.

The ordinary role of the speculator is to provide for a future demand by competing with today's would-be consumers. If the speculator is mistaken about the future demand, then the property-tax measure would improve the overall availability of land. To the extent that the anticipated future demand will be realized, however, the property tax would increase today's land supply and diminish tomorrow's. While this is really an "optimization" issue, it does point up an additional dimension to the question of the availability of urban land for housing, that of successive time periods. The speculator's role is to create an equilibrium in this supply over time by "reserving" useful land. He is the market's equivalent of a long-range land planner, and gives the future population of an area a species of effective demand in today's market. The market allocation of land occurs over time as well as over competitive contemporaneous uses.

BUILDING MATERIALS

House-building materials are, in general, among the most abundant and the most primitive of economic resources. Thatch, stone, clay, wood, or other materials close at hand are used in the construction of dwellings, often with very little processing. Industrial products (such as hinges, glass, pipes, wires) and processed materials (such as wallboard or tiles) tend to be assimilated where they are available but are not indispensable. Housing, almost by definition, is made of material which is available.

It is easy to generalize, then, that the "traditional" form of housing in a particular community is that which employs materials long available in abundance for the use of that community. We should have to add that of several materials which might be used, one, or a combination, would be selected which best suited environmental conditions. Thick adobe walls serve well in a hot, dry climate. Masonry is unsuitable for areas where earthquakes are common. The availability and suitability of materials tends to define a community's traditional concept of housing structures.

Building materials are likely to represent restraints on the creation of new dwellings only if the supply of such materials is exhausted or preferences (or technological requirements) with regard to dwellings change, and only then if there were no adaptation in the technology of housing construction. A common and important type of problem is the necessity to use heavier structural forms for high-density dwellings (apartment buildings) when the growth of community population makes complete dependence on individual dwellings unfeasible.

The demand for housing construction materials is also generally massive. Since large quantities are required, it is convenient for the community if the supply of such materials is relatively elastic. Otherwise fluctuations in the rate of construction—almost inevitable from demographic causes or migration as well as for economic reasons—would raise and lower costs from time to time and thus encourage periodic substitutions in materials or techniques. This would produce a mix of construction types within the community, but the conventions of urban living seem to discourage significant departures from an accepted housing type. Thus, a material which is in relatively elastic supply, as well as abundantly available and suited to the environment, seems the natural choice for the basis of traditional housing styles.

When the housing product has come to incorporate substantial amounts of particular industrial products—such as cement or steel—then the expansion of residential construction requires either new capital investment in those industries or an increase in the share of their output going into housing. The housing sector has some important competitors for such materials. The construction of office buildings, dams, ships, highways, and even automobiles may impose constraints upon expansion of the housing sector. The problem of building materials then becomes one of reallocation of the current outputs of the steel or cement industry, etc. At this point there may arise the possibility of capital-saving innovation, introducing a new product which does not have these indirect capital requirements.

In short, we seldom expect to find that housing construction is inhibited by a scarcity of building materials alone. This sector cannot be built around a resource which is in thin or precarious supply.

It almost goes without saying that transportation costs are very significant in limiting the range from which housing construction materials can be taken. It might be said that a large part of the cost of the raw materials in a finished dwelling is a transportation cost, for the resources themselves tend to be easily extracted but bulky and heavy. Transportation technology is thus linked to residential construction concepts so that a substantial change in the former may eventually cause a shift in the latter. The use of exotic woods in finishing some homes, for example, clearly depends on transportation facilities. It is reasonable to suppose that the chief and earliest effects of changes in transport technology would be on refinements or supplemental parts of dwellings rather than on the main elements of the structure.

In general, we might expect that as a community grows, its

housing sector consumes building materials of essentially the same type from an expanding area, until a major shift in technology or tastes (such as a switch to multiple-dwelling structures) changes the pattern of resource requirements. When this change in pattern occurs, it will tend to conform with and involve new resources having many of the supply characteristics of the old. Thus, building materials should present limitations for the housing sector only on occasion, but then in a rather serious way.

LABOR FORCE

There are many reasons why limitations in the supply of labor occasionally ought to have a restrictive effect on the level of residential construction, though there seems to be little evidence that such a restriction has operated. To begin with, as an industry with little "modern technology" to employ, housebuilding is usually quite labor-intensive. An individual house is virtually handcrafted on the spot, requiring numerous special skills and continuous coordination. Nonwooden, multifamily buildings usually represent somewhat less direct labor per dollar of housing product, but the volume of labor is still important and its complexity may be greater. Where prefabricated components are used, an increasing practice, the labor requirements may be in part reduced; in principle, however, they are simply moved back from the construction lot to the processing plant. The aggregate size of the labor force involved in house building is always substantial.[20]

In the second place, the aggregate level of residential construction is notoriously unstable. Seasonal factors make house building in many of the heavily populated areas of the world a part-of-the-year occupation. When the weather limits outdoor construction activity, the worker must be idle or move over into another occupation with compensating seasonal fluctuations. Business-cycle fluctuations have also had particularly severe impact upon residential construction, sometimes due to the decrease of final demand and at other times resulting in a "countercyclical" way from credit scarcity while manufacturing sectors of the economy build up their facilities during a wave of general prosperity. Instability in employment is a principal characteristic of the market for house building labor.

To compound these difficulties, the location of housing construction activity necessarily varies with differential regional growth and, within regions, with the selection of sites to meet new housing demand. House building labor must migrate inter-regionally and accept long and varying commuting burdens within a particular region. A by-product of this aspect of his employment is the fact that the worker seldom finds traditional urban amenities near his place of employment. In the extreme example, the worker who is employed in a "new town" project must put up with temporary or makeshift housing for himself, and virtually no facilities for his family.*

In view of these considerable drawbacks, it is surprising that labor shortages do not seem to inhibit house building on occasion, or that the cost of labor in this industry is not higher than it is. The supply of labor in this industry appears generally to be very elastic, expanding or contracting substantially as the otherwise-determined volume of housing activity changes its requirements for labor. This elasticity suggests that the skill requirements for labor in this industry are not so high as to prevent large-scale entry into the labor force at relatively short notice.

BUILDER'S EQUIPMENT

As an input in the house-building process, builder's equipment must be distinguished from the requirement of "finance" which has been discussed above. If houses were produced primarily on factory assembly lines, then it would be clear that the factory itself and the machines within it were a necessary input in the construction of dwellings. However, most of the capital equipment employed by house-building firms consists of movable tools and vehicles. They represent inputs for the housing product and it is conceivable that a severe shortage of such equipment could limit the output of housing. In the present state of technology this equipment is relatively uncomplicated and, in the aggregate, not overly significant. Labor or simpler tools can be sub-

---

* The construction of Brasilia is a case in point.

stituted effectively for much equipment (e.g. hand saws instead of power saws), and the supply of this equipment is usually fairly elastic. Earth-moving equipment is a major exception to this generalization, particularly as it may mean the difference in some areas between availability and nonavailability of land for housing.

ENTREPRENEURSHIP

The entrepreneur is the input in the housing industry most often overlooked, yet one of the most limiting factors in the equilibrium size of the housing sector. He is often confused with the investor, though his investment activities are distinctly minor. He is also confused with the builder, though he may or may not operate a building business. The entrepreneur is the person (or firm) who perceives (or thinks he perceives) a market demand for new housing and organizes all the resources necessary to meet that demand. He is, in essence, a middleman—one who buys components, assembles a product, and sells that product at a profit which represents his wage.[21]

It is possible for a family seeking a new home to secure land, financing, and the services of a building firm, dispensing with the middleman entrepreneur. It is possible for a person, group, or firm wishing to make a long-term equity investment in rental housing to find and acquire land, secure mortgage financing, and arrange with a builder to construct the investment property. The entrepreneur's function is not indispensable in the housing sector. His opportunity and value stem from the fact that he has skills which ultimate users of housing or long-term investors in housing often lack—a sense of the immediate market and a knowledge of the residential development process in intimate detail. He is often called a "developer" for this reason. He usually backs up his judgment of the market by taking a substantial risk; he owns the property during the development process and until it is sufficiently proven to attract a long-term buyer.

The activities of the entrepreneur may be inhibited by scarcity of any of the other inputs for housing development. The supply of open or redevelopable land, the availability of long-term mortgage funds and of permanent equity investment capital, and the extent to which the local building industry is willing to work with him determine the maximum scope of his activities in attempting to meet a market demand. The supply of entrepreneurs themselves is a more intricate question, however. They are businessmen who operate, typically, on a relatively small scale. Their individual success is always in doubt on one score or another and their fortunes fluctuate. There are substantial segments of the world in which a business class adapted to this sort of economic environment has never really emerged, let alone involved itself in residential construction.

From very limited information it appears that housing entrepreneurs arise from more settled trades associated with housing—real estate brokerage, law, architecture, appraising, construction, and lending. They must be individuals who feel they have discovered and understand an opportunity to pay going prices for land, financing, labor, materials, etc., and to put together a product which exceeds in value this combined cost. More than that, they must have the credit, or the credibility, to persuade backers to get the project going.

The entrepreneur is not essentially an investor. He wants a relatively liquid form of wealth in return for his activities. The equity in the completed property is his, but he may expect to use this equity as his working capital for the next undertaking.

An entrepreneurial role is assumed by someone in every instance of residential construction. Someone must always make the microeconomic decisions about what to build, when, where, and how to get it done. The behavior of the residential sector may be more "deliberate" if these decisions are left to the final user or to the mortgage lender. This implies that they will be sluggish, however, and not that they will necessarily be more appropriate to the needs of the market. The entrepreneur's specialized function is to be very close to the market and the involved process of serving it.

This completes our general comments concerning elements of supply which affect the equilibrium scale of activities in the housing sector. It is useful, in review, to visualize a "recipe" for housing which specifies how much of each of these six inputs is required per house. The quantities of each input available then indicate which requirement is the most limiting. For example, consider the following hypothetical set of numbers:

5

Input	Available	Requirement per 1,000 Houses	Maximum Output (000's)
Finance	$1 billion	$10 million	100
Land	1 million acres	200 acres	5,000
Materials	$8 billion	$8 million	1,000
Labor	120,000 man years	1,000 man years	120
Builder's equipment	$50 million	$200,000	250
Entrepreneurs	1,000	10	110

These assumed numbers indicate that finance is the most limiting factor. A demand in excess of 100,000 houses cannot be satisfied. (Of course, if the demand is limited to 95,000, none of the supply limitations will be effective.) If the available finance input were doubled, the table suggests that entrepreneurs would become the limiting factor. Estimates of the supply and unit requirement of entrepreneurs must be considered very uncertain, however, in the usual case. If the number or effectiveness of entrepreneurs increases quickly, labor takes over as the limiting factor. In this table, land is unlikely to become a "bottleneck" to housing development.

Equilibrium

In conventional microeconomics, the equilibrium output of an industry, such as the housing "industry" or sector, is determined by a process which brings supply and demand into balance. The balancing or equilibrating device is price. If the quantity supplied at a given price would exceed the quantity in demand at that price, the price tends to fall; if the initial price encourages a supply of the commodity which falls short of the demand at that price, the price tends to rise. This "Marshallian" equilibrium is illustrated in Figure 10.

This familiar diagram is, in effect, a geometric solution to a pair of simultaneous equations in two unknowns—price and quantity of output. Values of P (price) and Q (quantity) can be found which satisfy both equations and this pair of values is the intersection on the two-dimensional graph of Figure 10. The equations can be written as follows:

$Q = d(P)$, expressing the demand schedule
$Q = s(P)$, expressing the supply schedule.

The economist knows very well, however, that the quantities demanded and supplied of a particular commodity are determined by many other things besides that commodity's price. In-

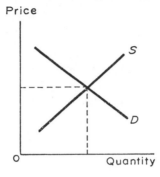

Figure 10

comes, interest rates, prices of raw materials, the size of the population, etc. are presumed to influence the actual behavior of the market. These other factors are implicit in the Marshallian equations, but they are regarded as being constant. This extended concept of Marshallian equilibrium can be represented by the following set of equations in which X, Y, and Z are factors which influence the equilibrium output but which are held constant:

$Q = d(P,\ X,\ Y)$
$Q = s(P,\ Y,\ Z)$
$X = \bar{X}, Y = \bar{Y}, Z = \bar{Z}$

The inference remains, however, that the critical and interesting variable is price. While this may be true for many commodities and while the price at which housing is available can influence the rate of new investment in housing, there are very practical reasons why the Marshallian equilibrium concept is not useful in the study of housing markets. In brief, we begin with the knowledge that several of the most important elements of demand and supply in the housing sector are not very price-elastic. The number of social households in the population depends primarily upon the age distribution of the population and customs regarding household formation. The relevant supply of land is virtually fixed in most cases and the amount of financing available for residential construction is almost everywhere influenced more by the institutional structure of the capital market than by the price of the housing product.

To represent equilibrium in the housing market by means of a price-quantity relationship would, therefore, overlook some of the most useful knowledge we have about this market. For example, if supply is reduced (the S-curve shifting to the left in Figure 10), equilibrium would be restored by an increase in price and a decrease in quantity of output. Which form of measurable demand will remain unmet? Specifically, will the formation of new households be discouraged? Will mobility and hence replacement demand be discouraged? Will the number of desired vacant units diminish? The answers to these questions, which may not depend very much upon prices, are of more interest than the knowledge of the price level change which will equate demand and supply. It is desirable to describe the equilibrium of the housing sector in such a way that the several components of demand and supply are not obscured.

The modern econometrician has developed a method of forecasting the equilibrium level of housing production which explicitly considers the several components of demand and supply. Rather than setting up a pair of equations representing the supply and demand sides of the market separately, however, the econometrician defines a primary equation in which the equilibrium—i.e. the actual level of housing output—is related to variables which represent influences upon demand and/or supply. For example, the econometrician might write the following expression, showing the quantity of actual output to be an equilibrium function of factors X, Y, and Z:

$$Q = e(X, Y, Z).$$

These factors might represent, for example, the number of new households, the rate of mortgage interest, and the initial number of vacant dwellings. The values for these factors might be determined through supplementary equations (making the number of new households a function of the age distribution of the population, for example). When the form of the function has been estimated by a statistical process using historical data, it can be used to forecast future levels of housing output.

The econometric procedure does not require that the factors within the explanatory equation be identified as elements of demand or supply. The rate of interest, for example, might conceivably affect both demand and supply, but in the econometric approach it is correlated with output regardless of how, in detail, it actually works through the housing market.

Any supposedly significant element of demand or supply can be fed into an econometric representation of housing sector equilibrium. No information about these individual elements comes out of the econometric system, however. We obtain a forecast of total housing output, but do not learn which type of the total possible demand is not satisfied by the market outcome. We do not know from this procedure how many dwellings are still "needed" or why specific demands were neglected. We do not learn how many dwellings *could* have been supplied except for specific, limiting factors. The econometric method produces useful gross expenditure estimates for macroeconomic forecasting purposes. However, it neglects issues of substantial importance for the housing sector, issues for which relevant information is developed in separate studies of housing demand. What is required is a procedure for comparing separate quantitative estimates of demand and supply.

A partial approach to such a procedure can be called a "feasibility solution." This approach ignores price-quantity relations per se and concentrates upon the quantity demanded and the quantity supplied in each segment of the housing sector. It recognizes that in equilibrium these quantities may not be equal and draws attention to the disparity and the manner in which that disparity may be resolved. Equilibrium output is determined not by a reconciliation of supply and demand functions, but, in the first instance, by the most limiting conditions which either of these functions contain.

The feasibility solution can be stated symbolically as follows:

$$Q_f \leq \bar{D}$$
$$Q_f \leq \bar{S}$$

That is, the actual output will not be greater than the quantity demanded nor greater than the quantity which can be supplied. The actual output is the output which is feasible, given the determinants of demand and supply. Quantities demanded and supplied are assumed to be substantially independent of the equilibrium outcome.

Another way of stating the feasibility solution is that the output is exactly equal to measured demand, less the demand which will be unsatisfied or "postponed," and the output is also exactly equal to measured potential supply, less the supply which is "redundant." Using P and R for the quantities of postponed demand and redundant supply, respectively, we can say:

$$Q_f = \bar{D} - P$$
$$Q_f = \bar{S} - R$$

Both P and R are real quantities and cannot be negative. In the aggregate, therefore, either P or R must be zero (in the coincidental case of $\bar{D} = \bar{S}$, both P and R would be zero). We are interested not only in the feasible level of output, but in the values of P and R, their reasons, implications, and consequences.

Looking back to our earlier example of demand, Equation (12) identified aggregate incremental demand and its sources. Table 3 disaggregated that demand into two sectors, urban and rural. The total of measured demand was 300 houses, and this is the quantity which we can now label $\bar{D}$. Let us assume initially that, from an analysis such as was illustrated by Table 5, the potential level of supply, $\bar{S}$, is 400. This produces a situation in which $Q_f = 300$, $P = 0$, and $R = 100$. The level of R indicates the redundancy of the *most* limiting component of supply, so that it is likely that other components of supply are even more redundant when the housing sector settles on a level of output of 300 dwellings. The varying degrees of resource redundancy can be traced by means of the supply concept of Table 5 and their implications studied. For example, if mortgage credit for new housing is in substantial excess, some weaknesses in the organization of the capital market may be indicated.

On the demand side, if $\bar{D}$ is fully satisfied by the actual level of housing construction, it is of interest to derive the implications of this output level for the housing stock. If we add the incremental demand of Table 4 (which, for the moment, we assumed to be entirely satisfied by actual construction) to the initial stock shown in Table 2, the resulting stock is as follows:

6

	H	$=$	F	$+$	V	$+$	$R*$
Urban	850		800		20		30
Rural	550		400		100		50
Total	1,400		1,200		120		80

The $R*$ column combines the R and M columns of Table 4, as was explained in connection with Equation (12).

This arithmetic produces an ambiguous result. It is easy to understand the implications of the F column, namely, that a total of 1,200 houses will be occupied. The V column indicates that 120 vacant units will be held as intentional investments. The significance of the $R*$ column is not so clear. $R*$ really means a demand to abandon units in favor of more desirable replacements. What effect does this accomplished abandonment have upon the stock?

In a physical sense, housing units abandoned by the market (but not necessarily by their owners) may be removed from the inventory by demolition or may be added to the number of vacant dwellings. The outcome depends upon a collection of microeconomic decisions, choices exercised by individual owners faced with particular sets of alternatives. Aspects of the microeconomic problem associated with abandonment by the market will be examined in a later chapter. For macroeconomic purposes we need only note that the final impact of new residential construction, Q_f, upon the housing stock depends, in part, on the manner in which replacement activities are absorbed. For example, in the above illustration we might learn ultimately that half of the

R^* houses were demolished in favor of some more attractive new use of the land. In that case, the adjusted inventory would consist of 1,360 houses of which 1,200 were occupied and 160 were vacant.

Next, let us suppose that the possible supply of new houses, $\bar{S}$, had been not 400, but only 250. In this situation the feasible output of the housing sector, Q_f, is 250, the redundant supply, R, is zero (though specific supply resources may not be fully used) and the postponed demand, P, is 50. The interesting question is which of the components of demand will be postponed? Looking again at the expression of demand, $\bar{D}$, in Equation (12), we find a total of 200 houses required by the increase in the number of families, 20 by investors' plans to hold vacant units, and 80 by various forms of mobility, including replacement in the usual sense. From one of these demands, or a combination of them, 50 houses must be subtracted, for only 250 new houses are feasible for the housing sector to produce.

Our feasibility procedure does not indicate which form of demand will be unmet (or to what extent). It does identify the necessity for postponing some form of emerging demand. The practical consequences of postponing any specific type of demand vary, so that the specific adjustments made to accommodate total demand to feasible output deserve ad hoc study. Also, for postponed demand, as for redundant supply, the ultimate consequences of the housing sector's current activities upon the housing stock require examination going beyond the determination of the level of new housing production. Thus, the equilibrium volume of new housing output is not the end of the story; a whole set of adjustments and impacts are implied by that equilibrium. The feasibility procedure facilitates further analysis of the behavior of the housing sector while, at least in principle, satisfying the need for a forecast of the overall level of the housing sector's activity.

"Normal Vacancy" and "Turnover"

The purpose here is to examine two concepts which are frequently employed in deriving estimates of housing demand but which can, in fact, be quite misleading.

NORMAL VACANCY

The concept of a "normal" vacancy percentage is related to so-called "frictional needs" of the housing market. According to this concept, unless some dwellings were unoccupied, no household movements could occur. It seems to follow from this that a certain level of vacancy is both desirable and inevitable, much as "frictional unemployment" is tolerated in the labor market since it represents workers' mobility.

In the housing sector there are two grounds for questioning the concept of friction and normal vacancy. In the first place, the practical manner in which vacancies could be produced in response to the frictional needs of households is not clear. Households undoubtedly benefit from the existence of vacancies because this facilitates their movement (as well as keeping rents down, perhaps). However, this benefit is "external" and thus creates no effective market demand. Households as a group do not compensate owners as a group for maintaining a redundant supply since no mechanism for this kind of bilateral transaction exists in the atomistic rental market.

The second point follows from the recognition of "intended vacancy" as discussed in the present chapter. There are several reasons why owners may choose to hold unoccupied dwellings. The aim of the owner is not to facilitate household movement, though that may be one effect of his decision. It is a self-contained investment choice. The monopoly element, for example, is rational ground for holding unrented apartments.

If a particular level of vacancies seems "normal" it is likely that the conditions leading to intended investment in vacancy are relatively stable. The satisfaction of frictional needs is a by-product of these investment decisions. It follows that the "normal" vacancy level can vary over time and among markets depending not on the mobility of households but upon the composite trend of several housing investment factors. This deprives vacancy of some of its accustomed meaning. There is no natural level of the vacancy factor to which housing investors must necessarily resign themselves. There is no ceiling to the rate which lending institutions or housing developers may consider appropriate. The correct interpretation of vacancy data requires a thorough knowledge of housing investment practices.

TURNOVER

"Turnover" is a concept used widely in conjunction with vacancy information to predict the rate at which a group of households waiting to be housed can be accommodated. The significance of turnover is obvious to people waiting patiently for a table at a crowded restaurant or to an ill person waiting for a hospital bed to become available. The correct application of the concept to the housing market is not so obvious.

Some mathematical symbolism is helpful. We can assume the following definitions:

$S =$ number of units in the housing stock
$K =$ present number of vacant units; $K \geq 0$
$V =$ number of vacant units at future time t; $V \geq 0$
$d_i =$ number of households departing from S in time period i
$a_i =$ number of households admitted to S in time period i
$\delta = d_i/S$, proportion of S vacated in time period i.

We can make the following statement:

$$V = K + \sum_{i=1}^{t} d_i - \sum_{i=1}^{t} a_i.$$

This says that the future number of vacancies equals the present number, plus the accumulated number of household departures, minus the accumulated number of admissions. Using the concept of a departure rate, δ, the statement becomes:

$$V = K + t \cdot \delta \cdot S - \sum_{i=1}^{t} a_i.$$

To illustrate, suppose the stock consists of 100 units of which three are now vacant, while 6 percent of the stock is vacated each time period and five households are admitted each period. At the end of four time periods, the number of vacant units is:

$$V = 3 + 4 \cdot 6\% \cdot 100 - (5 + 5 + 5 + 5) = 7.$$

Alternatively, seven additional households could be accommodated within this stock by the end of four time periods.

Occasionally the turnover concept is erroneously used as a "multiplier" of existing vacancy. Within each time period some units initially occupied become vacant, so that the total number of units which experience vacancy during the time period is a multiple of the initial number of vacant units. The multiplier, using the above symbols, would be defined as d/K, or 2 in the example. The turnover-multiplier concept then develops a prediction of the number of additional households which can be accommodated by the stock in a number of time periods, the number being $m \cdot K \cdot t$ (where m equals the multiplier, or d/K). In four time periods, making the other assumptions of our example above, the multiplier concept says that $2 \cdot 3 \cdot 4 = 24$ households could be accommodated.

It is clear that the multiplier concept merely assumes that the number of admissions will be zero in the time periods under consideration. Its prediction of the capacity of the stock to accommodate additional households is simply the accumulated number of departing households, even omitting the number of units initially vacant. The question is whether the circumstances warrant the assumption of zero admissions to the supply.

The ordinary functioning of a housing market—for a building, a neighborhood, or a city—assumes approximate equality between the number of departures and the number of admissions during a period of time, so that the number of vacant units remains unchanged. If there is a list of households to be rehoused from, say, an urban-renewal clearance project, these households can be given priority in a publicly owned housing project, but only by excluding some or all of the households which would have been admitted from other sources. In the private market it is usually not feasible to give specific households priority for vacated units and, in the local market as a whole, it is impossible to reduce admissions of nonpriority households without curtailing departures. In a local market the departure of a household from one unit means that the same household is admitted to another. If admissions of nonpriority households to vacant units is suspended, the departure of those households from their present units must cease, and thus "turnover" ceases. The multiplier is an invalid procedure of "finding" vacant units to house relocated households.

In an extreme case, the multiplier would say that more households could be accommodated by the stock of housing than there are units within that stock. For example, with a stock of 100 units, three initial vacancies, and a departure rate of 60 percent, the multiplier (d/K) would be 20 and the number of households which, according to the multiplier concept, could be housed within five time periods would be $20 \cdot 3 \cdot 5 = 300$, three times the size of the stock. Housing shortages could be solved very quickly if reality were so careless about its arithmetic.

4 · ▰

THE OPTIMUM SIZE OF

THE HOUSING SECTOR

The question of how much housing investment is "enough" has many complicating subissues. It involves the establishment of norms and the reconciliation of these norms with the availability of resources. It touches upon the normative rate of household formation and of normative housing expenditure per household. It touches upon the geographic distribution of the population in terms of mobility and differential concentration—i.e., the size of specific cities, and even inferentially upon the size and rate of growth of the aggregate population. Most fundamentally, it poses the problem of allocating resources in terms of aggregate social usefulness.

Evaluating Feasibility Constraints

There is a quick and superficial way of resolving the entire question. We may posit a set of indifference curves representing equally satisfactory combinations of housing investment and of "all other" resource uses, plus a "trade-off" relationship between the uses of resources in these two compartments of the economy.[1] The point of tangency is the optimal allocation. The following diagram illustrates this concept:

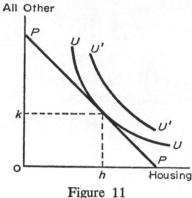

Figure 11

Points along the *U-U* function are combinations of *Housing* and *All Other* goods (or increases in the amount of goods in these two categories) which would be equally satisfactory to the community. More of *All Other* compensates for less *Housing,* and vice versa. The *P-P* line indicates the combinations of *Housing* and *All Other* goods which it is possible to produce, given the community's resources, the slope of this line depending on the quantity of resources which would have to be taken from one sector to expand the other. The position of the *P-P* line depends upon the aggregate quantity of resources available which might, in our particular instance, be interpreted as the volume of savings per year produced by the economy for investment purposes. The optimal scale of housing investment is *h,* the level at which the possibilities' line is tangent to the utility (i.e. satisfaction) function. With this allocation of available resources, the highest possible aggregate level of utility is attained. Until this distribution of resources is reached, the incremental, or "marginal," utility of more investment in one sector is greater than the incremental utility in the other so that total utility can be increased by transferring resources from one sector to the other. At the point of tangency, marginal utilities in both sectors are equal. With more resources, the *P-P* line would shift outward (in parallel fashion, it could be presumed) and some point on a higher aggregate satisfaction function such as *U'-U'* could be attained, involving increases in the scale of either or both sectors.

This is an abstract but, at the same time, valid statement of the manner in which optimum sector size is determined. Nothing in the following discussion is inconsistent with this manner of presenting the problem, nor could it be and still purport to be a discussion of optimization.

To leave the problem at this point, however, would be to ignore much that is of specific value and usefulness in our practical knowledge about housing and its place in economic life. The indifference diagram and statements derived from it—the equimarginal principal, mainly—leave it to the student or administrator to decide for himself what "Housing" is made of and what it is for. In these matters, imagination is a poor substitute for the real knowledge that has been accumulated. Without taking this knowledge into account, we might find virtual unanimity on the theoretical definition of optimum sector size but marvelous diversity of opinion about what this optimum size means in practice.

If we do take this more specific knowledge about the housing sector into account, however, we spoil the elegant tautology of the indifference or equimarginal description. A more complex representation of optimization is required.

To move gradually toward a more informative system, consider a situation in which only the technical trade-off function between housing and all other goods is known—i.e. the P-P line in Figure 11. This function is represented in Figure 12 and on it at point A,H, is some possible division of resources between the two sectors.

The optimization question can be expressed in the following terms: would an increase, ΔH, in the scale of the housing sector at the cost of a reduction, ΔA, in the scale of the remainder of the economy represent an overall improvement in the use of resources? This is simply an application of the concept in Figure 11, for if we deem ΔH more valuable than ΔA, then the starting point, A,H, must have been to the left of the point of optimum allocation and at the intersection of P-P with a lower level of satisfaction (indifference curve) than our available resources permit us to attain.

The real task is to reduce the subjectivity involved in weighing ΔA against ΔH. What is the real cost of enlarging the housing sector and what specific form will this enlargement take? The "feasibility solution" to the question of *equilibrium* size of the housing sector, which was developed in the preceding chapter, provides basic answers to these optimization questions. If the allocation *A,H* represents the equilibrium division of resources, then we know that there is among the various inputs into housing (such as finance, land, labor, etc.) one which is actually critical in limiting the scale of housing output. The real cost of

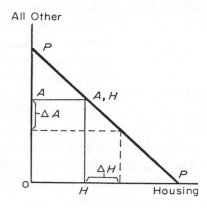

Figure 12

enlarging the housing sector involves primarily that one critical input, whichever it may be. Thus, concern about the sacrifice of "all other goods" boils down to a study of alternative uses made in an equilibrium solution of a certain quantity of one particular type of resource. If the most limiting supply factor in the feasibility equilibrium solution is finance, our study of the optimality of enlarging the housing sector will involve a review of the nature of capital allocation decisions, problems of economic theory, and of business institutions. If, on the other hand, the factor of entrepreneurship was most limiting in equilibrium, a study combining aspects of sociology and personal and business motivations would be in order. The concept of feasibility is instrumental in describing an equilibrium solution for the size of the housing sector and it is a meaningful starting point for the study of optimization as well.

On the demand side, feasibility suggests that in equilibrium certain types of need for additional housing will be met while other latent demands will be passed over. An expansion of the sector (which might be contemplated as an optimization issue) would presumably serve these passed-over needs. For example, if the equilibrium solution failed to meet some needs for upgrading the housing stock but did satisfy needs arising from changes in the number of households and in their mobility plus needs arising from vacancy investment, etc.—then, by devoting more resources to the housing sector, we would simply be improving the quality of the stock in some fashion. In this way, an "increase in the scale of the housing sector" acquires greater realism and meaning for the ultimate subjective process of making a decision about optimum resource-allocation.

The method for arriving at a concept of optimum housing-sector size, then, is a review of the critical components of the equilibrium solution. Which inputs will actually be difficult or costly to increase? What form of additional housing activity will result? The same basic market information which is required for estimates of equilibrium sector behavior is also vital in analyzing questions about modifying that behavior in the public interest.

It is a little more convenient to consider the requirements for housing—i.e. the Demand side of the problem—before taking up the resources or Supply side. If requirements turn out to be very modest, then resources may not represent a substantial impediment to achieving optimum size of the housing sector. It is true also that one aspect of supply, the element of finance, involves questions of some complexity which at this point would seem to be tangential to our principal interest. Let us turn, then, to the components of demand which emerged in the discussion of sector equilibrium and reexamine them from the point of view of optimality.

Optimum Population and Number of Households

The expression of demand (in the preceding chapter's discussion of equilibrium) involved three main elements. That expression was:

$$\Delta H = \Delta F + \Delta V + R$$

Thus, the desired level of new housing construction is the sum of the number of units arising from changes in the number of households (i.e. "Families"), the net increase in desired vacancies, and sufficient units to abandon portions of the initial housing stock which, in one respect or another, no longer serve the needs of the population.

The first term is the resultant of two very distinct factors, the size and characteristics of the population itself, and the pattern of grouping to form separate households out of that population. This "pattern" is expressible as a percentage, r, which links population, P, and the number of households, F, as follows:

$$F = r \cdot P$$

e.g. $250 = (25\%) \, 1,000$

Separate issues of optimization surround each of the terms on the right, r and P. Moreover, we are forced to recognize that the optimum rates of separation into households may differ for different subgroups of the population. If half of the population were under age 30, for example, and half above, and if we thought it proper for only two out of ten among the younger group to be heads of separate households, but that three out of ten among the older group should be household heads, then our example could be broken down as follows:

	$F =$	r	P
under age 30	100	20%	500
over age 30	150	30%	500
Total	250	25%	1,000

The population might be broken down into any number of groups according to any meaningful characteristics (such as income, cultural preferences, etc., as well as age) and an optimum percentage would have to be conjured up for each. It is clear that the overall percentage, 25 percent in our example, is simply the mathematical result of the percentages assigned to the subgroups and the population weights of those subgroups. It cannot be determined independently of its components.

What is the optimum size of the population? This very large question has troubled economists, scientists, theologians, and politicians for ages; surely it cannot be resolved in our present limited-purpose study. This is not a dodge, however, for we can say with some confidence that the housing sector represents a critical part of the population question only under some particular circumstances—for example, when there is a problem of congestion. Otherwise, the optimum level of population and the pattern of some of its main characteristics such as the age and income distribution are determined in a conceptual framework much broader than the housing sector. For that sector the optimum population is, then, simply the actual population, together with many of its most important characteristics.

On a global level, or even on the level of a national aggregate, the situation in which a pending shortage of sheer space makes the housing sector an important aspect of the population question is contemplated more in entertainment than in active concern. Some analysts and writers produce extrapolations of population growth which result in "standing room only." [2] Others estimate the number of planets in the universe (some fraction of which must be habitable) to be many, many times the human population of earth. Whether the future will see humanity so crowded that no one has room to lie down or so dispersed that everyone has a planet to himself remains unknown. Only in the first eventuality will the housing sector assume prominence in the optimum population issue; this, moreover, could occur only if barriers arising from all other sectors were overcome. It is quite safe to leave this larger question to later studies in housing economics.

When we raise the optimum population question with respect to an area smaller than a nation, however, the jocular aspects of the discussion quickly vaporize. Cities, neighborhoods, houses, and even rooms which are too crowded for comfort can be identified with ease in the world today. Dense torrents of pedestrians swirl through urban commercial districts, too thick, sometimes, to let an individual change his mind and go the other way. Automobiles converge predictably into massive paralysis in a growing roster of affluent metropolises. Patches of straw-covered floor serve for beds 24 hours a day as humans sleep in shifts.[3] The pessimistic prophecy of global congestion is already realized in microcosm on the urban level, and on this level the housing sector does become significant for the question of optimum population. How large should the population of a given city be? This is already a real question in the world and to which our analysis should be relevant.

Optimum Urban Scale

The size of a city has at least two important dimensions, the "scale" or absolute number of people and the *density* at which they live and work. A population of 10,000 persons might seem too large for a settlement which is confined geographically to a small island or peninsula or otherwise bound within a small area of land. A population of ten million might seem comfortable if spread over a vast plain served by a rapid and efficient system of transportation. Density thus affects a judgment of the population size which is desirable. The absolute number of people in a city also raises a question because there are significant costs—mainly in transportation—and remarkable economies of urban scale. Economies result from the fact, for example, that groups of interrelated factories and business services function best when located close to each other.

We need to resolve both issues—that of scale and that of density—and it is convenient to treat them separately. We look first at the question of scale, holding density constant. Then we shall consider variations in density while urban scale remains constant. After this, we shall put the concepts together.

TRANSPORTATION COSTS IN URBAN GROWTH

When the population of a city increases, the aggregate cost of residence-oriented transportation expenditures within that city will rise. More people will be traveling to and from work and shopping. Some people will be making longer journeys than were previously required of the city's residents because new residential development will be at the outer edge (unless increased density exactly offsets the gain in population).

The extent and characteristics of the increase in transportation costs to the city as population rises can be quite complex. The elements can be portrayed, however, in an illustration involving several simplifying assumptions. Suppose that our city is a flat, circular plane with all employment and shopping facilities at its center, and with a transportation system such that the direct cost of a trip to the center is a linear function of the radial distance to the place of residence.* Suppose further (at least to begin with) that residential density is uniform throughout the city, with every household occupying as much ground area as every other household.

The advent of additional population will cause the following four transportation-related events to occur:

1. Aggregate, direct transportation costs will rise.
2. Density may tend to rise, particularly at the center.
3. Congestion may appear in the central area.
4. Land values or "location rents" will rise.

We are concerned with the net effect of these factors in combination. Some qualitative feeling for this net effect may be gained by considering the nature of each of these factors. First, with respect to the change in aggregate community transportation costs, our assumptions imply that the aggregate will rise, and the marginal cost will rise at a diminishing rate.† The area of a circle (and, hence, the population of our constant-density city) increases faster than the radius (and hence, transportation costs), so that the average transportation cost per household will rise, for as the city expands, the average household lives farther and farther from the center. The marginal transportation cost lies above the average cost.

It is natural to suppose, as we have already suggested, that in the face of generally rising transportation (or location rent) burdens, some households would consider sacrificing a portion of their space to "double up" with others close to the center. If we

---

* For convenience we define the psychic and time costs of commuting as offsets to the benefits produced by urban growth rather than as resource costs.

† That is, the increase in total cost occasioned by the newcomer is greater than that occasioned by his immediate predecessor since the newcomer lives farther from the center. The excess is less and less as the population expands, however, so that for a very large population the marginal cost will be nearly constant.

worked this into our mathematics, the rate of increase in aggregate transportation costs would be lower, suggesting that expanding population creates little in direct new transport cost. The loss of space, however, would certainly be a cost in terms of household utility. It is reasonable to retain our constant-density assumption on the grounds that density increases induced by higher transport costs approximately cancel out the saving in direct-transport cost which they permit.

Congestion may build up at the center of the city as population grows, for three basic reasons. There may have been imperfect foresight in laying out of durable transportation systems. The positive cost of capital would, in any case, cause less weight to be given to future population than to present users in transportation planning. There will be also some technological limitations on the nature of transportation systems so that effective means to relieve congestion are not always apparent. Counting the inconvenience of congestion as a real cost of intraurban transportation, we would suppose that the congestion element of marginal cost would remain positive but perhaps be subject to erratic fluctuations as foresight or technology improves or capital becomes more abundant. In part, the costs of congestion can be held down by decentralizing some of the original functions of the urban core.

Finally, the increase in location rents creates a burden which is either "distributional" as landlords receive higher incomes from tenants, or "real" as owner-occupants become less mobile in an economy of "inflated" property values. The first may be offset, at least in part, by programs of recapture. The second problem will arise if the credit institutions do not adapt to the higher structure of urban "land" prices and so require higher and higher equity investment of purchasers. It will be compounded by variations in the wealth position of households not perfectly matched to locational needs and preferences, for the low-wealth households will be frozen out of home-ownership in central areas.

Taking all four elements together, we can conclude that the composite marginal transportation cost to a community as population rises will almost certainly be increasing. The first factor will tend to cause a slowing rise in this marginal cost; the second we have discarded; the third and fourth will tend to make the composite rise unless there are continuing, fortunate improvements in technology and institutions. There are real costs associated with expanding urban scale.

ECONOMIES OF URBAN SCALE

Output per capita of valuable goods and services—i.e. income—increases as the population of a city (or metropolis) grows.[4] This is true for several reasons. Individual enterprises, such as manufacturing plants or department stores, enjoy technological economies of scale from lower costs of production, distribution, inventory, and general management, so that large labor forces tend to be employed at the same site. Even beyond the scale economies of the individual firm, when several complementary firms are grouped together in a city, they contribute willy-nilly to each other's efficiency. For example, several factories using the same type of labor create a labor market of such size and flexibility that one firm can expand or contract its individual work force with little difficulty. Or the several firms may create a joint demand for long-distance transportation which is large enough to permit that transportation system to operate at low cost to the benefit of all its users. Joint or large-scale demand also creates opportunities for suppliers, subcontractors, and business service operations (banks, law offices, etc.) to achieve efficient levels of output.

One major category of "external economies" produced by large urban populations is in the diversity of consumption goods and services among which residents may choose. Theaters, hospitals, complexes of retail shops, consumer credit facilities, etc. are more accessible to people living in large cities than to residents of smaller cities. The magnetic attraction of the city through the ages and in virtually all cultures derives from the variety of opportunity for employment and for consumption which the city provides; this magnetism seems to increase with the city's size.

The sturdy, nearly irresistible growth of major cities in the world today suggests very strongly that the direct economies of scale have no end, and that further agglomeration is always in the self-interest of urban businesses. If this were the only factor to be considered, we might have a "marginal benefit curve" of urban growth which continued above the linear marginal cost curve which we have spoken of in terms of transportation needs within the city. The optimum urban population would be infinite.

Maybe this is really so. Conditions in many cities today, however, force us to consider that the marginal benefit curve does peak out and start to decline beyond a certain population size— if we subtract from direct-enterprise benefits the disadvantages to public-service activities and to households themselves which accumulate in a growing city. That is, local government functions seem often to experience substantial diseconomies of scale, including impersonalization, confusion about the locus of responsibility, and imperfect public vision about the consequences of public and private activities. Households may well find their incomes rising enough to cover increased money costs of transportation in the expanding city, but no rate of economic progress can give them more time or patience to endure long trips to work and to shop.

Figure 13 thus shows marginal costs associated with expanding population to be level and marginal benefits to be more or less bell-shaped, crossing the marginal cost function at two points. Urban scale may be said to have a minimum population level, below which some economic inefficiencies must be compensated for by semirural amenities, or else the population would tend to drift away to larger cities. It has a maximum point beyond which an expanding population is detrimental to the national well-being.

We might call this maximum level the optimum scale of the city. An interesting problem arises, however, when we consider the per-capita or average benefits and costs, which are also shown in the diagram. Maximum average net benefit (average benefit minus average cost) occurs at a lower scale than the maximum indicated by marginal curves. Whose interests should be considered in setting a ceiling on the growth of a particular city—the people who live there or the people of the nation as a whole? If the former, then the "maximum average" point on the diagram is the place to stop. If the latter, then the "maximum" scale indicated by the marginal curves is preferred. The economist rather naturally inclines to take the broader, national point of view, and so prefers expanding City A until it ceases to make a net contribution to national well-being. However, the point is really moot.

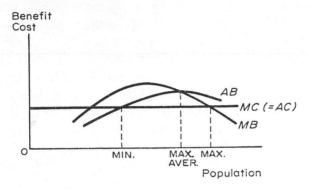

Figure 13

Supposing that decentralization of the growing city, with respect to employment, shopping facilities, and government, can proceed, then the logic of limiting the size of the city is weakened. With such decentralization, however, we begin to wonder whether it is still just one city or a family of related cities, a "megalopolis," in the new terminology.[5] Further pursuit of this question would be beyond our present limited purposes, however. There are essentially economic forces which encourage urban communities to grow in scale, but with some penalties which may or may not ultimately outweigh the gains. That is all we want to say for the moment.

Optimum Urban Density

We turn now to the density aspect of urban size. Given the total population of the community, over what area will they be spread? Again, we are concerned with residential density primarily, though other density issues may appear inferentially. And, again, we assume that the city starts, at least, as a uniform plane with a single center. We also assume that households in the community are homogeneous, or that we are describing an "average" household with respect to housing preference, income, etc. At this point we are not concerned with differences in density for different types of households nor with the geographic pattern of densities within the city.

Figure 14 is concerned with the quantity of land which will be consumed by the average member of the population—i.e. the density—in relation to the distance which that consumer will travel to obtain that land. In effect, we have a demand curve for land-per-person, labeled *MU* (for marginal utility or incremental satisfaction) which is downward-sloping. The less land costs, the more the household will use. We assume that land itself is a free good so that the cost of obtaining more of it is for transportation, including resource costs and inconvenience. (The value of outlying land for agricultural uses may represent an opportunity cost.) This incremental cost is represented by the *MC* curve, which may or may not be horizontal, depending on the scale economies of the transportation system.

The intersection of *MU* and *MC* tells us that the average person will consume 0*d* land, thus establishing the average density of the community. Given the size of the population, we then know the spatial dimensions of the community. Thus, if the average density is fifty persons per acre and the population of the city is 50,000, the city will have an area of 1,000 acres. (In the interest of simplicity, we can consider that the average use of land represented by our diagram includes industrial, commercial, public, and other land uses, besides residential.)

A dashed line, *MC'*, in the figure represents a different concept of the cost element which can be called marginal *private* cost. If the transportation system, including utility lines and all else that is necessary to service an extensive residential area, is subsidized in a way such that the private user of outlying land does not pay the full resource cost which is occasioned by low density, then consumption of land is encouraged. Equilibrium density would be 0*d'* while optimum density would be 0*d*. Transportation subsidies would then have to be offset by controls preventing density from falling below a certain level in order to assure optimum density. It is possible, on the other hand, that transportation or other private costs associated with lowering density might be artificially high, resulting in equilibrium densities above the optimum. For example, poor organization of the residential capital market might deprive families of the opportunity to acquire single-family homes, thus imposing higher density patterns than would be optimal under conditions of efficiency in the housing sector generally.

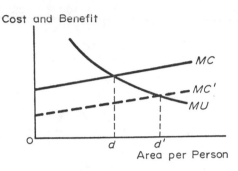

Figure 14

If the *MU* curve of Figure 14 is relatively steep or inelastic, this would imply that density would not rise very much as the size of the city—and with it the cost of preserving that density— rose. The source of such inelasticity could be a cultural predisposition toward the occupancy of relatively definite amounts of land per person or per family—perhaps reinforced by functional requirements associated with child-raising. Thus, if there is such a thing as the optimum residential density for a city, it probably arises out of a cultural or functional characteristic of residential demand. It is not primarily a "cost-minimizing" concept. Of course, the cultural notion of the amount of space which is "proper" for an urban resident—the level around which the *MU* line is nearly vertical—may be the result of long association with cities of a given total population and with a relatively stable transportation technology. So long as people are willing to pay in transportation costs for lower densities or in discomforts of crowding (alleviated by efficient high-rise construction) for high densities, there is really no one level of density which is optimal for the community. It is the attitude of consumers which creates such a concept, and this attitude is probably the product of customs developed by earlier generations in more stable communities. Technology—of transport, and of residential building —influences the "price" of lower density to the urban land consumer but does not tell the consumer how much he must use. Optimum density is not a technological concept such as, for example, the optimum population of a nation might be (given the relationship between population and per capita GNP). The density optimum is decided in the consumer's mind or, perhaps, decided for him by public or private planners. The "value system" underlying it necessarily derives from traditional urban experience rather than from the prospective scale or activities of the community in question. In this way, residential density is somewhat like a society's dietary habits in which those things which have been available in ages past seem necessary in spite of their cost to the present generation.

We could, of course, have a situation in which the *MU* curve of Figure 14 was nearly horizontal but at a very high level, while the *MC* curve became nearly vertical when the given population had exhausted the land physically available. For example, if the total available area consisted of a small island or a plain hemmed in by unbuildable mountains or swamps, then, a leftward shift in the *MC* curve (representing an increase in the total population of the community and rising scarcity values for land) would cause average density to rise. This would not mean that density was technologically determined, however, since the condition would imply that consumers wanted to use all the land which was physically available to them. The optimum density here is simply the minimum level which is physically attainable.

The slope of the *MC* curve in Figure 14 may not be affected by the scale of the city—i.e. by the total number of people living there. It is likely, however, that the position or height of this line will be affected by scale. The larger the city already is, the greater will be the transportation cost of spreading the existing population out. We would expect, then, that the optimal average

residential density in our simple example would rise as the scale
of the city rises.

We must consider, however, the durability of structures
and the question of foresight concerning the "ultimate" total
population of the city. Future densities can be planned for—even
by the inchoate market process, through what is known as "speculation." Once a judgment of future population potential is settled on, though, and buildings constructed accordingly, it will be
difficult and costly to remake the density pattern of the community.

In Figure 15 we show the population of a city increasing
along the vertical scale and the land area of the city increasing

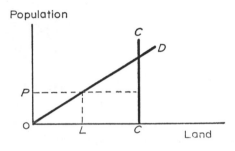

Figure 15

along the horizontal scale. A straight line, *OD,* expresses the optimal or anticipated density relationship, for example, 50 persons
per acre. A vertical line, *C-C,* represents the limitation imposed
upon the usefulness of land by maximum commuting time or cost
or by physical barriers, so that *OC* land is usable.

Suppose that the city's actual present population is *OP.* At
optimum density this population will occupy only *OL* land, leaving *LC* land idle or in uses such as market gardening which will
retain it as a reserve for future population growth. Any tendency
for the population to spread out at densities lower than the optimum, which would mean that the actual density was a line
from 0 with a smaller slope than *OD,* would use up some or all of
the land reserve for growth at optimum density. If this spreading
out has actually occurred and then population growth begins, the

manner in which actual density is raised may be unfortunate or acceptable, depending in part on the durability of existing residential structures and the speed at which the population growth occurs.

Alternatively, in Figure 16 we can suppose that population density remains optimal while the city is growing. Then we can

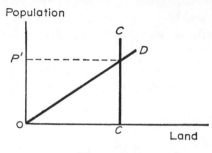

Figure 16

say that the population P' is optimal for this city as long as two conditions are met: economies of urban scale do not disappear with rising population, and no urban scale economies would justify a change in either the optimum density or the maximum commuting range.

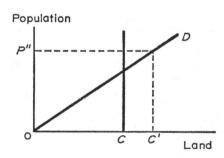

Figure 17

In case the net benefit of greater scale turns negative at some point below P', we have then merely defined a horizontal line at some level in our diagram which indicates the maximum population which should be sought.

Suppose that urban scale economies are so strong that population grows beyond P' in Figure 16 to at least P'' in Figure 17. We might consider P'' to be the minimum level of population for this city in the sense that efficiency requires it or public officials are unable to hold the city's population below this level.

Clearly, something must give in this situation. The community must learn to live at higher densities than originally deemed optimal, perhaps searching for new ways to make such densities attractive and livable, or it must improve its transportation system so that the maximum commuting range increases to $0C'$ (but not beyond, or it might encourage either spreading out of population $0P''$ or further increases in population!)

New Towns

There might be cultural situations in which a city with the greatest net benefit from population growth attracted residents from cities with less net benefit, much as a factory with higher wages attracts workers from factories where their productivity and wages are lower. This would lead to a redistribution of urban populations among cities until the incremental net benefit was the same for each city, following the equimarginal principle of neoclassical resource allocation. Certain interesting regularities in relative size and rate of growth among cities have been observed around the world, but the evidence that a truly rational "urban population market" exists in any nation is not very satisfying.

There are also some intuitive reasons to doubt that urban population distribution follows this equimarginal principle very precisely. Both the costs and benefits associated with urban growth arc distributed in ways which may not readily persuade a citizen to move to City A rather than to City B. Among the principal beneficiaries of growth are shareholders in existing urban department stores and other large-unit consumer facilities and owners of well-situated real estate. These groups are often found among a city's "boosters," and with good business reason. More intensive use of their facilities may represent efficient use of resources for the community as a whole, but it produces monetary gains for specific individuals in the process. Commercial enterprises are sometimes in an oligopoly position and owners of specific real estate have effective monopolies, so competition will not redirect all of this urban benefit toward the expanded population which really makes it possible. On the other hand, costs of urban facilities are shared through tax systems by property owners, businesses, commuters, and general income tax payers in such a way that the connection between population expansion and additional public costs is irregular and obscure.

If a city's population—and by this we imply its sources of employment as well—grows or does not grow without regard to net benefits and costs of that growth, then some type of public action is needed to achieve optimum size. On the one hand it may be wise to encourage population to grow in a city with a promising relationship of marginal benefits and marginal costs, that is to bring such a city up to its minimum level. On the other hand, a city may tend to expand beyond the maximum size (in the sense of Figure 13) and, in that case, public action may be concerned with checking further increases for that particular city. Both of these considerations are involved in discussions of "new town" development which are heard in many parts of the world. A major city, such as London or Tokyo, is thought by some to have grown beyond its inherent maximum population, so efforts are made to draw off future growth (at least) to some area which must achieve substantial size before it can compete effectively with the older metropolis. British New Towns provide, perhaps, the best laboratory for this concept.[6]

The economics of the "new town" movement is not really a housing market problem, in the narrow sense of the term, though it often seems to be one, and though it is usually the housing agencies of government which are most deeply involved. Additional housing would be required for a growing population whether that population concentrated in the original city or is drawn away to a new community. (The types of new housing to be built might be part of the problem, however.) The elements of the problem are external economies of urban growth, on the one hand, and the feasibility of expanding or improving urban services in the older city. It is clear that external economies (before public costs are netted against them) will be sacrificed by holding down the expansion of the older city. Residents of the new town will have less choice of retail and service facilities and less range of employment opportunities than they could have by living in the older city. Production, distribution, and other business economies of scale will not be realized to the fullest with a policy of drawing off population growth to new towns.

These losses are outweighed, in the minds of many urban theorists and administrators, by the costs necessary to expand the older city. The process of expansion would be either *extensive* (outward growth at constant density) or *intensive* (increasing the density of the existing area) or some combination of the two. Either method encounters certain barriers of public cost. Extensive growth of the older city—that is, expansion at its periphery —raises the average resident's distance from the center. When commuting time has reached a limit (it is not too subjective to concede that a two-hour journey each way is "too much"), further growth requires a technological innovation which safely speeds up commuting traffic, and such technology may not be available. If it is the money cost of commuting which has reached a limit (particularly if much of this cost is borne by a public subsidy of the transportation facilities), the needed technological breakthrough is one of efficiency rather than speed and safety. Again, the new technology may not have appeared. Extensive growth then drains the energy of commuters or the fiscal capacity of the community. Decentralization of shopping, service, and employment activities may hold in check the potential increase in intraurban movement, but this also sacrifices some of the external economies of urban growth.

Intensive growth creates very different types of problems. Density can increase within the original confines of the city by overloading the original facilities, including housing, schools, service establishments, and channels of movement. Alternatively, these facilities may be reconstructed at higher densities. Overloading has a superficial attractiveness to most urban decision-makers, for it tends to redeem any planning or business "mistakes" such as the establishment of a post office or restaurant at a poor location, and it minimizes the need to raise capital sums for new buildings. The general public is not unaware of overloading, however, and the ultimate political response to complaints may be a deluge of construction efforts which "temporarily" disrupts life even more and may not be finely attuned to the precise needs for expansion. A certain pace of replacement is inherent in the form of every piece of urban capital (the mechanics of which for housing will be examined in a later chapter), so problems arise primarily when the growth rate of the city's population overtaxes this technically efficient capital-replacement rate. In brief, the remaining value of facilities which would have to be scrapped will enter into the scale against further external benefits of city growth.

We may note in passing that a public commitment to preserve "open space" outside an existing city means that the city can grow in population only by solving the inherently complex problems of reconstructing itself at higher densities.

These comments do not perfect the case for new towns. Far from it, for a major "benefit" of clamping a lid on the population of a given city is postponed replacement of its facilities. Sometimes these facilities need to be replaced and the form of replacement is feasible, only the public decision being deferred. Failure to improve the efficiency and capacity of communications networks within the older city may be the result of lassitude or inadequate study on the part of public officials rather than a lack of technological knowledge. It is always easier for those who plan capital development projects to start with a clean slate, but the losses of urban external benefits resulting from this attitude could be substantial.

Headship Rates

The number of housing units which a population of given size requires involves a factor, discussed previously, which is called the "headship rate." It states the proportion of any given population or subgroup within the population (such as people age 23, or married males age 23, or married males age 23 with incomes between $3,000 and $5,000 a year) who are heads of separate households. If the rate is 75 percent for a population group numbering 1,000, there will be 750 households headed by members of that group and, by definition, 750 occupied housing units. A "household" is any group of persons, whether relatives, lodgers, roommates, or even a single person living alone, who occupy a separate housing unit. This is the concept used by the U.S. Census Bureau. A "housing unit" may be defined for our purposes as the smallest unit of residential space which is separated by a legal concept of property from all other residential space, and which contains facilities which are used in common only by its occupants. This definition obviously encompasses the single-family house and the separate apartment unit. It includes rooms in a residential hotel, but not the room of a lodger within the home of an otherwise "normal" family. This arbitrary definition may or may not be statistically useful, but it will help us to be reasonably clear in the abstract about what we mean by a "housing unit." Again, the person or persons living within one such unit constitute a "household," by definition.

Since we are interested in the optimum number of housing units, we must look for optimum headship rates to apply to our estimate of the optimum population. One overall rate will not be very useful, for a change in the characteristics of the population could easily affect the desirable number of separate housing units. For example, if the population of 1,000 persons consists entirely of families—each family including husband, wife, and three children—we might easily decide that the desirable number of housing units was 200 and the optimum headship rate was 20 percent. If the population of 1,000 consisted of husband-wife families with only *two* children each, we would probably say the headship rate should be 25 percent. This would represent a rule to the effect that every husband-father should be the head of a separate household. Perhaps we would want to amend this rule so that it applied only to cases where there was more than one child, or the children were at least one year old, or we might wish to make an exception for families living as servants in the household of some wealthy family or sharing the home of some other relatives because of choice rather than economic need, etc.

There are many characteristics of the population which influence the practice and the desirability of establishing separate households. Age, marital status, employment status, health, and other factors affect popular judgments as to whether a particular individual is "entitled" to be the head of a household. For each such characteristic, a rule—with complex amendments and exceptions, perhaps—needs to be stated. Such rules emerge out of the context of social practice and the society's theory of its own organization and are determined by economic factors only in the long run, if at all. For example, in agricultural societies it has been efficient over the ages to maintain "extended families" consisting of grandparents, unmarried adult brothers and sisters, perhaps some uncles, aunts, cousins, and hired hands—all living under the same roof. The efficiency lies in the operation of a relatively large-scale farm; after many generations, however, this arrangement comes to seem "proper," and an effort to maintain it carries over to the age of urban living in which the "efficiency" basis has disappeared. Another current problem is the position of widowed grandmothers, for only a few generations ago the life expectancy and the independent income of such people were both quite limited, and it was regarded as a moral (sometimes a legal) duty of the woman's married children to take her into their home. Recently, though, the health and life expectancy of widows have improved and in some societies such as the United States the widow typically has both property and income which may suffice for independent living. The feeling persists among many people that it is "wrong" for the married children not to take in the widowed grandparent.[7] Sociologists are sharply divided on the issue, but the economist's carefree solution is to say that a person who shows the inclination and the (physical) ability to establish a separate household ought to be able to do so.

It would be beyond our purpose to provide headship rates for specific classes of the population. Customs and points of view vary substantially on every point. Yet ad hoc determinations of satisfactory headship rates for planning purposes are not difficult to arrive at if the planner is familiar with practices and ideals of the local population.

One aspect of headship which is distinctively economic is its relationship to the income of the potential household. In actuality, headship seems clearly influenced by income, so that a high-income family is more likely to have a separate housing unit than a low-income family which is identical in all other significant respects. Which rate is optimal? The question is more difficult if the lower-income family is more nearly typical of the population as a whole, for it would not seem reasonable to establish as a norm a headship rate which was not realistically attainable.

This question runs headlong into the ultimate problem of equilibrium in the housing sector, for it asks, in effect, if particular potential households should be subsidized so that they can enjoy separate dwelling units. Indeed, it might raise the question whether some or all households are paying more or less than they "should" for housing, with the result that too many or too few separate households are established. This larger question will be taken up in our subsequent discussion of the "replacement demand" for housing.

Unless we can specify an optimum income distribution for the population, it is likely that the community's income distribution, like its age distribution, marital pattern, etc., will be exogenously determined. It is then appropriate to develop separate headship rates for different income groups—that is, to let income enter into the determination of the optimum headship rate for a particular group. The thinking is that the individual households or potential households allocate their income, in general, in a manner best suited to their own tastes and circumstances. Thus, as a first approximation to housing demand, the optimal-income relationship can be taken as the actual relationship. Revisions in this pattern of headship are thus one of the mobility elements of replacement demand and in that guise become the concern of public policy.

Optimum headship rates are thus quite subjective, though, in practice, they do not occasion wide disagreement. They represent fundamental patterns of social behavior which are not hard to identify.

Vacancy Rates

Creation of vacancy is a significant effect of equilibrium behavior of the housing sector. In our examination of equilibrium, various motives for intentional investment in vacancy were described and several reasons for unintentional investment in vacancy were presented. As a first approximation to the *optimum* level of housing vacancy, we can offer the following statement: the housing stock embodies and represents scarce resources and should not be allowed to become redundant; the optimum vacancy rate is zero.

There are three major reservations to this appealingly simple prescription. One of the principal reasons for the emergence of vacancy is imperfect knowledge of the market, not all of which can be offset. Vacancy in the housing stock also provides some external benefit for housing users as it simplifies the task of arranging shifts of users within the stock. Finally, vacant units at the bottom of the inventory may not have economic value. Some discussion of each of these sources of optimum vacancy is warranted.

Housebuilders would not overbuild and they could minimize investments in preempting future markets if correct forecasts of housing user demand were available to all members of the industry. Owners of existing units for rent or sale could adjust their prices and market their properties without delay if housing users were made aware of the full range of opportunities in the local housing stock. Customary methods of analysis, and of disseminating information about local housing markets, leave much to be desired; there would be an opportunity for community investment in housing information to pay off handsomely in lowering the drain of vacancy on housing resources. The "real estate industry"—as the occupation of brokerage is sometimes called—is generally too fragmented to develop or transmit market information as effectively as might be done and is unable to produce improved analytical tools. Research is conducted by financial institutions, both public and private, and occasionally by specialized research companies, but the quality and coverage of such research is, to make a very general statement, uneven and difficult to interpret, to say nothing of its being rather closely held. Local business organizations, such as chambers of commerce, are more concerned usually with basic factors governing the expansion of local employment than with careful working out of the implications for housing markets. At best, there would be some uncertainty or information gap which would lead to housing vacancy, and this we might regard as an "optimal" form of vacancy. Almost universally, however, there is much positive action which might be undertaken before this irreducible minimum is encountered.

Frictional vacancy is a concept which pertains to optimum, rather than equilibrium, behavior of the housing market, though it is usually discussed in connection with the latter. If investors were so competitive and so well informed about user demand in the housing market that no units were vacant, it might be appropriate for public agencies to cause some redundancy to appear. Otherwise, households seeking to change locations or to upgrade their housing would have a difficult time identifying units which would be available to them, and moving dates for all the households in a circle of adjustments would have to coincide. The practical difficulties in such a situation are easily imagined; one result could be a slowing down of optimal mobility and replacement construction. Vacancy represents slack which can absorb random shifts in demand. Since it results from market forces unrelated to this external benefit, however, it is difficult to identify from empirical data how much slack is really useful. As a theoretical exercise, we could imagine that, with ideal market information on all sides, a household's complete search and move could be completed within one day. Then the average number of vacant units required for this purpose would be the average number of households moving per day. This ambitious minimum would assume that lease arrangements and prorating of rents and other housing expenses raise no significant barriers. No doubt this degree of tightness in the market is impossible to achieve, but it may serve as a kind of benchmark for evaluating actual levels of vacancy. Since the "information" and the "friction" types of optimal vacancy are not additive, it is probable that the former will inadvertently serve at least some of the latter requirement. A large issue of the distributional coincidence of such vacancy—information vacancies spread around the market in proportion to frictional needs—remains, however.

Housing units which have "dropped out" of the useful inventory will be vacant until the land which they occupy is turned to another purpose. In a sense, this portion of the inventory is a slack which permits an unpredictable influx of population to be accommodated—a function long associated with urban slum areas. If this aspect can be overlooked, vacant units in this description are neither assets nor liabilities. So long as the appropriate moment for reuse of the land under these housing units has not arrived, their vacancy does not represent economic loss. Appropriate reuse of the land, however, raises other normative questions about the efficient behavior of entrepreneurs, investors, and others who are involved in the relatively complex process of changing land uses. In part, this efficiency is a matter of market information, so the data and analyses developed on that score can help in rationalizing the process of land redevelopment. Since many other conditions for optimal adjustments in land use exist, however, this is true only in part.

Replacement Rates

Housing replacement has both quantitative and qualitative aspects. Even if the qualitative standard remained unchanged, certain events would occur which would require that specific numbers of units be built just to maintain that standard. For example, some structures are made unusable by fire or other disaster, while the passage of time, plus sheer physical usage, makes most of the inventory wear out. On the other hand, new housing construction may have the effect of raising the general quality of the stock, scrapping old dwellings in favor of better ones, the improvement being in the form of location, design, size, or comfort.

One form of quantitative replacement commands particular attention. The rate at which the inventory "wears out" depends on the extent of the initial investment, and there is an optimization issue concerning the durability of housing and the replacement rate which is inherent in that durability. Our discussion of optimum replacement housing demand will, thus, be in three principal sections: durability, casualty, and improvement.

DURABILITY AND CASUALTY

If we pose the optimum durability question in terms of the minimum cost of a particular quality of housing, then the elements of the question may be illustrated as in Figure 18. As the structure is made more durable, the initial or present capital cost rises, while the present value of future replacement outlays falls. The sum of these two components provides a total cost function for variation in durability. The low point of the total cost function could be construed as the optimum durability or optimum economic life for the selected quality of housing.

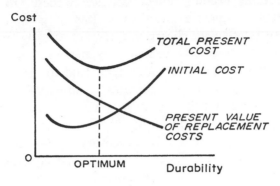

Figure 18

This highly simplified figure permits us to draw at least one practical conclusion. Suppose that we expect capital or other housing resources to be more abundant in the future than at present. Then the opportunity cost of replacement capital will be less than the money costs in today's money, and the replacement-cost curve of Figure 18 will fall more steeply from its cost-axis intercept. This expectation will shorten the optimum economic life of present buildings, because the low point of the total cost curve will appear at closer to the origin on the durability axis. The greater the prospects for general economic improvement, the shorter the planned economic life of the buildings should be.

Figure 18 assumes that the dwelling in question and its replacement retain the same degree of usefulness regardless of their durability. As we have previously observed, housing in general, and urban housing in particular, is a commodity which can be expected to remain in demand over a long period of time because it is a necessity which does not become obsolescent rapidly, and because normally a population of potential users can be expected to be present far into the future. Supposing that future usefulness for the selected quality level is in question, however, less expenditure on replacement will be anticipated and the replacement cost curve in Figure 18 will shift downward. This will shorten the optimum durability of the building. At the extreme, no replacement at all (at this quality level) may be contemplated, in which case the low point on the initial cost function (or its intercept on the vertical axis if this function has no downward-sloping section) becomes effective. Clearly these are only symbolic comments upon a practical matter of great complexity. However, it is often the directional impact of exogenous factors —such as a pending improvement in general economic capacity —which is least clear and which may lead to errors of policy. The creation of short-lived structures in an expanding economy sometimes arouses misunderstandings as well, and they are condemned as "slums of the future."

Casualty losses from the inventory of housing, resulting from such events as fire, flood, windstorm, earthquake, and other such exogenous factors produce a one-for-one optimum replacement demand, with two qualifications. If the stock of dwellings prior to the loss was excessive, then, at least in a quantitative sense, the resource impact of the disaster is nil and no replacement is needed. If the casualty loss is widespread, as in the Chicago fire or as the aftermath of wartime bombing, the community's resource base is diminished and a general reallocation of resources must be devised. The housing sector would be obliged to establish priorities for casualty replacement here as it must do also in the "improvement replacement" example to be discussed below.

Losses of dwelling units because of a change in the use of land is quite similar to casualty loss in its effect upon optimum replacement demand. This is true even though the source of the demolition (or "merger" of units previously separate) is housing construction. So long as the unit is occupied or actively desired as a part of the vacancy cushion, its removal from the inventory is premature with respect to its usefulness and a replacement is needed. Casualty and land-use losses from the housing inventory may tend to occur with disproportionate frequency in the inventory which is redundant, so replacement implications of each loss need to be examined. In terms of scale, it is also unfortunately true that these types of replacement needs are not readily predictable, particularly for a single community.

QUALITATIVE IMPROVEMENT

A third important source of replacement demand for housing is the desire to improve the quality and usefulness of the stock. We can usefully divide this into two subissues—the improvements which are associated with exogenous events, such as changes in locational orientation, and those which are housing-market phenomena in the narrowest sense, such as the response to a general change in the level of income. That is, the existing inventory may become less suitable because its environment changes, or because households have the means and desire to improve the intrinsic quality of their dwellings.

With this concern for quality, our discussion becomes concerned with the resource content of the housing unit. Up to this point, our discussion of optimality in the housing sector has been in terms of numbers of units, though it is obvious that the "housing sector's" optimum size must be in terms of resources rather than numbers of units. So, in effect, we must now ask the question, "What is the optimum house?" It has been possible to postpone this weighty question to this point because we have been dealing in incremental terms—that is, with additions to the inventory of housing rather than with the condition of the inventory as a whole. Our welfare concern that the de facto condition of the housing stock may not measure up to the standards of the community resolves itself conveniently into the question of how far we should attempt to go in improving the quality of housing, and this is a replacement issue.

In the abstract it is not difficult to define the community's overall housing standard or "norm" from the economic point of view and, at the same time, define the optimum "budget ratio" for housing, another sometimes troublesome point. In fact, we did this at the outset of this chapter. The abstract answer appears in Figure 19. This is simply an indifference diagram showing the rate at which satisfactions derived from various amounts of housing resources can be substituted for the enjoyment of other goods, and the combinations of housing services and all other goods which can be purchased at current prices with current income. The point of tangency describes the optimal budget allocation; by considering this amount to be available at each period in the future, it can be capitalized into a particular quality of housing. This quality is expressed in terms of resources available to the housing sector and which must be divided up among the optimum number of households in order to arrive at a concept of the "optimum house."

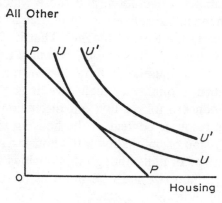

Figure 19

The manner of distribution, whether all households should have an equal amount of housing space or housing of equal quality, is a microeconomic question which can be deferred for the moment. (This problem is treated in Chapter 6.) The often troublesome issue concerning the proportion of individual household budgets which should go to the housing sector is a problem in the management of the housing sector rather than a problem of the size of the housing sector, and concepts of housing sector management will also be treated later. The macroeconomic question of overall resource allocation among housing and other sectors of the economy can be separated from the problems of distribution and of management. Of course, if the actual or equilibrium distribution of housing resources produces housing conditions which violate the concept of a normal standard, this might imply that the optimal size of the sector—its share of total economic resources—is greater or less than the equilibrium size. On the other hand, housing deficiencies for some groups might be remedied by redistribution of housing resources without enlarging the size of the sector. The manner in which distributional equity is attained influences optimal sector size.

Improvement demand for housing is less a matter of what the norm is than the rate at which that norm is changing. In one sense, public actions in the past have implicitly defined an acceptable standard, despite partisan appeals for greater attention to the housing sector. In the same way the current trend of public action might be said to define an acceptable rate of improvement in the housing stock. This, however, would be begging the question, for it is precisely at the point of today's policy-making that economic analysis must be active rather than passive. We cannot avoid making some less abstract observations about the rate of improvement in the housing stock which best serves the public interest.

The relevant concept is income elasticity of demand. When a household's income rises by $100, its expenditures on various types of goods and its savings will rise by dissimilar proportions. The nation as a whole will allocate increases in output among the sectors of consumption and investment, and the marginal shares will probably differ from the average shares. Goods which are considered "necessities" will have a marginal share which is less than their average share. If "food," for example, took 40 percent of the initial level of income, it may be expected to take less than 40 percent of the increase in income. Another way of stating this is that the amount spent on "food" increases by a lower percentage than the percentage increase in income. This concept is known as "Engel's law"—its application to housing, as "Schwabe's law." [8]

We put "food" in quotes because it represents a collection of commodities rather than a homogeneous item of consumption. As income rises, the kinds of food consumed will probably change more rapidly than the total expenditure on food. Starches give way to inexpensive proteins which, in turn, are partly replaced by better quality proteins—from potatoes to hamburger to steak, for example.

Housing is often put in the necessity category along with food. Every household, indeed every person, must have some form of shelter or place to sleep, so that the demand for housing takes precedence over most other consumption demands. As income rises, the household can spend more for housing, but the amount would not rise as rapidly (percentagewise) as income if the demand for housing were truly income-inelastic.[9]

Housing, like food, is a mixed bag of commodities. To mention only the major components of housing as an item of consumer demand, it consists of shelter, privacy, comfort, convenience, environment, and accessibility. The mix which is appropriate to a higher-income level includes a smaller proportion of simple shelter than the mix at a lower level. More space, more weatherproof walls, indoor plumbing, quieter streets, and better busses are objects of housing demand to be expected when the level of real income rises.

To accommodate this change in the composition of housing demand, it might literally be necessary to replace the whole existing housing stock. The increment in current consumption levels means, in effect, that the existing inventory of dwellings does not meet the requirements of the population. To take a simple example, suppose that the initial inventory consists of identical dwellings, each containing $1,000 worth of resources, and that income per household rises by $100 per year. Demand for housing would be income-inelastic in one sense if the housing sector's fraction of this extra income, say 20 percent, is less than the initial ratio of housing expenses to total income, say 25 percent. However, the $20 extra now to be spent on housing represents an investment demand for some multiple of this amount. The housing investment demand resulting from this gain in expenditure in an income-inelastic sector might, for example, be ten times the increase in annual expenditures, or $200. This is twice the increase in income, so that the concept of income inelasticity in the housing sector needs this important qualification. A more important qualification results from the fact that it may be necessary to scrap the entire initial inventory of housing in order to replace it with the product which wealthier households now require. Thus, the housing investment resulting from a gain in household income of $100 per year might be not $200, but $1,200. The amount of "leverage" exerted by the housing sector on aggregate investment because of its durable nature is greater the larger the initial value of the housing stock and the smaller the income increment.

CONTINUOUS OR SPORADIC IMPROVEMENT?

Clearly, this implication that the housing stock must be replaced totally and continuously with continuing increases in household income requires a searching look at what "housing improvement" means in reality and how it can actually be accomplished. There are, in principle, two ways in which these considerable adjustments in the stock of housing capital can be accomplished. One is to concentrate the capitalized increment in aggregate housing budgets on the production of relatively few new dwellings which are superior to elements in the existing stock, causing the average quality of the stock to rise in a gradual and continuous fashion, but leaving the bulk of the stock unchanged in the face of increasing demand. The other approach is to defer the investment required by rising income until some point at which much or all of the stock can be replaced together.

There are problems in each method. The "continuous" method of improvement produces a stock of dwellings which is qualitatively differentiated, thus raising the issue of equitable distribution. If this problem is to be solved—as through the adoption of a price mechanism which awards better dwellings to those who offer more for them, or through administrative rationing of the housing supply—a substantial degree of mobility must be achieved among households. There must be nearly continuous movement of housing users out of poorer housing toward housing of better quality, so that the general level of housing enjoyed by users is constantly rising. The more differentiated the housing stock has become in terms of intrinsic quality, the more pervasive this mobility must be.

The alternative "sporadic" method of housing improvement has one major advantage and three significant drawbacks. The advantage is that massive replacement of housing permits periodic rationalization of utility and transportation systems, improvements which otherwise would be carried out less efficiently if at all.

The drawbacks include a possible leakage of housing improvement demand as the desire to raise housing standards in response to an increase in income is not realized. Given the choice between an immediate increase in consumption of non-housing commodities when income rises and the opportunity to put aside a portion of the higher income for future "big-step" housing improvement, many households in many types of economies and cultures would probably choose the former. Housing demand can thus lose income elasticity and over time the prevailing proportion of housing expenditure in the average household budget will fall. The housing investment demand which is latent in increasing income is drained away into a consumption demand for the products of other sectors. A society without effective thrift institutions, or with regularly depreciating currency, is not likely to preserve housing improvement demand for "sporadic" investment waves.

Another drawback of the sporadic method may be its impact on general business and employment conditions. Replacement waves are at the heart of at least one theory of business cycles, and as a rule housing is a large enough sector of the economy to have noticeable impact upon business conditions. By chance or by design, sporadic improvements in the housing stock may occur counter to fluctuations arising in other sectors of the economy. Thus, the cycle-inducing characteristic of sporadic housing improvement may be of great or little consequence, depending upon the structure and management of the economy as a whole. This complementarity of housing and nonhousing cycles may work with less precision at the level of a city or region, however, than at the level of national aggregates.

The third drawback to sporadic improvement of the housing stock stems from the fact that the land required for the new dwellings is likely to rise in price during the period that housing-improvement demand is postponed. We are not referring to the long-run rise in land prices which is supposed to be an inherent characteristic of a commodity in fixed supply. Rather, it is the specific parcels of land on which older housing is situated which derive particular benefit from the neglect of housing improvement when household incomes rise. We have previously referred to this phenomenon as the "urban land ratchet" (see Chapter 2). To illustrate, consider a community in which household incomes are rising but housing investment is held in check. Owners of housing are able to ask higher and higher prices from tenants or purchasers because these consumers have more to spend. The asset value of the housing stock rises even though the stock itself is deteriorating. Purchasers do not hesitate to pay higher prices because they correctly consider the increase in asset values to be permanent. When reconstruction of the housing supply is contemplated, however, the asset value of the older stock becomes the price of land for replacement construction. Unless reserves of equally useful land have been held during the period of deferred improvement demand, the owners of older dwellings have an effective monopoly of an essential input for replacement housing. They will provide the land only if the enlarged value of the housing structures to be replaced is paid over to them. This can increase the money cost of the improvement effort substantially, frustrating some of the expected real improvement as a result. Thus, the deferment of housing improvement can itself cause an inflation in the price of "land" (i.e. parcels on which the existing building is to be demolished) and, hence, in the money cost of that improvement. The community's housing standard may then stagnate despite rising incomes and genuine desire for better housing.

There is some question whether the money cost of land under such conditions is a "real" cost of better housing. To the individual it certainly is a real sacrifice for the owner of a new home must undertake a larger investment than was anticipated or settle for a lesser degree of housing improvement. The tenant in the new housing must contribute to the servicing of an investment which is greater than might have been necessary without the inflation of "land" prices.

To the economy as a whole, however, these payments are "transfers." They do not represent or compensate for the loss of valuable resources. The older structures which capture increases in housing expenditures while improvement investments are deferred are, when the time for replacement arrives, no longer of economic value. This is simply a matter of definition, for the desire to expend resources on new structures implies a desire to abandon the old structures. In a sense, the increasing asset value of the initial housing stock in such a situation represents the accumulation of deferred demand for housing improvement, as a sort of "savings bank." The operation of this accumulation device is perverse, however, since it ultimately obstructs the real object of rising outlays for housing rather than helping to achieve it.

This discussion is pertinent to the much discussed "cost benefit" problem of urban renewal activities. The pattern of such activities in the United States and a few other places is for government to assume the financial loss of buying expensive but deteriorated housing to make the land available for improvement investment. The rationale for such public subsidy has ranged over a variety of considerations, including the fiscal benefit to the city of higher property taxes from new buildings and the exposure of relocated families to social services. No supposed benefit of the urban renewal process as described here is free of serious question, and the uncomfortable fact remains that possibly inflated values are confirmed rather than negated, and assumed by the public action.[10] Transferred purchasing power is spendable, and the system of making substantial transfers an inherent part of the process of housing improvement imposes an income-distribution problem on the housing sector. Accepting this burden, or introducing a device to overcome it (no examples of which are readily available) is bound up with a sporadic improvement proclivity on the part of the housing sector. It may be noted that the problem is not limited to an economy in which urban real estate is privately owned, for collective ownership faces the same dilemma in the demolition of income-producing assets.

The fact is that deteriorated housing stock under such conditions does produce income, whether for private or public owners. It is useful as housing until replacement is actually available, and such replacement cannot be made available until the income-producing properties are destroyed. In real terms, housing improvement—whether of the sporadic or continuous types —discards assets which still have some usefulness, just as a man who wants a new overcoat must, in effect, discard the old one.

It is slightly paradoxical that urban renewal operates on the implicit assumption of deferred and sporadic replacement demand in the United States where, on all evidence, the housing sector probably comes closest to providing improvement housing on a continuous basis.

REPLACEMENT IN RESPONSE TO EXOGENOUS FORCES

Exogenous events also lead to the desire for improvements in housing quality and, hence, for replacement construction. In contrast to the income-elasticity case, however, in which the outcome is an upgrading of the housing stock, replacement which is stimulated by exogenous events aims merely to restore the stock to an earlier degree of usefulness. For example, the migration of population from one area to another causes housing to be abandoned at the first location and replacement-housing demand to appear at the second. Exogenous events such as this, in a way similar to physical deterioration, effectively diminish the supply and call for new construction.

Locational shifts form a wide class of replacement-inducing exogenous events, of which actual interregional migration is the extreme case. Less dramatic, but essentially similar, are changes in the transportation system within a region which raise the real cost of reaching urban destinations (congestion, increased fares, or gasoline taxes, for example). Relocation of urban employment focal points or of urban services relevant to particular households (such as the dispersal of a middle-income retail complex) will also change the usefulness of the existing housing stock, creating a latent demand for physical alterations in the inventory.

One of the most interesting types of exogenous change affecting the replacement of housing is a shift in the age distribution of the population. As a matter of custom and preference, younger households often require relatively smaller housing units and will accept higher land densities than will child-raising families. If the composition of the population shifts so that the proportion of younger households rises, a whole section of the housing inventory becomes unadapted to its demand. Elderly people, too, as a proportion of all households, have a similar impact upon the housing sector when they change, though their specific housing requirements may be unique. Since this is a matter of different preferences for housing types, it might be said that virtually every household has a unique set of housing requirements and a change in the preference composition of the population implies a demand for some degree of inventory replacement.

This raises again the question of how rapidly or how often inventory adjustments in response to preference changes (such as we often associate with a change in the age structure) should be undertaken. The immediate, complete response to a substantial, exogenous change of this sort could require the scrapping of much previous investment in favor of new investment which would soon meet the same fate. This problem seems to have been resolved in practice by converting it into the question of which types of unique preferences should be recognized by the housing sector. Hence, our question becomes one of the optimal level of differentiation of the housing stock and the rate at which further differentiation occurs.

There are substantial economic costs of differentiation for a commodity which is durable. The pioneer mass-producer of automobiles, who is said to have remarked that his customers could "have any color they want so long as it is black," was reflecting the economies of scale production which may be lost when the product is differentiated to suit a variety of tastes. Even the buyers who did want black would pay more for their cars if all buyers were free to choose colors. In housing, the most significant source of scale economies for a homogeneous product probably lie in distribution rather than in production. The great heterogeneity of housing makes the purchase of any unit or the investment in any structure a task of great complexity and unavoidable uncertainty. One cannot be quite sure what one is getting nor how readily it can be disposed of to a subsequent buyer or investor. The inherent risk is an economic cost which, other things being equal, deprives the housing sector of some resources which might be appropriately allocated to it.

One policy might be to standardize housing, much as certain critics perennially wish automobiles to be standardized. Problems of adjusting to some types of exogenous changes, such as age-distribution shifts, would be eliminated, along with the improvement in general efficiency of housing distribution and of particular investment decisions. The cost of such efficiency, however, is the neglect of specialized demand. Many, if not most, households would be living in units representing resources which, if put together in a different fashion, would produce substantially greater satisfaction, or they would have to live in units which tie up more resources than the occupants really need.

Differentiation in the housing stock is a luxury which is purchased at some cost in the trouble of operating the housing sector. This luxury appears to have an income-elastic demand, so that communities of greater affluence may choose to cater to a variety of specialized housing needs. This is optimal in the macroeconomic sense so long as the external costs of the individual options are taken into account. That is, widening the variety of housing units in the inventory hinders the management of the entire inventory, requiring resources to be expended in overcoming this (for appraisals and for transmitting lengthy property descriptions) and creating individual risks for which no remedy is possible (such as uncertainty about future resale value). If the benefit from differentiation exceeds these costs, then the exogenous influence on demand can be recognized by the optimally functioning housing sector.

In effect, preference shifts, such as those arising from the age distribution of households, create a multiplicity of opportunities for differentiation which enjoy some inherent economic ranking at any one time and place. Recognition of a specific need may be long delayed, with the result that the exogenous cause of housing replacement and differentiation may be simply an age distribution which has long persisted but which has not exerted optimally effective demand (or we might say that the marginal efficiency of its investment requirement was below the social cost of capital) until a general economic advance by the community uncovered this relatively low-priority demand.

Some exogenous demands, such as a change in the age distribution of households, may be predictable but not subject to control. Others, such as geographic mobility, may be essentially less predictable but more readily subject to public control. The housing-investment consequences of controllable exogenous events should certainly be a part of whatever system of control (say of factory or shopping-center location) the community may attempt to create.

Supply Constraints—The Social Cost of Housing Inputs

Our approach to the problem of optimizing the size of the housing sector takes the form of reconsidering elements of demand and supply which enter into market equilibrium. The reconsideration adds public benefits and costs of housing construction to the private benefits and costs which become effective in the market. Having looked into social and "external" aspects of housing demand, our attention now turns to the supply side. What is the real cost, to the community as well as to the individual, of each of the inputs required for the production of additional housing?

LAND

The supply of land is often represented in textbooks as perfectly inelastic, i.e. as a vertical line. Certainly the amount of usable ground in any one place or region is effectively fixed, at least in the short run. Land reclamation has produced major changes in the physical supply of urban space in many areas of the world, but the opportunity for reclamation presents itself in a pattern conditioned by natural endowment, which in itself is fixed also. Real costs of reclamation obviously vary with technology and with the scarcity of other factors such as labor and earth-moving equipment.

A less dramatic method of extending the supply of land than filling bays or draining swamps is "site preparation." This term covers the clearing and leveling of building lots, even to the terracing of relatively steep slopes. This wide spectrum of activities is represented in almost all urban residential construction and it would be only a matter of definition to divide site work between activities which are part of house building per se or part of a program of increasing the supply of land. Suffice it to say that under almost any circumstances, the local supply of usable land can be augmented by the expenditure of other resources.

The supply of residential "space" can also be increased by multistory construction. Again, other resources are used to compensate for a shortage of land, subject to the limitations of technology on the supply side (and to density preferences on the demand side). The same can be said for extension of transportation systems which makes land at substantial distances from the urban center part of the local, effective supply of land. All the foregoing concepts of elasticity in the supply of land involve expenditure of other resources, so the issue is not one of the real cost of land itself.

The concept of cost associated with the supply of land for housing construction which is relevant for our discussion is "opportunity cost." Land, however provided, can be used for a variety of urban purposes and its use for new residential construction makes it unavailable for other uses. New housing tracts may remove land from agricultural use. The construction of a dwelling means the space which it occupies is not available for a retail store, an office, a manufacturing plant, a public building or park, a right of way, or any other prospective use. Further, the use of an already-developed site for new residential construction means that some or all of the previous investment made in that site must be scrapped. Thus, the supply of land for residential construction is elastic to the extent that land is transferable from other actual or prospective uses, including existing residential structures. The market price or other de facto limitations on transferability of land are not necessarily correct indicators of the real or social cost of the transfer. Allocation of specific sites to specific uses is a microeconomic question, but there remains a macroeconomic question about the total amount of land to be transferred to residential construction, for any particular time and region.

The concept of opportunity cost really defines the supply cost of land for one type of use, say new housing, as the value stemming from the demand for other uses, such as farmland, factories, or existing housing. Demands for nonresidential land uses are "derived" demands, coming from the desire of consumers for products or services through systems of technology and management. Variation in the ultimate demand or in the methods used to satisfy them can result in changed derived demands for urban space. An example is the change in industrial technology which encouraged land-consuming, one-level operations, a change which resulted from the introduction of assembly-line techniques, together with the use of electric power for machines instead of power delivered by belts and shafts from a central engine. Changes in urban transportation systems, such as the use of private automobiles, also affect the availability of land for housing purposes. Changes in agricultural technology, such as the development of long-distance transportation of fresh produce, alter the availability of land for housing. Changes in the demand for products of local industry and agriculture, under which we might subsume the whole matter of optimum regional economic development, likewise impinge upon the supply of (as distinct from the demand for) residential land.

What matters is that the process of rationing land for new construction should involve a measurement of the incremental value of land to these various industries and should also respond to significant changes in underlying technology or final demand. The market, of course, does have just these functions, so it is a matter of judging whether each of these industries is particularly favored or disadvantaged in the market for urban land. This, in turn, raises the question of whether there is imperfect communication or ineffective competition where land transfers among classes of users are concerned.

The demand for existing housing also serves to check the availability of land for new housing. This is interesting for two reasons. It is often a very substantial form of use-transfer in urban land and one of the main sources of land for new housing. It also reduces the land-supply problem for new housing into a question concerning the demand for old housing. This is the replacement-rate problem, and the answer is very clear and useful. Replacement demand creates its own land supply, for it represents a demand to abandon existing units. The demand for existing units, in a real sense rather than in market terms, thus ceases to exist when the decision to effect replacement has been made.

This is strictly true if there is no change in land density as a result of the replacement activity. If density is to fall, then replacement demand must, to some extent, compete for land from other uses, presumably excluding all other existing housing. That is, if ten acres of old housing are to be replaced, but densities are to be cut in half, then ten additional acres must be found from the nonhousing land in the community. Intraurban location factors may help to determine which old housing will be replaced by which kind of new housing—a microeconomic question—but do not require additions to the supply of residential land in the community as a whole.

Existing housing commands a price in the market, unless it has been unmistakably and irrevocably abandoned. The social decision to abandon a portion of the existing supply does not transmit itself into entrepreneurial decisions. The old buildings will be valued by sellers and buyers as though the abandonment decision had not been taken.

The social cost of land for replacement housing represents a unique problem for the urban economist, particularly with respect to the possibility or likelihood that this cost will differ from the market value of such land. The problem arises because portions of the housing stock become redundant immediately when the decision to abandon it in favor of newly constructed dwellings is taken. Land under the putatively redundant housing is not available until that housing is actually made redundant by the new building. Before the new building occurs, the value of the presumptive site for it—the land occupied by the buildings slated to be replaced—has a value based upon the market situation prior to the decision to replace. That is, we may wish to scrap house X and build a better one, Y, but we cannot have the land for Y without paying a value for X based on its value in a market in which X does not exist. Given the social decision to scrap X, its social value is nil; its market value is not changed until the decision is actually implemented (by the construction of Y), but this value becomes a part of the money cost of Y.

The solution to this problem may be seen in a highly simplified case. Suppose that in a community there are ten separate houses, each on its own lot, each occupied, and each numbered according to relative quality from 1 (lowest quality) to 10 (best quality). Suppose, also, that the social decision has been taken to replace house 1. The social value of lot 1, including its house, becomes nil with this decision, but as long as it is desired by the households in the community, it will have a market value.

Realistically, it will be necessary to build the replacement house on additional land, lot 11, to be obtained from another use at its opportunity cost. Directly or indirectly, this leads to the actual abandonment of house 1 and the destruction of its market value. Lot 1 can now be used to effect the abandonment of house 2, when the decision to replace that dwelling is made. The practical necessity of this procedure arises from the need to have all households accommodated at all times. Lot 11, however, and later lots 1, 2, etc., in their turn perform another important function of driving the market value of putatively redundant housing and the land it occupies to zero, the social value. To use an appropriate label, this useful inventory may be called "swing" land, for it bridges replacement construction needs and indispensable land supply.

The amount of "swing" land which a community requires depends mainly on three factors. In the first place, there is a minimum requirement which is determined by the "gestation period" for housing construction (the time from actual abandonment of the old dwelling to the first occupancy of the new house constructed on the same lot) and the rate at which the community is replacing its housing. Defining S as the minimum number of lots of "swing" land required, G as the number of gestation periods in a year, and R as the number of housing units to be replaced per year, we can say that:

$$S = R/G.$$

For example, if six houses are to be replaced this year, and it takes six months to produce a new house, then we need at least three lots in our "swing" inventory. If R is variable, then the value of S should perhaps be based upon the maximum value of

R; it may not be possible to expand and contract the swing inventory according to housing replacement needs.

This suggests the second factor determining the size of the swing inventory. If replacement occurs in a continuous fashion, the swing inventory may be close to its minimum level. If replacement is undertaken sporadically, however, the swing inventory must be relatively large, at least during the actual replacement activity.

The third factor is the efficiency of the housing sector's administration (whether public or private). If, through lack of knowledge or institutional weaknesses in arranging for the reuse of land, some abandoned portions of the housing inventory are not available to replacement builders, the need for swing inventory is augmented.

The concept of swing inventory infers that the social value of land under housing to be replaced is nil (apart from its distinctive location or amenity value). Unless such an inventory exists, however, the market value of that land will be positive and will for that reason discourage replacement construction. In the market, land which becomes a part of the swing inventory may derive value from the fact that it is a substitute for the land currently in use but which is next scheduled for abandonment and reconstruction. That is, it is part of the supply in the market for open land. If that supply is great, the market price of the swing inventory will be low; if there is very little open land within the reach of the community, the swing inventory will command a relatively high price (close to that of some developed properties). Always, however, the appropriate concept of value for land which becomes a part of the swing inventory is that of its opportunity value for nonhousing purposes (a subject already considered) or, in the absence of this, nil. The land-cost problem in housing replacement is one of income or wealth distribution, since confiscation may be considered undesirable; the price of land is not otherwise a real economic cost.

LABOR

In some societies the social or opportunity cost of labor for house building is considered to be nearly zero, with the result that people are encouraged to perform the labor required for the production of their own housing. Indeed, even in so complex an economy as the United States, it continues to be true that a significant number of houses are built by the owner's personal labor (except for more complex elements such as the electrical work).[11] Under particular circumstances this "do-it-yourself" application of labor to house construction makes fine economic sense. It is an efficient practice when the labor thus used has no other practical employment, as for seasonally employed persons who can work on a home during the off-season, or for householders in a society or community which has not developed a construction labor force. Often wives and children, who would ordinarily not be in the labor force at all, can perform much of the work when given adequate instruction and supervision.

There are, however, several drawbacks to this way of reckoning the social cost of labor. The true opportunity for seasonally unemployed farm laborers, for example, may be migration to an area or industry of continuous employment. Skills acquired by persons who help to build their own homes could, at much less cost, be converted into permanent assets by creating a specialized, mobile, house-building labor force for areas where none exists. Housing constructed in areas remote from population centers may represent illiquid assets of questionable market value should the builders subsequently desire to leave the area. In general, if it is feasible for the society to remedy unemployment or poverty by improving the mobility of the labor force and improving conditions of productivity and aggregate demand, such a course of action makes better sense than the development of make-work housing construction programs. Specialization of labor has a very general form of economic merit and it would need to be shown in each particular case that its merits were not attainable before the self-help approach to housing construction could be endorsed.

At the other end of the spectrum, it is sometimes difficult to expand the residential-construction labor force because of institutional restrictions such as exaggerated apprenticeship requirements, limited participation in unions, or geographical immobility. Where entry into the building trades is artificially limited, the wage which prevails may exceed the opportunity cost of additional labor, and here the effective question of social cost concerns the desirability of weakening the restrictions upon entry. This is largely a political question, the cost being one of alienating the trade groups or of devising a compensating inducement. Geographical immobility is, in essence, a resource barrier, though it may be presumed that the competitive wage in the house-building industry reflects those costs of mobility which regularly fall upon the worker.

Seasonal "immobility" of construction labor represents an opportunity for the substitution, in effect, of technology or other resources for labor. Devices which extend the building season have the effect of expanding the labor force, though at the additional cost of some off-season secondary productivity which individual members of the labor force may have been able to develop. It is also increasingly possible to substitute other factors for construction labor—such as elaborate capital equipment or prefabrication technology.

With these few qualifications, the social cost of labor for housing construction is approximated by its competitive wage.

BUILDING MATERIALS AND EQUIPMENT

Out of historical necessity, housing has usually been constructed from readily available, abundant materials. Hence, the basic house-building material varies considerably from society to society—from blocks of snow in the arctic to cloth tents in the desert, from mud-covered sticks in the tropics to adobe or baked bricks in the temperate zone—so that the social cost of this essential material is very low.

There are several important exceptions. Urban gigantism of the industrial and modern ages has overtaxed the supply of traditional materials in some places. In present-day Japan, for example, wood has become so scarce that it has become more expensive than ferro-concrete construction, suggesting a marked departure from traditional building forms. Urban safety requirements, such as fire prevention and earthquake safety, have also ruled out some customary materials and building styles. New materials such as aluminum, and rising labor costs (encouraging the use of plywood panels rather than plastered walls, for example), have altered the physical nature of dwellings, while the proliferation of household appliances has required that the dwelling itself become more and more complex a product.

Nevertheless, the demand for house-building materials is so large and relatively stable that supplying industries must develop materials which are generally abundant. The social cost of expanding such industries is less likely to be a scarcity of raw materials per se, for new materials can and must be adopted if old materials grow scarce, but rather is the scale and form of capital goods required by these materials-producing industries. Thus, a demand for additional housing creates a derived demand for investment in certain materials industries, a problem best considered together with the social cost of housing finance itself. Physical raw materials for housing are, almost by definition, seldom scarce, for if certain materials become scarce, others simply must be employed.

The social cost of ordinary house-building equipment—carpenters' tools, small mixers, simple hoists, etc.—can be presumed to be small in any case and probably closely approximated by the market price of such things. The kind of equipment used in constructing high-rise buildings and in large-scale land clearing is of a totally different order. Not only may this latter type of equipment require heavy financial investment, representing an additional derived demand for finance as a result of housing demand, but it also embodies technology which must either be discovered or borrowed. The necessity to import such machinery may be a valid deterrent to its use. This is a problem of the mix of high-rise and conventional low-density construction rather than a problem of overall housing-sector size, however, unless it should be the case that high-rise construction is necessitated by other factors such as an insurmountable scarcity of buildable land.

ENTREPRENEURS

The social cost of entrepreneurship is a very elusive matter. Some societies are well endowed with entrepreneurs, others depend upon "alien" minorities and many others simply seem to lack such a group altogether. The problem of creating entrepreneurial proclivities in a population whose culture is essentially antithetical to entrepreneurial behavior is a delicate and important matter of a sociological nature.

One aspect of the problem which presents itself in the larger "middle-class" nations, however, is incontrovertibly economic. The willingness of entrepreneurs to engage in housing supply in such nations (as the United States) is affected by financial inducements which can be provided through the legal, monetary, and tax systems. The assurance that one can profit by prudent, entrepreneurial effort rests upon a stable system of real estate property rights; relatively unambiguous systems of transferring titles to property; reasonable access to the main arteries of the money market; and a tax system which is free of whimsy or the intent to expropriate—all these are essential preconditions to entrepreneurial interest even where the spirit of entrepreneurship flourishes. Greater inducements can be provided by special tax benefits (accelerated depreciation, for example), or privileges in the financial market (mortgage insurance, low-interest, government-assisted loans, etc.).

The social cost of basic institutional systems, one might argue, is zero or even negative. They can be created by fiat and operated on the basis of fees. They may encourage all types of competitive enterprise—not just housing. Of course, this presumes that the system of private property and private business is acceptable to the society as a whole. The social cost of special tax or money market benefits for housing entrepreneurs is, in part, the burden of transfer which may result if entrepreneurs realize profits and, in part, the social or political unrest which may result if these profits reach "scandalous" proportions (as in the FHA 608 apartment-building program of the late 1940's in the United States).[12]

As a very general statement it is perhaps useful to say that if a nation possesses an entrepreneurial class, that group can be encouraged through well-tested devices to increase the production of housing. If such a class does not exist, it is a problem far transcending the development of the housing sector for the society is confronted with the choice between endeavoring to bring such a class into being and developing bureaucratic structures which will substitute for entrepreneurship.

Finance as a Constraint

The social cost of finance for the expansion of the housing sector is a many-sided subject. It touches upon a large current controversy and we must develop the issue with some care.

HOUSING AS A "SOCIAL" PROBLEM

The literature of economic development abounds with references to the "social" nature of housing requirements. This phrase is used to distinguish the housing sector from other capital-using sectors of developing economies such as manufacturing. The implication, which is often made very explicit indeed, is that while there is no "economic" need for housing investment, since the market demand for it appears very weak, it ultimately must be provided in order to solve a "social" problem.[13] The housing sector is regarded as a drag upon the process of economic growth. While it is admitted that housing must be provided or improved eventually, many national economic development programs regard housing as a form of investment eminently able to be postponed. The longer it can be put off, the reasoning goes, the better the result for the nation as a whole.

The background for this peculiar point of view is that where economic development is occurring, this process is almost necessarily accompanied by expansion of urban areas and increasing urbanization of the population. Cities grow to provide a labor force for expanding industry, business, and government. Swollen urban populations press against the supply of housing and other urban resources which do not expand in parallel with population. The society is increasingly confronted with a paradox of rising indices of per capita GNP and deteriorating standards of urban accommodation. Privacy, comfort, sanitation, and safety fall victim to an unevenness in the form of economic progress. For those who do achieve even minimal amenities in their housing, the price is usually extravagant, so that others become pessimistic about improving their woeful conditions. In this context a con-

tinuing plank in the platform of economic administration promises to correct "social evils" such as bad housing. To keep the
hope of improvement alive, some well publicized housing programs are undertaken, but the economic administration remains
committed to a system which throttles the housing sector until
such distant time as affluence will permit the luxury of dealing
with "social evils"—such as insufficient housing.

How does housing come to be excluded from the category
of an "economic good" so that it must be bestowed as a kind of
social-security benefit? Surely this is not the universal position of
the housing sector within an economic system. There are portions
of the world in which the satisfaction of demands for housing,
and housing improvement, is a rewarding private business which
does not lack eager participants and which seems to produce, as
in the United States, a general level of housing welfare which is
widely envied. Nevertheless, in many other parts of the world,
housing is regarded as a demand which cannot and should not be
satisfied by the market and, hence, must be distributed as a form
of public largess.

It is our task to examine the extent to which housing production is a "social" rather than an "economic" activity and,
indeed, what these terms mean and why they are in use.

To begin with, we must make a definitional, but highly
significant, point. Any useful commodity is an "economic good,"
no matter whether it is labor-, land-, or capital-intensive in its
production, and regardless of whether it is distributed through
the market or by public agencies. No one disputes that housing
is useful and desirable. As such it has some inherent position in
the scheme of priorities for the use of resources, depending upon
the degree to which additional or improved housing is wanted,
and on the relative desirability of alternative products which
could be produced with the same resources. The question as to
whether housing construction should be postponed is a question
about its priority, not about its essential nature as an object of
valid economic demand.

A misconception regarding the strength and importance of
housing demand can and apparently does arise from the fact that
in many portions of the world the market—i.e. private business

—does not respond very effectively to such demand. If the entire economic system were administered by a "perfect" market (in the economist's complex sense of that term), then a system of priorities in consumer demand would be reflected without distortion in the actual pattern of production. If government administrators study the behavior of business enterprises with the assumption, perhaps subconscious, that the market does, in fact, approximate the conditions of "perfection," then they are bound to conclude that there is too little consumer demand for housing to justify the further diversion of resources to that sector. While they can hardly escape the chorus of complaints about housing conditions under these circumstances, they tend to ascribe the desire for better housing conditions to a "social" awareness rather than an individual preference. That is, public officials may convince themselves that it is *they* who desire ultimately to improve the housing conditions of the people rather than the people themselves. "If the people really wanted better housing for themselves," one can almost hear these public officials say, "they would buy it in the market at its present price. Unfortunately they don't want it as much as they should, so eventually we shall just have to give it to them some day as a gift." *

The assumption that the market place actually responds to economic demands in accordance with their intrinsic priority is never entirely justified. It is characteristically erroneous in just those parts of the world which are self-conscious about their economic development. It is, in any part of the world, less justified in connection with the housing sector than for almost any other major component of an economic system. Thus, it is simply incorrect to measure the strength of the economic demand for housing by the past or current performance of that sector. In seeking other measures for this demand, we do not, however, rob housing of its attributes as an "economic good."

Nor, of course, do we imply that by detecting a stronger demand for housing, we establish that the market itself—i.e. the

---

* For example, The Economic Planning Agency in Japan includes housing in the category of "social overhead capital" along with roads, ports, water supply, etc. See *Economic Survey of Japan* (1965–1966), Japan *Times*, Ltd., 1966, pp. 123–128.

system of private business—must be expanded to meet that demand. The system of production and distribution, whether public or private, is essentially unimportant in the establishment of resource priority for the housing sector. An "economic" good can be produced by a socialized sector of the economy. The real difficulty is that the behavior of a very imperfectly organized sector of the market seems often to set the guidelines for the actions of even the more aggressive public efforts to meet the demand of that sector. It is possible and, under the circumstances, appropriate to measure housing demand before we decide whether the satisfaction of this demand should be a public or private responsibility. Even if we choose eventually to restrict the function of supplying housing to social or public agencies, this does not infer that housing demand is social rather than private.

Market demand for housing is substantially weakened by market imperfections characteristic of the housing sector. Among these imperfections are those which arise from the nature of housing itself. Systems of property rights and orderly methods for the exchange of real property must exist before private housing investment is warranted at all, and where these systems are of dubious strength, the terms for the investment are relatively discouraging. Control over land uses and the provision or encouragement of facilities which serve residential areas—transportation, utilities, education, and commercial establishments—also condition the quality and strength of housing demand. That is, housing demand is inherently bound up with parallel demands and unless the latter are satisfied concurrently, the demand for housing per se is diminished. It is noteworthy that many of these parallel demands call for supply through public rather than private agencies. Thus, unless the community is alert and sympathetic on this score—in matters not directly relating to the construction of housing itself—it exercises a partial veto over private housing demand and forecloses the opportunity for private supply to meet that demand.

Other imperfections which diminish the apparent strength of housing demand lie in the process by which housing is created. If there are conditions which inhibit the use or reuse of land for residential construction or the flow of capital to the housing sector, then the market response, even to an intense demand, will be weak. Complex, flexible, and specialized business institutions and skills are required to operate this sector of the economy. Information about the existence, availability, and prospective value of land for residential construction must be produced and distributed. Financial organizations which are capable of attracting and administering with prudence some portion of the community's savings must be integrated into the capital market so that investors as a group have reasonable opportunity to weigh the housing sector against alternative yield-producing portions of the economy. Devices to overcome some of the risk and illiquidity of housing investment are also elements of an "ideal" supply response to housing demand. All these business devices do not spring automatically from the mere existence of housing demand, but rather, where they exist at all, they have evolved only slowly, greatly dependent upon nurture and guidance by public agencies. In this respect, too, it seems that an economic administration which is not familiar with and wholly sympathetic to the complex, supplementary requirements of the housing sector will effectively prevent that sector from functioning according to the "ideal" principles which would make the market a proper indicator of housing demand.

In addition, there may be any of a great variety of specific legal or cultural barriers to business activity in housing supply. Traditions of rent control, erratic investment markets which encourage holding of underused land, tolerance of squatting and perpetuation of tenant leases, outright prohibition of certain kinds of residential building (either as "extravagant" or "substandard") are among those conditions which can be expected to weaken the apparent demand for housing. In the opposite direction, tending to enlarge housing demand, are subsidies and tax exemptions directly or indirectly favorable to greater consumption of housing.

The net effect of these considerations is twofold. The observed behavior of the housing sector is unlikely to be a meaningful indicator of housing demand. Nevertheless, housing demand is an economic force which is valid in calling for the employment of resources in preference to some other uses. It is virtually necessary, even in an economic system most closely approximating the concept of an "ideal" marketplace, that housing demand be estimated by a synthetic process which is cognizant of past market behavior, but aware of its limitations as a guide to efficient overall allocation of resources.

The answer to our question regarding the "social" nature of housing demand can be put in these words: housing demand is not fully effective in the marketplace unless a set of institutions has been created in which that demand can be expressed. In the absence of these institutions, the market will incorrectly register apathy toward housing improvement and, in the face of this apathy, public agencies are likely to assume reluctant responsibility for the housing sector. The confusion between "social" and "economic" needs arises from a misreading of market behavior.

HOUSING AND ECONOMIC DEVELOPMENT

The foregoing discussion of the validity of housing demand might be accepted by economic planners in developing nations who would nevertheless favor restrictions upon the size of the housing sector, for they have another argument. "All right," they might concede, "housing is a desirable consumer good which ought to be available in the marketplace in competition with other uses of resources. However, the public welfare requires that housing demand be suppressed. Housing is very capital-intensive, but it does not create conditions favoring economic growth as other forms of investment do. Even if market institutions existed which tended to respond effectively to demands for housing and related facilities, capital should be withheld from the housing sector in order to foster economic development."

This is a multifaceted argument of substantial practical importance. It must be examined with great care. With some oversimplification it is summed up in the concept of the "capital-output ratio" as a guide to the allocation of scarce savings in a country which hopes to increase its per capita economic output.[14]

The capital-output ratio idea may be expressed as follows: a developing country's principal avenue to economic growth is through the prudent use of available savings, including what may be obtained from other, more affluent nations. These savings expand the capacity of the nation to produce goods beyond the limitations imposed by the size of the labor force and the existing stock of raw materials. Different types of investment, however, cause different degrees of the expansion of national economic capacity. The investment of $1,000 (to use an arbitrary unit of savings capital) in Industry X may permit GNP in each subsequent year to be $500 greater, while the same investment in Industry Y may result in additional annual output of $400, and in Industry Z of $100. The capital-output coefficients are then 2.0 in Industry X, 2.5 in Industry Y, and 10.0 in Industry Z. The economy will grow fastest—that is, per-capita GNP will show the greatest possible percentage and absolute gain from year to year —if available savings are employed in Industry X until investment opportunities in that industry are exhausted (or "diminishing returns" causes the capital-output ratio in that industry to rise above 2.5). Then, further savings will be allocated to expand the capacity of Industry Y. Industry Z has a very low priority for investment and its development will have to wait. In practice, the housing sector often plays the role of Industry Z, and the administrative decision to check the flow of savings into housing is regarded by many "development economists" who serve as advisors to governments in developing countries as a prudent device for fostering rapid economic growth.

In practice, the pool of available savings may be allocated among sectors of the economy according to significant modifications of the capital-output ratio concept. For example, an industry which promises to improve the foreign-exchange situation of the nation (producing a net inflow of gold or "hard currencies") may be favored even though its simple capital-output ratio would not give it a high priority. Secondary industries servicing or supplying high-priority industries share in the latter's favored position. Various public facilities such as transportation systems are necessary "inputs" into many industrial sectors and so they, too, may receive generous allotments of savings.

The capital-output ratio for a particular industry may not correspond to the "yield" of investment in that industry for a variety of reasons. For example, the high-priority industry may not yet exist in anything approaching the scale contemplated by the national development plan. Individual investors may have no way to know that their small contributions would be matched by a sufficient number of other contributions so that the new industry will be viable in a world of intensely competitive trade. Hence, the market yield prior to development may misrepresent the real productivity of investment in the industry. The administrative allocation of capital (based upon rules such as the capital-output ratio) is a substitute for an inadequate or inefficient capital market, or for a capital market which is oblivious to such governmental needs as the opportunity to accumulate foreign exchange or to commence the training of an industrial labor force.*

The housing sector's "output" generally shows up as quite low in relation to the amount of capital invested in it. Its capital-output ratio is, therefore, relatively high (many dollars being required to produce an increased output of $1) and development plans thus accord a low priority to this sector. The output of the housing sector may be measured simply as the net increase in rents which will be collected when the additional housing investment is made. We can show that this treatment of the housing sector understates its output and overstates the output of other sectors and that, as a consequence, systems of capital allocation which seem to be maximizing the rate of economic growth may, in fact, use scarce capital inefficiently.

There are many adequate reasons for suggesting that the housing sector's share of the limited investment potential of a developing country should be substantially greater than that arrived at through the use of capital-output ratios. Let us examine several of these.

Housing as Input.—As a user of capital, the housing sector differs qualitatively from other principal capital-using sectors.

---

* We need not be troubled by the fact that an investment in one industry, say a machine for Industry X, may have a shorter useful life than a similar investment in another industry. These aspects of the specific investment choices can be represented in the capital-output ratio by estimating the net addition to permanent output capacity which is possible in each industry. Many such technical matters make the actual administration of capital allocation in a developing economy very complex.

Investment in housing is tied up in a durable consumer good, while investment in machines or factories creates the potential to produce greater quantities of other consumer goods. Industry's use of capital is "productive" in this sense, while housing capital is an elaborate form of consumption. Industrial capital makes a relatively permanent improvement in the technology of production, while housing does not affect technology. A nation's productive resources are not expanded, therefore, if available capital is used for housing.

We note, however, that industrial development requires the enlargement of the urban labor force. Population pressures and housing complaints in developing countries arise primarily in cities which are growing in response to expanding industrial capacity.[15] To realize the benefits of greater industrial capacity requires labor as an input. This labor may have been underemployed in agricultural areas before, so that most of its product appears to be a net gain.

What seems to be overlooked in very large measure is the fact that "labor" is in fact not as mobile as, say, electric energy. The strength and skill which a laborer brings to industrial employment cannot be distilled away from the man himself. The physical human being represents a need for a complex of facilities and services, many of them capital-intensive, and when the individual is moved, all his needs move with him. If there is an expanding factory in an urban area, there is a need for more workers; but if there is a need for more workers, there is a need for facilities to serve those workers. Just as the demand for urban labor is derived from the creation of urban industry, the demand for urban facilities—including housing—is created along with the industry. Housing is an industry which "subcontracts" for urban industry. It is a real input in the process of industrial production. A portion of the value of the industrial output is created by the housing sector. Just as an industrial enterprise will not function unless a physical system is created to provide food to its workforce, the enterprise does not function unless there is physical housing.

Just as a matter of economic accounting, then, we have not really finished building a new factory until we have built houses, schools, stores, and streets to serve the workers who will serve the factory and make the capital investment pay off. The cost of these labor-oriented facilities is a hidden cost of industrial development; but if we ignore this cost, we exaggerate the value to the society of the new industry. Its capital-output ratio may simply appear favorable because too much of the output has been assumed to be net—that is, inadequate provision has been made for the production costs associated with that output. This would be bad accounting and it would be bad economics. A major source of the indirect economic cost of industrial development arises from changes in the location of employment opportunities, for these changes bring in their wake the need—at least in an economic sense of optimal resource use—to recreate a set of living facilities to accommodate the "mobile" worker and his family in their new environment.

Workers as Forced Savers.—If a worker migrates to a city during a period of urban industrial expansion, he is automatically "housed" in some kind of definitional sense. He sleeps somewhere. It may be in a previously vacant house or apartment or in one which has just been constructed. It may be in a dormitory or hotel, or in an empty lot or on the street. Wherever he is we may say is his "home." This is not the end of the matter as far as the economist is concerned (nor the political scientist!) for we want to know whether the economic system is sensitive enough to any unsatisfied needs which this man may have to divert resources in his direction. If his initial housing in inadequate, will better housing be provided?

The provision of better housing, no matter who arranges it or what form it takes, will call for the channeling of investment into housing and hence away from further industrial growth. While no "development economist" can hope to avoid some diversion of capital into housing, he naturally desires to keep that "unproductive" use of scarce capital to a minimum. It is a question of the quality rather than the quantity of new housing facilities. What is the minimum kind of accommodation which will still permit urban industrial growth?

This is, in effect, the question, "how much will it take to keep this man from moving back to the countryside?" How much squalor, jostling, noise and lack of privacy, how much danger on the streets and filth in the sewers, how much commuting time and difficulty in hauling the necessities of life for his family will this man (and his family) endure for the privilege of participating in his benevolent government's "economic miracle?"

Both sticks and carrots are available to achieve the optimum result—a stable urban worker who makes the factories produce GNP without expending more than the barest minimum of investment capital to satisfy his own needs. The most effective stick is the lack of nonurban employment to which to return. Changes in agricultural technology coinciding with urbanward migration may have obliterated his former livelihood or removed the niche in which a superfluous family farmhand could previously maintain himself. The rural housing in which the worker lived earlier may also have ceased to exist so that he would have a "housing problem" wherever he went.

The largest carrot is undoubtedly the city itself. Over the centuries and in every culture which has created cities the variety and possibilities inherent in urban life have exercised a magnetic pull upon much of the rural population. Mercantile England, feudal Japan, and communist China have all adopted stern measures to discourage migration into cities. It is primarily in the city that human beings are exposed to the full range of choice of occupation, association, consumption, and entertainment which civilization has devised. Once the rich banquet of urban activities is seen—even though very little is tasted—the provender of rural life seems dull to most of us. Humanity will apparently endure much—because it has, in fact, endured much—just to be near the color, delights, and surprises of the city. Wise men have lamented this mothlike instinct and science adds some tentative condemnation. The impulse is strong and enduring, however, and is one of the major, permissive factors which help us to account for the existence of dense human settlements. Industrial development is able to draw in a very substantial way upon this human tendency to prefer urban to rural life and, thus, to excuse its neglect of investments which might make that urban life decent as well as delightful, safe as well as surprising, and comfortable as well as colorful.

Another kind of carrot is the proliferation of factory goods which industrial development, secured at the expense of housing, is able to offer as a partial substitute for housing and related capital-intensive urban facilities. Flimsy shacks contain transistor radios; pointed shoes in the latest Italian mode step across open sewage ditches. A man can stand before an unsanitary and unprivate washstand to shave with a stainless-steel razor blade and lather spurting from an aerosol can. Children who are fed a diet of sugar-frosties and cola, plus pills with modern, medical magic inside, sleep in sweaty clusters on bug-ridden straw or burn their flesh trying to crowd around live coals. Industry, indeed, provides many compensations for the housing which it regards as inimical to the national design for better living.

The ultimate carrot which persuades the urban family to stick it out is a game of chance. Once in a while some reasonable housing is put up, and some lucky families will find their circumstances instantly transformed from the dark age to the space age. Of course, there is the question of who will receive this prize. Years of faithful service to a prosperous employer (especially the national government) may be the winning ticket. Often enough the system of distribution is quite literally a sweepstakes. A household head who meets various conditions of alert citizenship enters his name on the list and crosses his fingers. If his name is not drawn from the gigantic basket, well, maybe next time. Meanwhile, home will be a decrepit heap of lumber and the right to wait to use someone else's toilet. The lure of the lottery is probably second only to the lure of the city as a force which impels uncomfortable men to hold on just a little longer. And it serves as an intangible but very effective substitute for the actuality of a modest improvement in one's housing. In this way it advances the national purpose of industrial development and a growth in the GNP measured in someone else's money.

So it is possible on a very large scale to induce urban populations to get along with rather little in the way of new housing or related facilities. Much more capital is available to be expended on industrial facilities which will be described on financial pages around the world. Available savings are stretched in this way, by drawing upon certain major reservoirs of human endurance. The arrangement has the delicate advantage of avoiding financial transactions between the virtual source of savings—the households whose housing needs are bureaucratically frustrated—and the emergent industrial complexes. Savings which might have gone into the possession of a family home are committed anonymously to facilities which provide no comparable source of security or well-being to those sacrificing families. There are no bonds, or deeds, or even tax receipts given in exchange for the domestic privations arising from the suppression of housing demand. It is a silent, unremarked transfer of resources; there is nothing on paper. The physical results, however, are incontrovertible.

This means, of course, that the economic cost of industrial plants financed in this manner will be understated. Without an explicit financial transaction to compensate households for their sacrifices, industrial development may seem to be a great bargain for the nation. When its real cost is counted, it may become only adventure or folly. This is not an egregious "social" judgment, but a commentary upon the inadequate arithmetic of economic decision. GNP is too amorphous a thing with which to measure the result of our economic labors and the application of our resources. The economist who disregards the composition of the national aggregate or the conditions inherent in encouraging that national aggregate to grow is more mathematician than social scientist. The economist's largest task is to detect implicit values, not to press for explicit accomplishments. "Economics" does not require that people with resources, ambition, and skill must live in hovels. To imply that housing conditions which can be observed throughout the world are "inescapable" is to prejudge the relative values of competitive commodities. That, assuredly, is just what the economist says he never does.

Nonexportability of Housing.—If the housing industry, aggregating all the functions which must be performed to make housing available to users, produced a product which could be loaded on freight cars or on ships and sent to a distant market, as an automobile is sent, the interest of developing nations in housing would be much greater than it is. If a housing shortage developed under such circumstances, the nation would be strongly constrained to stimulate housing construction so as to become "self-sufficient" in housing and minimize the drain on foreign exchange reserves. Developing nations would vie with each other to solve each other's housing problems and, perhaps, an international cartel would have to be created to prevent excessive competition in housing supply. Workmen would be sent abroad to learn how to repair foreign-model homes. The capital-output ratio for the housing industry would improve dramatically since the long-term investment in housing would, naturally, be undertaken by the distant consumer; thus, domestic capital in house construction could turn over at least once a year and probably more often.

In fact, of course, housing is the most immobile of consumer goods. Housing produced in one city cannot be sold in the neighboring city, let alone be exported. Conversely, housing needs in one city cannot be met by housing production anywhere else. Housing is not a commodity of inter-area trade and each separate community is a housing sector unto itself.

This means, obviously enough, that whatever latent advantages there might be in really large-scale specialization and production in the housing sector, such advantages cannot be enjoyed. This is little more, perhaps, than an accident of nature and need not be lamented, as it cannot be helped.

The nonexportability of housing also means, however, that local suppliers have a captive market. This is a circumstance which may, indeed, produce avoidable diseconomies affecting housing, not least of which is a set of market conditions which diminishes the effective demand for additional housing and makes its apparent capital-output ratio less favorable.

By its very nature, housing is a commodity without close substitutes. One can drink tea when coffee is scarce, but if housing is scarce, no other category of consumption goods can even approximately replace it. If coffee from Brazil is too expensive, coffee from Java may be used instead, but a dearth of housing in City X cannot be satisfied by entrepreneurs in City Y. In two very significant respects, housing demand is characterized by this lack of substitutability.

The textbook term for a demand of this type is "inelastic."

This means that the commodity will be bought with less regard to price than might otherwise be the case. If the price of local housing rises, the quantity purchased will fall relatively little. If the quantity supplied were then to increase, the aggregate sum paid for housing will increase little or may even fall.

Housing is durable also and thus—considering short periods of time—its supply (locally) is relatively fixed. Its price is thus determined not by past production cost, but by present demand alone. An increase in demand (an upward shift in the demand schedule reflecting an increase in population or in purchasing power) is translated entirely into a higher level of prices. If suppliers of local housing decide not to respond to this higher price the quantity available will not increase and the higher price level will remain.

Once again the concept of an "urban land ratchet" helps in understanding the hesitancy of the local housing sector to reply to an increased demand for houses, this time by holding down the profitability of new housing construction. This situation can be represented in diagram form, making some simplifying assumptions. In Figure 20, the supply of housing, S, is the stock available to the community at the time of an increase in demand. The increase in demand, we might assume, takes the form of a doubling of the number of households. There is no change in the pattern of household incomes or in household preferences for housing. The new demand, D', is simply twice as far from the vertical axis as the original demand, D.

Let us suppose, also, that the initial equilibrium of the market provided a level of rent, $0C$, just sufficient to compensate the investor for all resources embodied in the housing stock. This is the minimum rent which would encourage independent investors to expand the housing stock.

It is important to note what has happened to household expenditures and to the value of the housing stock as a result of the increase in number of households. Each household pays one-half of the new rent per unit—that is, $\frac{1}{2}0R$. However, two households are now sharing each dwelling in the original supply. The rent per dwelling is much higher than before, the height of $0R$ depending on the steepness or inelasticity of the demand curve. If rent, $0C$, previously represented the maximum housing expenditure each family could afford, its demand curve, when faced with a virtual reduction in supply, may be of unit elasticity so that $\frac{1}{2}0R = 0C$, approximately.

The area CRSE is economic rent which is created by the increase in demand for the fixed housing stock. This value is transferred from housing users to housing owners. Any measures to relieve the housing shortage will reduce this economic rent. The owners of the original housing stock would not be motivated

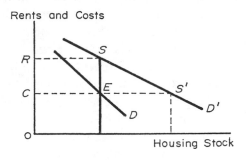

Figure 20

to invest in additional housing if they acted in their joint interest. Even acting as individuals, the owners of existing dwellings control land which may be needed for higher-density redevelopment. They would be unwilling to demolish the existing valuable building unless this meant a gain greater than their present economic rent, an unlikely situation.

Independent investors might endeavor to meet the housing demand of this city by constructing new housing at cost $0C$. Without the doubling-up of families which has taken place in the original stock of houses, these new dwellings will rent for $\frac{1}{2}0R$. This may or may not be attractive to potential housing investors.

The real benefit of the new housing, however, must be measured by the reduction in economic rent, CRSE, which is transferred back from housing owners to housing users. This transfer will be completed when the housing stock has, in our example, doubled to S'.

This simple illustration has been constructed so as to emphasize that the effect of housing shortage on individual households may be a reduction in housing conditions rather than an increase in housing expenditures. Therefore, the market return from offering a new dwelling to an individual family will not really measure the improvement in housing conditions which that new dwelling will provide. An important part of the benefit of new housing investment is the transfer of economic rents from owners, who have been placed in a monopolistic position, to housing users. This is an external benefit and it is, perhaps, a paradox that economic development planning which stimulates urban population growth often discourages housing investment, so that these economic rents remain in the hands of owners of the original stock of housing. If the social benefit of reducing these economic rents were perceived, economic development plans might allow considerably more capital to flow into the housing sector.

An individual private supplier who produces additional housing for the city which has absorbed a population influx does so at the cost of lowering the market value of the existing inadequate supply. This cost will be absorbed by the owners of that existing supply who may endeavor to discourage competitive building. If the entire local supply is under the control of one agency—a complete monopoly or a socialized housing sector— then that agency has every financial incentive *not* to increase the supply of housing. The marginal return on housing investment for such an agency is very low or even negative.

The fact that housing is not an article of inter-area trade makes it unnecessary for the economic administration to respond to an increase in specific local demand. The same fact discourages entrepreneurs in one locality from attempting to profit from a scarcity in another locality, though both may be part of the same nation or planning region. The housing industry has strong inherent tendencies to monopolistic behavior and it is a characteristic of monopoly to exert little demand for additional investment. The present investment will do very well to extract almost compulsory expenditures from a market with no alternative sources of supply.

It is just as true of a monopolistic situation, however, that its output tends to fall short of the optimum. Where demand is exploited by the existence of a monopoly at its equilibrium, the incremental benefit of greater investment exceeds the incremental cost. The market or monetary return on this investment will be inadequate but the return in terms of economic value (i.e. utility) will be more than sufficient. In general, the capital-output ratio concept is invalid in the case of a monopolized industry, and housing has at least one major characteristic—nonexportability —which makes the housing sector relatively monopolistic.

Costs of Delay.—A flat refusal to incorporate housing in national economic plans would be too brutal in most political circumstances to be tolerated. A preferred expression is "later." This is consistent with the basic capital-output ratio concept which expects diminishing returns in the industrial sectors eventually to elevate the priority of the housing sector as a recipient of rationed investment. While the concept itself is inapplicable on several counts to the housing question, the issue of delay is separate. Postponing of housing investment is a policy choice which, far from saving resources, is likely to involve substantial waste and makes the ultimate answer to the problem of housing far more costly than it need be.

In the first place, a large influx of new households must be met by "temporary" dwellings or additional investments to the existing stock of dwellings if full-scale response to the new housing demand is discouraged. There simply must be places for the entire population to bed down. This means committing some resources immediately which it is expected will be scrapped in due time.

It means somewhat more, however, in the scarring impact which makeshift devices will have upon the supply of usable land and upon the structures which existed before the influx occurred. A tangled web of fragile, but sensitive, tenure relationships and routes of supply will adhere to the soil of once expansive and manageable domains. Defenseless amenities will perish before they ever have a chance to serve decently housed families. Structures of intrinsic worth will be pounded to pieces by wasteful intensity of use. The whole utility structure of the community will be replaced piecemeal to relieve excessive use, but in the process it is likely to evolve into a makeshift maze. In the face of permanently enlarged demand, investments wil be made in a manner more rational for a community of Bedouins. Emergency measures are inherently wasteful but excusable in economic terms if the emergency is likely to pass. Such measures in the face of a virtually irreversible change in the fortunes of a sprawling urban community are inexcusably wasteful.

A third, more subtle form of permanent damage is done to the local economy through administratively determined delay in meeting housing demands. Land values throughout the community are pushed up to levels which become new "floors" and which distort all future activities of the local housing sector. We have described this earlier as the problem of the "ratcheting" of urban land values. Serious delays in meeting new housing demand mean that future generations of households in the community will serve turns in paying tribute to the early landowners whose fortunes were created by a piece of economic sophistry and a government eager to improve the welfare of its citizens.

Housing's External Benefits.—There are several respects in which adequate or convenient housing benefits society above and beyond the satisfactions it provides to people who live in it, and to this extent society, rather than the individual user, would be justified in paying the cost of such housing. That is, to some extent housing is a social commodity the benefits of which are shared by the general public.

Perhaps the clearest instance has to do with the location of urban housing with respect to the householder's place of employment. If a housing shortage in the city forces workers to live far outside the city, they may be obliged to cut short their working day in order to make the long commuting trip, and they may arrive at work with their energies depleted by the protracted discomforts of simply getting there. The efficiency of the labor force then suffers, and the economic output of the community as a whole declines. It will reward the community up to a point to arrange for workers to live closer to their places of employment; this might mean, for example, subsidizing the reconstruction of nearby areas at higher densities.

Similarly, if the discomforts and hazards of poor housing interfere with the application of labor to business or industry, the community may wisely assume part of the cost of housing improvement. Lack of sanitation or shelter from the elements can weaken members of the labor force physically and deny the economy some of its scarce resources. Quite apart from the humanitarian aim of relieving suffering, additional housing investment is, in such a case, "good economics." As an additional benefit, the expenditure of resources on medical care might be reduced and schoolchildren might be able to derive greater benefit from the community's educational investment if better housing means less illness and more chance for quiet study and adequate sleep.[16]

It has long been the fond belief of "housers"—people who advocate government action to improve housing—that social behavior is improved by the provision of adequate housing. Families taken from slums, for example, are thought likely to acquire better housekeeping and child-rearing habits when placed in decent dwellings. Crime and delinquency, marital breakdowns, and chronic dependence on public doles are associated with substandard housing so that, in the housers' arguments, community investment in better housing will result in better citizenship and lower community welfare costs.

All of these suspected "external benefits" of housing investment suffer from being rather difficult to measure unambiguously. Serious, careful efforts have been made, but the factual case does not yet appear strong. Particularly in the last group of effects mentioned above, it seems questionable that personal habits and harmful attitudes toward society which one does find in areas of bad housing are caused by that housing, for rehousing projects have, in practice, provided serious disappointments in this respect.[17]

One less ambiguous type of external effect is the opportunity of accelerated household formation which is afforded by increased investment in housing. To perceive this effect we must make a definitional distinction between what might be called "family formation," representing primarily marriage or the arrival of adults at a normal age for marriage, and "household formation" which means that a "family" obtains separate housing so that it can carry on its functions such as homemaking and child-raising with independence and privacy. Now, if the housing sector operates in such a fashion that families have to accumulate substantial equities before they can acquire separate housing, it is clear that household formation usually will be delayed. Young families will exist without household status, remaining in one or the other parental households perhaps. The extreme example would be that in which the only way to establish a household was to pay all cash for a house. The young family would (without some parental assistance) save year by year toward this goal, meanwhile sharing the home—and the homemaking expense— of the previous generation. Eventually the price of a separate dwelling would be accumulated, but by that time many of the essential tasks of family life would have been completed, for the family's children would be at least partly raised and might even be starting to form families—but not households—of their own. The family might never have really exclusive control over its own private destinies. Clearly, a net addition to the supply of housing in the community would make it physically possible to let young families function as households, and a system of distribution of this housing to young families (sale for a small down payment with a long-term mortgage, for example) could be created.

The elements of this problem are the following: the young family living in a parental household is able to pay the cost of its present housing needs, because the accumulation of the ultimate cost of housing is evidence of this ability. The housing is not provided, however, until its entire capital cost has been accumulated. When that sum has been saved up, much of the need for separate housing has expired. The system as it stands exhausts the housing budget of the young family so that the market yield on a net increase in the housing stock would be low or negligible. If the community sacrifices other objectives to enlarge the stock of dwellings, it receives in return whatever social benefits there are in having young families live in privacy and independence. The community is reimbursed for its initial financial investment as independent families repay the capital cost of the housing they currently occupy. Should the community arrange to enlarge the stock of housing in anticipation of a long-term economic need?

A similar problem exists in the field of education. A child eventually repays the cost of his public education for, when he is grown, he participates in the labor force and produces taxable product, a product which is presumably larger because of that education. If he were required to pay in a lump sum the capital cost of all the educational facilities he requires on the day that he enters school, his education would be delayed. Eventually when it began, that education would have lost some or most of its potential usefulness. If someone—the community in some sense —will advance to the child the cost of his education, then the potential value of education will be realized to the maximum possible extent. Society, including the children themselves, will benefit from providing facilities needed by people whose ability to pay is several years off.

One may argue, certainly, that separate housing for a young family is a luxury rather than a productive necessity such as education. It is, however, a distinctly social judgment. If the society is aware of the way in which it can benefit young families by enlarging the scale of the housing sector, then a rational judgment can be made, pro or con. The judgment of many societies seems to be that such social investment is of great value, though other societies may view the independence of young families in a different light.

It is important to note that the social cost of providing independent dwellings for young families is not the entire resource cost of these dwellings, but only the differential rate of money return on this public investment versus the most rewarding alternative use of social savings. The capital cost of the investment will be repaid with interest as the young families amortize the public investment. Supposing that the money rate of return provided by the amortization of such additional housing is 7 percent, while the investment of scarce savings in industry would yield 10 percent, then the social cost of accelerating household formation is the 3 percent differential. If the community values the independence of young families at more than this 3 percent, then enlargement of the housing stock to achieve this goal is a rational choice.

Another kind of external effect of housing investment is

simply a matter of scale and has to do with the rate of replacement or housing improvement demand which may ultimately arise spontaneously from the housing market. In an economy which has known a relatively stable level of income for generations or even centuries there may be little in the way of aspirations for better housing. Housing replacement in such an economy simply means putting a substantially identical new building where a very old and no longer useful house has been standing. In a wealthier society, housing replacement more characteristically means scrapping one structure with years of physical usefulness left in favor of a "new model." The transition of a society from stable, low living standards to rising and relatively higher standards often seems to alter the concept of housing replacement from that of qualitative stability to one of continuing qualitative improvement.

The practical importance of this is that the immediate market demand for improved housing may not be very strong in a developing economy, for most households are unfamiliar with any other type of housing. When substantial improvement in the inventory occurs, however, tastes for housing change, or so it seems, and the desire for upgrading the family residence is awakened. This is sometimes called a "demonstration effect," and might be reduced to the jocular concept of "keeping up with the Joneses." Family X becomes interested in a better house only when Family Y obtains one. Until someone starts the trend for housing improvement, the market demand for such housing investment does not exist and the "capital-output ratio" of the housing sector is made relatively unfavorable by this fact. The ratio is improved, however, once substantial improvements in the stock have actually been made. There is a latent demand for the better product, but the private market will not respond to such a demand with much vigor. It is possible for the community investment in better housing to tap this latent demand and, far from violating the "equimarginal" principle of capital allocation, cause the capital-output ratio or the "yield" on housing investment to improve. The critical element is the scale of the undertaking.

Housing replacement rates of this sort are markedly higher

in the United States than in most other nations. In general, the rate of housing replacement seems to rise with per capita income when nations at different stages of economic development are compared.

Accomplishing Optimization

From the demand side we note that the aggregate need for housing investment is the sum of several qualitatively distinct elements, each of which in its turn has quantitative dimensions. These elements include population growth; a change in non-economic population characteristics (such as the age distribution); preference shifts; geographic mobility; intraurban location, and transportation developments; and changes in income. In order to perceive the form of a socially optimal scale of housing sector activities, it is necessary to rank these types of needs in order of priority, and it makes practical sense to consider them in incremental terms. That is, given the present state of the inventory and some limitations on the supply of additional housing resources, which kinds of needs are most deserving of the new resources which can be allocated to this sector? The quantitative problem—how many new houses we should provide—is harder to deal with in the context of social optimization than is the qualitative problem—which kinds of demands are most urgent. Social judgments (and they must in large measure remain just that) come more readily when the problem is one of ordering or ranking qualitatively different demands than when the problem is simply that of selecting one total level of investment on a scale which is, in principle, infinite. What is more, a solution to the qualitative problem goes much of the way toward solving the quantitative problem, since the decision to meet one category of incremental demand implies a quantitative commitment, and the cutting off of some categories of demand releases specific quantities of resources from a putative use by the housing sector.

The manner of ranking follows from consideration of the social or external benefits associated with the satisfaction of each type of need. One portion of this chapter has examined some of these benefits.

From the supply side we can somewhat more readily distinguish qualitatively different categories of inputs which are used in the housing sector. Land, labor, materials, finance, and other inputs have been discussed in this chapter in terms of their probable social costs. These elements must be ranked in terms of their respective social costs, a process which necessarily rests upon presumptions about community values but which is made easier by the fact that we need establish only an ordinal and not a cardinal ranking. That is, we must be able to say that factor X has a higher social cost than factor Y, but we do not need to say how much higher.

The selection of an optimal description of housing-sector scale then becomes a matter of comparing the highest-ranked need with the most limiting (i.e. highest social cost) input, and the decision as to whether the specific need under consideration warrants the use of the specific limiting input. In outline this is not different from the equilibrium system described at the close of the preceding chapter. Here, however, the indicators of benefit and cost are social rather than market relationships.

Supposing that a significant discrepancy appears between the equilibrium scale of the sector—resulting from market processes—and the optimal scale, how can the optimum be realized? This is a broad question of political policy toward the housing sector encompassing the questions of socialization, marginal control, and the inherent degree of competitiveness in housing business. This large subject will be given a chapter of its own after the microeconomics of equilibrium and optimization are considered, for the political view of the housing sector cannot deal only with the aggregate scale of the sector, but must look into the inner workings of the housing economy as well.

5 · ▞

ENTREPRENEURIAL

BEHAVIOR IN THE

HOUSING SECTOR

The essence of a market economy is that individual producers
and consumers act and react in their own individual best interests, unconcerned with the consequences of their aggregate behavior. Under some conditions these consequences will include
an optimum use of resources, but whether this occurs or not is
beyond the power of the individual to determine. Since each market decision is influenced by social stipulations—i.e. by public
prohibitions, taxes, and rewards—as well as by the availability
of resources, a change in those stipulations can move the collection of individual decisions closer to the optimum as society perceives it.

Before we can design or implement an optimal plan for the
housing sector, it is necessary to achieve an understanding of the
way in which an individual housing producer or consumer responds to the market and institutional conditions which confront
him. Housing investors, developers, and users do not engage in
business to fulfill a social plan but, rather, to achieve their individual goals, so the mere pronouncement of community goals
with respect to housing will have little influence upon the manner

in which housing is supplied and distributed. Nor can individuals in the market place be counted upon to respond to public acts— new laws, subsidies, taxes, etc.—as though they understood and were in sympathy with the framers of such acts. The response of the market to a change in the background of public regulations is not self-evident nor simple and may include effects quite contrary to the intention of the regulators.

This is one important reason for making a close study of market performance at the level of the individual producer and consumer. The design and implementation of community housing programs requires realistic perception of market behavior, just as the development of synthetic materials requires an understanding of chemical reactions.

Of course, there is value in understanding the interdependent mechanics of the housing market even if our interest is not in the design of public programs related to housing or community development. A local housing market is inherently dynamic, constantly absorbing and responding to changes in elements of supply and demand. Population, income, housing preferences, mortgage availability, building technology, and other factors do not remain constant. The mere passage of time creates a dynamic of its own as it causes buildings to deteriorate in particular ways and brings a change in the age structure of the population. Business practices are modified over time, sometimes quite independently of public controls. To anticipate the effects of such changes within the market or responses in the market to new social programs is to make wiser individual decisions. The durability of housing requires the builder, the investor, and the user of housing to look ahead, foreseeing events which will influence the value of particular houses and divining the nature of this influence. The need for business forecasting creates a need for analytical understanding.

This chapter investigates a number of situations which call for business or consumer decisions with respect to housing; it describes in principle the manner in which each such decision is made if the decision-maker can define his own interest and is rational in its pursuit.

Types of Decision Situations

An individual may be confronted with the need to make a housing market decision in a variety of different ways. He may represent a household which is seeking a dwelling unit, confronted with a choice among locations and specific dwelling units at those locations, a choice between renting and buying (or acquiring a share in a cooperative), and the problem of deciding how much to spend on housing.

The individual may be a seller, faced with the task of setting a price upon his property or, more broadly, with the problem of deciding whether to sell or to rent out his property and when he should do so. The property owner has a continuing need for decisions concerning additional investment or expenditure for improvement or upkeep.

The housing developer needs to decide which piece of land to acquire and which kind of dwelling (whether single-family or multiple dwelling, which architectural style, what degree of quality) to construct. A large-scale developer must decide how many dwellings to place on the market in a given period of time.

The mortgage lender must decide how much to lend against a given piece of property, whether existing or not yet completed. The equity investor must decide among alternative income properties and among alternative financing arrangements such as the proportion of equity to debt when the choice is his.

There are many subquestions which must be answered in the process of making these principal choices and, indeed, there are many other primary issues which may arise in particular cases. The immediate point is that the housing market represents a variety of decision situations, each of which may require a specialized form of analysis. In general, however, each individual "actor" upon the stage of the housing market is confronted with a set of alternatives. Analysis of the market from a particular point of view can be helpful in selecting the alternative which maximizes the gain of the decision-maker.

The form of the gain varies. There can be income or capital

appreciation from housing just as there are in the securities market. The field of housing provides entrepreneurial income as well and, of course, the more or less subjective enjoyment which housing users seek. Each kind of potential gain has its converse in costs, losses, and discomforts. It is a fallacy to think of housing decisions exclusively as problems in investment, for there are numerous situations in which the analogy to the search for a return on capital is inappropriate. We shall be careful to specify the form of the gain as we discuss each type of decision situation.

INDIVIDUAL OR SOCIAL EQUILIBRIUM?

Gains which individuals seek in the housing market are defined, with a few important exceptions, in terms of the well-being of those individuals only: The impact which my decision makes upon the other people in the community can be disregarded by myself. The calculus of gain versus cost which concerns the individual involves only the gains and costs which that individual will experience.

From the viewpoint of the community, the alternative which is preferred by the individual directly involved may be less desirable than another alternative. The housing market is notorious for giving rise to situations in which gains and losses from a transaction are measured by the community in a different manner than they are by the individuals immediately concerned.

We do not need to define the "public interest" in detail in order to justify the above statement. Every private action or transaction in the housing market affects other persons in the community besides the owner, occupant, seller, buyer, builder, and lender. When an apartment is built where an old house stood, new competition is created for apartments already existing in the community and the character of the neighborhood is changed. When a homeowner sells out and moves away, the social relationships among his neighbors will have to adjust and the value of adjoining properties will be influenced by the price at which the sale is made. Expenditures on improvement, or the absence of expenditures on maintenance by one property owner, contribute to a broad pattern of changes in the qualitative distribution of the housing stock in the community. These only suggest the myriad repercussions of individual behavior. "Society," then, or the "community" (which we have said measures the effects of an individual housing-market decision in different terms from those employed by people directly concerned) simply means all the people who are *indirectly* concerned.

COMMUNITY PATTERNS AND THE INDIVIDUAL DECISION-MAKER

One useful way of looking at this problem is to consider that certain community patterns arise from the whole assemblage of private decisions. These are patterns of the distribution of the housing stock itself—qualitatively, locationally, and among different types or styles of housing. Residential areas assume particular physical forms as a result of the whole collection of private market decisions, and the dwellings within them serve the variety of household needs for housing with varying effectiveness.* There are also patterns of residential impact upon other community functions such as retail stores and personal-service activities, and upon the transportation system.

The community as such sees these patterns as the result of individual decisions made in the private housing market. It is concerned with guiding the large pattern, not with directing the individual decision.

Up to a point, the individual sees the community pattern as fixed. His decisions or his forecasts about what can be realized from his property or his expenditure are based implicitly or explicitly upon the condition of the community as it is, and as it is evolving independently of his decision. The individual is correct in his presumption that the pattern of the community is beyond his control. If John Doe does not put up the first cheap apartment building on fine old Maple Street, well—Richard Roe probably will. The nature of the community is one of the inputs in private housing-market decisions, not one of the outputs.

The businessman or other private decision-maker in the

---

* An early and influential study of housing patterns in American communities is Homer Hoyt's *The Structure and Growth of Residential Neighborhoods in American Cities* (Washington: Federal Housing Administration, 1939).

housing market may, of course, wish to consider the impact of his own decision upon others than himself. His decision criterion then becomes a blend of his own costs and gains, and his judgment of costs and gains to others. He must attach various weights to different kinds of effects, some of which—such as the esthetic impact of a proposed building—will necessarily be quite subjective. He must select these weights himself; the manner in which various kinds of external effects are taken into account will bear no necessary relation to the views of other citizens or other housing market decision-makers. A principal problem, of course, will be to forecast all relevant community repercussions from his individual market decision, including some estimate about what other private decision-makers will do.

It is possible for the community to choose to ignore the external effects of individual housing-market decisions but, where they are not to be ignored, it is poor community policy to place the burden of coping with these effects upon the conscience of the individual market participant. With the best public spirit, the individual is unable either to foresee the consequences of his actions for the entire community or to evaluate each and every effect upon persons other than himself. To expect that the collectivity of housing market participants will look upon all these external effects in just the same way is to take the short end of some very long odds.

The community's function is to establish explicit conditions upon the behavior of housing market participants, whoever they may be. This avoids paralysis of public decision-making due to assuming responsibility for the endless consequences of minute adjustments in the use of housing resources. Also it prevents the paralysis of private decision-making compounded with exhortations for community concern as well as the potentially disruptive consequences of individual behavior which are totally unchecked by the interests of the community at large.

The market, then, is a stage for private decisions based upon simple judgments of individuals for their own individual welfare. Certain general constraints are put upon the performers, not in the form of vague, moral directives, but in the "yes or no" and "how much" language of market decision-making. As the pattern of the community evolves, these public constraints can be modified to inhibit or encourage results previously unforeseen or mistakenly anticipated, or to accommodate a change in the community's perception of its own responsibilities.

Household Decision Model

Microeconomics describes the elements of decision-making which may lead to increases in income, particularly for businesses, or to increase in the consumer satisfaction obtained from a given income, particularly for households. Households and businesses are faced with many alternative ways of producing products or meeting consumption needs and there is, in principle, a systematic way of examining each set of alternatives to select that which is best from the decision-maker's point of view.

In the following pages we wish to discuss the manner in which decisions are made in the housing market by consumers, developers, property owners, and real estate lenders. Our object is to perceive the essential steps in reaching such decisions, not to provide a formula for automatic decision-making. It will be seen that information relating to the individual—his housing tastes, his tax bracket, his attitude toward risk, etc.—plays an important role in every final decision and in many intermediate ones. With the great diversity of individual situations which exists, a single formula might not be very useful. It is useful, though, to look at the common procedures which might be followed by anyone faced with a particular type of housing market problem.

The flow-chart diagrams to be presented in this chapter serve such a purpose. They trace a question-and-answer sequence from an initial inquiry to a decision to act, showing what kinds of information will be required at each point and what intermediate decisions need to be reached along the way. We can offer also some suggestions on how each of these intermediate decisions can be made.

The decision flow charts indicate how decisions "should" be made (on the basis of rational self-interest), rather than the manner in which they actually are made. No one is forced to make strictly logical decisions but, to the extent that people in a market economy wish to use their limited resources to maximum advantage, their actions are forced into some general pattern of rationality. The flow charts are such general patterns.

The first chart, Figure 21, deals with the householder's decision about a change in housing. In brief, the chart says that the householder should look around to see if something better is available. Some interesting subquestions arise, however, when we try to show how to decide whether something which is available is actually better. Thus the household flow chart serves to introduce the decision-making "model" concept with a relatively simple situation.

We start with the inquiry: Is it time to consider a change in the household's housing arrangement? In practice, the active search for housing improvement is expensive in time and money. It cannot be carried on continuously. The first issue, then, is whether the time has arrived for a serious review of housing possibilities.*

If the household's last housing move was "rational," then presumably it now occupies the optimum housing based on the market conditions and the needs, resources, and tastes of the household at the time of the previous move. Another move at the present time could not improve the household's housing circumstances unless there has been some significant change in market conditions or in the household's needs, resources, and tastes, or in the expectations about those things. Perhaps the family has grown, or its income has increased (or decreased) substantially. Perhaps the present dwelling has deteriorated in some respect, or a number of attractive dwellings have been placed on the market. The decision A answers the initial inquiry. A "no" answer shelves the inquiry for some later time.

A "yes" answer requires that the household do some careful preliminary thinking about its housing objectives. Certain broad limits on the prospective housing search must be defined. This

---

* Some interesting recent research on this subject is Sherman J. Maisel's "Rates of Ownership, Mobility and Purchase," in *Essays in Urban Land Economics*, James Gillies, ed. (Los Angeles: Real Estate Research Program, University of California at Los Angeles, 1966). An earlier study is Peter H. Rossi, *Why Families Move* (New York: The Free Press, 1955).

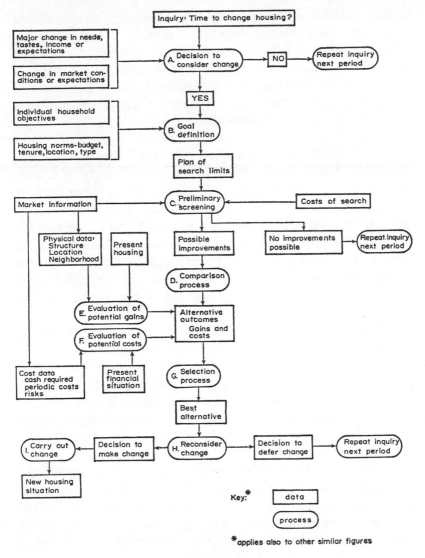

Figure 21
Household's Housing Decision

includes financial matters such as the range of rent or mortgage payments which the household's budget is likely to support, and its cash resources, including proceeds from the sale of the present home; great diversity can be seen in household budget ratios for housing.[1] An objective with regard to ownership may be drawn from community customs, with either renting or purchase alternatives being excluded from the outset. In principle, though, the process B should be as open minded as possible. Broad limits on locations to be examined and on housing types (e.g. number of bedrooms) are also established at this point. The result of process B is a set of limits for the proposed search.

Process C is a preliminary screening of available units which fall within the limits defined in B, eliminating all those which are clearly unsuitable. This screening is costly so it may, in practice, be a sampling of available dwellings rather than an exhaustive review. If no available dwellings survive this screening, it may be desirable to repeat processes B and C, revising the limits of what will be considered until some reasonable prospects emerge. If no such prospects appear and further repetition of process B produces no change in the limits of the search, then further action is deferred and the inquiry put over to a later time period.

If the screening process, C, produces a number of housing prospects which promise some improvement over the household's present situation, a selection process, D, is required. This process requires the assembly of exact physical and financial data regarding each of the prospects in turn. Financial factors must be interpreted in the light of the household's current and expected budget and asset situation, including proceeds expected from the sale of the present home. Physical factors concerning each prospective housing alternative must be weighed against the present housing. Process G brings these evaluations of incremental costs and gains from each housing prospect together. The result is a ranking of these prospects, identifying the one which offers greatest net improvement in the household's housing situation.

The costs of moving should be considered as a result of process D and further considered in process F. However, a housing change is a major event in the lives of most households; before the final decision is made, then, some final reflection about the emotional and worrisome aspects of moving is warranted. The chart provides process H for this purpose. A "no" answer to this additional inquiry—"Continue present arrangement?"—is an action decision. The household has decided to change its housing situation and has selected that available alternative which offers the greatest degree of improvement in its housing circumstances consistent with other budget requirements.

Housing Equity Decision Model

Dwellings, whether single-family or multiple, are purchased for various reasons, including the desire to occupy them, to enjoy the status and security which are associated with home ownership, to receive spendable income from tenants, or to accumulate capital value. The decision to purchase a particular property is inherently more complex than an investment in, say, corporate securities since the owner of housing is normally directly involved in basic management of the property itself.

Once a particular property is purchased, a sequence of decision-making situations commences. Short-term operating plans may have to be modified; long-term capital improvement undertaken; or, it may become prudent from the owner's point of view to demolish the existing structure and redevelop the land for some different use; or, conditions may suggest that the ownership be terminated by a sale of the property.

In a sense, every economic aspect of ownership is subject to continuous review. Daily, even hourly, changes occur in the conditions of the market, in the availability of loan funds, or in the circumstances of the owner which should lead to new decisions concerning the management of housing equity. It is convenient, and probably realistic, to look upon this continuing task as one of monitoring the relationship between specific expectations concerning the ownership and the market environment which helps to determine these expectations. That is, certain sets of policies and expectations are established by the purchaser at the time of his purchase, and these are reviewed only when something happens "outside" the property itself to suggest that the policies or expectations were wrong or have become outdated. When such information is received, a process of review and policy reformulation is begun which concludes in any of a variety of actions

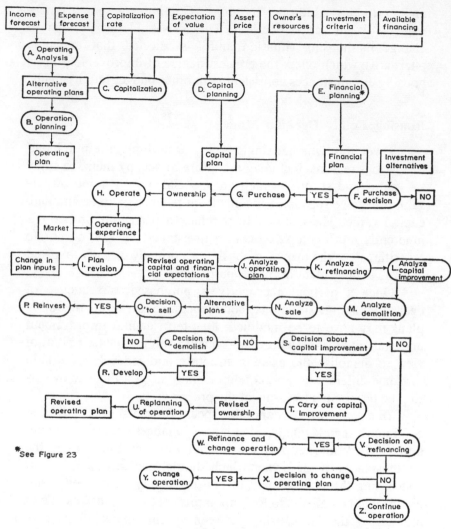

Figure 22
Housing Purchaser—Owner Decision System

such as the sale or refinancing of the property, its demolition or improvement, or simply a reinstatement, perhaps with revised expectations.

This treatment of the ownership situation is symbolized in the second of our flow charts, Figure 22. We begin at the time when the purchase of a specific residential property is contemplated. Before the decision concerning purchase can be made, three basic sets of forecasts must be made. One is the "operating plan," a short-range view of income and expenses. Another is the "capital plan," which foresees changes in capital value over the economic life of the property. The third is a "financial plan," which defines the manner in which acquisition and other outlays are to be financed and projects ultimate disinvestment.

THE OPERATING PLAN

Process A is the assembly and interpretation of data concerning incomes and expenses. The prospective owner-occupant who excludes the possibility of buying the property for investment alone needs only to consider the value of the property to his own household; this value will be largely in subjective terms. The intrinsic appeal of the dwelling itself and of its neighborhood; the quality of local schools, public facilities and commercial services; and the location of the dwelling with respect to places of employment and other frequent destinations form a package which need not be expressible in terms of monthly rent so long as these terms are visualized with some degree of accuracy by the household itself. Any reasonably probable change in the kinds of satisfactions which the home can produce should be investigated and considered—such as changes in transportation facilities or in the density or character of nearby land uses. Impending changes in the size or needs of the household itself have to be anticipated also.

Against these benefits of ownership—i.e. occupancy—must be set the operating (but not the financing or depreciation) costs of the property, such as taxes, insurance, and maintenance.[2] The level of maintenance expenditures implies a projection of the property's state of repair which, to the extent that it is a variable, makes the as-yet-undetermined capital and financing plans variables as well. This complication can be deferred for the moment, and it is often reasonable for the home purchaser simply to envisage a program of repair consistent with his own desire to retain occupancy of the home. If this occupancy is expected to continue for a considerable period of time—over five years, say —it is practical to consider that the level of maintenance costs will be approximately constant. Should a short occupancy be considered, then the preparation of the property for the tastes and requirements of its subsequent occupants (presumably those representing the optimal disposition opportunity) becomes the determinant of the maintenance scheme.

For the short-term occupant, the problem of optimum marketability arises in much the same way it does for the prospective owner of rental property. The housing market is significantly segmented in most cases, so that a variety of management plans are possible and it is the prospective owner's task to identify that plan which would be best for his own purposes. It is by no means true that the best plan always involves serving the highest-rent segment of the market as the following hypothetical situations illustrate:

	Alternative I	Alternative II
	$	$
rent	150	110
operating costs	90	40
net income	60	70

Higher rent in the first alternative is more than offset by higher operating costs, so that the second alternative produces better net income. The difference in operating costs may reflect the superior market position of those who would be able to pay a rent of $150, meaning that this group might require higher levels of maintenance and other management service and might also give rise to higher levels of vacancy.

If a change in the rental market for the area is to be expected—say, from a group paying $150 to a group at the $110 level—then it may be possible to offer the dwelling to the first group, but trim the maintenance outlays to a pattern which, in effect, prepares the building physically for the later, lower-rent market. Upkeep expenditures are by nature forward-looking rather than strictly current outlays; where the future best market is less demanding of physical quality, then, some capital-withdrawal through diminished upkeep may be optimal from the owner's point of view.

It might be objected that the increase in net income achieved by a reduction in maintenance expenditures may result in a decrease rather than an increase in capital value, since the accelerated deterioration of the structure seems to imply a shortening of the building's economic life. While no doubt possible, and even likely, in many circumstances, this impression is also subject to some important reservations. The near future may offer little hope of retaining the higher-rent tenants in any case. The lower-rent tenants may represent a virtually captive market little able to resist declining physical dwelling standards. If the greater net for low-rent tenants is the result of lower vacancy losses, then no physical impairment of the structure need be implied by the lower rent.

Vacancy also is a variable for the operating plan of the multiunit building. Low rents and good maintenance may assure low vacancy, but it is not always necessary that the final result be an improved net income. This can be illustrated with the following set of alternatives:

	Alternative I	Alternative II	Alternative III
	$	$	$
rent	140	120	120
operating costs			
maintenance	40	30	10
vacancy	20	0	10
other	20	20	20
net income	60	70	80

Here the low-maintenance, relatively high-vacancy alternative (III) produces the best net income at a rent of $120. The alternatives II and III represent quite separate markets despite the similarity of rents. If the market reflected in II is unlikely to be available for this property in the near future, then the higher-maintenance program appropriate for that group has no real benefit for the asset position of the prospective property owner.[3]

These situations are not constructed with a view to implying that a rental property owner's best alternative is always to let his property run down so that he can exploit a low-rent but undemanding market; the object is merely to challenge some stereotypes which often suggest the opposite, namely that unwavering programs of scrupulous maintenance and rents low enough to minimize vacancy are always in the owner's best interest. Circumstances may sometimes lead an owner to prefer a situation which seems imprudent to an unsophisticated observer or to one who confuses market equilibrium with social optimization or even with some utopian image which overlooks resource limitations and the dynamics of capital formation and destruction.

The owner of rental dwellings may anticipate vacancy from several sources. A relatively high rent level, given the nature of the structure, can produce vacancies which, nevertheless, are acceptable to the owner because rent reductions to achieve full occupancy may more than offset the reduction in vacancy losses. This implies that the owner occupies the position of a monopolist, to some extent, since his best net income situation may involve keeping a portion of his "capacity" idle. In the case of a rented, single-family dwelling, this may mean longer stretches of vacancy when turnover occurs and possibly higher turnover as well. For the owner of a multiple-unit structure, it may mean a relatively constant proportion of vacant units. The multiple-dwelling owner can attempt to discriminate among his tenants, charging less rent for the last unit rented than for those taken previously. The opportunity to do so removes the incentive to maintain vacant units, but is limited by the prospect of discontent among the earlier occupants. Their discontent, in turn, is diminished if the units within the structure are not homogeneous so that rent differentials will not be unambiguous discrimination, but instead may be explained by the owner as related to differences in space or amenity among the several units.

In some situations, such as resort areas or college towns, seasonal fluctuations in the general level of demand for rental housing must be anticipated. In any rental market, the possibility of vacancy due to competition from new structures must be borne in mind. This means that the vacancy allowance must increase over time if more difficult competition is expected, or it may decrease over time if community demand seems likely to rise more rapidly than competitive supply expands.

It needs to be emphasized that within a certain range the level of vacancy which a rental dwelling will experience depends on operating policies of the owner. The owner's self-interest and personal perception of the market may lead to high vacancy for one and low vacancy for another.

Information concerning rent levels which can be achieved in a particular structure, and the vacancy and upkeep factors which are associated with each relevant segment of the rental market, must be drawn primarily from the current experience of the market. For already existing buildings, historical or reproduction costs are not meaningful determinants of rent levels, since obsolescence, changes in incomes and spending patterns among renter households, and changes in the "tightness" of rental markets may cause present rents to differ substantially from rents which previously justified a particular form of construction. Comparisons drawn from the present market—rents paid for similar dwellings —must serve as the basis for estimating the gross income of the property.

Either of two approaches may be taken to the task of rent comparisons.* One involves the identification of generally similar dwellings, preferably bracketing the property in question in each significant respect—size, condition, location, neighborhood, and other amenities. Rents established for each of these comparison units, and the direction of recent rent changes then provide a range within which a feasible rent schedule for the property under study may be established. Recent rent experience for the property itself is very important, but this rent may reflect management abilities or interests which are not typical of the market or not similar to those of the prospective purchaser. A broader view of the market is always warranted (unless, of course, the property at hand is leased or subject to some form of rent control).

A major difficulty with this approach is that there may be some impending shifts in the market which will bring a different type of renter household into the type of dwelling which is being studied. The alternative method of examining rental accommodations currently enjoyed by several types of renter households in the community not only reveals relationships between various

* The following paragraphs represent a re-interpretation of customary practices of real estate appraisal. For a description and discussion of these practices, see Paul F. Wendt, *Real Estate Appraisal* (New York: Henry Holt, 1956), or such texts as Alfred A. Ring, *The Valuation of Real Estate* (Englewood Cliffs, N.J.: Prentice-Hall, 1963).

housing amenities and rent levels, but also may disclose pressures or vacuums in markets for slightly different types of dwellings which foreshadow changes in the market for the property under consideration. For example, if rents are creeping up in a nearby district of lower-rent, but less well-maintained buildings, then the prospect of a shift "downward" in the market for the present building must be considered.

One approach, then, is to find units bracketing the characteristics of the unit under study, but serving a single segment of the market. The other approach is to find comparison units which bracket that segment of the market. The second approach may involve a more extensive study, but is likely to produce much greater understanding of the operating alternatives for a building under consideration for purchase.

Information about operating costs and vacancy can be developed in the same way—i.e., via a study of comparison dwellings. However, a somewhat more analytical approach makes good sense. Taxes and insurance costs, costs of heating, and similar items may be peculiar to the individual building and relatively fixed, so that such costs associated with other buildings may not be relevant. Vacancy and maintenance costs may be influenced by the peculiar features of the property under study, but the range of rent-vacancy-maintenance mixes which are feasible alternatives for this property can best be determined by empirical study of the broader rental market.

The output of this collection and analysis of information is a set of alternative operating plans. At the extreme of simplicity is the owner-occupant's plan which recognizes the serviceability and amenity of the dwelling as "income" and the estimate of tax, maintenance, and other costs as operating expenses, with no alternative uses of the property considered. The prospective rental proprietor should consider several possible markets to be served, each with its peculiar mix of rent, vacancy, maintenance, and other costs—including whatever uncertainty surrounds any of these items. In a fairly volatile market situation the list of alternatives should have a time dimension as well, indicating, for example, that the property may be operated in a certain fashion for a while and then shifted to a different scheme.

Process *B* selects one "best" operating plan from among these alternatives. The criterion may be very simple if the long-term implications of the several alternatives are similar in principle. That is, the alternative which produces the greatest net income may be selected. The prospective purchaser's criteria may be more complex, however, if the burden or opportunity of subsequent capital expenditures on the property differ greatly for different operating plans (as, for example, the expectation that additional parking space or an additional bath should be provided later). The financial implications of the operating alternatives may also differ, producing different opportunities for mortgage loans (often less available for low-income, undermaintained structures) or tax advantages, with consequent variation in financial outcome for the owner.

The complex situation in which operating alternatives involve capital and financial alternatives may be attacked in either of two ways. We may try to reduce all three aspects of the problem to a single set of simultaneous equations. Even conceptually this is difficult, so the practical value of such an elegant approach might generally be limited. The other approach is to select two or more of the most promising alternative operating plans and follow each through to the ultimate description of financial results, finally selecting that operating approach which produces the best capital and financial outcomes.

Since the operating plan is by nature relatively short-term, however, the current net-income criterion has much practical merit. External forces are likely to alter the long-term ownership strategy—occasioning redevelopment or sale of the property, perhaps, before the expectations of a complex, long-term operating plan can be realized.

THE CAPITAL PLAN

Process *C* is the translation of the short-term operating plan into an estimate of current property value. Two steps are involved. The net income as forecast must be capitalized into a present value, and to this must be added the present value of the property when the income stream ceases, the latter value often being given the name "reversion," or "reversionary value."

Capitalization of income is a familiar and thoroughly mathematical operation, and numerous precalculated tables are available. The formula for the present value of a series of net-income receipts, say, I dollars per year, with the first payment due one year from now and continuing for a total of n payments, discounted to the present at discount rate r is:

$$PVI = \sum_{i=1}^{n} \frac{I_i}{(1+r)^i}$$

in which the symbol i designates a particular year in the sequence. This formula applies even when the income payments are not all in the same amount, though tables of present value generally assume a constant level of income.

The formula also is useful for finding the present value of the reversion, R, which will be received when the property is sold at the end of the nth year, or otherwise realized at that time. In reversion, however, only one payment is expected, so the summation sign, Σ, is not needed. The combined value of income and reversion can be written compactly as follows:

$$PV = \quad PVI \quad + \quad PVR$$

i.e. $$PV = \sum_{i=1}^{n} \frac{I_i}{(1+r)^i} + \frac{R}{(1+r)^n}$$

The significance of discounting is the assumption that a dollar of future income is less valuable today than a dollar of present income. This preference for today's money over money to be received in the future is usually explained in terms of natural impatience, plus whatever uncertainty there may be concerning the actual receipt of money in the future or doubts about our ability to enjoy it when received. Thus, the promise of $1.10 one year from now may seem worth only $1.00 today, in which case the implied discount rate is 10 percent, for,

$$\$1.00 = \$1.10 / (1.10)$$

at simple interest. If we consider 10 percent the proper discount factor given our individual preferences for present over future money and our assessment of the risks involved, then we would be warranted in paying no more than $1.00 for the promise of $1.10 one year from now.

The discount factor which is appropriate in process C is a market rather than a personal rate. What is desired at this stage of the analysis is a perspective on the worth in the market of the entire property. The prospective owner's evaluation of that worth is not as relevant as his evaluation of the equity—which is to be determined at a later stage. Thus, a property with a net income (assume, for simplicity, that it is perpetual and that there is no reversion) of $10,000 per year and with an asking price of $100,000 is not necessarily to be rejected by a prospective purchaser whose personal discount factor is 20 percent. Financial terms may limit his initial equity to $20,000 and provide him with net income of more than $4,000, making it at least a reasonably acceptable investment.

The market discount factor can be determined by observation and, indeed, what is desired is a judgment of what the general trend among residential investors seems to be. Evidence may take the form of discount rates or of rental "multipliers" which imply particular discount rates.

The rate which is chosen represents a combination of factors, principal among which are the "pure" or "riskless" rates of return, such as the rate on long-term government bonds, and a risk factor appropriate to residential real estate in general and to the particular property in question. It is common to identify the components of the discount rate in this manner, adding the several elements to obtain the total rate which is to be used. The factor of illiquidity—reflecting the difficulty of disposing of housing property—is often separated from other aspects of risk, and a separate factor for "management" (of the investment, not of the property) is frequently specified.

An alternative method of arriving at a discount rate is to make a weighted average of the returns expected by suppliers of different portions of the purchase price of a normally financed property. Thus, if a $100,000 property would usually be financed by an $80,000 mortgage loan at 5 percent and equity investment of $20,000 for which 10 percent return would usually be expected, the weighted average discount rate would be 6 percent (80/100 x 5 plus 20/100 x 10).

It is mathematically incorrect to incorporate an allowance for "depreciation" or for "return of principal" in the discount factor. The fact that a given property's usefulness may diminish over the years and eventually disappear is adequately reflected in the forecast of net income and reversion, against which the discount factor is to be applied. Capitalization establishes the net worth of specified future receipts, and if it is properly done, it determines the price that could be paid for a potentially "wasting asset" while producing the required rate of earning on investment. To show the decline in productivity in the income forecast and also in the discount rate is to double-count the loss and thus to understate the investment value of the property.

The value of the reversion means, in principle, the amount which can be expected to result from the sale of the property when the economic life of the present improvement comes to an end. To determine such a value requires, first of all, some estimate of how long that economic life will continue, but this information is presumably provided by the short-term operating plan. In addition, we need to establish what the probable next use of the land will be; this must come from knowledge of the direction of land use changes in the immediate area, projected to the time of the reversion. Then the value of land for such use at that time must be estimated; this can be done by supposing that land so used at the present correctly indicates, through a study of the factors likely to change its value, what the value of the reversion will be. Finally, as indicated before, a discount factor must be applied to this reversionary value when it is added to the present value of the income stream. The sum is the estimated present market value of the property.

Process *D* represents analysis of this capital value and related information to produce a projected "life history" of the values contained within the property and the aggregate sums which will be paid out to realize that value. Paul Wendt has done an interesting, quantitative exposition of this entire process.[4] The asking price of the property provides one important datum, for this—or something related to it—will be the initial total outlay to establish ownership. Other aspects of the capital plan include forecasts concerning capital alterations and their effects upon capital value over the lives of successive improvements on this land, and the sequence of uses separated by demolition of one improvement and the construction of another. The construction costs of these succeeding structures also fit into this long-term capital plan, not only for the property as it stands, but as far into the future as practical foresight enables us to see.

The purchaser of real property may or may not be aware that the residual land value which helps to determine the market value of his purchase implies a forecast of successive uses of the land and the value of such uses. Because of the uncertainty surrounding such forecasts and, of course, because of the large time discount which applies to the more distant changes in use, this residual value may be only a very rough approximation of real future values. Nevertheless, if the purchaser is able to grasp the long-range opportunities associated with the property to be acquired, he may obtain considerable advantage in his negotiations. On the other hand, if he fails to understand the land-use changes implicit in the property's present value, he may experience substantial disappointment with his purchase.

Just as the value of the existing use is the present value of the income stream which it is expected to produce, the residual land value is the present worth of the income expected from a subsequent use or uses of the land, less the capital costs required for implementing the later use.*

Some symbols will make this discussion more precise. We can express the present value of the property, V, as the sum of the present value of the first or current use's income, I_1, and the present value of the first reversion, R_1, or:

$$V = I_1 + R_1$$

The value of the reversion is itself a property value with similar components, in addition to which the construction cost of the second use of the land must be considered. Remembering that all terms are defined as discounted to the same point in time,

---

* The following discussion is a condensation of the author's *Aspects of Housing Demand,* Ch. IV.

"now," we can say, concerning the value of the first reversion, that:

$$R_1 = I_2 + R_2 - C_2$$

where C_2 is the cost of constructing the building which will follow the present use.

The values of R_2, R_3, etc. can be expressed in a similar fashion.

This permits us to define property value without explicitly employing the concept of "reversion." This value is simply the sum of all future income streams less the capital costs needed to realize these incomes, all appropriately discounted to the present. The existing improvement has no capital cost, since its resources represent "sunk" capital. The expression we are seeking is:

$$V = \sum_{i=1}^{\infty} (I_i - C_i), \qquad C_1 = 0.$$

The subscript i indicates a discrete land use, not, as often in similar-appearing expressions, a particular period of time.

Thus, the present market value of property is, at least in theory, a value derived from anticipation of a chain of specific events, the operation of the present improvement over a definite period of time, the demolition of the improvement at the end of that period, the construction of a particular type of new improvement at a specified cost at that same time, the operation of the subsequent improvement at particular net income levels during its own economic life, and so on perpetually into the future. The purchaser of existing property is acquiring the opportunity, or perhaps even the obligation, to develop and operate the land itself many times over in the future.

The discount factor reduces the immediate value significance of even major errors in forecasting land use changes if these changes are to occur in the distant future. At a discount rate of 6 percent, a value or difference in value of $100,000 forty years from now has a present value of only $9,722. This significance will increase, however, during each year that the present purchaser continues to own the property, and when the time comes to sell the property, its value will depend more heavily upon those prospective later uses of the land which seem so remote at the time of purchase. At 6 percent, the same $100,000 future value is worth $17,411 after the property has been held for ten years. This does not mean that today's purchaser should pay more for the property but, rather, that he should consider whether he is well enough informed to manage the disposition of the asset in the market which will subsequently be appropriate to it. A home which is in an area almost certain to remain residential for the distant future is in this sense different from a home in an area likely to see complex commercial or public land-development activities, even though the latter are two or three ownerships away.

In a more immediate sense, the economic life of the existing improvement may end within the period of ownership contemplated by today's purchaser. It will be necessary for the owner to recognize that the time for demolition and redevelopment has come and to undertake this. The criterion for demolition can be defined in the same terms as the above expression for value, since the effect of demolition and redevelopment should be an increase in that value. The following expression defines the value, V^*, of the property on the assumption that the existing improvement is to be demolished at once and replaced with an improvement designated by the subscript 2:

$$V^* = \sum_{i=2}^{\infty} (I_i - C_i).$$

If V, in the preceding expression, is calculated on the basis of a continuation of the present use, then the test for immediate demolition is:

$$V^* > V$$

for unless the total value of the property is increased by immediate redevelopment of the land, it is in the owner's interest to retain the existing structure. However, the capital plan must contemplate a point in time at which V^* will exceed V, and, hence, a time when the current improvement must be demolished.

Again, the reason for such foresight is not so much that it can affect present value, but more that it tells the prospective purchaser what the nature of his ownership responsibilities will be.

This demolition criterion also implies that structures with some remaining usefulness may be destroyed because it is in the interest of their owners to redevelop the land. Conversely, properties which seem quite "obsolete" or ill-suited to the land they occupy may continue in use because they have not yet passed the microeconomic demolition test. Interesting questions of public policy are raised by either; these questions will be discussed in the following chapter.

The relationship between the physical condition of a structure—its state of repair—and its economic life-expectancy is fairly complex, even from the point of view of an owner's narrow self-interest. The possibility of shifting a structure to a less and less demanding market may, as we have seen in earlier examples, encourage the owner to carry the property well beyond the point at which it has ceased to be attractive to the original class of occupants, even causing him to accelerate the physical demise of the building by reducing "normal" maintenance activities. On the other hand, a shift in the local land market may cause the time of succession to arrive suddenly, resulting in the demolition of a structure still in its physical and architectural prime.

If shifts to less demanding markets are not rewarding and if, in addition, there is no sudden upsurge in the demand for land for other uses, the physical condition of the property is a relevant influence upon the structure's economic life. In such circumstances, the acquiring owner must obtain information about the approximate date when the present structure will cease to be attractive to the market segment which it presently serves. This will be a function of physical deterioration and various forms of obsolescence in some combination.

Physical deterioration or obsolescence in style or function may be arrested by capital expenditures, renewing the attractiveness of the property—perhaps to the extent of shifting it into a more demanding market segment. The desirability of capital improvements is tested in a manner very similar to that for demolition and redevelopment. That is, the effect of the capital expenditure must be to produce an increase in total property value greater than the amount of the expenditure. The process of capital improvement may be regarded as equivalent to demolition and redevelopment, for analytical purposes.

One aspect of capital improvement which may be obscured by the immediate problem of designing and financing it is its impact upon subsequent changes in land use. That is, demolition of the present use may, and presumably will, be delayed as a result of the renovation of the existing structure. In turn, subsequent land uses may be altered, at least with respect to timing and perhaps with respect to the nature of those later land uses as well. This, in fact, can be a major deterrent to capital improvement, for the postponement of attractive, pending, new land uses can seriously detract from the present value of the property. To employ a familiar analogy, we may hesitate to resole an old pair of shoes if we wish, and expect shortly, to acquire a new pair. The delay in enjoying the new is a cost which must be added to the resource cost of repairing the old.

Capital improvement, in effect, inserts a new form of land use between that which presently exists and that which is expected upon the expiration of the economic life of the present structure. Such expenditure pushes the whole structure of subsequent redevelopment and operation further into the future, a process which in itself lowers the property's present value. The near-future gain in net income from the capital improvement, however, may more than offset this loss and the cost of the improvement.

Another manner in which use-succession may be deferred is by holding the property vacant, with the structure either demolished or standing idle, for a period of time necessary for the nearest redevelopment opportunity to "mature." Often there may be a reasonable expectation of major increase in the productivity of a parcel of land, for example, in its use for a retail store, but the market conditions or other factors (such as zoning) which will make such a change feasible will not appear for some time after the economic life of the present improvement has ended. That is, vacancy may be a form of land use, with its own place in the expected pattern of use-succession for the property under consideration. Unrentable properties may continue to exist, or cleared land may stand vacant, pending the proper moment for the institution of the new use. Short-term uses for urban land are not common, for a variety of reasons, including public regulation and the difficulty of providing short-lived structures which can compete with more conventional, durable buildings.

A prominent source of delay in redevelopment, and hence a reason for the existence of substantially unused structures or cleared land, is the characteristic of residential land markets which makes the opportunity for one owner dependent upon the nature of surrounding developments. It may be logical to expect, for example, that the next use of land on which an unrentable old dwelling stands is a small apartment building for middle- or upper-middle income families. However, such families may not be willing to consider such a building if it is situated among a cluster of similarly unrentable old dwellings. Until a wave of rebuilding activity sweeps over the entire district, the practical choice of the individual owner may be to wait, to hold off on the next stage of the land's history of uses.

The appraisal term "highest and best use" can now be interpreted with somewhat more fullness than might be found in the layman's understanding of the term. The capital plan envisaged by the prospective purchaser involves various uses of the existing structure for some period of time, followed by a sequence of changes in land use. Within the economic life of a given structure, opportunities for supplementary capital expenditures are likely to arise. A physical life history of the property—and particularly of the land—is projected into the remote future, selecting that chain of events which at the moment of purchase seems to promise the maximum benefit to the owner. At some phases this optimal capital plan may require active disinvestment in the structure, allowing it to adapt to uses of a different order, or the plan may require intervals of idleness and apparent neglect. The condition of the improvement at any moment of time, or the current level of gross rents, do not form the basis of the owner's view of "highest and best use." In his view, that phrase means a plan of successive uses, each anticipating the uses to follow. What the property is at the moment is much less important than what the property is in a condition to become.

The output of process D is the capital plan. This is a forecast of property value and capital expenditures as far into the future as it seems reasonable to peer. In its early stages the plan must be consistent with the short-range operating plan already selected. In its entirety it provides information essential for the development of a financial plan and, ultimately, for the decision concerning the purchase of this particular property. One significant and relatively concrete item in the capital plan is the acquisition price, as this heavily influences the owner's investment base against which the benefits of ownership are to be compared.

The capital plan which first appears out of process D may be treated as a "benchmark" plan only. Its purpose is to provide inputs for the financial plan which will really determine the worth of the property to the prospective purchaser, as distinguished from its value to the market in general. Considerations about finance may suggest that portions of the capital plan, or, indeed, aspects of the short-term operating plan, are not optimal for the would-be purchaser. If so, a new look must be taken at these preliminary plans with the possible result that the financial outcome might be improved by revising either or both of those plans.

The benchmark capital plan serves its purpose best if it is drawn up as a picture of what the present market of housing users and housing investors sees as the opportunities latent in the property under consideration.

THE FINANCIAL PLAN

The financial plan interprets the operating and capital forecasts into terms directly relevant to the decision regarding purchase. Housing is relatively complex as an investment good, just as it is from the consumer's point of view. It produces a variety of useful results and these may be secured in a combination of different ways. Analysis of financial options is indispensable if the prospective purchaser is to conserve his own resources and maximize his gain.[5]

In brief, the financial plan must indicate how much debt is to be incurred against the property and how this indebtedness will affect the income and asset positions of the owner. Taxes levied against the income from the property (as distinguished from taxes on the value of the property itself, which are considered as operating costs) may also affect financial outcomes in an important way, and these effects would be part of the financial plan.

An owner who pledges his property to secure a debt will often find the earning power of his equity enhanced as a result. For example, suppose a property can be purchased for $100,000 and will produce annually a net income of $8,000. This would represent a return (ignoring depreciation) of 8 percent if the purchaser used only his own funds. If a mortgage loan of $70,000 at 6 percent interest were obtained, this loan interest would consume $4,200 per year (assuming no amortization), leaving $3,800 as a return on equity of $30,000, or more than 12 percent. As long as mortgage financing is available at less interest than the inherent rate of return produced by the property as a whole, it is advantageous for the owner to "leverage" his purchase—that is, to employ a small equity to control the income from a large property. (Depreciation and amortization do not affect this outcome.)

The purchaser who has funds to be invested equal to the full acquisition price of the property sacrifices the earning power of those funds if he neglects an opportunity for leverage. In the above example, the purchaser might be able to make similar investments in additional properties so that his entire $100,000 was in this type of equity, producing perhaps in excess of $12,000 yer year.

The purchaser with only $30,000 to invest obviously benefits from leverage in a market consisting of properties priced at $100,000 or more, and the same logic applies to the prospective home owner. Access to long-term credit provides real economic benefit to housing purchasers, regardless of motive.

Many investors are less concerned with a percentage rate of return on their investment that they are with the increase in the value of their equity. This is particularly true in the housing market, among both homeowners and the purchasers of rental property. Mortgage terms usually require or permit repayment of the indebtedness before the end of the expected income-producing lifetime of the property, so that some or all of the operating net income, after mortgage interest, is used to pay off the indebtedness. At some point in time the property is owned "free and clear," and the owner who purchased the property with a limited equity comes into full possession of a substantial asset. Any expectation of an increase in the basic market value of the property during this period, whether it reflects monetary inflation or the normal tendency of urban land to get increasingly scarce, is further inducement to acquire such property regardless of short-term income as a percent of initial cash equity.

It may easily be seen that "equity growth" is a financial benefit from this type of investment which is quite distinct from the conventional investment criterion of a "rate of return." It is not inconceivable that this type of property can be acquired with zero equity, financed with a mortgage equal to the entire purchase price. Any income to the "zero-equity" owner must, in reality, be a "capital gain," an increase in his net worth, for it cannot represent a return on invested capital. (Such view, however, is not shared by the U.S. Department of Internal Revenue.)

Having made an attractive case for leverage, we must now point out some of the pitfalls in placing liens against property. The larger the mortgage on a given property, the more of the net income of the property which will be required to service the mortgage. Debt obligations are contractual and thus fixed over time, while property income fluctuates with the market—with vacancies, changes in operating costs or shifts in rents, etc. Where the equity is "thin" a sharp decrease in net income, even though temporary, may mean the income is not sufficient to meet scheduled payments on the mortgage. Unless the owner can carry the debt from other sources or secure refinancing, the equity, with all its prospective value, may be lost in foreclosure. The purchaser must therefore weigh the advantages of extreme leverage against possible exposure to loss of the equity. If he has sufficient other resources to carry the property through poor times, the purchaser may feel that no substantial risk is involved, but the less favorably situated owner must regard this problem as one of some gravity. For the home owner it is a fluctuation in his own income or earning power which may threaten the equity which has been accumulated or is expected, though if the remainder of the home market is strong, the loss of equity may not be complete.

The opportunity to employ borrowed funds for the purchase of residential property transforms the relatively straightforward operating and capital aspects of the property into financial aspects which may not be obvious at the outset. The outlay of capital sums by the purchaser can be substantially reduced through mortgage financing, operating income will be diverted to debt service, and spendable funds may be received in amounts and at times bearing little relation to the actual employment of the proprietor's own capital. Thus, methods of financing change the outcome of the purchase. The alternative methods of financing which are likely to be present confront the potential owner with an important and complex decision situation.

The basic elements of this situation can be seen in the accompanying simple graphs, Figure 23. Diagram 1 shows the manner in which operating net income is expected to change over the years, information provided by the operating plan previously discussed. At some point in time a capital improvement occurs, an event prescribed by the capital plan, and the consequence of this is an increase in the level of net income. The lower line in this diagram is the amount of debt service required by the financing arrangements. The position and shape of this line depend on the financing terms which are made and these, in turn, should depend on the terms available and the prospective borrower's assessment of the final results which various financing alternatives would produce. For the moment, let us suppose that a particular financing plan has been adopted for study and that the lower line in Diagram 1 reflects the obligations under this plan. The space between the two lines is spendable net income, except for income taxes as we shall next indicate.

Diagram 2 portrays a pattern of income tax costs associated with the property. This aspect of the problem is treated separately because the tax treatment of residential real estate is far from standardized. The situation represented here is basically that under tax laws prevailing in the United States for about the period 1955–1965, and this period is of interest because it saw perhaps the strongest and most direct relationship between in-

I. Operating Expectations

Income
Expense

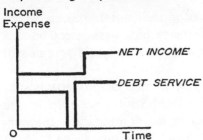

NET INCOME

DEBT SERVICE

O   Time

2. Income Tax Costs

Tax
Cost

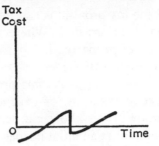

O   Time

3. Cash Income

Income

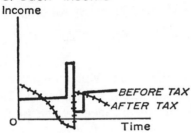

BEFORE TAX

AFTER TAX

O   Time

4. Equity Expectation

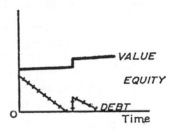

VALUE

EQUITY

DEBT

O   Time

5. Equity Transactions

Recovery and
Realized Gain

+

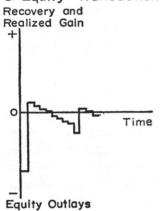

O   Time

−

Equity Outlays

Figure 23
Financial Planning Elements

come tax provisions and investment in residential property which has been created. Where income taxes have less effect on this kind of property, the appropriate revisions of these diagrams will be nearly self-evident.

So long as income produced by residential property is subject to taxation, or expenses associated with ownership of the property are allowable deductions in tax computation, the purchase of residential property will have "tax consequences" which alter what would otherwise be the financial outcome of ownership.* We may define the "tax cost" of ownership, following the broad outlines of procedures in the United States, as follows:

tax cost = tax rate x (net income — depreciation — loan
interest).

The "rate" which enters into the formula is that which applies to the receiver of the income, the corporate rate if the ownership is held in that form, or the personal rate determined by the total income situation of the owner(s). "Net income" is gross income less operating expenses including property taxes, vacancy, and normal maintenance. "Depreciation" is the amount allowable under tax laws, which may bear little relation to loss of economic value and may be substantially higher in earlier years of ownership than thereafter under "accelerated depreciation plans." "Loan interest" means whatever financing charges are allowed as tax deductions. The formula above defines tax cost for a single fiscal period.

The sum of depreciation and loan interest may exceed the net income from the property in a particular year. The tax cost of ownership may then be negative, with resulting "tax shelter" for income of the owner from other sources. In fact, this has proved a powerful inducement for highly leveraged ownership of residential property. Diagram 2 shows the tax cost to be negative in early years, becoming positive as depreciation allowed under "accelerated" plans falls. If capital improvements qualify for favorable depreciation allowances, then the pattern of low or

* This is a very large subject in itself, and several informative publications relevant to taxes in the United States are available, such as Paul F. Wendt and Alan R. Cerf, *Real Estate Investment Analysis and Taxation* (New York: McGraw-Hill, 1968).

negative but gradually rising tax costs may be repeated following such capital alterations, as Diagram 2 indicates.

Loan interest, though often a deductible expense for tax purposes, is only one element of debt service, the other being amortization (if any). Debt service may consume income available from the property, particularly when the advantage of tax shelter from accelerated depreciation is used up, to such an extent that the flow of cash from the property is low or even negative. A simple expression for the cash flow during a single operating period is:

cash income = operating net — debt service — tax cost.

A highly leveraged property with a fairly short amortization period will produce little cash for the owner during the loan term and may even require that owner to supplement the property's own income with money from other sources to meet tax and loan obligations. If the owner is dependent primarily on income from this and similar properties, ownership under such terms will be disadvantageous. Many purchasers, however, may be less concerned with current cash income than with such income beginning, say, twenty years from the date of purchase, treating the property as a form of retirement annuity which will be added to rather than drawn upon for several years after acquisition. Thus, a given property and a given set of tax and financial arrangements may represent a foolish purchase for one individual but a prudent choice for another.

Diagram 3 combines the information of the previous two diagrams. Spendable income before taxes, reflecting operating results and debt service, is shown as a solid line. Cash flow, spendable income after taxes, is shown as a dashed line (to facilitate overlooking it if the underlying assumptions about income tax treatment of residential property do not apply). The end of the amortization period brings a sharp increase in spendable income before taxes. This continues, in our illustrative situation, until capital improvement and the refinancing associated with it increase both operating income and debt service levels. The "after-tax" picture is quite different, with large cash flow in the early years becoming negative in the latter part of the amortization period, but rising again when extensive capital improvements restore the shelter from depreciation.

Diagram 4 shows the time-related changes in the market value of the property as a whole, based upon the capital plan previously elaborated. It also shows the unpaid portion of loans used for acquisition and improvement of the property. The gap between these is a measure of the value of the equity at various points in time. The sense in which equity is used in Diagram 4 is that amount which could be realized by the owner upon sale. Total property value is shown rising over time, suggesting a gain in "land value" anticipated by the market (and embodied in the capital plan) which more than offsets actual economic depreciation of the current structure. Value jogs upward upon the assumed capital improvement, and such change in value must be expected if the prudent owner actually makes a capital improvement. The line indicating indebtedness slopes downward to indicate amortization, but jumps to a higher level when the capital improvement is financed.

Diagram 5 depicts the history of equity capital transactions associated with the property. In the first year a substantial outlay is recorded, representing the purchaser's contribution toward the acquisition price whether in cash or in the surrender or hypothecation of other assets. Since the market value of the equity in our example is shown to be increasing, there is no real need to indicate annual return of capital out of property income. In some sense, however, favorable tax treatment of "depreciation" may provide income in the early years of ownership which refunds initial investment and, in fact, the theory underlying depreciation tax deductions is precisely that they permit invested capital to be recovered. The diagram reflects this theory of the matter and shows some capital repayments in early years. These become negative, however, because depreciation allowances soon diminish, the underlying equity increases in value, and possibly the owner makes additional cash contributions to the property to carry the debt and pay the necessary taxes. If the value line in Diagram 4 were downward-sloping, recovery of equity would have to be provided out of income and this recovery would be shown as positive entries in Diagram 5. Diagram 5 shows additional equity committed at the time of capital improvement, though it is perhaps common to limit such improvements to the amount of available loans.

From Diagrams 3, 4, and 5 the prospective purchaser can foresee the consequences of a decision to purchase the property at hand under a specific set of assumptions about operation, capital planning over the lifetime of the property, and financing. It may well be that a feasible change in one or more of these assumptions would provide a total outcome more to the liking of the would-be purchaser, so the several plans should be reformulated to test the change in assumptions.

These last three diagrams, or equivalent information in some other form, describe separate aspects of property ownership which can be combined into a single index of the wisdom of purchasing it only if many specific assumptions about the purchaser's motivations are introduced. For our purposes it will be best to leave the financial considerations about the property in the relatively flexible form suggested by these three diagrams. The prospective purchaser must consider all three—the ebb and flow of cash, the variation over time of the value of ownership, and the timing of equity outlays and their recovery—in terms of his own circumstances, objectives, and aversions. The final product of these considerations will be a financial plan, specifying the kind of financing arrangement preferred and identifying the several consequences for the owner of his purchase. Multiplicity of development motives has received the attention of American housing economists in recent years.[6]

The financial plan may, as we have illustrated, include a substantial capital improvement during the period of ownership. It might provide for significant refinancing of the property at some point even without additional capital expenditure. It should recognize the possibility, at least implicitly, of demolishing and replacing the existing structure and it should determine, at least tentatively, the point of time at which the property will be sold.

The financial plan of the household purchasing its own home will have the same features in essence. Tax depreciation may not be relevant, but the tax treatment of mortgage interest will be. Return of capital, if required by diminishing value of the equity, must be accounted for in terms of the satisfaction of ownership and use, but these housing services must provide a return *on* equity invested as well. The wisdom of later capital alterations, or of refinancing or sale, must also be given thought.

THE PURCHASE DECISION

This completes our discussion of Figure 22, Process *E*—formulation of the financial plan; the next step is the purchase decision, process *F*. This involves the comparison of alternative purchases, including the retention of assets currently held. Other residential properties which enter into this comparison should be analyzed in the manner described at some length above for an individual property. The comparison may involve alternatives in the nature of financial investment, such as corporate and government securities and deposits in thrift institutions or purchase of insurance or annuities. The comparison may, on the other hand, be in terms primarily of the "investment" of the prospective purchaser's skills rather than of his savings, such as the desire to speculate in attractively priced properties in anticipation of a change in market or financing conditions, or simply the plan of spending one's time physically managing an apartment building. The form and timing of the financial outcome may be more significant to the potential purchaser than the rate of return on equity, as is true for the professional man seeking tax shelter for his high present income from other sources, and accumulation of equity which will begin to produce significant "free and clear" income only some years hence, upon the owner's retirement from his profession.

The essential aspect of the purchase decision, Process *F*, Figure 22, is that the person making it have a realistic view of the complex financial outcome which is possible under each of his purchase alternatives. The development of a "machine" to process this information is less important than the development of the information itself.

If the outcome of the purchase decision is negative, the flow chart suggests that the property at hand be excluded from further consideration at the time. Attention should be directed to other alternatives, including (to repeat for emphasis) the retention of the present set of assets and obligations.

A "yes" response to the purchase inquiry of Process F sets in motion two processes which require little comment in this treatment. Process G (Fig. 22) is the actual purchase, a step which in its usual complexity may inadvertently change some of the significant assumptions about the property. Unanticipated expenses may occur or loan terms may prove to be somewhat different than anticipated. There is a "point of no return" in the purchase transaction and this should be known in advance so that all information and expectations can be brought up to date before the final act is completed. Process H (Fig. 22) implements the operating plan and here, too, care must be exercised to assure that no significant worsening of the results of ownership occurs at the outset by a careless renting program or other sorts of mismanagement.

With ownership established and the property in operation there arises the question as to whether any or all three of the basic plans developed for the purchase decision should be altered for a new major ownership decision. Such thoughts should, in principle, always be in the mind of the owner, for events occur daily which improve or worsen his ownership position and which present him with opportunities to do other than his initial plans projected. In practice, such reformulation needs to be undertaken only when there is some external evidence which suggests that the initial plans are obsolete.

This evidence may be watched for from two directions. The operating experience of the property may show that basic market conditions have changed or are not as initially expected. Outside the property itself there may be a significant change in local demand for housing or in items of cost such as property taxes, fuel, etc. The condition of the mortgage market or the provisions of income tax codes affecting the property and its owner may be changed in important ways. When any of these is known to have happened, then it is appropriate for the owner to commence a series of analyses and decisions which will result in his making significant alterations in the property or in his ownership, or perhaps in ultimately deciding to continue under the initial set of plans. Processes I through Z, Figure 22, trace one possible manner in which the problems raised by a change in circumstances concerning the ownership may be thought through.

Process I indicates a reformulation of the operating, capital, and financing plans under the new circumstances, plus the assumption that no change in the overall "ownership plan" is undertaken. That is, what will occur in terms of the physical condition of the property and its financial results if no action is taken in response to the new external conditions? The outcome of process I is such a set of revised projections.

Processes J, K, L, M, and N prepare operating, capital, and financial plans based upon five principal, alternative types of actions which the owner may take at this juncture. The five types are change in operating plan; refinancing (replacing the original financing, reducing it, or extending it); capital improvement in the present structure together with an appropriate financing plan; demolition and replacement of the present structure; and sale of the property. Two or more variations on any of these types might be considered as separate alternatives. The outcome of all these investigations is a set of alternatives including a "status quo" plan which results from Process I.

A decision may then be reached by considering first the alternative of selling the property as is. This should be done if the sale alternative is the most attractive of those just developed. If the decision in Process O is for selling, then a reinvestment problem may arise which, in effect, is considered in Process N but is here shown separately as Process P.

If the result of O is negative and the property is retained, the next issue is whether to demolish the existing property. Again, this will be done if this alternative is best of those remaining (i.e. refinancing, capital improvement, and change in operating plan) as viewed from the criteria of the owner. A "yes" answer on demolition in Process Q implies that the owner will assume the position of developer. This introduces a new mode of behavior, Process R, which is the subject of the following section.

A rejection of demolition next raises the issue of capital improvement, an alternative considered in Process S by comparison with the results of simple refinancing or simple adjustment in the operating plan. A decision to make capital improvements calls upon Process T to accomplish this and, subsequently, upon Process U to adapt the operating scheme to the new conditions in the most suitable way.

A decision against capital improvement leads to consideration in Process V of simple refinancing versus adjustment to or retention of the original operating plan. A "yes" answer introduces Process W to implement the refinancing and adapt the operating plan. A "no" answer on refinancing leads to Process X which compares an adjusted operating plan (without refinancing or capital improvement) with the original operating plan, always in terms of all three sets of forecasts—operating, capital, and financial—on which ownership decisions are based.

A decision to change the operating plan introduces Process Y to implement the new plan. A decision to retain the original plan reinstates that plan, an action labeled Process Z.

This portrayal of policy review by the owner of a residential property does not exhaust the complications which may be present, nor is it the only manner in which the several alternatives may be compared. It merely illustrates a type of problem organization which represents common aspects of the problem.

Residential Developer Decision Model

Urban land is "developed" when it has some useful structure upon it. "Development" is the process of creating that structure, and this process involves decisions about the "best" type of capital improvement for a particular parcel of land. In the context of residential development this means a choice concerning the basic structural type—single-family house, duplex, small multifamily apartment building, etc. It also means a decision about the economic stratum by which the dwelling or dwellings are expected to be used. The development process itself involves business functions such as negotiating for land and for construction financing as well as dealing with the suppliers of labor and materials for the physical construction of the building.

The "best" type of residential building for a given parcel of land depends on who is making the decision. The housing user—the ultimate occupant—may perform all the functions of development and tailor the new structure to his own needs, though even here the pattern of surrounding land uses and the opportunity to use borrowed funds, among other things, will influence the choice of structure type. Generally the user is rather remote from the immediate development decision and is instead in the ordinary position of a consumer in the market place, reacting favorably or unfavorably to what is available for his use and thus indirectly influencing subsequent housing development.

IS THE DEVELOPER AN INVESTOR?

Development is often thought of as an investment activity, conditioned by the objectives of investors and by the structure of investment markets. Again, the investor in new housing influences development decisions about the type of housing to be built, but only a very special type of "investor" actually makes such decisions. Since the determination of how land is to be used is a proprietary right—a privilege of ownership—the development decision falls upon the owner of the land (or land-use rights, for ground-leased space). If the investor is also the owner of these rights, then he is the developer. However, the very common practice of using borrowed money for the construction of housing and for the purchase of houses in being means that a large portion of investment is separated from ownership and thus from the opportunity to make development decisions directly. The lender, the mortgage investor in a familiar class of situations, has a power to veto his investment if he disagrees with the developer's notion of how the property is to be improved. In this way the lender can influence the owner's decision, particularly if all lenders take approximately the same view about which types of development will be the most appropriate sources of security for loans.

Investment, in the broad sense of advancing funds for the creation of a capital asset, may be shared between lender and owner. It is the owner's contribution of funds which seems to make development an act of investment, for one might suppose that the owner, like the lender, looks upon the property to be created as an income-producing use for his own investable funds. If the equity, or ownership, proportion of the required investment is substantial, then, indeed, development becomes a part of the process of investment and investment criteria such as the maximum rate of return on invested funds will directly determine the "best" use of land which is acquired and perhaps the choice of land for development as well.

There are several reasons why development criteria for housing types may differ from investment criteria. In the first place, the ownership position, and hence the opportunity to select a mode of development, may be acquired with relatively little equity capital. Land may be acquired by means of a purchase-money mortgage, building materials by suppliers' credit, and funds for labor costs from mortgage lenders. When the size of the developer's own capital is the base for measuring the success of the development, the rates of return so calculated are likely to be so high (infinite in the case of zero equity—a not impossible situation) as to be meaningless. The appropriate basis for evaluating the development involves all the developer's inputs into the undertaking, and financing alone may be one of the least important among these inputs.

Second, the owner-developer's financial investment in a particular property may be very short-lived. The funds which he uses may be considered "working capital" rather than part of an income-producing investment portfolio. The main purpose of his equity investment may be to allow him to engage in profitable employment, much as a merchant requires an inventory in order to exercise his skills as a trader. The equity capital may be little more than a license to engage in a trade or profession, the trade itself being the source of gain. When this is true, the developer's equity investment is moved from each project upon its completion—i.e. upon construction and sale of the building—and into the next development undertaking.

The successful developer may accumulate a net worth which in itself requires to be put to productive use; and, beyond a point the opportunity for one developer to employ all his personal financial resources as working capital may not be realistically available. Then the developer, perforce, becomes an investor as well. Though he may decide as an investor to provide long-term debt or equity financing for properties which he as developer has created, the two functions are intellectually separable. The prudent business person recognizes that his personal, creative ability does not necessarily produce things which his personal investment needs require. Investment and development are distinct functions, calling for different criteria, even if they involve a single person and a single property.

The developer is an entrepreneur, and it is the entrepreneurial functions connected with the production of housing which will next be portrayed. The developer is represented as a producer of a commodity for sale. He formulates a plan, assembles resources, manages the transformation of these resources into a product—new housing—and sells that product. His own inputs are his knowledge of the "market," skill in business and legal matters related to the production of housing, knowledge of housing technology and design in a broad sense, and a willingness to bear the risk that his efforts may yield less than was expected. In addition, he may supply some circulating capital.

The "market" of which the developer must have knowledge is three-sided. It involves the users of housing, for their acceptance or rejection of the product he makes is likely to have a great influence on the salability of the developer's product. The product is actually sold to investors, however, either of the equity or lender types, or both; knowledge of the state of competition for investor's funds is another aspect of market knowledge which the developer must possess. Finally, the developer must have intimate familiarity with the rather specialized markets for physical inputs into the housing product and the short-term financing of its production.

Development may result in outputs for the entrepreneur in a variety of forms and combinations of forms. Outright sale of the completed property will produce cash (probably taxable as income) representing the difference between the sale price and all his costs for land, materials, labor, taxes and fees, financing, and marketing. He may "take back" a mortgage (especially a junior mortgage) as part or all of his development gain and the mortgage, in turn, may provide either a deferred and somewhat illiquid and uncertain form of cash, or a source of income for the term of the mortgage. He may retain the equity in the completed dwelling but refinance the property in such a way as to realize most of his entrepreneurial profit in cash. He may trade the equity for other property, particularly for land suited for his next development. He may retain a portion of the equity in the form of a partnership in the completed property or shares of a new corporate entity. He may retain the right to live in the property or a portion of it. The forms in which the developer may realize gain from his activity are many, and each property has some inherent characteristics which limit these options or differentiate among their availability. A type of development which appeals to a broad class of equity investors may, for example, readily produce cash proceeds upon sale but offer little opportunity for trading and less for retaining the right to live in one of the units. The individual developer's income tax position, plus the complex of rules which govern tax treatment of development gains, may affect the manner of disposition in an important way also, for "tax shelter" may be of less value to the medium-bracket developer than to a potential high-bracket purchaser.

Most of the possible forms of developer gain might be translated into the difference between value of the completed property and the sum of all land and development costs. It is reasonable to suppose that the typical entrepreneur wishes to maximize this difference, that is, to develop the property in such a way that per unit of his own resources committed to it the maximum equity value is created. This criterion requires amplification on two counts. First, it must be emphasized that it is the developer's inputs only which serve as the base for measuring profitability, and only the equity in the completed property which is measured against that base. Total costs and total property value are not directly relevant, nor is their difference. The developer's inputs may include some financing but the most significant input cost will probably be the developer's own entrepreneurial skills and knowledge—his capacity to make decisions concerning the property in such a way that his own interests are served.

The second point concerns the measurement of those costs of "management." Clearly, the time dimension must be borne in mind, for a project which takes two years to complete and

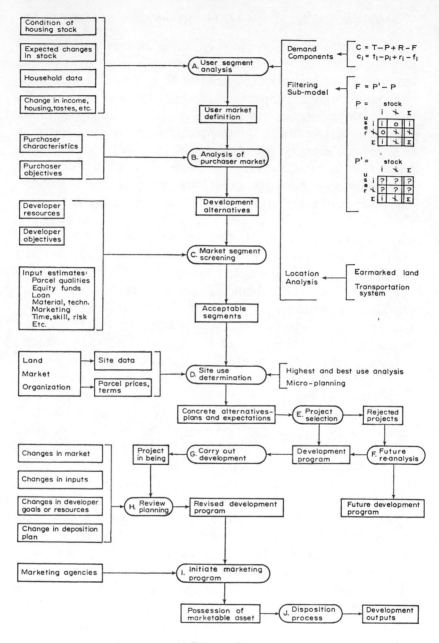

Figure 24
Housing Developer Decision System

yields a gain equivalent to $100,000 may be less attractive to a developer than a one-year project producing a gain of $75,000, assuming that other developer inputs would be the same and that both projects would require the maximum available effort of the developer. Another most interesting assumption is that when the second year begins, a new project producing more than $25,000 for a year's efforts would be available.

The developer who is described by the foregoing comments is ordinarily called a "speculative" developer—one who undertakes the construction of new housing in anticipation of a market for it, a market of users or investors, or both. Thus, the developer owns the product while it is being created, much as an appliance manufacturer owns refrigerators on the assembly line and in the distribution channels. Not all housing is constructed by speculative producers, for governments, financial institutions, and individual long-term investors, including home owners, sometimes prefer to make all possible entrepreneurial decisions about residential property which they intend to own. Entrepreneurial decisions are to be made in the production of all housing, however, and the speculative developer simply represents a specialist in the entrepreneurial side of housing creation. He brings business concepts and methods into the housing market and the value of such approach is an appropriate object to study. Whether the entrepreneurial approach to housing development produces housing which is "best" in other senses remains to be seen. First, however, the characteristics of the entrepreneurial approach must be examined. The flow chart in Figure 24 and the discussion which follows describe this approach in an "idealized" fashion, indicating the several basic areas for decision by a developer, the information which is relevant to those decisions, the output of each analytical or action step, and at least one possible sequence in which the several components of the problem may be handled.

ANALYZING THE MARKET

The first stage, which we might suppose is more or less continuously in the mind of the would-be developer, is familiarization with and analysis of basic information about community housing-user demand and about the stock and flow of housing supply. This means the collection of factual information about the number of households in the community; about the composition of households—the age and sex distributions of household heads; about the size distribution and makeup of households—numbers of children by age, the presence of persons outside the two-generation, parent-child system, etc.; about the income and perhaps the wealth distributions of households; and, about the social characteristics of neighborhoods. It means also information about the manner in which households choose to spend their incomes and use their savings, and about consumer tastes concerning housing—with particular regard for attitudes toward ownership, toward residential density, toward housing location, toward neighborhood amenities (such as schools), and toward particular physical aspects of the housing commodity (such as the amount of space per person or the kind and quality of plumbing fixtures). It means very particular concern about changes in progress or in prospect regarding any of these elements of housing user demand. In essence, the developer needs to know the sources and extent of dissatisfaction with the existing supply of housing. He must, therefore, be aware of the condition of that supply, the way it is distributed, and the ways in which it is changing. The age and location of principal types within the supply are part of this picture. Other parts are the state of repair, the kinds of integral equipment (plumbing, heating, and electric fixtures, for example) in the housing, the convenience of common floor plans, and the amounts of space per person or per household. Residential density and ground area available to household members are relevant information as is the degree to which residential land in each particular neighborhood is insulated from other land uses, yet provided with accessible nonresidential facilities such as shops. The terms on which the housing supply is available to users and the degree of ease with which a household can adjust its housing consumption to a change in housing needs are also aspects of supply which should be within the prospective developer's general ken. Again, it is the changes in these factors which are of particular importance.

This is a rather large order and it might be asked whether the developer can focus his attention on particular segments of the housing market with which he is already familiar or can most easily learn about, thus economizing on information-collection costs. To a limited extent this is possible, but the far-reaching interdependence of segments of the housing market precludes much appealing simplification. Segments which are substantially independent of one another, such as the single-family and apartment markets in most American cities, may still be linked through the use and reuse of land. Geographic segmentation is even less likely unless we are talking about virtually impassable barriers—such as an unbridged river—or two separate communities not actively competing for housing demand. Price segmentation for given structure types is no doubt the least valid of the simplifying assumptions which the tyro developer might think of making, for competition here is often most direct and intense. Segments involving specialized housing requirements, such as elaborate facilities for the convenience and safety of aged occupants, or housing serving a market which is generally excluded from the bulk of the supply, as in the case of minority groups, might permit some simplification of the search for background information.

The basic question is, assuming that the developer has a particular type of housing in mind or a particular area in which he wishes to confine his activities, what other housing in the community is or will become competitive with his projected development? From what types of dwelling units in the existing stock and from which geographic areas will competition for the proposed new housing be felt? Beyond that, these immediately competitive parts of the supply may themselves be under competitive pressure from still other portions of the market, so that many, if not most, of the distinguishable segments of the housing market are directly or indirectly tied together by threads of substitutability—threads either taut or slack, brittle or elastic.[7] In principle, the housing developer needs to know most of the principal facts and trends in the housing market of his community.

Of course, a market system may not only exist, but may even achieve substantial efficiency without imparting comprehensive information to entrepreneurs. The willing but uninformed entrepreneur is free, within limits (such as the availability of credit or zoning), to "probe," to produce a product and see if it sells and, if it does, to see how many more can be sold. There are some important questions about the external effects of entrepreneurial mistakes, which must be left for later. But the venturesome entrepreneur who relies on little more than intuition may contribute innovations of sufficient value to offset some of these external costs, and it is in the nature of an entrepreneurial society that the person with the least official expertise may have the most sensitive "feel" for emerging needs, but he will not be able to prove these needs to a smothering bureaucracy either public or private. Thus, the "entrepreneur" whose thought processes are represented by this flow chart may, in reality, be not one individual, but an entrepreneurial system, without a compact library of urban data, but with hundreds of pairs of eyes, hundreds of curious minds, and a score or two of utopian reformers and con men. The aggregate of their successes and failures over the whole spectrum of opportunities will reveal a pattern of market conditions with greater accuracy, perhaps, than will result from any feasible program of deliberate data-gathering. Such, at any rate, is one view of a "market economy" which applies with rather special logic to the complexities of housing affairs.

The background information thus assembled can be converted into an estimate of market demand for new housing construction in terms appropriate to the developer's situation, by means of the rather complicated process labeled Process A. Two basic sources of demand are considered, the numerical growth of the community—that is, increases in the number of households —and the desire for improvement in housing conditions. The "direct" incidence of such demands are estimated first. Then, by means of a supplementary process, the actual or indirect demands from each source are estimated for the community as a whole. These demands are subjected to a locational analysis which yields the desired description of market demand. Each of these steps will now be described in somewhat more detail.

Growth demand results from an increase in the number of house-using social units, i.e. households, in excess of the number of units in the stock of dwellings. Clearly, if the employment base of the community is increasing, the number of households can be expected to grow. Even without an increase in the total number of persons in the community, changes in customs and economic circumstances may cause additional households to be formed—such as earlier marriages among young people—or older household to persist in the housing market—as in the case of widows who enjoy pensions sufficient to let them retain their family homes so long as health permits them to live independently. From whatever demographic or economic cause, it is necessary to anticipate changes in the number of households— not in total, but in as fine detail of household type as seems relevant. Nor should decreases in certain categories of households—e.g., in the number of lower-income families during a period of economic improvement or in the number of young households two decades after a drop in national birth rates—be overlooked.

Another source of "growth" demand, in a sense, is the loss of dwellings from the usable stock through other means than obsolescence. Fires and earthquakes, floods and windstorms take dwellings from the inventory and leave specific households immediately homeless. The result upon housing demand is much the same as if these families had suddenly migrated into the community. Major disasters may bring associated changes in employment and in income distribution, but "casualty losses" occur constantly on a small scale in every community and so constitute part of the regular requirement for housing production. Losses from the inventory are also occasioned by land-use changes— intentional demolitions of usable dwellings to make room for a different type of building or for some public use such as a highway.

"Direct growth demand" thus means an enumeration of the types and numbers of households which face an immediate need for housing as a result of demographic and economic changes and because some dwellings are removed from the supply.

"Direct improvement demand" means an enumeration of the types and numbers of households having the desire and the economic means to upgrade their housing standards. These households must be identified first by the types of dwellings they presently occupy and secondly by the nature of the improvement anticipated. The immediate source of the demand for improvement may be accumulated obsolescence in the present housing, increases in real purchasing power, a change in tastes regarding housing, or a combination of such causes.

The object at this initial stage in the flow diagram is to identify those segments of the local housing market in which a demand for new units can be expected in the period anticipated by the forecast. Segments are defined in terms of household characteristics such as family type, income, and tenure. The developer wants to know how many new housing units can be disposed of to each of these segments over a certain future period. This period can be any planning period which is meaningful to the developer, though a very long-range forecast, say ten years or more, is likely to involve greater likelihood of error in the basic data than a shorter-range forecast. The developer may wish to make a short-run *annual* forecast—that is, to estimate the number of new units which the market will absorb each year over the next few years. He may make successive one-year forecasts or he may make a single forecast of new construction demand over a period of, say, five years and estimate roughly how that total will be distributed over time. Since an individual developer is likely to meet only a small fraction of the actual annual demand, his rough estimate of the total may be enough to assure him that he will have a good chance of selling what he produces.

The flow chart incorporates some symbols representing a method of identifying new construction demand for particular housing market segments. This is, in effect, a "segment demand model" which formalizes the numerical relationships which translate background data, such as we have already discussed, into forecasts of the opportunity for selling particular types of new housing. At this point the entire community is treated as one market; a further stage considers the separate and very important factor of location.

The first line in this model expresses the components of new housing-construction demand for the community as a whole. The terms are defined as follows:

$C =$ the total number of new housing units which can be marketed—i.e. for which there is user demand

T = the total number of households expected at the end of the forecasting period

P = the total number of households at present

R = the number of occupied units in the present inventory which will be removed during the period, being either demolished or added (net) to the present inventory of vacant units

F = the number of units which will be supplied to one segment of the market from another segment.

To provide a simple numerical example, suppose a community now has 10,000 households and occupied housing units, and that in the next five years we expect the number of households to rise to 11,000, while 2,000 of the present units are either demolished or added (net) to the supply of vacant dwellings. Then:

C = 3,000

T = 11,000

P = 10,000

R = 2,000

F = 0, since the net of transfers from one segment to another must be zero.

Thus, there is an expected market demand for 3,000 new housing units during the period. The developer's basic problem is to determine *what kinds* of new units should be built, i.e. which segments of the community will move into new housing during the period.

The above set of symbols may be construed as vectors—i.e. as lists of numbers pertaining to the several segments of the market, as well as aggregate sums of all segments. Let us focus our attention on one particular part of the community, "Segment i," which may, for example, represent those households which have annual incomes of between $5,000 and $6,000 and may be expected to occupy single-family dwellings. The other segments of the market we can lump together for purposes of illustration as "Segment non-i" or "$\bar{i}$". How many newly constructed dwellings will be purchased (or rented) by Segment i households over the next five years?

The second line in the model on the flow chart expresses the demand for new housing units by the i segment, by lower-case letters and subscripts. To continue the numerical example, we can complete a table of numbers showing all the relevant entries for both segments of the market and the sum of the two segments.

Segment	C =	T —	P +	R —	F
i	500	1,200	1,000	100	(—)200
i	2,500	9,800	9,000	1,000	200
Total	3,000	11,000	10,000	2,000	0

In order to determine C, the market demand for new construction, we must provide numerical estimates for T, P, R, and F, not only for the total of all segments, but for each segment individually. Once the arithmetic of the situation is clear, providing the estimates is the real problem. We may consider them in order.

T, t_i, and t_i are forecasts of the future number of households in the community by characteristics which define the segments under consideration. Thus, our example says that we expect the community to consist of 11,000 households five years hence and that 1,200 of these will fall within the description of Segment i. To make such a forecast we must be able to anticipate changes in the scale and type of employment within the community, changes in the income distribution, and changes in preferences for types of housing as influenced, for example, by the availability of mortgage credit to home buyers. Economic, demographic, cultural, and institutional expectations must be combined to produce segment-by-segment forecasts. Exactly what type of information must be developed depends on the manner in which the several segments are defined, and each data requirement will probably lie within the domain of a specialized study. Economic-base analysis, discussed briefly elsewhere in this book, is an elaborate subject unto itself and is of such general community interest that public or private community agencies are likely to have made such studies, in greater or lesser degrees of refinement. Income-forecasting may be incorporated in the economic base study, linking the various kinds of employment to typical and projected wage levels. Age composition of the population and forecasts thereof are normally available from public statistical documents. Knowledge of trends in housing preferences and in housing credit practices may be well developed but not widely disseminated, being best understood by major public and business participants in housing activities. The types of information germane to the forecast and the sources from which such information may be secured will obviously differ from one community and one period to another.

P, p_i, and p_i are simply the numbers of households now in the community and in the several segments of the housing market. Once the segments are defined, these numbers can be obtained, if necessary, by direct survey. Useful estimates may be garnered from recent public or private surveys, adjusted for changes since the survey date. Problems may arise (particularly in the lack of cross tabulations by desired segment characteristics) in published information.

R, r_i, and r_i are numbers of housing units now occupied which it is expected will be physically unavailable at the end of the forecast period, plus the net increase in vacancy in the presently-occupied stock. "Net" means that a negative figure results when units now vacant are taken up by households.

F, f_i, and f_i are numbers of housing units transferred during the period from one segment of the market to another. This process is often called "filtering" and means that housing which has served one group of the population is "handed down" to another group. Lower-income households, it is often observed, live in obsolescent dwellings originally constructed for a higher-income group. There is no inherent reason why the process cannot work in reverse and, when incomes rise generally in a community, many dwellings "filter up" to higher-income groups even though physical movement of households may not occur, the original occupants simply undergoing a statistical transfer to a higher-income category.

In the aggregate such transfers cancel out and the filtering process does not meet any of the community's total requirement for new housing. The importance of filtering comes in its ability to determine the composition of that new housing construction. One segment of the housing market may expand by thousands of households over a period, but have its entire additional housing demand satisfied by units from another segment. The latter segment, in turn, may make up its loss (if any, for it may have decreased in size) from another segment or segments. The final impact of new housing demand may be considerably removed from the segment which expanded in size. Thus, for the developer who must decide not how many new dwellings the community as a whole needs, but how many of a particular kind he should attempt to place on the market, the filtering process may be of overwhelming significance.

The numerical illustration shows a loss of 200 units from Segment i to Segment $\dot{\imath}$. The former is expected to "sell" (perhaps literally) this many of its present dwellings to other portions of the community. The reasons for this may be several. Increased requirements of other groups may be met more readily by expansion into initial Segment i than by paying the price for new construction. Segment $\dot{\imath}$, for its part, may find that newly built units satisfy its own demands more effectively than some portions of its initial supply. Households within Segment i initially may, through income changes or changes in other characteristics which serve to define the segments, become part of the $\dot{\imath}$ community without physically moving.

In estimating the scale and direction of this and similar filtering changes, care must be exercised to make all such forecasts within the community not only reasonable, but also mutually consistent. For this reason, a filtering submodel is described in the last two expressions of the market-analysis model. The first, $F = P' - P$, expresses the fact that the vector of filtering changes, F, which may also be written $\begin{pmatrix} f_i \\ f_{\dot{\imath}} \end{pmatrix}$, is the difference between P' or the number of housing units presently in each segment which we expect to remain within that segment, and P, or the number of households now in each of the specified segments.

In our numerical example, these terms would have the following values:

$$
\begin{array}{ccccc}
F & = & P' & - & P \\
i \begin{pmatrix} -200 \\ 200 \end{pmatrix} & & \begin{pmatrix} 800 \\ 9{,}200 \end{pmatrix} & & \begin{pmatrix} 1{,}000 \\ 9{,}000 \end{pmatrix}
\end{array}
$$

This says that of the 1,000 dwelling units presently occupied by Segment i households, 200 will shift to a different segment of the housing market in the five-year forecasting period.

With more than two segments, consistency and meaningfulness in the filtering forecast may be protected by regarding P and P' as matrices, the form of which is shown in the final portion of the market-analysis process. Entries in the matrices to reflect our example would appear as follows:

		P' Stock			P Stock		
		i	$i̇$	S	i	$i̇$	S
	i	800	0	800	1,000	0	1,000
User	$i̇$	200	9,000	9,200	0	9,000	9,000
	S	1,000	9,000	10,000	1,000	9,000	10,000

These may be called "stock-user" matrices, for they show the manner in which the stock of dwellings, classified by the market segment of present occupants across the top, is distributed among households, classified by segments along the side. The S columns and rows are summations. The meaning of the P matrix is easier to understand, since it merely states the present arrangement of the housing market, with all 1,000 of Segment i households occupying Segment i dwellings, by definition, and 9,000 $i̇$ households living only in $i̇$ dwellings.

The P' matrix represents a forecast of changes in occupancy of the present stock of dwellings. Only 800 Segment i households will be found in dwelling units presently classified (by the category of their occupants) as Segment $i,$ and the other 200 units of the initial Segment i stock will be occupied by Segment $i̇$ households.

This pair of matrices makes the forecast of filtering quite clear. The occupancy of certain portions of the housing inventory is expected to change in a particular fashion, either because of physical movement of households or because of reclassification of occupants' households. The net effect of such change is that fewer units of the present stock are occupied by Segment i households at the end of the forecast period and more are occupied by households of a different category.

The number of segments may be increased by finer distinctions among household types without overburdening this arithmetical framework. The real task is that of deciding just what the scale and direction of filtering changes will be.

When the output of the filtering model is added algebraically to other demand components, we have a forecast of the demand by users for new housing construction during the forecast period, broken down among all the defined market segments in such a way that the developer can understand, in general, what type of dwellings are required and what manner of households will purchase or rent them. The model thus far does not indicate where within the community such new housing should be built. The next stages of analysis takes the factor of geography into account.

Within a community which has existed for a substantial period of time, each district has acquired attributes which attract certain types of residential use and discourage others. If we suppose that owners of land, wherever situated, want to receive the highest possible price for that land when it is developed (or redeveloped), then the land uses which offer the highest price would have first call upon available land. And presumably those land users—housing occupants, really—who have a choice would select land and location most agreeable to themselves. Parcels of land in districts with pleasant views, favorable historical or social associations, good neighborhood services, and convenient access to other portions of the city are in this way "earmarked" for high-priced residential development. Land with somewhat less to offer in any or all of these respects will be available for middle-range residential development. Lower-priced dwellings will be feasible for the developer in areas with some pronounced disadvantage which discourages higher-income households, such as poor drainage, inconvenient street patterns, obsolete public and commercial facilities, unkempt neighborhood appearance, disturbing mixture of land uses, poor air, lack of attractive greenery, etc.

Earmarking may exist in several other dimensions than price. Districts without attractive elementary schools may have positive attraction for elderly households and, hence, for developments of housing for elderly people. They may also attract young households without children of school age. Land near water recreation areas will appeal strongly to families whose interest lie in this direction and who have the means to enjoy this form of recreation. Other groups will prize housing sites on high ground with an interesting view. Some groups in the population prefer relative solitude above all, and will seek districts which in one way or another afford privacy. Housing developments which are experimental, either in architecture or function, not only may have inherent site requirements, but may also need to avoid areas where the preservation of traditional patterns is priced, for local opposition in various forms may otherwise add to the developer's difficulties.

Multifamily structures serve households which do not prize exclusive ground area and so, by pooling their demands for whatever locational advantage a site may have (i.e. the capacity of a site to substitute for transportation expenses), these households can pay more for a given site than other households can afford. This additional land-purchasing power means that multifamily residential developments can acquire sites which are priced beyond the reach of many or all other types of residential development. The most obvious example is the purchase of obsolescent, but still useful, low-density houses which are then demolished so that apartments can be constructed on the site. The strong land-market position of multifamily housing developers allows them to select land of substantial amenity as well, such as hillside areas or prestigious neighborhoods, as long as other factors do not arise to offset the advantage. Among such other factors are local opposition to the increase in density and traffic, possible loss of economic status, and concomitant loss of neighboring land values associated with placement of multifamily dwellings in established high-amenity, single-family areas. Another deterrent may arise in the marketing of completed apartment units, since the rental or apartment market has traditional methods of communication which narrow its effective range, relying much on direct, visual appeal rather than on description through intermediaries. These factors have long tended to restrict multifamily development to central districts and thus to the redevelopment of land which was built upon in an earlier period of the city's history. If the forces of obsolescence are not strong, however, the central areas will be less available to multifamily housing developers than land on the fringes of the city, leading to a pattern familiar in many European communities.

Expected changes in transportation systems will affect the choice of land for specific developments. Since transportation is usually a more variable circumstance affecting the usefulness of land than other characteristics of land (such as amenity), a particular study of pending alterations in transport facilities or in habits of intracity movement is warranted. Roads or transit systems may improve or deteriorate; proliferation of two-car families may occur; shopping, commercial, and industrial centers may decentralize—all of which will affect the relative usefulness of each particular parcel of residential land. The expansion of the city into hitherto nonurban areas depends quite fundamentally upon transportation factors, though the prior existence or likely creation of basic urban facilities such as water systems and schools may not only bend the pattern of such expansion, but also cause it to occur in a scattered or "leap-frog" manner.

At this stage of the analysis the developer thus knows what types of new housing units can be disposed of to users and where these several varieties of new housing are likely to be located. He has a forecast of feasible developments in sufficient detail to permit him to consider variables arising from his own situation and preferences.

The housing market opportunities identified by the process just described represent effective demand by housing users. The developer, however, in the role assumed for him in this portion of our study, will dispose of his output not to housing users directly, but rather to long-term investors in housing. The latter may, of course, include purchasers who wish to occupy the dwellings themselves, thus combining investment and use functions. Every unit must have a long-term holder, however, and it is the group of such potential owners of newly produced housing who make up the developer's direct market.

Consequently, the user demands for new housing must be interpreted by the developer into investor demands. This means understanding what aspects of housing are of interest to particular types of long-term holders, and recognizing that the several

housing types for which user demand can be forecast offer different attractions to long-term holders. Stable income and modest
opportunity for land appreciation will characterize some types of
housing in some locations. Other portions of the user market will
seem to have management problems but promise generous operating margins for the skillful owner. Tax advantages may be
prominent features of ownership in some properties but less so
in others. The same may be true of basic liquidity or the acceptability of the property for highly leveraged financing.

The developer thus is required to scrutinize each segment of
user demand from the viewpoint of ownership or investment.
When he has grasped the important features of each segment as
they will appear to purchasers of the completed properties, he
needs then to survey the population of potential purchasers, to
see how many are interested in each type of ownership benefits.
This tells the developer how he would have to market any of the
potential new housing projects and whether the purchaser market
for any particular type of new housing would be thin or well-
populated. Knowing this, the developer may decide to limit his
activities to market segments for which he understands the purchaser market and the amount and type of sales effort which will
be required. For example, if properties are sold to relatively unsophisticated purchasers with little credit, the seller (developer)
will be at an advantage if he can offer financing commitments
and has a reputation for quality developments and honest trading.
An inexperienced developer may prefer a market segment in
which purchasers will be able to satisfy themselves of the property's inherent worth by their own knowledge, and will have adequate personal credit to obtain suitable financing without difficulty. Some purchasers will be likely to offer other properties in
trade and, if the developer understands the resale market and its
procedures, he may have an advantage in such a market; lacking
such special capacities, another developer would fare poorly in
such a market segment despite a strong demand for the new
dwellings from users. The intervention of the purchaser between
the housing developer and the final market for housing, the
user, adds another dimension to the analytical and data problems
of the developer, shown as Process *B* in the chart (Fig. 24),

but in return, may assist him in selecting the market segment in which he will operate most successfully.

The output of Process B is a description of the several market segments for which user demand was previously seen to be present, with additional information regarding ownership appeal and necessary marketing effort for developments of each feasible type. This list may be somewhat narrower than the input list of user-demand segments, because the developer's desire to avoid certain marketing problems may have eliminated portions of the user market from consideration. It is now necessary to narrow the list further—indeed, for the developer to select the market segment (and the geographic area) in which he will work.

INPUT-OUTPUT ESTIMATIONS

The next step is a more exact study of each development alternative, identifying specific input requirements and judging them against the developer's own abilities and objectives. What is already known at this stage is the nature of the market to be served, including the general, physical aspects of the dwellings to be constructed. What needs to be made clear next is the complete bill of materials and services required to produce such dwellings, plus comprehension of the business procedures necessary to transform these inputs into completed products.

The physical production of the building, perhaps including preparation of the site, may be put in the hands of one or more contractors.[8] The developer's principal tasks and personal inputs are selection and negotiation with the contractor, participation in selection of materials and layout, and proprietary supervision of the contractor's activities (meaning that the developer should try to be sure the builder does what he is supposed to do).

The developer may himself play the role of contractor, being directly responsible for all or part of the physical process of construction. Indeed, it may often be said more appropriately that established contractors choose to play the role of developers; skill in the building trades often leads to participation in development ventures because the contractor learns to perceive development opportunities. Two sets of skill requirements exist, however, whether one person or two are required.

Land requirements for specific developments include considerations of minimum and, perhaps, maximum lot or parcel size. Some types of housing developments permit the use of irregularly shaped lots or lots which are not level. Distance from particular facilities such as a rapid-transit stop may be of great importance for one type of housing development (such as one intended for elderly residents) but not for another. Each market opportunity has some specific limitations on the kind of land which can be used and may impose certain types of costs to prepare land. A study of these requirements enables the developer to visualize the completed property more effectively and to prepare for the search for sites on which to carry out his development program.

Time and financing inputs also tend to vary with the nature of the development. Land acquisition and construction-period financing present different sorts of problems, depending on the type of market segment to be served. An expensive, custom-built home or luxury apartment may move so slowly through development that substantial interest accumulates on funds expended and much attention must be given by the developer to each variation of materials or performance from his initial concept. The search for land may also be time-consuming for specialized types of housing and bargaining for land may prove critical in determining the overall profitability of the development. These problems must be anticipated by the developer and incorporated into his more exact evaluation of the several opportunities among which he has still to choose.

Changes in input requirements, particularly those affecting land, building design, and financing features (both for construction and marketing) may significantly alter the developer's perception of market opportunities, placing some apparently available market segments virtually out of reach or bringing some doubtful market opportunities into an attractive new light. There is thus a degree of feedback between the market analysis previously discussed and the description of development input requirements. Generally, the market analysis should reflect recent major changes in housing input requirements of whatever sort, material, technology, financing, land, marketing, or entrepreneurship. Assumptions implicit in the market analysis can and should be re-examined at the stage of input analysis, possibly requiring a revision of market estimates.

Process C (Fig. 24), which is called "segment screening" in the flow chart, converts relatively specific input requirements for each type of marketable new dwelling into a description of the task which the developer will face in producing that type. At this stage, the time, skills, and equity funds he must contribute and the risks he must bear must take fairly definite form in his mind. The results of each type of development for his own position can also be anticipated in general outline at this point. The probable timing, the amount, the taxability, and the liquidity of his earnings should begin to emerge from the shadows. Giving attention to his own strengths and weaknesses, he may decide that some segments of the residential construction market would be well within his capacities, while other portions would represent a perilous misapplication of his resources. Taking into consideration the form of the developer's inputs and the form of the developer's outputs, he can now produce a limited list of development alternatives which lie within his area of competence and meet his general objectives for earnings.

The actual earnings of the developer from a particular undertaking will depend, in part, upon the price paid for land. If land prices and characteristics can be determined in advance of actual purchase, then these factors may be considered as part of the information input for Process C in Figure 24. Often, though, the price of land and the terms available for its purchase are set only in the process of actively shopping for that land, so that relatively firm land costs may be unknown until at least options or, perhaps, actual titles to property are acquired. Process D is inserted into the flow chart, Figure 24, to describe the search for and selection of land, implying also the selection of a definite development plan—i.e., the decision about the segment of the user market which the developer will attempt to supply.

The essential new informational inputs for this process are, of course, the characteristics of the several sites which are currently on the market and the prices and terms for which they can be acquired. These prices and terms may become "firm" only when negotiations have reached an advanced stage, so that Process *D* includes active efforts on the developer's part to secure information of this sort. The organization of the local land market, however—meaning the business and public institutions which serve to communicate information about properties which are on the market—may substantially amplify the developer's own efforts to learn about available sites for residential building.

Two important analytical problems arise in Process *D*. One may be called the issue of "highest and best use," meaning that land offered to the developer may really be better suited to uses which he is not currently contemplating. The other problem is that of adjusting generalized housing plans developed in Process *C* for specific sites which the developer decides he may be able to use; this second problem may be called "microplanning."

Sites available for residential development may not necessarily be suitable for the kind of improvement which the developer has in mind. Indeed, they may be best suited for some nonresidential use. An interesting question arises as to whether it is prudent for the developer to improve any parcel to other than its "highest and best" use. This concept, widely used by appraisers, ordinarily means that use which results in the greatest "residual" value of the land—residual value being defined as the difference between the market value of the completed property and the cost of the improvement. Thus, if a building which costs $75,000 to construct results in a property with a market value of $100,000, the residual value of the land so used is $25,000. Of the several ways in which a given parcel of land may be employed, one will produce the maximum residual value. From the landowner's point of view, that is the highest and best use.

A developer acquiring land for residential development of a specific type may learn that the land he has come to own would have a greater value if used for some other purpose than he himself intends to carry out. Suppose, for example, that he had purchased the site for $20,000, and that its residual value with his contemplated improvement would be $30,000, but the residual value in some other, perhaps nonresidential use, would be $50,000. He would be most prudent to sell this land—which was presumably underpriced when he bought it—unless three conditions are met. First, there may be no other land available to him for his contemplated development. Second, the expected gain from his development may be greater than the profit he could actually realize from reselling the property, due perhaps to a poorly organized land market. The third condition is that he is not able to carry out the highest and best development himself.

Land for which the highest and best use is of the type contemplated by the developer needs to be screened for its potential residual land value, so that the property having the greatest excess of residual value potential over acquisition price can be identified. In a well-organized land market, the price of land for generally similar development purposes would be similar in comparable locations, so the developer may perceive similar "land-value profit" potential (residual value less acquisition price) on several sites. This will provide him with an opportunity for bargaining or for selecting the site which most closely corresponds with his physical building plans.

The nature of highest and best use is often subject to some misunderstanding which can be clarified at this point. For example, if a given site is capable of being developed in three ways, A, B, and C, we might have the following situation:

	A	B	C
Cost of Building	$40,000	$60,000	$80,000
Market Value	60,000	85,000	95,000

Many casual commentators on urban affairs assume that the building which is most expensive (or of best quality) is the best use for any site. Plan C, above, would probably seem to be the most "intense" and perhaps the most attractive use for the site, for it involves the most costly building. However, C provides a residual land value, the difference between market value of the completed property and the cost of the building, of $15,000, whereas A provides a residual of $20,000 and B provides $25,000. On the basis of residual value, C is least attractive. "Highest and best use" does not necessarily mean the most elaborate building, for circumstances of location and environment might make the more expensive property more difficult to sell.

Another misunderstanding concerns the basis for measuring

residual value. Plan A's residual of $20,000 is 50 percent of the cost of the building, while B's residual is 42 percent of its building cost. It might seem that A, providing the highest percentage return on the invested cost of the building, is the preferred use. Such is not true, for percentage returns are appropriate for determining the use of capital, while the question at hand concerns land. The land input is the same for any of the three uses, so the landowner would prefer that use which gives him the highest dollar price, or residual value if he retains the property through development. Thus, B is the "highest and best use" of the land in question. The cost of the building includes the cost of money borrowed at its own market rate and the payment for the use of money is not the residual value of the land. The prudent landowner in this case should set a price on his land as close as possible to $25,000, thus excluding uses A and C.

Still another misunderstanding arises when land considered for a new development has an obsolete but still income-producing improvement upon it. Suppose that the land in our illustration was currently occupied by an obsolete building with income valued at $30,000. To demolish the building in favor of some new and more attractive use would mean the sacrifice of $30,000 in value and this amount would have to be added to the "building" cost in our example. This would reduce even the most promising of these alternative new developments, Plan B, to a money-losing proposition. An obsolete building may represent the "highest and best use" of a parcel of land. Further obsolescence would ultimately bring its value below the residual land value as calculated in our example, so that a succession of land uses would ultimately occur, and at that time, if market conditions remain unchanged, the new use would be Plan B. The concept of highest and best use rations land over time as well as among competing development programs.

MICROPLANNING AND DEVELOPMENT OPERATIONS

"Microplanning" means the adoption of specific construction designs and input details. Until land is identified as available for and suited to the general type of development planned, precise architectural planning may not be feasible, for individual sites may require or suggest variations from more or less standard forms. The placing of the building on the lot and the design for improvements outside the building proper (walks, shrubbery, etc.) may be influenced by characteristics of the lots available. Exterior building design may be influenced by the neighborhood, either conforming on behalf of protecting a neighborhood "image" or seeking contrast for the sake of attention. Each element of the building itself presents problems of choice as to the quality of structural materials and fixtures, of color scheme, etc. Choices involving greater or lesser expense should be made, in principle, on the basis of marginal contribution—that is, selecting those components which add to the value of the building more than they cost. Choices without cost differences can be made in favor of the material or design or combination of elements which adds most to the final value.

The output of Process D (Fig. 24) is a set of concrete alternative development plans. Each parcel of land suited to the developer's needs and capacities is represented on this list, together with nearly final plans for construction, financing, and marketing. For each alternative in this list, the anticipated form and scale of developer gain should be clear enough to permit comparison.

The actual selection of a particular site and development scheme is indicated in Figure 24 as Process E. The developer must, at this point, reflect upon the inputs required by each alternative project, in conjunction with the nature of the output as it affects himself—i.e. his cash profit, tax shelter, source of income, mortgage proceeds, or whatever other results he contemplates from each prospective development. Then he must simply select that parcel and that development which best suit his capacities and his interests. If there were a single dimension to this evaluation, it might be the present value of all the benefits which he expects any given project to produce, perhaps divided by the number of months during which the developer will be occupied to the exclusion of other projects. The output of Process E is a development program which may include one or more sites (or none, if the developer's best judgment suggests that some delay in the most attractive undertaking would be productive). A development program which includes more than one project may indicate a sequence or other form of time scheduling if the circumstances preclude simultaneous undertakings.

Rejected projects may warrant future reconsideration, so Process F indicates that they may be included in a later development program. The nature of Process F is essentially similar to the whole of the flow chart now being discussed, though it would make sense for the developer to be alert primarily for changes in strategic factors which were responsible for the elimination of any feasible development alternative from his current program. That is, each rejected alternative should, in a sense, be "tagged" according to the principal factor leading to its rejection.

The development program which actually results from Process E needs, of course, to be carried out. This vast group of activities is shown in the chart, Figure 24, simply as Process G. The first output of this latter process, indeed the immediate consequence of initiating actual development, is that the developer becomes the proprietor of a project in being, with many commitments which to varying degrees are irreversible. Since development is by no means instantaneous, however, many circumstances may arise during development to encourage a change in some aspects of construction design or in plans for the disposition of the development at completion or during development. Process H is a review of the project under development, and this process is essentially the entire development decision-making scheme once again, with two major simplifications. Only changes in strategic considerations which led up to the development program chosen in Process E need be considered. Also, presuming that a site has already been acquired, only the potential uses of that one site (which may include its immediate disposition) need be considered. The output of Process H is a revised or current development program. Obviously, revisions during development may be numerous.

After the last revision which circumstances permit, the time arrives to put in motion efforts to market the property. This effort may, of course, be started well before the structure is completed and may itself, as already suggested, be subject to change in midstream. Process J is the actual disposition of the property, meaning the negotiations and formalities required. At last the developer realizes the output of development as Process J is concluded.

Lender Decision Model

Lenders on residential real estate are of several different kinds, including thrift institutions, short-term financing specialists, and individuals.[9] The accompanying flow chart, Figure 25, suggests the main structural elements in U. S. residential finance. Thrift institutions are, in effect, indirect investors, for they accept savings from individuals and relend these funds to other individuals who wish to apply leverage in the purchase of real estate. These institutions perform the valuable service of pooling small amounts of funds and making investments based upon specialized knowledge of investment opportunities and of legal and technical aspects of what are often complex financial transactions. Because they act thus in an intermediary and inherently fiduciary capacity, they are usually subject to public supervision in some form. Often this supervision, or the institutions' interpretation of this supervisory interest, extends to particulars of individual loan applications, making it necessary to exclude many potential borrowers and classes of collateral.

The thrift institutions provide something more than investment expertise for depositors. An insurance company, for example, collects premiums primarily as a means of permitting policyholders to share some specific form of risk and only secondarily to manage the investment needs of those policyholders. The person who "saves" via such a company gets insurance protection and investment services as a part of a package. The saver who contributes to a pension fund does so to meet specific income objectives in later life, and the amount of that future income is often stipulated at the time that he first joins the pension scheme. The saver who deposits funds in a bank or savings association has somewhat less certainty about the ultimate return, for deposit interest rates are changed periodically, keeping this type of saver in closer contact with actual direct investment opportunities. Depositors in banks or savings associations, however,

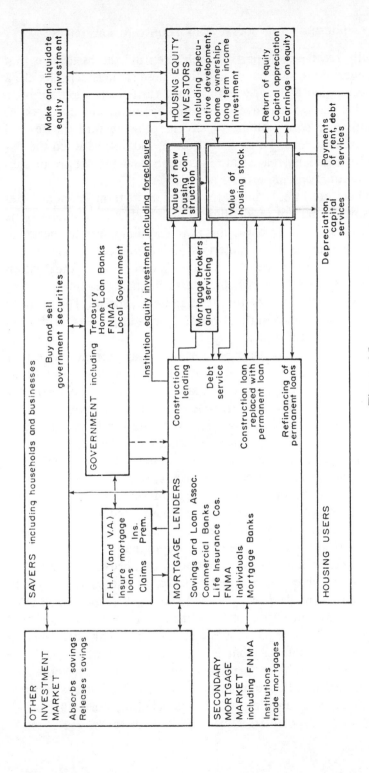

Figure 25

Flow of Housing Investment Funds in the United States

generally receive as a part of their "return" the assurance that their funds are in safe hands and that these savings deposits are a relatively liquid form of wealth. Thus, thrift institutions provide something more than investment management, and these other functions affect the volume of savings flowing into the several types of institutions. To an extent, then, the link between the demand for funds by real estate borrowers and the supply of savings is indirect and imperfect.

There are three principal types of short-term financing specialists in the field of residential financing. The developer who is improving land or constructing new dwellings usually needs to finance his purchases of materials and labor, etc., expecting to sell or refinance the property when it is completed. Construction loans are thus one form of short-term financing calling for very specialized knowledge of the development process. The lender's security in this case is in the form of "goods in process" with only conditional market value.

Other specialists arrange mortgage loans for purchasers or developers of residential real estate, advancing their own funds to these purchasers pending the sale of the mortgage loan thus created to a long-term lender. These "mortgage bankers" are not savings institutions; they have limited funds and must turn these funds over as rapidly as possible. Sometimes the expectation of improvement in the price of newly created loans will lead these intermediaries to hold such loans briefly, but their basic function is more in the nature of market communication—linking borrower and long-term lender—rather than investment per se.

Mortgage loans which have been held in a long-term lender's investment portfolio for a period of time may be placed on the resale market when that investor's liquidity needs or other investment opportunities make it wise to change that portfolio. Such resales may be made directly—say from Bank A to Bank B. The communication problems of the market are such, however, that short-term holders of mortgages can perform a valuable function by "making a market," that is, by standing ready to purchase existing loans (subject to price negotiations) which sooner or later will be placed once more in the hands of a long-term investor. This liquidity-creating function is generally not highly developed, though its potential value is widely acknowledged.

Individuals make real estate loans as a form of personal investment or as a means of facilitating the sale of real estate, or some combination of these aims. Individually held loans created through the sale of a home are often junior liens, representing some portion of the purchase price which cannot be financed advantageously through a first mortgage. Thus, the seller of a home priced at $30,000 may find a buyer who can obtain a first mortgage of only $20,000 and can provide no more than $3,000 in cash. The seller may accept a second mortgage of $7,000 (or more) to facilitate the sale. The seller's ultimate cash needs and investment goals, plus the condition of the market for such junior loans, will determine the length of time during which the seller will hold this loan. Loans arising in this way give the investor little opportunity to compare investment alternatives, since the transaction revolves around a single, unique property as collateral.

Residential mortgage lending is distinguished from other common types of debt investment by the fact that the debt is held in a small number of hands. Indeed, because housing assets are small in value in comparison with typical business assets, there is very often only one lender involved with a given piece of property. In case of default, the entire burden of ownership and management can fall to that lender. Thin equities increase the likelihood that the lender will have to assume total responsibility for a very specific item of durable capital, so it behooves the mortgage lender to learn something of the entrepreneurial aspects of housing ownership and to provide a contingency plan for managing and disposing of the collateral property. Thus, the residential mortgage lender assumes substantial proprietary interest, and investors who lack familiarity with the problems of housing ownership are normally reluctant to make residential mortgage loans. If the workings of housing markets, both specifically and generally, were better understood, and if the market itself were well enough organized to facilitate liquidation of ownership responsibilities inadvertently acquired, the sources of mortgage funds for housing would be broadened. Of course, legal protection for borrowers and users are often both complex and strong in the field of housing, which makes the lender's position in case of default particularly difficult.

POLICY FORMULATION

That being said, the broad logic of investment decision-making with respect to residential mortgages corresponds very closely to that for other types of debt investments. The accompanying flow chart, Figure 26, can be read, perhaps, in terms of loans secured by other assets than housing, and this generality is quite intentional. At certain points, specific knowledge about housing is required, but we presume that basic investment criteria for loans secured by housing are the same as criteria for other types of loans.

The first process on the chart, Process *A,* is the development of a set of policies to govern the evaluation of specific mortgage loan opportunities. Informational inputs for this process include the lender's own internal requirements and limitations imposed by external factors. The cost of funds to the lender can be quite explicit as in the case of interest rates paid to savings bank depositors. For an individual lender, it may be best understood as an opportunity cost, the rate which could be earned by alternative investments of equal risk and liquidity or the utility which could be realized by the use of the funds for immediate consumption purposes.

Liquidity requirements must be weighed rather carefully by prospective mortgage lenders for residential investments of this sort are typically quite illiquid. A thrift institution which is subject to substantial withdrawals of deposits will have to select any mortgage investments with caution. Some types of lenders have the opposite view about liquidity, preferring investments which will continue to be productive for many years without requiring reinvestment of funds.

Most institutional lenders are regulated in one way or another by public agencies, to repeat a point made earlier. These restrictions, for example, may permit the institution to make mortgage loans only within certain geographic limits, or for only certain maximum amounts, maximum interest rates, maximum ratios of loan to property value, or maximum terms. The nature of the property which secures the loan may be limited, for example, to single-family homes or, conversely, the institution may be

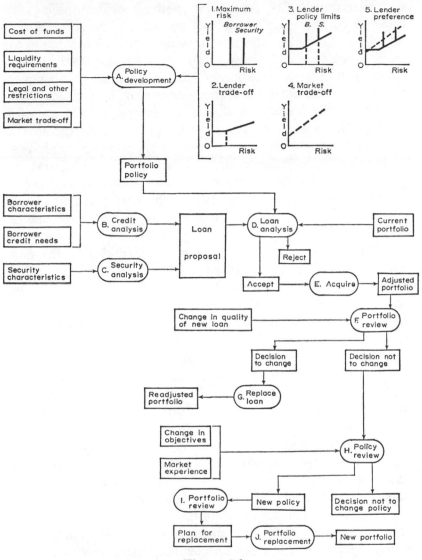

Figure 26
Residential Lender Decision System

permitted to engage in certain other types of business and consumer financing. Legal protection given to borrowers and lenders may differ for different types of loan contracts, with the effect of dissuading lenders from making some legally permissible types of loan arrangements. Acceptable methods of determining the credit of borrower-applicants or of the value of property offered as collateral may be defined with some degree of exactitude by public regulations. Such specified methods may provide the lender with valuable guidelines for the performance of a complex task but, on the other hand, they may depart importantly from realities of the housing market. For example, public agencies seem prone to overlook the contribution of developers to the value of housing and land, thus understating the economic cost of housing. Speculative values also are poorly understood by public regulators, it often seems, so that productive and useful lending is discouraged. Nevertheless, the lender cannot fail to consider legal prohibitions or inducements, whether profound or shallow.

Another type of consideration not identified in the flow chart but of potential significance for lenders might be called the "public relations" aspect of their business dealings. Housing has social implications in most communities, so that lenders who favor or discourage one type of housing market activity (such as sales to minority groups or the construction of low-priced dwellings) may variously benefit or suffer in public esteem.

The last item identified as an input into Process A in Figure 26 is information concerning the "trade-off" between investment yield (the interest rate on the loan, in the simplest case) and the risk inherent in specific mortgages. The implications of this trade-off will become more apparent shortly, but the prospective mortgage lender must have some information about the manner in which the local market converts the natural characteristics of residential debt financing into yield-equivalents.

With informational inputs of these several types, the lender is in a position to establish the major framework of an investment policy against which mortgage lending opportunities can be tested. The flow chart (Fig. 26) shows some essential parts of this process in the form of diagrams.

The first of these, Diagram 1, represents absolute limitations of risk acceptable to the lender, as determined by public regulations, personal attitudes of decision-makers, or the nature of the lender's responsibilities to depositors. Thus, vertical lines arise at some levels of risk to indicate that no increase in yield would compensate for the acceptance of risks beyond such points. In our two-dimensional discussion we shall have to consider that "risk" is a complex of negative aspects associated with particular loans, including illiquidity. Two vertical lines are shown to indicate that the lender may find it necessary to decline lending opportunities because the prospective borrower is too likely to lead to default—perhaps because of uncertain income, doubtful management ability, or poor sense of financial responsibility—or that a loan may be declined in spite of the borrower's qualifications because the property offered as collateral is too subject to sudden loss in value which cannot be guarded against through normal loan terms (especially as to the rate of amortization). Different lenders may assign priority between these two sources of risk in different ways, some wishing to lend, perhaps, in a risk-prone residential area but, at the same time, to avoid the less responsible borrowers, while other lenders may feel that their assessment of the collateral is so skillful that large uncertainties about individual borrowers can be overlooked.

Diagram 2 shows the lender's "trade-off" policy between yield and risk. The nature of the lender's business may require him, on the one hand, to make at least a certain net rate of return (as in the case of a savings association which must pay depositors at the rate of 5 percent) and, on the other hand, permit him to ignore risks up to a certain point because, perhaps, the scale or specialized form of lending provides a form of self-insurance. Thus, this diagram shows a horizontal line projecting some distance past the vertical axis. Beyond some risk level, however, the lender may feel it necessary to require progressively higher yields to compensate for additional risk, so that this trade-off function slopes upward in the right-hand portion of the diagram. The degree of slope will reflect the individual lender's perception of his responsibilities, including some recognition of the fact that operations in residential lending which assume significant scale inevitably call for the acceptance of some risk on individual loans, but that the form of loan contracts will permit such risks to be matched by yield-increasing provisions such as the payment of loan fees.

Diagram 3 combines the first two into a set of boundaries within which the lender will endeavor to conduct his investment activities. These boundaries, shown by the solid line, include minimum yield requirements and alternative maximum risk levels, either of which may be operational in any particular case. These boundaries enable the lender to make "yes or no" decisions with respect to individual loan applications.

Diagram 4 represents the lender's perception of the yield-risk trade-off which prevails in the market, as distinguished from the trade-off relationship appropriate to his own set of values. An active, competitive market with well-developed systems of communication will provide the capable lender with information of this sort. Without such resources, the lender must either develop reliable internal substitutes or accept the business risk of investing funds less advantageously than conditions actually would permit.

The last diagram in Process A combines Diagrams 3 and 4. Depending on the relationship of the two trade-off curves' slopes, their maximum vertical separation will occur at various points within the policy boundaries. This point, wherever it does occur, indicates the loan policy which the lender should prefer if he is to place his funds most advantageously. That is, given a degree of risk, the lender should want to make loans with actual yields exceeding the risk-compensating yield requirements of his own trade-off curve by as much as possible. As Diagram 5 is drawn, this lender would prefer loans which are on the margin of acceptability as to borrower. If the slopes of the lines were otherwise, the preferred policy could come well below this level of risk and, of course, it could be the property-risk rather than the borrower-risk which dominates the lending policy.

LOAN SELECTION

The output of Process A (Fig. 26) is a set of policies which enable the lender to do two things. He can screen out loan applications which fall outside his yield-risk boundaries. He is also able to direct his attention to particular portions of the market in which mortgages of the preferred yield-risk combination are likely to be available. This set of policies prepares him for the evaluation of specific loan opportunities, but before the actual "yes or no" decision can be made with respect to an individual application, that loan proposal must be subjected to preparatory analytical steps, indicated in the flow chart as Processes B and C.

Process B is a credit analysis of the borrower. As informational inputs, it requires data about the borrower and his credit needs in the contemplated transaction. At this point it may be useful to view the proposed investment as an unsecured loan, for the essential questions about the borrower's credit relate to his capacity to satisfy the debt from sources other than the operation of the property to be offered as collateral, and his probable disposition to make effective and honest efforts on behalf of repayment. This type of analysis is a specialized business field and services may be available which the prospective lender can employ. The problem, with or without professional services for credit analysis, is that stereotypes may be substituted for legitimate information about income stability and general credit worthiness of certain segments of the home-buying or housing-developer population.

Process C, labeled "security analysis," considers those aspects of the property offered as collateral which are of interest to the lender. One of these aspects is the inherent capacity of the property to produce income above operating costs which will permit debt service payments under the contemplated loan contract. It may be useful for the lender to view the question as one of determining the nature of the loan contract—its amount, term, and interest rate—which the expected income stream from the property will amortize, for the least liberal loan which the property will support may be more liberal than any loan the prospective lender is ready to consider.

Another aspect of security analysis, of course, is a forecast of the value of the property over the life of the proposed loan. The expected "loan life" may be substantially less than the term or amortization period of the loan, particularly in a community which has a housing market sufficiently well organized to make equities liquid, for this factor will encourage adjustment in equity investment portfolios and adaptation of homeowner housing to changing family needs. Any probability that the value of the security will fall below the amount of unpaid indebtedness must be considered by the lender as an invitation to the borrower to abandon the property, bringing, at least, management difficulties and, very likely, some economic loss to the lender. Essentially, the lender has no interest in the probability of increases in the value of the security except as this diminishes the likelihood of foreclosure losses, for the lender's financial interest in the property is commonly limited to the amount of unpaid debt. Thus, the value forecast might be reduced to a set of nonsymmetrical questions: Is the property value likely to fall and, if so, by how much? Is the property value likely to rise? The lender must anticipate the direction of change, but he needs to know the degree of change only when the direction is downward.

Another less obvious aspect of security analysis in the case of residential mortgage lending is the probability that the proposed loan may produce additional lending opportunities in the future. If the loan is "open ended," the borrower may wish to turn portions of accumulated equity into cash by additional borrowing. The borrower may also have the opportunity to make capital improvements and find that extension of the first mortgage provides more favorable financing than alternative methods would. To some extent, the nature of the property indicates whether such additional lending opportunities will arise.

The output of Processes *B* and *C* is a description of the loan proposal in terms relevant to the lender's position. This description includes material about the credit worthiness of the borrower, his ability to carry the proposed debt from the income of the property and, if necessary, from other sources. Of central importance in this description is the forecast of the relationship between the value of the property and the unpaid balance of the loan. The terms of the loan may be stipulated by this description if either the prospective borrower or the lender himself have rigid preferences concerning terms. Otherwise, the negotiating range of loan terms will be a part of the description.

The object of loan analysis, Process *D*, is to decide whether to add the proposed new loan to the lender's portfolio. This involves first screening the loan proposal to determine whether it corresponds to basic portfolio policy, previously developed.

Presuming that the proposed loan meets these qualifications, the question next arises whether it represents the best of the presently available alternatives. Among the alternatives is the retention of the existing portfolio, for the lender may not have new investment funds to place, but may find it possible to liquidate some previously acquired loan or loans. If the only point of difference is yield, then the criterion is obvious. Differences as to liquidity or to the degree of uncertainty regarding loan quality may be resolved almost as readily by exercise of the lender's judgment, whether to keep the present portfolio or make a substitution.

New funds or funds returning from the amortization of previous loans clearly require the lender to consider net additions to his file of loan papers. Then his choice is among the available loan applications which meet the lender's basic portfolio policy. Again, the criterion may simply be the highest yield, or it may require a subjective ranking of loans according to a set of characteristics such as liquidity, risk of foreclosure, borrower capability, etc.

An interesting and distinctive feature of loan analysis by mortgage lenders stems from the interaction of property values within the housing market. The "ideal" collateral, from a lender's point of view, might well seem to be a property which is certain not to decrease in value, and a single, small-scale lender may find it possible to select only those loans which represent such "sure things." This means, in effect, that the mortgaged property has characteristics which assure a steady, unchanging demand over a period well in excess of the loan term, such as a home which is durably constructed in perfectly traditional style and located in a neighborhood which has great socioeconomic stability. Hence, many lenders consider that community policies such as land-use controls, building regulations, and even official socioeconomic segregation, which have the effect of stabilizing property values, represent desirable and efficient practices. We shall have the opportunity to examine this question of optimization at a later point, but we can note here that, in principle, the lender would prefer to have as loan collateral totally risk-free properties. In fact, it may be possible for prospective lenders to find situations corresponding closely to this ideal.

A monopoly lender, the only source of residential mortgage loans in a community (or a public agency which effectively controls all private mortgage lending in that community) may be able to create conditions in the local housing market which maximize the value of mortgaged property. For example, a monopoly lender may freeze out developers whose new housing would compete effectively with existing housing, causing the value of the latter to fall. Since the intermixture of socioeconomic groups within neighborhoods sometimes can result in lower overall housing rents and prices (if user preferences for homogeneous neighborhoods are strong), a monopoly lender may be able to control residential mobility in a manner advantageous to the value of his loan portfolio. Where new housing is to be built, the monopoly lender may be able to dictate certain aspects of its design, and particularly of neighborhood design, so that the loan portfolio is enhanced. Whether these efforts will result in an optimum housing program for the community as a whole remains to be seen, but lender criteria for community housing development and housing market operation have acquired strong public support in some areas.

An open, competitive housing market with many developers, many lenders, and mobile households will tend to produce a pattern of housing which is more fluid than either the "sure thing" lender or the monopoly lender would prefer. Energetic entrepreneurs will entice households from even the most stable of neighborhoods into more attractive developments, weakening demand and, hence, value for many interdependent segments of the local housing market. Competitive lenders will facilitate these new developments, adding attractive loans to their own portfolios but indirectly causing the value of other lenders' portfolios to decline.

These questions regarding the impact of a given new loan application upon the value of other loans in the lender's own portfolio arise principally because housing markets are confined within narrow, geographic limits, and the share of a given lender in this market may be substantial. Lenders are thus inclined to be concerned about the "soundness" of the local housing market —concerned about "blight" and "overbuilding" and other qualitative matters of broad community interest—but the nature of that interest, at least as far as housing loans are concerned, coincides with simple, financial advantage. Whatever the competitive structure of local mortgage lending, any one lender must consider in his evaluation of a new loan proposal the likely effects of future acts by other lenders (and developers) upon the value of the proposed collateral. That is, the organization of the local housing market has an important bearing on the quality of mortgage collateral.

Process *D*, loan analysis, must produce a decision regarding the acquisition of the proposed loan. This is essentially a "yes or no" decision. The process must also establish terms for the loan if it is to be accepted and if the description of the loan proposal has left open some elements of the contract. If there are no terms on which the proposed loan would meet the lender's portfolio needs, the loan application must be rejected. On the other hand, the loan analysis may produce a range of acceptable terms, leaving the exact arrangements to be decided in negotiations with the borrower. Process *E* represents these negotiations, and the result is a change in the lender's portfolio.

PORTFOLIO MANAGEMENT

Process *F* (Fig. 26) is a review of the portfolio occasioned by any significant change in the quality of loans held by the lender, or loans available in the community, which meet the general portfolio policy of this lender. This review is, in effect, an application of Process *D*, loan analysis, to each possibility for replacing presently held loans. The outcome may be the sale of the loan which served as our hypothetical investment problem, so that the life history of a loan must not be considered completely determined when it is acquired and taken under management. Removal of a given loan from the portfolio is an investment decision of not less importance than its acquisition and possibly of greater practical difficulty if the secondary market for mortgage loans is imperfectly developed.

Process *G* represents merely the act of disposition if a loan in the portfolio is deemed inferior to an available substitute (including, perhaps, short-term holding of cash), and if resale opportunity is present, plus the acquisition of a substitute via new loan proposals and Processes B, C, and D. The outcome of this is an adjusted portfolio.

The story for a given loan is not quite ended when it passes a succession of portfolio reviews, for the lender may subsequently alter his basic portfolio policy. This is indicated by Process H, a repetition of the steps of Process A, and would be undertaken whenever the preferences or capacity of the lender change significantly or his investment experience persuades him that he must change his objectives.

The outcome of the policy review may be a decision not to alter that policy. If the choice is in favor of a new portfolio policy, however, a new portfolio review is indicated. This is shown in Process I, identical to Process F, and produces a program for adjustments in the portfolio. These adjustments must then be carried out in Process J, which is, in essence, the same as Process G. The final result is an adjusted portfolio.

Equilibrium Characteristics of the Residential Inventory

The aggregation of individual decisions which we have just considered produces a physical, social, and economic pattern in the community which cannot be perceived by looking at one decision at a time. If we stand back a bit from microeconomic processes, what will the residential community look like? What major patterns will emerge in the kinds of housing which the community offers to those who live there?

One characteristic of the inventory implied by the private decision-making process is that it tends to expand and improve at the fringe. Central areas, those which are built up first in the city's history, remain relatively obsolescent, while demand for housing improvement is drawn off largely to the periphery of the city. A "gray area" of older and less desirable dwellings appears at the center and spreads, over time.[10] Unless there is strong, personal attachment to the central areas and a correspondingly weak desire for substantial innovation in housing types, the central area sees relatively little modernization and, perhaps, a declining level of maintenance. The reasons are implied by the decision-making process. So long as the older structures in the central city have some economic value, they cause the price of "land" for new residential developments there to be high relative to raw land at the periphery (unless the transportation system is quite inefficient). In addition, there is a "scale effect." The owner of one centrally located property hesitates to improve it substantially for the appearance of its neighbors will detract from any increase in value. Unless large central areas were improved at the same time, this deterrent would be present, and it is in the nature of residential property decisions that they tend to be made in isolation from one another.

When households and entrepreneurs have made their decisions, a pattern of occupancy will emerge in the city. This "pattern" should be understood in dynamic terms, for it will have some tendency to move about over time as population characteristics change and the inventory becomes obsolescent. An intricate set of "priorities" will determine which family lives in which dwelling, the best houses being occupied by households which rank high in income, housing tastes, social status (perhaps including ethnic or religious characteristics), and other factors. Many discrepancies in the broad pattern will arise from differences among individuals with respect to residential mobility. The program of occupancy, together with the qualitative characteristics of the stock just mentioned, will induce a certain clustering of household types. That is, "neighborhoods" will emerge in which generally similar households will predominate in subareas of the city, and the housing stock in these subareas will also exhibit general similarities.

Less visible, but of substantial practical importance, will be a "map" of residential property values. Land and building prices, including unit rents, will appear out of the mass of individual transactions and assume geographic regularities. In turn, this price information will play a very important role in the ongoing decision processes of entrepreneurs and households.

The transactions themselves—and the various patterns arising from them—will not be "rational" or "purely competitive" in the textbook sense. Investment motives and the desire to use, trade, or produce dwellings will be tangled together by the institutions of local real estate business. The type of housing which is developed and used will be determined, in part, by institutional reliance upon equity investment, often screening out from the developer role or from the role of housing user people who happen not to have access to sufficient equity funds, despite their other qualifications for conducting housing market business. Lenders will tend to impose a certain amount of conformity upon the physical nature of the housing stock, in the interest of long-run liquidity, though this will discourage adaptation of the stock to variegated and shifting housing needs. Market decisions will tend to be skewed in the direction of certainty in many particulars; families of uncertain probity, borrowers with insecure employment, builders with unproven instincts about the market, and dwellings with obscure pedigrees will be less welcome everywhere than those who arouse no doubts in the minds of the seller, buyer, lender, or whoever. Each market participant's options are restricted to some extent by these transactional interdependencies. Options are further restricted by any existing imperfections in the system of market information, imperfections which must always be present to some degree and which will lead decision-makers into nonoptimal choices.

All of the above characteristics of microequilibrium in a private housing economy might be defended on the grounds of effective compromise or improved by innovations of a technical nature—such as the multiple-listing service which enlarges the communications range of buyers and sellers. (The problem of the "gray area" might be considered as the consequence of externalities.) Thus, they may be consistent per se with a generally acceptable notion of optimal and efficient resource use by the housing sector. Private decisions have the characteristic, however, of overlooking external costs and benefits, and it is from this source that reservations about the optimality of microeconomic equilibrium in the housing sector really can arise. In the absence of public measures, for example, it is likely that private decisions will provide impoverished families with little or no housing. The market process works its calculations on the income a person has, without raising the issue of whether it is enough—or too much. A city with impoverished people in it will have, at least eventually, some poor dwellings in it as well, unless public programs to offset the one or the other are in effect.

Individual land users are hard put to control the environment outside their legal property boundaries, so that noisy, noxious, and unsightly activities may sprout in places where residential amenity has been created at substantial cost. Even if mixture of land uses does not appear, the architectural style of neighboring residential buildings under complete individual control may be so inharmonious as to be detrimental to all. The community may ultimately feel that the clustering of socioeconomic groups which results from microeconomic housing-market processes is damaging to the vision of open economic intercourse.

Private decisions tend also to overload public facilities which are related to the use of housing. If the street is there, or the water line, and so on, one more dwelling attached to it will hardly be noticed, perhaps. But in the aggregate this assumption will produce congestion and inadequate service for the many. The marginal private cost of utilities often approaches zero, but the marginal social cost may be both positive and rising. These things bear mightily upon the usefulness and value of housing but are beyond the reach of the individual housing market participant's personal means to determine.

Private decision-making can be very sensitive to individual wants and individual capacities, so that the housing sector of the city which is produced by these private decisions may be very finely tuned to the shades of need and ability, tangible and intangible, within the compass of individual transactions. Yet the outcome may, in some respects, fall well short of what these individuals might do with their housing resources given some other or some auxiliary decision-making devices.

6 · ▧

OPTIMUM

CHARACTERISTICS OF

THE HOUSING STOCK

The Dimensions of Optimality

The housing stock of a community is multidimensional. Given its aggregate spatial size and value, the stock of housing units may exhibit varying distributions of density and of quality. At one extreme the stock may consist of perfectly homogeneous dwelling units, each as large, as well made and equipped, and occupying as much land area as any other, differing only as to location within the community. At the other extreme every unit may be unique, not only with respect to its location—which is an inevitable point of difference—but also with respect to the amount of ground area appurtenant to it, the materials used in its construction, its age, its design, its intrinsic quality, and the use for which it is primarily intended. In most communities the stock of dwellings comes closer to the second extreme than to the first, though the most common situation is one in which particular dwelling units are unique or nearly unique combinations of limited classes of characteristics.

Thus, we might find one dwelling unit in a community which falls into the class of being of "prewar construction," and also into the classes of "wood frame," "large lot," "two-story with basement," "suburban," "six-room," "well-maintained," and "for middle-income families." Perhaps it is the only dwelling in the community which has this particular set of characteristics. Usually, however, if the classifications employed do not exceed those which have practical significance, there will be several dwellings which share a common description. The community housing stock will consist of a number of distinguishable types of dwellings, and the "microoptimality" question is concerned with how many there should be of each type.

Suppose, for example, that only three characteristics are of interest—location, quality, and density of dwelling—and that each of these characteristics has three meaningful levels. We might then have twenty-seven classifications or "cells" into which every housing unit would fit, as for example:

Location	Quality	Density
central	poor	apartment
intermediate	medium	duplex
suburban	good	one-family

and all their combinations, which could be arranged in a three-dimensional box diagram, or in a list such as the following, using a three-letter code to represent the categories of location, quality, and density, respectively:

Code	Number of Units (000's)
c-p-a	6
c-p-d	2
c-p-o	1
c-m-a	4
c-m-d	1
c-m-o	1
c-g-a	1
c-g-d	1
c-g-o	1
i-p-a	1
i-p-d	1
i-p-o	1

Code	Number of Units (000's)
i-m-a	4
i-m-d	3
i-m-o	8
i-g-a	1
i-g-d	2
i-g-o	3
s-p-a	1
s-p-d	2
s-p-o	3
s-m-a	2
s-m-d	1
s-m-o	9
s-g-a	3
s-g-d	3
s-g-o	24
total units	90

Total by:	Location:	Quality:	Density:
	c 18	p 18	a 23
	i 24	m 33	d 16
	s 48	g 39	o 51

This hypothetical list might represent the *actual* distribution of the housing stock according to the three illustrative characteristics, or it might represent "optimum" distributions. Whichever is so, a few more or less mechanical aspects of this classification and distribution process are worthy of mention. The locational distribution implies a pattern of transportation facilities and movement. The greater the proportion of housing units in "suburban" areas, the more total resources will be expended, day by day, as workers travel to jobs and as shoppers move between homes and retail districts.

The qualitative distribution must be consistent with the community's distribution of housing purchasing power and preferences, for dwellings of "poor" quality are likely to command lower prices (other features being the same) than dwellings of medium or good quality, and medium dwellings to command lower prices than good dwellings. It might be pleasant to wish that all of a community's housing stock could be "good" in quality, but some of it must be available on some basis to households with less to spend than others. So long as there is inequality among households with respect to their ability and desire to command housing, there must be qualitative differentiation of the housing stock.*

The density distribution also must be consistent with the pattern of ability and preference among households with respect to ground area. Density affects the functioning of households; and, the desire for relatively low density usually appears to be greater among some types of households (usually for child-raising families) than for others (such as recently married couples). Thus, the distribution of certain social characteristics is relevant to the pattern of density.

It is also necessary that cross classifications of quality and density be consistent with the social and economic characteristics of the community. For example, the total number of "good single-family" dwellings, 27,000 in the illustration, must bear some relationship to the number of households within the community for whom such dwellings are appropriate and attainable. The same applies to the 9,000 dwellings which make up the composite category of "poor-quality apartments," and so on.

Clearly, if a greater number of dimensions is employed, and additional stratification is desired within each characteristic, the number of relevant combinations increases geometrically. The complexity of interrelationships and the difficulty of ascertaining that any apparently desirable distribution of the housing stock is consistent internally and externally with social and economic facts must increase accordingly. It is helpful to begin the discussion of optimum characteristics of the housing stock by simplifying the problem as much as possible. Our first task, then, is to

---

* The word "command" is used here to suggest not only effective demand in the ordinary sense but augmentations of private purchasing power in the form of rent control, tenant protection laws, and subsidies based on an income or means test.

select dimensions which are relevant in practice and to apply whatever analytical tools are available to the study of optimality in simplified dimensions.

One problem which lends itself rather well to analysis is that concerning the relative location within a community of different density types. Should apartment buildings be in the center of the city or in the suburbs—or does it matter? We can call this the "location-density" question.

Another question involves the qualitative composition of the housing stock or, more exactly, the relative quality of additions to the stock. Should new houses be inexpensive, relatively luxurious, or of medium quality and price? This question may be combined with the problem of location, but it may also be analyzed without regard to where within the community the new houses are to be constructed. An answer to this question, or a formula for answering it, means that we can answer the broader question of what the qualitative composition of the housing stock should be, for the stock acquires its qualitative character through the accumulation of additions and through physical wear and tear, but the latter is largely a function of the passage of time and is thus not a policy question. We can call this question about the quality level of new housing units the "increment-quality" problem.

A third dimension of the housing stock, apart from where different density types are located and what the quality distribution is, has to do with the adaptation of housing units to particular types of housing needs. Should all dwellings be of the same size —two bedrooms, for example—or should there be a range of sizes? Should there be some units which are specially designed for aged people, with nonslip flooring and waist-high electric outlets, and some units specially designed for bachelors who can't cook, but who would like to have a commercial cafeteria in the building, or should every unit be designed to serve the modal household consisting of a middle-aged couple with three children? * Should all units be for rent, or all for sale, or should there

---

* Interest in the housing of elderly people in the United States in the late 1950's led to the development of a set of dwelling unit specifications along the lines suggested in this paragraph. See *Housing Requirements of the Aged— A Study of Design Criteria* (Ithaca, N.Y.: Housing Research Center, Cornell University, 1958).

be some of each? Clearly, this is a catchall dimension, and we can refer to it simply as the problem of "differentiation." We shall have to deal with it in rather general terms and not attempt to create a special kind of analysis for each conceivable manner in which, apart from density and price class, dwelling units may be different from one another.

A subproblem under the question of qualitative distribution is the question of how the households of the community should be distributed among the available dwellings. Should poor families live only in the poorest quality dwellings? Should the fact that some families are poor lead to the creation of a poor-quality segment of the housing stock? In fact, this question of the distribution of users among the housing inventory is inseparable from the question of how much qualitative variation there should be in the physical inventory, and so it does not call for a separate kind of analysis.

These three problems are relevant for most communities, and they include the issues which ordinarily seem of greatest importance from the community point of view. Hence, if we can provide some theoretical solutions to these problems, we will have some fairly practical tools to use in the development of community housing policy oriented toward the characteristics of the stock. (Recall that macrooptimization issues, the size of the community in terms of space and population, and the aggregate amount of resources used for housing were discussed in an earlier chapter.)

Ultimately we wish to integrate these three dimensions into a multidimensional analysis, to make sure that the conclusions from analysis of each separate dimension are consistent. We also want our conclusions to have the quality of being dynamic; that is, we should be able to visualize the optimum composition of a community's housing stock not just today, but one year, two years, five years, or more from now. We want to have some idea of the manner in which the optimum characteristics of the housing stock change when various external factors change—such as the income level of the population or the distribution of income, or the age distribution—or when some important improvement in urban construction or transportation technology occurs.

Before attempting a multidimensional analysis, we must

take a series of simpler views of the three basic issues identified above. Before undertaking even these simpler analyses, however, we must consider an obscure but ultimately essential aspect of all three issues (and of any other major issues which we can identify). Criteria are needed by which we can judge one composition of the housing stock to be "better" than another, from the community's point of view. Which criteria are realistic and useful? Which criterion is best? How do the institutions of the community help to determine its housing goals?

Criteria

Decisions about the use of resources, in general, are rendered complex by two phenomena which may be labeled "incommensurability" and "externality." The first refers to the fact that the person or group of persons responsible for the decision —say the development of a new apartment building—may be motivated by several aims rather than just one, and these various objectives cannot be compared by a single yardstick. The entrepreneur of elementary economics textbooks is supposed to be interested solely in maximizing his profit, so he selects the output which makes marginal cost and marginal revenue equal. In more advanced textbooks, however, the entrepreneur may be described as being interested in obtaining a larger share of the market as well as in realizing profit. He may also want to maintain a favorable public image. These and other objectives may be essentially incompatible and, indeed, they would very often be expected to be mutually exclusive. To get a larger share of the market, for example, may require price cutting which would result in less profit than otherwise might be obtained. We might try to put a dollar value on the size of the market share or on the rate of increase in this share, and so make it comparable with the simple goal of money profit. But this would involve assumptions which would be often only dubious approximations to reality. In fact, the various objectives which any businessman may have are like the proverbial apples and oranges which cannot be added.

Business decisions about housing almost inherently involve incommensurable goals. Most entrepreneurs in the housing field want to be "proud of" the physical results of their efforts as well as to be financially satisfied. Financial satisfaction itself includes a blend of short-term net income, long-term increase in capital value, entrepreneurial profit by quick completion and sale of housing properties, avoidance of risk, and reducing of illiquidity. Any housing enterprise produces as output a whole set of financial, physical, and psychological results (not just "profit" or "rate of return"), and these various consequences of housing business are too different in nature to be added together. The decision process is not just a problem in arithmetic, but also an introspective act in which the complex results of alternative decisions are recognized and compared. We might rationalize that the "best" decision for the entrepreneur is the one which provides him with the greatest "utility" or sense of overall satisfaction, but the scale of utility or satisfaction, if it exists at all, exists only for the individual. Ultimately the entrepreneur must choose one set of results as preferable to any alternative set of results. Incommensurability does not make his decision impossible, but it does make it less easy to predict.

The private entrepreneur thus is compelled to consider not just one but usually several results of any anticipated decision. Some things will happen as a consequence of his action, however, which he may ignore. When he decides to build medium-rent apartments, for example, he dilutes the market for existing medium-rent apartment units and, by causing vacancy rates to rise, he denies some economic value to the owners of those existing buildings. He denies the housing resources at his command to families which cannot affort the rent he will require, though his action may result in some older, medium-rent apartments becoming available to low-income families. He uses land which might have been suited to buildings of greater quality, thus implicitly reducing the housing alternatives available to higher-income families. These are some of the "external" effects of his action, and the list of such externalities may be virtually endless. Complex as the entrepreneur's decision problem is, it is far simpler than it might be if he were obliged to evaluate every direct and indirect consequence of each alternative business proposal. The freedom to overlook many of these consequences simplifies his problem greatly and permits him to reach action decisions which might otherwise be next to unattainable.

The community as a whole, however, cannot ignore the external consequences of private business behavior. Certainly not in the field of housing, which so closely affects the welfare of individual households, the physical appearance of the community, and the mechanical way in which the urban area functions. The collective impact of individual housing business decisions produces physical and economic patterns, but no single private decision-maker controls the manner in which these patterns develop. If there is any likelihood that the external effects of accumulating private housing-market decisions will be unfavorable to the community as a whole then it is up to the community to provide redress.

So, we might say that the community needs no active housing program if it can be assured that the external effects of private housing market decisions tend to produce patterns of location-density, increment quality, and differentiation in the housing stock which correspond to community goals under resource constraints. Since it is likely, for a variety of reasons (which will be explored shortly), that private housing market decisions will not automatically add up to community patterns which satisfy all the aspirations of that community, some deliberate community effort is required to restrain private activities in some instances, to encourage them in others, with the aim of coordinating the whole in the pursuit of jointly perceived goals. It follows that community housing criteria should be couched in terms relevant to private market behavior.* In other words, community goals in the area of housing should not be presented merely in the form of "this is desirable," but rather in the form of "this is an inherent direction of private activity which produces thus and thus undesirable external effects." Public concern arises from the external consequences of individual market behavior and it is useful to know the manner in which these externalities are produced. Community criteria thus are judgments of private

---

* Even in nonmarket economies it is generally true that consumer motivation and satisfaction with respect to housing are relevant in the allocation of resources.

behavior, and it is the unfavorable judgments which call for community programs. Before programs can be designed, private behavior must be judged, and before these judgments are possible, the norms or ideals must be identified.

For our purposes we can define the "community" as the entity which is conscious of and responsible for all the direct and indirect consequences of its several and joint actions; thus, there are no external effects of community behavior. Effects which are external to the entrepreneur can be ignored by him, but all the effects of both private and public housing market behavior must be considered as part of the community's housing decision problems. Consequently, the public decision problem is much more complex and involves more far-reaching incommensurability than private decision problems do. In principle, the welfare and aspirations of every citizen (and future citizen) must be respected in the delineation of public policy.

It follows that public criteria are essentially different from private criteria. For the individual the costs and benefits of a single-housing enterprise may be of paramount importance, while the broad picture of housing supply throughout the city is a blurred image of uncertain meaning. For the community, though it is composed of individuals, it is the situation of the individual which is blurred while the broad contours of welfare and amenity in general are clearly in view. Though the community's housing circumstances are an aggregation of individual enterprises, it cannot be said that there is a community housing enterprise, for the community as a whole is neither selling nor buying. Its function is to assure that the total effect of individual transactions is productive of general equity, wholesome environment, and amenity which no individual entrepreneur can bring into being. We cannot produce the public or community counterpart of the decision-making flow charts of the previous chapter, for the community's essential role is to evaluate the manner in which resources are used, rather than to make direct use of those resources. It must compare the aggregate effects of private behavior against a public template. What kinds of templates may be used?

One test of housing market behavior is esthetic. Early discussions of urban renewal in the United States often made the argument that unsightly slums were clustered around downtown railroad terminals so that persons arriving in the city received an unfavorable first impression. Some communities or sections of them impose architectural standards on housing, limiting the choice of building styles, so that the appearance of the area is homogeneous and perhaps suggestive of pleasant historical associations. It is common in the United States for communities to insist on broad front lawns not hidden by fences, so that passers-by may enjoy the greenery. Visitors to Hong Kong are impressed by the orderly rows of massive apartment blocks, not because they represent housing improvement (which they may) but because they look nice from the harbor. Partisans of the esthetic point of view sometimes seem anxious to convince others that a housing stock which meets their visual standards is also ideal in social, economic, and other terms as well, but in this they may err on the side of modesty. Beauty is of value in its own right, even to the abstraction of the "community interest" and a positive sacrifice of other values may at times seem most appropriate to individual citizens for the sake of a good community appearance.

Another genre of criteria is based on ethics or equity. The behavior of the housing market may be held up against distributional norms which consider marked disparity in housing conditions among households as a fault. Perhaps the most common of public outcries about housing is concerned with crowded or substandard living area occupied by families of low income, implying that less dispersion in the qualitative distribution of the housing stock is publicly desired than is privately created. Exclusion of racial or social minorities from some portions of the city or from access to credit facilities also may rank as a fault in the overall performance of the local housing market. Uses of individual dwellings or residential land which create discomforts or dangers for other persons, such as careless burning of rubbish, giving raucous and prolonged parties, harboring dangerous or unsanitary animals, and the like, may be considered unethical private acts.

It would be difficult to distinguish public standards which are political in nature from those which seem to be concerned with ethics. It may well be the structure of political power and the desire for material advantage on the part of groups which possess political power that determines what is "fair" and "in the public interest," rather than some transcendent moral code. The community is, after all, a political entity, and its aims in the control of urban development must necessarily be consistent with the sources of its authority. Zoning is a case in point for, when the freedom of one person to make use of land is restricted, then some other member or members of the community stand to make material gains. The fact that a system of land-use controls may improve the aggregate usefulness of land does not alter the fact of private gain. However the most "rational" zoning system is administered, some individuals will lose while others gain. This is inevitably political. Nor is it necessarily cynical to reduce urban morality and its concrete expressions to the articulated bones of political truth. Generosity, as well as greed, is a private spirit which can be realized only by a public act. Except to the mystic, the "community" is an abstraction which has no morality. It is a vehicle for the exploitation of resources in the material interests of real persons, and the system which guides this vehicle is politics. This is an unchangeable aspect of reality and a source of disappointment to those who fancy that their private views of urban justice have been adopted by the god of cities. Life in a city is highly interdependent, and it is natural that people who live there would like to impose some restrictions upon one another. In one way or another, they manage to do just that, calling the process "morality" on Sunday and "politics" the rest of the week.

Some criteria for housing market behavior are largely technical. Houses should not be located where water cannot be supplied effectively or where sewage cannot be disposed of safely. Nor should houses be inaccessible for fire-fighting equipment or exposed unnecessarily to the dangers of fire, earth slides, or flooding. Residential areas should be organized physically in a manner consistent with means of transportation, with safe streets, and sufficient parking area if that means is primarily the automobile, and with reasonable access to public transportation if otherwise. By nature housing is linked with a number of public services which cannot be performed effectively unless public "servants" have the opportunity to discourage unwarranted demands.

The literature of urban economics puts great emphasis upon transportation cost as a criterion of market behavior. That is, many writers seem to believe that land uses within cities should be so arranged as to minimize the aggregate use of resources for transportation. The economist is ordinarily uncomfortable about ethical, esthetic, or political matters and is often shaky on the technical aspects of production, but he feels confident in his judgment that the "community as a whole" is better off when it does not use up more resources than necessary to achieve a given goal. Thus, a city which is greatly spread out consumes more transportation resources than an otherwise comparable city which is compact. In his simplest view of the matter, the economist is almost bound to recommend the compact urban form. This has often been expressed as "minimizing the costs of friction," where "friction is understood to be the cost of transportation." [1] However, the nature of the argument can become more complex and in many ways more useful, as we shall see below. The phenomenon of transportation cost is of such obvious importance in urban resource management and is so measurable (at least in comparison to other aspects of urban economic behavior) that much economic theorizing has been done centering around transportation.[2] The initial hypothesis, again, is that the pattern of land uses in a city should cause total transportation costs for the community to be as low as possible. This provides at least the starting point for a fairly specific set of criteria for housing market behavior.

While one set of economists may want to be chary of gasoline, asphalt, subway rails, and other physical requirements for urban transportation, another set of economists is concerned primarily with the resource cost of buildings—the wood and steel, wiring and plumbing, shingles and tile, bricks and concrete out of which the existing city has been fabricated and which will be required if the city is to grow or change, or even to stay as it is. The urban capital economist sees the profile of the city and knows that every structure which already exists can serve functions which otherwise would require the expenditure of new capital resources. Where the transportation economist wishes to conserve future gasoline, the capital economist wishes to make the fullest use of past construction labor still embodied in the stock of buildings. Thus, another type of economic criterion for the behavior of the housing market is maximization of the value (in terms of useful effects on humans) of existing buildings.

The interplay between considerations of transportation and capital stock is more fruitful of economic insights into urban housing-market behavior than either aspect alone. The remainder of this chapter will show that these two resource issues provide the central elements of a theory, and the theory, in turn, is relevant to the three selected dimensions of the problem of establishing community criteria for housing market performance. Those dimensions are the relative locations of the housing stock and the extent of differentiation among housing unit types within the stock.

Theories of economics do not provide criteria but they do, if well constructed and properly understood, show how various criteria are interrelated. There is no law of nature which compels us to minimize transportation outlays or to provide subsidized housing, but we might, as a community, decide that we would like to do these things. Theorizing—whether it is moralistic, esthetic, political, or economic—suggests various possible criteria, and so makes it *necessary* rather than unnecessary to make community decisions. Theories may clarify the nature of a choice, but they do not bear the responsibility of choosing.

Some Early Theories About Patterns of Land Use

The price of land was a matter of great concern to the earliest economic theorists. It was the principal subject of Ricardo's writings and a subject upon which he made an enduring and important conclusion.* To be sure, he was dealing with some problems concerning agricultural land, but his argument was so fundamental and his conclusion so basic that they clearly

---

* David Ricardo, *The Principles of Political Economy and Taxation* (London, 1817). For a discussion, see Raleigh Barlowe, *Land Resource Economics* (Englewood Cliffs, N.J.: Prentice-Hall, 1958), p. 152 ff.

apply not only to all types of land uses, including urban, but to many other economic resources as well. At the time most farming land in England was rented to tenant farmers by landowners, and it was widely believed that a sharp increase in the price of food (at the time of the Napoleonic wars) was caused by increases in the rent of land. So it was Ricardo's problem to explain how the level of such land rents was determined. Today economists generally continue to use the word "rent" or "economic rent" in the sense of "price" for resources which are fixed in supply, thus paying tribute to the important theoretical work which Ricardo did.

Ricardo's conclusion was that the price of wheat (the staple food crop of the time) was not determined by the rent of land, but rather the other way around. Land rents were determined by the price of wheat. The manner in which he showed this can be represented by two diagrams, Figures 27 and 28. In

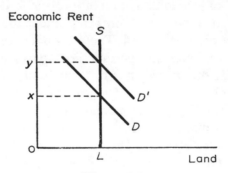

Figure 27

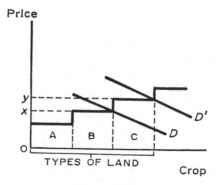

Figure 28

the first, the supply of land is a vertical line since it is a resource peculiarly beyond human capacity (usually) to create or destroy. There is just so much of it, and the existing supply is neither increased nor decreased by changes in the price of land, labeled "rent" on the diagram.

Demand is shown by the downward sloping line, D. This demand for land is "derived" from the demand for foodstuffs such as wheat, because land is a necessary input for the production of food. Since only OL land is available, there is a fixed amount of food which can be raised on this land (there are more complex cases which do not change the substance of the argument). This amount of food will, according to the derived demand curve, bring in a rent, OX, per unit of land to landlords. If the demand should rise, shifting the demand curve from D to D', this equilibrium rent would rise from OX to OY. Landlords would be enriched because demand had risen in the face of a fixed supply. Or, if demand should fall from D' to D, rents would fall and landowners would become relatively worse off. The level of landlords' incomes is governed by demand for the product of their land, not by their own actions. If demand is at the level of D, landlords cannot raise rents above OX.

Rent, in Ricardo's sense, is a reward for ownership, not for production. Landlords control the use of land, but they do not create land. They might withhold it from use but this would do them no good, for they can only receive rents if crops are grown on their land. If the demand for food were relatively small, in proportion to the supply of land (imagine the demand curve of Figure 27 falling toward the horizontal axis), rents would be very low. If the rents charged by landlords were almost entirely taken away by a tax on rents, the same supply of land would still be available. Landlords are thus passive in the determination of the price of land and the prices of things which land helps to produce.

Why, then, should land have a price, since the price does not determine the quantity of land and especially since the price which is paid goes into the pockets of landowners who, by themselves, do nothing to earn those payments? One answer to this question was supplied by Ricardo and is shown in Figure 28. The supposition here is that the total supply of land consists of several types which vary in fertility. On Land A the labor requirements for producing wheat are low, since the fertility is high. On Land *B* the fertility is less and the labor costs correspondingly higher. Land *C* is still less fertile, and so on. The axes in this diagram represent the quantity of wheat to be produced and the price of wheat per bushel.

If the demand for wheat is represented by the curve, *D,* it would make sense to use Land *A* and Land *B* but not to use Land *C,* on which the production of wheat is relatively costly. Thus, the supply curve for wheat takes the form of a step-function which is labeled *MC* (for marginal cost). With demand *D,* the equilibrium price of wheat will be 0*X,* a price which is just sufficient to pay for the labor expended in growing a bushel of wheat on Land *B.* Owners of Land *B* will not be able to charge rents to their tenant farmers.

Owners of Land *A,* however, find that farmers can produce wheat on their land at a labor cost less than 0*X* per bushel. In the market place, however, all bushels of wheat are alike, so each will sell for price 0*X.* The owner of Land *A* can charge his tenants rent up to the difference between the labor cost of one bushel on their land and price 0*X.* Rent results from differentials in the inherent productive capabilities of different types of land.

If demand for wheat should rise, because of an increase in population, perhaps, to *D',* then Land *C* would have to be brought into production. Costs, in terms of labor, are higher on Land *C,* however, so the price of wheat will have to rise to 0*Y.* Now the owner of Land *B* can begin to receive rents and the rents of Land *A* can rise. Consumers do not pay the average cost of production for the wheat they buy, but rather the marginal cost, for they must pay enough for each bushel to cover the costs on the least fertile land which the level of their demand requires to be cultivated. In so doing they create rent income for owners of better-endowed land. Owners of marginal land—that which is just worth cultivating at the prevailing market price—receive no rent.

From this emerges Ricardo's central point. Rent is not a cost of production. It is a consequence of differential productivity of a type of resource which is fixed in supply. The amount of Land *A* cannot be increased by entrepreneurs who are attracted by the rents being received by the present owners of Land A.

A corollary of this point is that rent is a "transfer payment." The rents received by owners of Land A, and later of Land B, in the example simply come out of the pockets of consumers and go into the pockets of landowners. Consumers thus have less purchasing power because of rent, and landowners have more. The total amount of purchasing power remains the same. When the owners of Land B begin to receive rent, there is no change in the use of any resources, land, labor, or any other, as a reciprocal action by these landowners. Payment for land does not measure the consumption of resources, for no additional resources are consumed when such payments occur. This makes the payment of rent fundamentally different from many other types of payments, such as that to a tailor for mending a suit, for the tailor's energies are actually used up in the process of mending. The stock of community resources is not depleted when land is rented or purchased. It is erroneous to consider that the productive capacity of a community or nation is reduced by payments for land.

Heinrich von Thuenen was a German economist of the 19th century whose theoretical writings have assured him a permanent place in the literature pertaining to the use and value of land.* Again, however, von Thuenen (as Ricardo) was interested in agricultural phenomena, so that this work may not seem to have a direct bearing on the issue of urban land uses. The principles involved are, nevertheless, of great interest, and we can shortly attempt to translate them into the urban context.

The essence of von Thuenen's idea can be explained by means of a simple numerical problem. In Figure 29 the vertical axis is a measure of money value of certain crops at the center of a city. The horizontal axis is distance from center of this city —in effect, the radius of the circular land area in which all the crops used by this self-sufficient community are grown. The problem is to decide where within this circular area—i.e. where

---

* For a biographical sketch and commentary concerning von Thuenen, see Joseph A. Schumpeter, *History of Economic Analysis* (New York: Oxford University Press, 1954), pp. 465–468. For a description of his theory, see Barlowe, *Land Resource Economics*, p. 249 ff.

along the horizontal axis of Figure 29—each type of crop will be raised.

We need consider only two kinds of crops, say, Wheat (W) and Vegetables (V) to make all of von Thuenen's points. Demand for food by the people of the community is such that the price of vegetables in the central marketplace is $20 higher

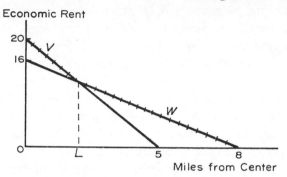

Figure 29

than the labor (and other nonland) costs of production, for the amount of vegetables which can be grown on one acre of land, and the price of wheat is $16 higher than its costs. To obtain vegetables from an acre of land one mile distant from the center requires the expenditure of $4 for transportation. This transportation cost per mile, T/M, for one acre of vegetables is assumed to be constant, so that the production of vegetables on land beyond five miles would not be feasible for farmers. The transportation cost per mile for wheat is only $2, so this crop can be grown as far as eight miles from the center. These facts can be summed up in a convenient table:

	R_0	T/M	$M_{max.}$
V	$20	$4	5
W	$16	$2	8

in which R_0 stands for the economic rent of land, per acre, at the center of the city.

What von Thuenen has done is to substitute transportation costs for Ricardo's differences in fertility, to explain the existence of economic rent for land and the reason for variation in the rent of different parcels of land. There could, of course, be differences in fertility as well, so that rent could result from either or both factors in particular cases, and, perhaps, from other factors as well. Ricardo treated transportation costs as the same for all land and explained rent on the basis of differences in soil fertility. Von Thuenen assumed equal fertility of land and based rent on location.

But von Thuenen took a long step beyond Ricardo when he composed an example involving more than one type of crop. For he was able to say that a competitive process involving farmers wishing to rent land for different purposes or a determination by landowning farmers to maximize their individual incomes would cause the two kinds of crops to be produced in a specific geographic pattern. At the center, the production of vegetables would reward the landowner (whether or not he did his own farm work) with $20 per acre, while the production of wheat would provide him with only $16. The production of vegetables would be preferred on this land, and on all other land up to a limiting distance, L, where both crops would be equally rewarding to the landowner. Beyond that point, the economic rent from wheat would exceed that from vegetables so that wheat alone would be produced in the ring of land enclosed with a circle L miles from the center and another circle eight miles from the center. Vegetables would be grown in the circular central zone with a radius of L miles.

Simple algebra tells us the value of L and the rent of land at this point. Two equations may be formed from the information of the preceding table:

the rent of vegetable land $R_v = 20 - 4M$
the rent of wheat land $R_w = 16 - 2M$

If $M = L$, then

$$R_v = R_w$$

so that:

$$18 - 3L = 20 - 4L$$
$$L = 2$$

and at distance

$$L, \quad R_v = \$12 = R_w.$$

This process rations land in the sense of deciding how it should be used. The rationing instrument is competitive bidding for the use of land and/or the self-interest of the landowners; one result is that the aggregate amount of economic rent received by all landowners in the community is as great as it can be. The "profile" of land rents or land values from the center of this theoretical community is the hatched, bent line indicated on Figure 29, a line which includes the maximum possible area above the horizontal axis.

Another, and in many ways far more compelling, result of this rationing process is that the aggregate expenditure on transportation by this community is at a minimum consistent with its demands for food. This is not immediately evident from Figure 29, but it can be proved without difficulty. Starting with the system just arrived at, with vegetables growing up to point L and wheat growing beyond that point, suppose that two acres of land, one on either side of L and being X miles apart, are transferred to the production of the other crop. Production of some wheat is moved X miles closer to the center of the city at a transportation saving of $2X. Production of some vegetables is moved X miles farther away from the center at a loss in transportation of $4X. There is a net loss amounting to $2X on the interchange of uses. Any variation from the competitive, rent-maximizing use distribution is wasteful of transportation resources.

This is an enormously important concept for the study of land economics, for it means that under the conditions assumed by von Thuenen rational self-interest on the part of private landowners serves the public interest at least as well as any "planned" system of land use. The competitive model of resource allocation, so widely used as a norm in the economics of most other resources, is thus carried over to the field of land-use determination. If we could be certain that the issues and circumstances of land use determination were always essentially as von Thuenen's model assumed them to be, we would not need to worry about what pattern of land uses was "best." The market would determine this, and the market would accomplish the distribution. We would only need to be assured that the market functioned competitively and on the basis of rational self-interest. So rarefied is von Thuenen's example and so remote from issues more germane to urban housing patterns, for example, that we would not be warranted in leaping to the conclusion that urban land markets can do no economic wrong. Yet the elegance of von Thuenen's logic compels us to be most circumspect in questioning the effectiveness of the market process with regard to any set of land uses. And its outline provides us with a starting point in the analysis of many land-use problems quite foreign to the context of von Thuenen's simple farming community.

Before leaving von Thuenen's concepts, it may be useful to consider certain of its implications. If the equilibrium pattern of land uses shown above—a circle with a two-mile radius for the production of vegetables and a surrounding belt six miles wide for the production of wheat—did not produce the two crops in quantities required by the market at the given prices, then we would expect that the market prices for wheat and vegetables would change, shifting the V and W lines on the diagram upward or downward (but not changing their respective slopes) and land on either side of L would shift from one use to another until the quantities desired by the consumers were actually produced. This might involve shrinking or expanding the total cultivated radius (of eight miles in the illustration) to suit the needs of the community's consumers. Thus, the model is flexible with respect to quantities of products.

It is also flexible with respect to changes in the transportation cost per mile for either or both of the crops. Such changes would at first change the slope or slopes of the lines on the diagram, and subsequent changes in the pattern of land use might mean the quantities of output became out of balance with demand, so that further adjustments in the position (but not again in the slope) of one line or the other was necessary.

If the structure of transportation costs which influences the decisions of land users is "false," the pattern of land uses may lead to a waste of transportation resources. Suppose that vegetable farmers were subsidized so that they had to pay only $2 per mile for transportation instead of $4. Then the pattern of land uses would be indeterminate; at first vegetable production would have first claim on all land, but the economic rents of vegetables would have to fall until, with its changed slope, the line V of Figure 29 came to coincide with line W. Land uses would be indeterminate, and though only the same amounts of land might be used for each crop as before (depending on the price elasticities of demand), the location of production of each crop would be indeterminate. Some vegetables might be grown too far away and some wheat too close to the center to permit actual aggregate transportation costs to be minimized.

Von Thuenen's model of land-use determination involves many important assumptions, most of which are made fairly explicit in the above example, such as the uniformity of the transportation system and the single center at which crops are sold. One vital assumption for our later purposes is that the uses of land are perfectly flexible. There is no economic cost of shifting an acre of land from wheat to vegetables or vice versa in response to a change in market demand or relative transportation costs. If there are such costs, such as the removal and reconstruction of an irrigation system (which might be necessary for vegetables but not for wheat), this would substantially alter the nature of optimum land uses.

Robert M. Haig was an American economist much interested in the pattern of urban land uses. His writings during the 1920's were, in effect, adaptations of von Thuenen's theories to intense commercial land uses of the American city, and of New York in particular.[3] Like von Thuenen, Haig based his theorizing upon extensive empirical research, first discovering what was the actual pattern of land uses and then endeavoring to explain the economic mechanics which determined this pattern. Because he dealt with a great variety and mixture of land uses, Haig was not able to present his theory in the simple and graphic manner which made his predecessor's analysis so appealing, yet the fundamental logic was the same. Land uses could be explained by a competition among potential users, with each parcel of land or each building going to the highest bidder, and with the bids arising from the peculiar advantages which each site possessed for each type of potential user.

The consequence of this competition, Haig observed, was not a neat system of concentric rings, but a helter-skelter patchwork of jewelry stores, law offices, furriers, and restaurants. Individual types of users did not concentrate all their activities in one place, but often scattered different business functions across the metropolis. At first glance, Haig observed, there seemed to be no logic whatever in this hash of land uses. But he convinced himself, upon very careful examination, and he made a persuasive argument for others, that there was an underlying rational system at work. It was the competitive process, but competition under circumstances much different from those imagined by von Thuenen. Each type of urban enterprise had its own locational orientation, sometimes to freight terminals for the receipt or shipment of goods, sometimes to the convenience of shoppers or those who used its services, sometimes to competitive enterprises whose customers it hoped to lure. Sometimes the primary locational pull was the cost of transporting goods, but sometimes it was the radius of consumer shopping habits or the form and condition of buildings suitable for the activities of a particular type of urban business. With such a variety of forces operating on a myriad of land-use types, it was understandable that the resultant pattern was more like an egg which had been scrambled than one which was fried sunny side up. But there was efficiency and logic behind the apparently chaotic pattern, Haig concluded, and well-meaning efforts to cure the "chaos" of city land-use patterns would worsen rather than improve the economic life of the city.

The very nature of the phenomena which Haig wanted to understand and explain prevented him from developing a meaningful, symbolic formulation or model. It is also true that appropriate, mathematical concepts and computational techniques were not available at the time of Haig's work, if, indeed, they might be said to be in usable form today. (The CRP model for San Francisco illustrates both the promises and the problems of computer techniques in this area of study.[4]) Thus, his analysis remained in verbal form and the appreciation of his insights has not been widespread. This is perhaps the most dramatic, single case of a condition which has always seriously impeded the development of urban economic theory. The inherent complexity of many-dimensional competition for the use of urban sites means that formal reasoning must employ such abstract and advanced mathematical expressions that it will not be understood by those to whom the urban issues are real, or it must go to the opposite extreme of verbal, unsymbolic reasoning which does not automatically test its own internal consistency and which loses its value when one of the informational "inputs" into the problem is changed. This dilemma still exists, though there are encouraging signs of new and specialized forms of economic reasoning applicable to urban land uses. Had a solution to this methodological problem been available to Haig, his pioneer efforts in urban theory would almost certainly have greatly facilitated the wise, public direction of urban development.

Homer Hoyt is an American scholar of urban development, and of housing in particular, whom it is necessary to characterize as an "empiricist." He made perhaps the most comprehensive compilations of urban land-use data which any single individual has ever put together, particularly in his remarkable study of Chicago.[5] From these masses of data, Hoyt tried to cull some general principles of urban land-use behavior. The most influential of his conclusions is often called the "sector theory," but it is not a theory in the sense of explaining *why* things happen. His "theory" is a set of general trends in the way urban land uses have changed. It has unquestioned, historical importance, but its significance for the prediction of future events or for the development of public policy for housing is very limited.

The sector theory's principal elements can be seen with the aid of Figure 30, a moderate simplification of diagrams actually employed by Hoyt. The inner circle is the area of a newly created city, and the outer ring represents the city's circumference after a period of growth. When the first settlement occurs, the circular area of the city is divided up into wedge-shaped "sectors," each sector housing a specific socioeconomic class. The higher class constructs its residences in the "most fashionable" part of town, and Hoyt has a great amount of information to show which characteristics seem to have made certain parts of cities "fashionable." For example, the well-to-do tend to prefer high ground, partly to enjoy a broad view of the community and its surroundings, but perhaps to represent a superior social status as well.

The middle classes cluster as closely as they can about the

"fashionable" sector, so that some of this status may rub off on them. The poorest class lives in areas which rank lowest in qualities prized by the higher class. They occupy land which is poorly drained, afflicted with the odors, noises, and hazards of industry and transportation centers. These generalizations are consistent with earlier sociological observations of American cities.[6]

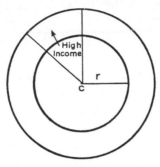

Figure 30

When the city expands, however, some very specific and interesting events occur. The higher class moves away from its original district, because the residences there have become obsolete. This group moves outward, and the direction of movement is one of Hoyt's major, empirical discoveries. This group remains within the sector or wedge which it originally occupied. That is, it simply moves outward, farther away from the center, but in the same compass direction. As successive waves of growth occur, additional outward movement by this leading group takes place, but the direction of movement remains unchanged. Looking at the city at one point in time we can draw two radii enclosing the high-income area, and by extending these radii beyond the present boundaries of the city, we can forecast, in Hoyt's conviction, where in the suburbs future, "fashionable" residential development will occur.

The other major aspect of the sector theory concerns the uses made of the dwellings left behind by the high-income group in the process of urban expansion. These, Hoyt observed, are converted to the use of the low-income group. The dwellings are too large to serve the needs of middle-income households, and are out-of-date in terms of style, equipment, and relation to the transportation system. By cutting them up internally, several smaller dwelling units can be formed out of each large, old house, and the combined rental budgets of several lower-income households can thus acquire a building which is out of reach of an individual middle-income household. This aspect of the sector theory is often called the "filtering" process (a term which Hoyt did not originate) since the homes of the rich eventually filter down to the poor. In a long span of time the low-income group is supplied housing by the marketplace almost exclusively in this way.

There are many aspects of the sector theory which bear witness to its peculiarly American origin. The continued growth of a city's population assumes urbanward migration such as occurred in 19th century America in particular. Lateral expansion of the city absorbs land on the periphery and requires constant improvement of local transportation systems, both of which situations existed in American urban areas in the period of Hoyt's studies. Simple, economic, class distinctions and class consciousness which are embodied in the sector theory also fit the time and place. The concept of housing mobility which encourages the wealthy to give up their residences in regular succession to an influx of poor families is a nearly unique aspect of American urban growth. There is nothing particularly invalid about the empirical generalizations which underlie the sector theory, but they cannot be said to apply to all societies at all times.

One of the most restrictive conditions for Hoyt's theory of the way in which residential areas change is the coincidence between the rate of obsolescence for the homes of the wealthy and the rate of population increase among the low-income class. If there were a sudden influx of low-income families an insufficient number of hand-me-down dwellings would be available for them, and then where would they go? * On the other hand, if the well-to-do became dissatisfied with their present homes, but the num-

---

* Indeed, American cities may be the exception rather than the rule with respect to the spatial distribution of social groups, for in many European, Latin American, and Asian cities low-income housing is found at the periphery while high-income families occupy the central districts.

ber of low-income families failed to increase or perhaps even decreased, what would become of the outward growth pattern? Rapid expansion of the middle class might mean that the potentially "fashionable" areas in the suburbs would fill up with moderately priced houses. It is reasonable to consider post-World War II "G.I. tracts" in the United States as an instance of departure from the "sector theory." The times and places observed by Hoyt did not exhibit these irregular but by no means unlikely patterns of change, so his theory seems to reflect a specialized historical coincidence. As such it cannot offer much to urban scholars of other times and places.

The strong coincidence between the rates of in-migration of the poor and outward movement by the wealthy, upon which the sector theory depends, might be an economic process. That is, we might suppose that an increase in the demand for housing by low-income groups made it possible for the well-to-do to realize such good prices for their old homes that development of new "fashionable" areas in the suburbs became feasible. Or, conceivably, the high-income families might be so anxious to sell obsolete, old dwellings that a surplus of "worker" housing appeared in the city and the expansion of local industries was encouraged.

Hoyt does not offer an explanation about the direction of causation, nor even imply that there is a causal, economic process at work. He limits himself to generalizing about the overt pattern of events. In this sense he fails to provide an economic theory of the distribution of housing types within a city, though his generalizations often seem to provide useful forecasts of growth patterns in contemporaneous American cities. His theory does not explain why these patterns emerge, nor whether they are desirable patterns.* For one thing, the aggregate cost of community transportation plays no role in the sector theory, so we cannot decide on the basis of Hoyt's own writings whether the sector theory or sectoral patterns of change tend to minimize those aggregate transportation costs. Looking at the problem in a different way, Hoyt's theory does not tell us whether the sector pattern and the filtering process provides the community as a whole

---

* See, for example, the criticism by Lloyd Rodwin, "The Theory of Residential Growth and Structure," *The Appraisal Journal* (July 1950).

with the best housing standards which its resources will permit. This has become a major issue in the emerging study of urban development and it seems that Hoyt's writing confused rather than clarified this point.

There is an interesting similarity between the concentric circles of von Thuenen's explicitly economic theory (minimizing transportation costs and maximizing land values) and Hoyt's empirical generalizations. One concerns agricultural production, while the other describes urban housing patterns, but both involve a set of concentric circles separating classes of land uses. In the search for broad patterns of land uses—seeing the forest rather than the trees—concentric circles are a recurring theme in the literature of urban development.

From this very brief look at some early work on the subject of land-use patterns, we see three distinct approaches. One, best exemplified by Hoyt, is an effort to generalize about past experience without necessarily explaining why it occurred, so that only a conditional forecast of future patterns can be made. (It is a conditional forecast since we must assume that past conditions, known or unknown, will be present in the future.) Another approach, most clearly reflected in Ricardo's writing, is to explain why certain things occur, such as an increase in the rent of land. This explanation is based upon assumptions of gain-motivated, competitive, private behavior. Haig also takes this point of view to see economic order underlying visual disorder in the land-use pattern of New York City.

A third approach, most clearly evident from von Thuenen's work, is an examiniation of the implications of private behavior for public welfare. This is very much the crux of our inquiry into the optimum characteristics of an urban housing stock, for it is one thing to know whether an emergent condition is good for individual landowners and quite another to understand whether it is also helpful to the community as a whole, and particularly to families in search of the best housing which available resources can provide. The question, "Does a housing entrepreneur's pursuit of gain cause economic resources to be wasted?" creates the need for a very particular type of economic theory, one which shows what entrepreneurs will be inclined to do for themselves and what their actions will do on behalf of others.

In order to make progress toward such theory, we shall need to define a vocabulary of urban economic concepts in two distinct "languages," that of the entrepreneur and that of the community. Sometimes the meanings coincide, but sometimes they do not. Where they diverge we can begin to see how entrepreneurially determined urban housing patterns may be different from patterns best suited to the needs of users. We can also use such theory to guide community housing policy by identifying cases in which difficulties which seem attributable to entrepreneurial motivation really are based upon institutions of society or government which could be modified to good effect.

Economic Elements of Urban Housing Optimization

Several of the concepts in the following enumeration have their roots in the pioneer writings summarized above. Such writings do not, however, provide an integrated model of urban housing behavior and polity sufficient for discussion of the three, major, analytical issues which we find in urban housing affairs. Additional concepts are needed to adapt basic earlier notions to housing issues perceived today and to blend all these concepts into at least the framework of a question-answering theory. The following sections develop a number of such concepts which in various combinations are strategic for evaluating housing programs within a community. We have had occasion to consider most of these concepts earlier, particularly as they bear on the question of equilibrium within the housing sector. (See Chapter 5.) Now we must develop them somewhat further so that the social or community implications of market-determined behavior can be revealed.

SITE RENT

A city, like a grocery store or a stock market, is a device for facilitating exchange. Things are brought into a central place, exchanged, and carried away. The carrying process involves the use of resources; that is, urban functions give rise to transportation costs. The spatial distribution of human activity is influenced by the technology and cost of transportation systems. Transport factors affect not only what cities are like, but how big they are, how numerous, where they appear on the world's surface, and, indeed, whether they exist at all. A considerable body of economic literature has to do with the influence of transportation on urban development.*

For one thing, we would expect that considerations of transport cost would tend to cause cities to be essentially circular in form. If exchanges occur in a central point, less total resources would be required for transportation by a circular city than by a long, narrow city of the same population. It follows that the location of various land uses along the radius of a circular city is one principal, analytical problem in urban economics. The radius appears in the "plan view" (i.e. from above) of the city in Figure 30, and as the horizontal axis of the "profile view" in Figure 31.

Suppose there is a continuous pattern of residential development from the center C all along radius r in Figure 31. Some families must be living at the outer edge of the city and if their daily activities take them to the center of the city, they will incur transportation costs of a definite amount, represented by the vertical height b or for numerical illustration, say $240 a year. Families living at the center will have no such transportation costs, and families living at in-between distances will have transport costs which vary with that distance at a rate of, say, α dollars per mile, per year. We can suppose that the radius is ten miles, so that the value of α in our illustration is $24.

A family living at a distance $\frac{1}{2}r$, or five miles, from C has an annual transportation cost of $\frac{1}{2}b$, or $120. If, for some reason, this family and one living at the outer edge of the city decide to switch locations, the first would be able to ask an amount equivalent to $120 per year from the second. The second family would be willing to pay this amount for this is what it will save by being closer to the center. This payment has been given the name "site rent" or "position rent." It can be demanded by anyone who controls the use of land within the margin of the city.

---

* For example, Lowden Wingo, Jr., *Transportation and Urban Land* (Washington, D.C.: Resources for the Future, 1961). Major empirical studies relating land use to transportation variables have been made recently in several American cities.

It rises from the center at a rate which may be slow or fast, regular or irregular, depending on the nature of the transportation system in use. (If transportation costs in one direction from the center are less per mile than costs in another direction, then the plan view of the city will not be perfectly circular as in Figure 30, but will bulge outward in that direction.) Figure 31 shows a constant rate of increase in transportation costs from the center, but this need not be so. Sherman Maisel has made an extended discussion of this.[7]

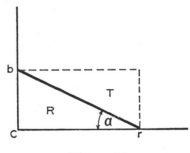

Figure 31

Whatever the technologically determined structure of transportation costs in the area of the city, the site rent at any one point will be equivalent to savings made possible by that location over the transportation costs of a resident at the fringe. Location rents at the fringe itself is zero, though as a city grows outward, rents will begin to appear on previously "marginal" land. (This is quite similar to Ricardo's argument about farm rents with differential fertility among farms and an increasing total demand for wheat.) The sum of site rent plus transportation cost is the same, *b*, or $240 a year in our illustration, at any point along the radius. Distance along the radius determines the manner in which this total is divided between actual transportation costs and the payment of site rent, but the total is always the same.

Now, to understand the significance of this concept, we must realize that the payment of site rent is a "transfer," while costs of transportation represent (at least in principle) consumption of scarce economic resources. The household which lives at the outer edge of the city uses up $240 worth of transportation resources per year, in our example, and these resources are physically consumed. They disappear, and the society becomes that much poorer because of the transportation expense. The family which lives at the center, however, and pays $240 per year in site rent, consumes no transportation resources. The community saves a certain quantity of gasoline, highway space, utility lines, and commuters' time because the family lives at the center.

It would be incorrect to say that the saving in real resources is caused by the payment of rent, however. The market creates a redistribution of income when the community chooses to live in a dispersed pattern rather than tightly clustered at the center. In a system of private ownership, the possession of favorably situated land means that spending power will be transferred from households to landowners (which might, of course, be the households themselves) whenever the residential pattern gives rise to transportation outlays. This is the basis for Henry George's "single tax" proposal.[8] A community may gain by saving transportation costs, but it does not gain by lowering site rents. Transportation activities use up resources, while site-rent payments only redistribute an unchanging quantity of resources.

Both site-rent and transportation costs are "prices" of urban residential location, but it sometimes happens that site rent is given greater weight in residential-location decisions than transportation costs. The payment of rent or the purchase of land is directly attributable to the need for housing in the eye of the typical householder and the housing entrepreneur, but the cost of transportation resulting from the selection of a site sometimes is not seen as a housing cost. It is paid in the form of day-by-day bus or subway fares, consumption of gasoline, expenditure of time, and payment of taxes and utility bills which go, in part, for the construction and maintenance of transportation facilities. A family or a builder may believe it will be prudent to buy "cheap land" in the suburbs, forgetting that the location will result in added transportation costs. When those costs are subsidized or paid in such a way as to be unrelated to transportation requirements (as might be particularly well illustrated by utility bills based on the amount of water, gas, etc. consumed by the household but not on that household's contribution to distribution costs), the private household or housing entrepreneur can be led by a transfer price (site rent) to cause excessive consumption of real community resources (transportation). Public enterprises, such as housing authorities, which should be conscious of the nonmarket real costs of location decisions, often seem misled in just the same way. Suburban land is not "cheap" to the community.

Some urban economists seem to confuse site rents with site *value,* and while the two concepts are related and both are quite significant, the distinction between them is marked. The household which lives halfway between the center of the city and the fringe of development, in our example, saves $120 per year in transportation cost and explicitly if it is a tenant, or implicitly if it owns the ground, pays $120 per year in site rent. If we use a simple capitalization multiplier of 10, we might say that the value of their site is $1,200.

This does not tell us what the value of the land they occupy is, however, until we know how many households share the same land unit. If this family lives alone on one-fourth of an acre, then we could say that the site value of land is $4,800 per acre. If this family lives in a two-unit building on the same quarter of an acre, however, or lives in a one-family house on an eighth of an acre, the site value of land is $9,600. Thus, to translate site rent, per household, into site value, per unit of land, we must know what the housing density of the location is. This brings us to the second of our concepts, density.

DENSITY

Let us build further upon the preceding numerical illustration to show the role of density. A perfectly circular city with a radius of ten miles has an area of πr^2 or 314 square miles. Let us suppose that the community includes 314,000 families, so that the average (and let us further assume at first, uniform) density is 1,000 families per square mile. (This allows plenty of room for each family's share of factories, stores, office and public buildings, streets and parks and other land uses, as well as residential.) Each and every family pays $240 per year because of its location. This amount is determined by the cost per mile of distance from the center (including costs of roads, utility lines, etc., and let us assume that it fairly represents the value of travel time and inconvenience as well), and by the radius of the city.

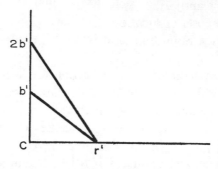

Figure 32

The radius is determined by the density, however. If the households of the community feel that $240 is too much to pay, they can, in principle, reduce this payment, which is a varying composite of site rent and transportation cost, by living at higher density. For example, if the same population inhabits a city half as large in area, or 157 square miles, their density will be 2,000 families per square mile. The radius, r', of such a city will be approximately seven miles, for $\pi r'^2 = \pi r^2/2$, $r'^2 = r^2/2$, and $r' =$

$$\sqrt{\frac{100}{2}} \approx 7.$$

Transportation cost for the family at the fringe of the city is therefore 7/10 of $240 per year, or $168. Families at the center pay $168 in site rent, so that the structure of site rent per household is lower than that indicated by the line in Figure 31. The slope of the line remains the same, since no change in transportation technology has been assumed, but the intercept, shown as b' in Figure 32, is lower.

In exchange for higher-density living, the residents of this community are able to conserve transportation resources and devote those resources to other forms of desirable consumption, either public or private. There is a "trade-off" between transportation outlays and the enjoyment of low-density living, and we may say that the density of every city in every modern epoch reflects some form of community judgment, deliberate or accidental, about how much to pay for transportation in order to achieve low density. (See Figure 24 in Chapter 5.)

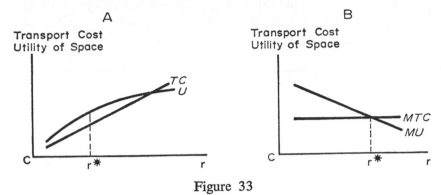

Figure 33

The nature of this trade-off decision is represented by Figure 33. The horizontal axis in Figures 33a and 33b is the radius of a city of constant size but varying density, while the vertical axis measures the cost of transportation and the advantage, or "utility," of land area per household expressed in comparable, monetary terms. Figure 33a shows the changes in aggregate or average transportation costs (i.e., resources expended for transportation as the radius of the city increases and density falls, and the increase in aggregate or average household utility as density falls. Transportation costs rise at a constant rate as the radius increases because as density falls families simply move outward along the radius of the circle. Total utility rises at a decreasing rate, assuming that the enjoyment of urban space without regard to its price is subject to diminishing returns. At point r^* the excess of utility gain over transport cost is a maximum, and this is the density-transport cost combination which would be optimal for this population. Figure 33b expresses the same idea in marginal terms. The marginal transportation cost curve (MTC) is horizontal, while the marginal utility of lower density is decreasing. The point of intersection, r^*, identifies the optimal area and density level.

The structure of site rent is lower for the community which will accept higher residential densities, as Figure 32 shows. However, the structure of site *values*—the location value of a unit of land area—is partly higher for the high-density community. This is shown in Figure 34, the vertical axis of which measures the value of a constant unit of land, say the amount enjoyed by each household in the low-density community, or .001 square miles. Using our convenient capitalization factor, this value would be $2,400.

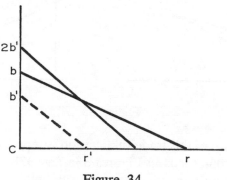

Figure 34

For the high-density community, in which each household enjoys only .0005 square miles of land, the capitalized site rent of the family living at the center is $1,680. There are two such families in each .001 square mile, however, so the site value at the center of the high-density community is $3,360 on a basis comparable to that of the first case. Site value falls to zero at a radius of seven miles in the high-density community and at a radius of ten miles in the low-density community. Hence, the lines indicating site value per land unit for the two situations cross. (The point of intersection has no special significance for the present argument.) Doubling the density of the city means site values will be raised for all land from the center to this intersection point and beyond that point they will fall.

Holding other factors constant, we would thus expect that a community which is either relatively poor, or in which the cost of transportation per mile is relatively high, would be built up at higher densities. That is, these factors would cause a city to be relatively compressed, though productive of absolutely higher site values in the central area. There is much in the way of international comparison and comparisons over time for cities in the same nation which would support this abstract theory. Early Boston or New York, for example, had narrow streets, small lots, small-scale and densely occupied buildings in comparison with cities developed later in the United States. These "miniature" urban dimensions are to be found even in "ghost towns" of the American west where there never was a scarcity of land. Perhaps the explanation is in cultural carry-over by settlers who assumed that the land economy of mid-19th century New York or Philadelphia was a universal "natural order." The association of small-scale urban buildings and streets with the past is evident in the nostalgic design of Disneyland. Tokyo today is a city of narrow streets, very small lots and houses, and probably the world's highest land prices at its center.

Thus far we have said very little of variations in building sizes as an aspect of residential density. For the moment we can suppose that density is determined before the buildings are built and that subsequently residential buildings are constructed to conform to this. Another trade-off situation is indicated, for a given population can be accommodated on a given amount of land in any of several ways. Each might have a single-family home on its pro rata share of the land, or dwelling structures may expand vertically, giving each household more floor space but at a sacrifice of privacy. There are also some increasing per-unit costs as the height of buildings is increased, and technology sometimes provides absolute barriers to vertical expansion (the development of the elevator represents a technological breakthrough in this sense).

The trade-off is represented by Figure 35, showing the rising marginal cost per housing unit as the number of stories in a residential building is increased. It also shows the marginal utility of the household, holding the land density of population constant, rising at a diminishing rate as the vertical expansion provides it with increased floor space. It might be supposed that some sense of privacy is sacrificed when a small but separate dwelling gives way to one floor of a multifamily structure. The shape of these curves is largely supposition, in any case. What matters is that high land density may be represented by many small buildings or a few large ones, the choice being a matter for the households involved. Presumably, the choice of structure type is a part of the process by which the density utility curve of Figure 33 is determined.

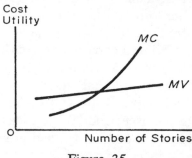

Figure 35

The significance of residential density for the economic welfare of the community lies partly in its ability to conserve transportation resources, for the community which accepts high density can economize on transportation resources. In part also the significance of density selection by households affects the physical pattern of the city's development, for some households may be willing to live at higher densities than others prefer. This is our next issue, the competition for specific intracity locations by different density groups.

COMPETITION

Where transportation cost is the criterion, land within a city is rationed among classes of users not by site *rent*—transport savings per user—but by site *value*—transport saving per unit of land. We can express the relation of rent and value in this way:

site rent x density = site value

Thus, it is density, or more specifically variations in density, which govern the distribution of various land uses within the city. Without differences in density, the market would not determine which user was located where.

Urban land users who respond to the cost of transportation by selecting different "trade-off" points between transportation cost and density have different competitive strengths for individual parcels of land within the city. This is a point suggested by the theories of von Thuenen and very particularly described in the writings of Haig. Haig, however, was concerned with nonresidential uses, so the concept of "density" would have to be understood as the space requirement of individual business enterprises. For residential users the meaning of density is simply the number of households who are willing to share a given ground area.

Figure 34 provides a starting point for a description of the competitive outcome in the residential market for land. Close to the center the site values generated by the high-density group of households exceeds that originating from low-density households. The opposite situation arises in the outer portion of the city. Hence, the high-density group could command the central district in a competitive market, and the low-density group would be accorded the outer ring.

The outcome of competition is not obvious from Figure 34. This diagram superimposes two independent situations, communities of like size but inhabiting a circular city at different densities. We must see what the residential pattern would be if both of these population groups inhabited the same city.

It is convenient to start with the assumption that the city is occupied by 314,000 high-density households only. They occupy one square mile for each 2,000 households for a total of 157 square miles. The radius of such a city, as we have shown, is approximately seven miles. The site value at the center is $3,360, decreasing at a rate of $480 per mile, reaching zero at the end of the seven-mile radius.

Now, suppose the population of the city increases by 314,000 households, all of whom prefer to live at a lower density, say 1,000 households per square mile. We must assume also that buildings, if they exist, are perfectly adaptable to either density pattern at no cost, and that every household is basically indifferent about the way in which its residential land budget is divided between site rent and transportation cost. That is, no household prefers a specific location or is reluctant to move.

The first effect of doubling the number of households in

the community is to expand the margin of residential development beyond the original seven-mile radius. Marginal transport
costs will rise as the city expands, and the whole structure of site
rents and values will shift upward. The area of the city will increase by 314 square miles (to accommodate the additional
households at their density) to a total of 471 square miles. The
radius of the expanded city will be approximately 12 miles.

The site value of centrally located land is $2,880 (per year)
per .001 square mile ($240 x 12) if rented to a low-density
household. However, if high-density families live on the fringe of
the city after the population change occurs, a central location
would have a value of $5,760 to them ($480 x 12) for the
same .001 square mile of land. Competition would award the
central land to the high-density household. As the next land
away from the center was considered, and then the next, high-
density households would continue to outbid low-density households until all of the former were situated in the central portion
of the city. Once again, this central portion would have a radius
of seven miles, but land at this distance now commands a site
rent, for there will be households living beyond that point.

To determine the structure of site rents in the expanded
community we have information which is summarized in Figure
36. Central site rents for the two population groups, high and
low density, are v' and v, respectively. We know the value of v
to be $2,880, but the value of v' (which is the actual value) is
unknown and to be determined. We know that the two lines, H
(for high-density values) and L (for low-density values), cross
at a radius of about seven miles and that the two lines decrease
at rates of $480 per mile and $240 per mile, respectively.

We can calculate the site value, v^*, at radius seven miles by
moving inward from the twelve-mile radius adding $240 per
mile. Thus, $v^* = \$1,200$. Moving back out from the seven-mile
point toward r' and subtracting $480 for each mile, we find that
H reaches zero when $r' = 9.5$ miles. Now we can find v' to be
$4,560 (9.5 x $480).

The site-value structure of the community finally achieves
the following shape: at the center it is $4,560 per .001 square
mile of land, falling at a rate of $480 per mile for seven miles to

a level of $1,200; beyond that point it falls at a rate of $240 per mile for five miles. All high-density households reside at the center, and all low-density households live in the five-mile wide outer ring.

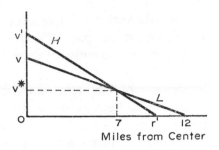

Figure 36

Because we started with high-density households occupying the central seven-mile radius circle, and ended with the same type of occupants, it might seem that the effect of additional population was simply to build up the fringe of the city to accommodate the newcomers of whatever density, leaving the original residents undisturbed. A careful rereading of the above argument will remove such suspicions, however. We could have started with a low-density community occupying a ten-mile radius circle, added high-density newcomers, and established a final pattern just as described above with high-density households taking over the center.

We might note, too, that the structure of land values in the community emerged only when the rationing process was complete. Households did not decide the place or the density at which they wished to live by considering the land-value structure of the community. On the contrary, the structure of land values was determined by prior density-transport cost trade-off decisions and a competitive process. Locational patterns were decided simultaneously.

A more significant point is that the competitive process produces a distributional pattern which minimizes the aggregate use of transportation resources by the community. We can show this in the same way that the point was made by von Thuenen.

Starting with the equilibrium distribution, with the two types of households separated by the seven-mile ring, imagine that occupants of one unit of land, .001 square mile, on either side of this line are switched. Moving the two high-density families out will add twice as much to total transportation cost as moving one family will save. Thus, where these simple conditions prevail a competitive process which awards parcels of residential land to the highest bidder will most efficiently conserve community resources.

The real significance of site rents and site values now emerges. These charges arise because some sites within a community are advantageously situated. The incomes which these sites provide for owners are in the nature of monopoly gains, for each location is unique and cannot be duplicated. As such, site rents seem sometimes to accomplish an antisocial effect, for they redistribute income on the basis of ownership, not creative personal effort. The existence of a system of site rents, however, where there are various types of users competing for the same parcel of land, excludes all but one class of users from each parcel. The pattern of rationing is determinate if each landowner seeks to maximize his own rental income, and the result of such unrestrained monopoly and greed is a pattern of land uses which, in simple circumstances which we have used to illustrate the argument, cannot be improved upon by any community-conscious, selfless, public administrator.

An important characteristic of site rents and values is that they represent potential or expected uses rather than uses and needs actually in existence. One reason for this is that users are not in practice perfectly mobile so that they cannot be replaced on a given site when a higher bidder for that site arrives in the community. More will be made shortly of this point, but the essence of the site-rent rationing process is that some users are excluded by high prices which some other user is merely *thought* to be willing to pay. Informed expectation may replace explicit communication in the auction market for urban sites without, in principle, distorting the outcome. Users who have not yet appeared on the scene must bid by proxy through the reservation prices of present landowners.

We could introduce other types of families into this hypothetical city and see additional rings formed by site-value competition. We could let there be more than one center or change the roundness of the circle with some natural barriers, or limit the transportation system to certain routes. Very quickly we would go beyond the bounds of plane geometry or simple algebra, but the essential nature of the market's land-rationing system would remain unchanged. Transportation savings create the opportunity for landowners to receive rents, rents create values, and the landowners' desire to secure the greatest value per unit of land establishes a system of priorities which allocates residential land among competing types of households. The nature of the competition is in the level of density acceptable to the household, and, in the more complex case, the peculiar locational interests of each household and its individual assessment of the transportation burden.

ECONOMIC LIFE

Unfortunately—and that is a very large word in this situation—transportation costs alone suffice to allocate urban resources efficiently only if no valuable structures have yet been placed upon the land, or if the structures are not durable, or, if durable, structures are identical, multipurpose buildings which use up all the area of the city. These conditions are not likely to be met—unless we are building an entire town all at once—so it becomes necessary to take into account the role of a stock of durable, heterogeneous buildings in discussing the economic determinants of urban form.

Suppose, for example, in the preceding illustration that one parcel of ground within the high-density, inner circle had upon it a low-density dwelling which had been constructed at an earlier time when, perhaps, its location was "efficient" in the sense of transport-cost-minimizing land allocation. Because this land is now occupied by a low-density household, there must be two high-density families living farther from the center than is in one sense appropriate. This causes total transport costs for the community to be higher than necessary.

The saving in transport costs can be realized, however, only by destroying the existing low-density building. For a period of time this building must continue to be the most "efficient" use of the land in a new, larger sense, for the transportation savings occasioned by changing the use will not be great enough to compensate for the loss of valuable capital stock. The value of the existing house is determined by its worth as a residence to present and prospective occupants.

The time will come, of course, when the low-density dwelling has so little value remaining in it—being deteriorated and obsolescent—that the site value for the new use begins to exceed the remaining value. Then that building will have come to the end of its economic life. Until that time arrives, the economist must plead that the building is more valuable than the extra transportation cost which its location causes; its premature removal would be a false economy.

We should note that the decision not to demolish the "misplaced" house implies that the potentially higher-density occupants of this site must locate in what otherwise should be the low-density zone. The new building will commence its own economic life and may retain a hold on this "inappropriate" land even after the economic life of the first, low-density house (in the inner zone) has ended. This chain reaction of "poorly located" dwellings is still, paradoxically, the best overall choice of land-use arrangements the community can make.

Perhaps we don't feel too badly about the inappropriate location of just one dwelling or one pair of structures. Chances are, however, that this situation will not be the exception, but rather the rule. Populations of cities can grow and change so rapidly that the great majority of the dwellings (and the other structures which relate to the location of dwellings such as streets, stores, and offices) which exist today are not located in patterns which minimize transportation cost. The durability effect of structures more than offsets the transportation effect of sites.

In years to come we have reason to expect that rising incomes will lead to more rapid obsolescence of dwellings, shorter economic life for structures, and a greater role for transportation costs in the determination of urban form. This assumes that people with the higher incomes will not choose to increase their transportation expenditures as much as they consume outlays on buildings. It will be interesting to watch shifts in technology and taste affecting both structures and the means of transportation, for these can be translated into predictions of change in urban form.

For the present and near future, if the value of structures already on the land dominates land-use patterns and the socio-economic form of the city, we need to know something of the way in which particular kinds of buildings come to be built, and why they are constructed where they are. In a growing city it makes sense to expect that newer buildings will be built mostly on the fringes, with the exception of those kinds of buildings which have an unusual intensity of site value, such as offices and stores.

FILTERING

One very interesting question concerns the relative price level at which new dwelling units are added to the city's stock of dwellings. We cannot answer this question without at least implicitly deciding what is going to happen to the older portions of the housing stock when the time comes to construct some net additions to the stock or to replace some part of the stock. Will the older dwellings "filter down" to economic groups less affluent or less demanding than the previous occupants? If so, then the new buildings will be built for the relatively well-to-do. On the other hand, if this filtering process does not occur, then the nature of the new construction—most of it being at the fringes of the city—will reflect the characteristics of the added population or that population which has decided to abandon its present housing.

In the early years after World War II the urban areas of the United States saw a great influx of middle-income families, and the fringe filled up with "G.I. tracts"—large housing developments for veterans who were favored with mortgage credit on very generous terms. Later on, the filtering process came back into play, and it was the outward movement of the upper-middle-income group in search of housing improvement which dominated suburban construction. Thus, more recent suburban residential construction has had a rather luxurious look.

How do we know when the filtering process will operate and when it will not? More important, perhaps, for our immediate interest, can we judge whether the filtering process serves some kind of social purpose? These questions relate to the manner in which urban resources are priced and rationed. A type of economic analysis similar in principle to the above discussion of site rent is needed. This time, however, the criterion of market behavior will not be the value of land and location, but the value of buildings and of capital. An urban economy rations capital as well as land among classes of users. Some of the capital is "sunk" in the form of durable structures which can only be used, demolished, or abandoned and which, like land, have no current economic cost. The community's broad interest will be served by using the stock of sunk capital to maximum advantage. Under some conditions we can expect that the competitive market process will secure this maximum use.

Another form of capital to be conserved is the supply of new savings. That is, buildings can be constructed to replace, improve, or supplement the stock of sunk capital, but to accomplish this, the resources must be diverted from some other purpose. To invest in new capital the community must divert resources from consumption. To invest in housing the community must divert these saved resources from the expansion of industrial equipment, inventories, office buildings, and other possible forms of new investment. To invest in luxurious, single-family suburban homes the community must divert new housing resources from low-priced home construction, from apartment building, and from reconstruction of the central area. Again, there is in principle a competitive market process which makes these decisions about the uses of currently available resources. The direction of these market decisions, and the likelihood that they will coincide with the direction of community interest can be analyzed.

A competitive private market tends to adjust the pattern of use of the existing stock so that new community housing demands are met with minimum new capital expenditure. That is, the nature of a private market is such that it tends to conserve capital, making the most intensive feasible use of the existing stock of dwellings with the result that additional capital requirements stemming from a change in the pattern of demand are minimized.

Consider first the methods of meeting a demand for replacement dwellings. Suppose that the community consists initially of 360,000 dwellings and households, and that we can classify and rank the dwellings on the basis of quality. Dividing this ranking into three equal parts, we can call one portion of the inventory "low quality," another "medium quality," and the last "high quality," so that there are 120,000 dwellings in each group. Now suppose that the community desires to raise its housing standards, either because it has experienced an increase in real income or because the present stock of dwellings has deteriorated. One method of satisfying this desire, which we may label "direct improvement," would be to provide each household with a newly constructed dwelling which is superior to its present dwelling by the desired degree of improvement.

This would result in the construction of 360,000 new dwellings, and a scrapping of the entire initial inventory. In Tokyo, two-thirds of the present dwelling units are smaller than the pre-war average size which is now considered a sort of "norm." To realize the norm by the "direct improvement" method would mean scrapping more than a million and a half dwellings and, at present rates of housing construction, would require about fifteen years. Another method, which we can label "indirect improvement," would provide 120,000 new units of "advanced quality" as replacements for the "high-quality" group, releasing the latter dwellings to the initial occupants of the "medium-quality group, and in turn releasing "medium-quality" dwellings to the initial occupants of the "low-quality" dwellings. This method provides housing improvement for all households, scraps only the poorest 120,000 of the initial stock of dwellings, and requires that 120,000 dwellings be constructed. No matter what weights are attached to these requirements for different construction costs or housing satisfactions received, the indirect method is more effective than the direct method in the sense of conserving capital.

A variation on the "direct improvement" method which recognizes the principle of conserving capital may be called "direct fair shares." In this method the total number of new units (or aggregate new housing capital in a more sophisticated situation) is held to the level of 120,000, but one-third of this amount is provided directly for households in each of the three initial dwelling quality classes. These three means of meeting improvement demand may be summarized by the following table:

7   DWELLING QUALITY CLASSES (000's of Units)

	Total	Low	Medium	High	Advanced
Initial Stock	360	120	120	120	—
Improvement Requirements					
Direct	360	—	120	120	120
Indirect	120	—	—	—	120
Direct fair shares	120	—	40	40	40

The "direct-fair-shares" method requires the continued use of 80,000 units of initial low quality, and less effectively improves housing conditions for any and all groups than does the indirect method. The indirect method enjoys a strong, presumptive superiority as a means of improving housing conditions for the community at minimum new capital expense.

The advantage of the indirect method lies in making household mobility a part of the response to a change in housing requirements. This is none other than the "filtering" concept, long a part of discussions and research on the economics of housing. It is a tendency which is inherent in the system of private, individual management of housing capital, for any market tendency to abandon existing dwellings induces the owners of those dwellings to compete by lowering prices and rents. This brings existing units into the reach of households previously unable to afford them and diminishes effective demand by those households for newly constructed dwellings.

The mobility of households is very important to the indirect method, and a more complicated phenomenon than it may at first seem. Not only must households be willing to physically transfer their places of residence, but they must be aware of the opportunities available to them. If they are home owners, they must find it possible to market their present homes without unnecessary sales expense and they must have access to housing credit for the purchase of better though not necessarily newly constructed homes.

The advantage of meeting housing requirements indirectly rather than directly is less obvious in the case of subsidized improvement, but the presumptive argument for the indirect method is strong, even here. Suppose, for example, that the community's initial stock of dwellings is divided into three quality categories as before, and that the community determines to subsidize the acquisition of medium-quality dwellings by households initially occupying low-quality units. That is, medium quality is to be made the actual minimum standard for the community. The direct and indirect alternatives are shown below:

8   SUBSIDIZED IMPROVEMENT

	Dwelling Quality Classes (000's of Units)				
	Total	Low	Medium	High	Advanced
Initial Stock	360	120	120	120	—
Improvement Requirements					
Direct	120	—	120	—	—
Indirect	120	—	—	—	120

Either method eliminates all the low-quality dwellings and provides medium-quality dwellings as replacement. The direct method requires no mobility and, indeed, assumes that the rest of the community is quite unaffected by the change in housing quality among the least adequately housed families. The subsidy is equal to the "replacement cost" of medium-quality dwellings (i.e. the amount necessary to reproduce quality equal to that of medium-quality dwellings in the initial stock) less the capitalized housing purchasing power of households initially in the low-quality dwellings.

The indirect method subsidizes the construction of dwellings of advanced quality, so that all households may, if they are mobile, move up the ladder of housing quality. The difference in resource cost between the indirect and direct methods is the difference between the resources (other than land) required for advanced as opposed to medium-quality housing, so that it is likely for the indirect method to cost more. However, the indirect method produces no less improvement in housing quality for the initial occupants of low-quality dwellings, plus housing benefits for the remainder of the community as well. It is not inconsistent with the principle of conservation of capital that more resources should be utilized if the result is a net gain in consumer utility. When the community considers it worthwhile to divert resources into the housing sector to raise housing quality, it does not necessarily have to stop at a particular level of initial quality.

The difference in resource cost between the two approaches may not be very large, in fact, because of cost-utility relationship which often seems to characterize the housing economy. New dwellings of high quality tend to have a close relationship between cost and utility, precisely because a competitive market will not provide them unless this is the case. Obsolescent dwellings, however, have replacement costs in excess of the utility provided, because of the factors of depreciation and obsolescence. In constructing a dwelling of "medium quality" it is difficult to save resources by imitating the forces of deterioration and obsolescence which have acted upon units of the older stock to reduce the latter's value. The needs of families which are most immediately in need of housing subsidy can be met with buildings which are to some extent depreciated and obsolescent, for the initial "medium-quality" dwellings in our example are such housing but remain within the community's definition of standard and adequate housing. It is not the fact of depreciation or obsolescence which makes a dwelling unsuitable, but only the degree of such faults. Since it is not feasible to reproduce dwellings which, though adequate, are depreciated and obsolescent, any subsidized construction produces better dwellings than the community actually requires for its direct improvement needs. The issue is how much better these dwellings should be and, hence, how large a segment of the community should be involved in the transformation of the housing stock. The relationship of total utility created to total new resources required is likely to be most favorable for a program which, in a sense, "overshoots" the initial, direct objective. If it is time to replace one sleeve on an overcoat, it may make better sense to replace the coat. Limited efforts can be wasteful.

Housing demand changes through population growth as well as through the desire for improvement. Again, there are direct and indirect methods for meeting such changes in housing demand. Suppose that 60,000 households are added to the community of our example and that all of these households are in the "medium-quality" segment of the housing market. The alternative methods of adding to the stock of dwellings are summarized in the following table:

9 GROWTH OF COMMUNITY HOUSING STOCK

	Dwelling Quality Classes (000's of Units)				
	Total	Low	Medium	High	Advanced
Initial Stock	360	120	120	120	—
Growth Requirement					
Direct	60	—	60	—	—
Indirect	60	—	—	—	60

The direct approach neither requires nor utilizes mobility on the part of the households initially inhabiting this community. Newcomers are provided for by means of newly constructed dwellings adapted to their specific needs. The indirect approach foresees improved opportunities for some household initially in medium- and high-quality dwellings to improve their housing standards. The mechanism might be price increases in the medium range which encourage some households to move up to high-quality dwellings. This, in turn, would create price pressure in the high-quality range, encouraging some households there to move up to newly constructed, advanced-quality dwellings.

The objective differences are similar to those of the subsidized-improvement case. More resources are employed, but the gains in utility are more widespread. Since we do not assume a subsidy here, the question is whether the new arrivals can secure units from the present stock, even at prices which are "inflated" by the increase in community housing demand, at less cost to themselves than they would experience by entering the new construction market. Again, despite the tendency toward some inflation of price levels, the factors of depreciation and obsolescence are likely to make older dwellings a better bargain for the new arrivals than new medium-quality dwellings would be.

The most important advantage of the private sector in meeting housing needs is its ability to perceive indirect opportunities for conserving resources. Its most important weakness is its inability to respond to externalities.

AMENITY AND SHELTER RENTS

The filtering process and the pattern of new housing construction can be illustrated by means of a geometric diagram if we make a few, simplifying assumptions. First, suppose that transportation costs (and hence site rents) are nil, and that residential densities are uniform over the city. Suppose, also, that the housing units are qualitatively differentiated, new ones being better than older houses. Further, assume that new houses have always been built on the fringe of the existing built-up area. Thus, as we travel outward from the center, C, along the radius, r, in Figure 37 we encounter progressively newer and more desirable housing units.

Finally, suppose that the households in the city fall into two groups as far as housing demand is concerned. One group is in the market for "shelter" alone, while the other group wants housing which combines "amenity" with shelter. Perhaps the first group has less income than the second, or perhaps it merely attaches less significance to housing in relation to other consumption goods. The exact reason for their lack of interest in housing amenity does not matter at this point.

The allocation of the stock of housing units between these two groups is represented in Figure 37. The "shelter" group offers the same price (or rent, in the ordinary sense) for every unit in the supply, an amount measured by CA. The "amenity" group offers different prices depending on the quality of the unit; hence, their demand schedule rises as we go out from C along r. The distance, CB, defines the inner portion of the housing stock occupied by the shelter group, and the outer ring, which is Br wide, is given over to the amenity-seekers. The reasoning behind this allocation of the stock is very much like the theory of von Thuenen. If we start from a market-equilibrium situation, all the shelter-seekers will be accommodated in the older, less desirable housing in the *CB* circle, and the amenity-seekers will live in the newer and better units in the *Br* ring.

In our previous discussion of transportation, site rents, and density it was readily apparent that a competitive market could determine residential land-use patterns in such a way that the use of transportation resources by the community as a whole

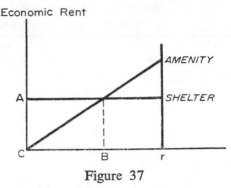

Figure 37

was minimized. Market prices having the textbook name of "site rents" are instrumental in bringing about this efficiency in the allocation of urban space. A very similar argument applies to the allocation of urban structures, but the reasoning may not be so obvious.

Thinking back on the problem of intraurban location, we realize that the way in which one fixed resource, land, was used affected the rate at which a variable category of resources, transportation, was required. Transportation, which uses up resources potentially available for many other uses, is a substitute for conveniently located land. The land is "free" in the sense that no sacrifice of present resources (labor, etc.) is necessary to make it available, but the manner in which this free gift of nature is utilized has a direct impact upon the requirement for the use of a costly resource, transportation.

Urban residential capital presents the same problem. The existing stock of dwellings is "free" much as land is free, for no current production is required to make it available. It exists and can be used. The manner in which it is used, however, can influence the amount of new resources, labor and materials, which will be used in the production of additional housing. The competitive process which rations buildings tends to conserve new housing capital.

Suppose that we reverse the allocation shown in Figure 37, putting the amenity households into the older dwellings and the shelter households into the outlying, newer homes. Unless a market process of exchange is possible, which would restore the original allocation, the first group of households will have a demand for housing amenity which is not satisfied by their present accommodations. This is tantamount to a demand for the construction of additional, new housing, a demand which is intensified if amenity-seeking households are excluded from the qualitatively superior portions of the existing stock. The end result, when new houses have been built to meet the amenity-seekers' demands, might be much the same as the initial equilibrium, with shelter-seekers enjoying shelter (albeit in newer dwellings than originally) and the amenity-seekers enjoying housing qualities. In exchange for the considerable expenditure of new resources for additional housing, the maximum, positive result is likely to be that shelter-seeking households enjoy housing amenity for which they had no effective market demand. This might seem like a kind of social or community benefit until we realize that the process could be repeated ad infinitum, always providing the shelter-seekers with the new part of the housing stock and encouraging the amenity-seekers to cause still more housing to be built at a limitless expenditure of community investment potential. The relative housing positions of the two groups would remain essentially as in the initial competitive equilibrium. We may take the community interest in minimum housing standards as being already represented in the initial stock of dwellings and concern ourselves only with the problem of deciding which household occupies which dwelling within that stock. If the criterion is the minimum rate of expenditure for new housing capital, that decision will probably conform to the competitive equilibrium.

Economic rents which are similar in principle to site rents emerge during the competitive process in which the stock of housing capital is considered fixed. Owners of dwellings can, at least implicitly, ask prices which measure the maximum benefit which any potential occupant would enjoy by living in a particular dwelling. This would exclude amenity seekers from the older portion of the stock and exclude shelter-seekers from the newer portion.

Our simple example puts all households in either of two groups, suggesting two distinct forms of prices. The price which the shelter group would offer for any dwelling can be called a "shelter rent" and the structure of prices which the other households would offer can be thought of as "amenity rents." The essence of this distinction is that each grouping of households which differs from others in its demand for housing has a potential bidding schedule for all the elements in the existing housing supply, a schedule which is different from that of any other group. Our example makes the simplest assumptions possible lest the complexity of the demonstration obscure that which is to be demonstrated. In principle we might say that every household in the community looks upon each unit of the supply in a light peculiar to the household's needs and income and to the unique attributes of the individual dwelling. Thus, in a community of one hundred households and one hundred dwellings there are ten thousand "rents." A perfectly mobile, competitive, "rational" market process would select that pattern of occupancy which maximized the aggregate economic rent of the present housing stock. This pattern also would minimize the utilization of new capital for housing.

To show how a fixed supply of dwellings might be reallocated to meet a changed pattern of demand (the total number of households remaining unchanged), suppose that there is an increase in the number of shelter-seekers which is just matched by a decrease in the number of amenity-seekers. Figure 38, which is the usual demand-and-supply diagram, shows that the first result of adding shelter-seeking households is to increase the shelter rent from $0a$ to $0b$. A greater part of the supply will become available to the shelter-seekers, but not until it is bid away from the amenity group. The latter are reduced in number but still put a price tag on each unit in the housing stock whether they live in it or not. Ultimately, the supply available to the shelter-seekers rises to S', and the new shelter rent becomes $0b'$ in Figure 38 or b' in Figure 39.

Shelter-seekers now take over a portion of the housing stock indicated by BE in Figure 39. The number of units in the BE ring is presumably equal to the increase in shelter-seekers and the decrease in amenity-seekers. Note that the remaining amenity-seekers will still live at the fringe of the city, occupying the more desirable units. The shelter-seekers' circular zone has expanded. Note also that rents of all units in the area with radius CB have increased by an equal amount, that rents in the BE ring have increased by diminishing amounts, and that beyond the distance E the unit prices are unchanged.

This was a simple reallocation of the city's housing stock; no house building took place. Sometimes, however, it may happen that a change in the composition of a city's population will

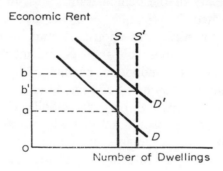

Figure 38

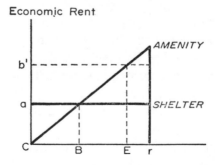

Figure 39

bring about the construction of new dwellings and abandonment of old units. These complex events are represented in Figure 40. In this case it is the amenity-seekers who increase in numbers and the shelter-seekers who decrease. The whole structure of amenity rents shifts upwards (just as shelter rents rose on Figure 38), reaching a maximum level of A' instead of A. The zone indicated by FB is given up by shelter-seekers and taken over by amenity-seekers.

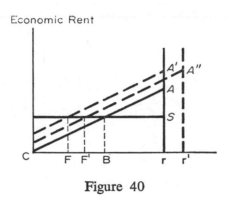

Figure 40

This could be the end of the story. However, the price A' now being offered for the newest existing houses on the edge of the city may exceed the cost of constructing even better dwellings just beyond that point. If this happens, the radius of the city will grow from r to r', the entire structure of amenity rents shifts part of the way down from A' to A'', and the zone FF' is given back to shelter-seekers. The shelter group now has more housing than it needs and we can reasonably suppose that they might abandon, not the FF' houses which are relatively desirable, but an equivalent number of houses at the very center of the city. These central houses are, by our convenient assumption, in the poorest condition.

Thus, we have one instance in which housing construction occurs along with a fairly involved rearrangement of families within the existing stock of dwellings. The number, location, price, and occupancy characteristics of the new units are specified in this very simple model of a housing market. This construction was induced by an upward shift in housing demand, such as might result from improvement in the income situation of a city's population.

It is more common to think of house construction occurring as a result of replacement demand or population growth, rather than as a result of an income shift. These two familiar sources of new construction demand can also be represented on our basic diagram.

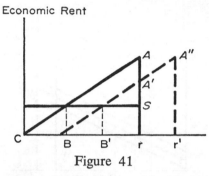

Figure 41

Replacement demand is portrayed in Figure 41. Here obsolescence of the housing stock pushes down the structure of amenity rents. All units yield progressively less amenity as time goes by. They provide unchanged shelter, however, so the level of shelter rents is not affected by obsolescence. If A is the price necessary to justify the construction of a brand new house, there is now an unsatisfied demand for new houses, and construction can occur in the zone between r and r'. An equivalent number of houses at the center of the city can be abandoned, as shelter-seeking families migrate into the zone BB'.

The possible outcome of population growth is represented by Figure 42. There is an upward shift in shelter rents and amenity rents, but the slope of the amenity rents may decrease since the demand for amenity is probably sensitive to price. The higher the cost of housing in general, the less each family can afford as a premium for extra housing quality. New houses are built at the fringe of the city, but it is not certain that they will be houses for the amenity market. Perhaps the shift of A to A' will not be sufficient to cover the cost of new amenity-type houses, so that most of the amenity-seekers will simply stay where they are.

If so, shelter rents must rise enough to cover the cost of

new shelter-type housing which will be built on the fringe. Thus, the zone *rr'* would be built up with amenity-type dwellings, shelter-type dwellings, or some combination of the two, depending on construction costs for the two house types as well as on the elasticity of underlying shelter and amenity demands.

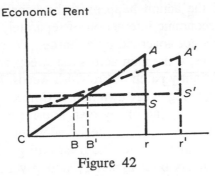

Figure 42

This nearly exhaustive use of a greatly simplified housing market model is directed toward a simple point. The stock of dwellings may be used in such a manner that requirements for the expenditure of new resources on housing are minimized and that, within this minimization task, the type of dwellings which are added to the stock is also influenced by the composition and use of the initial stock of dwellings. If the market is to carry out this capital-conserving function, it will create economic rents for units of the stock existing at any one point in time and will administer the use of this stock by means of these prices. As is true for site rents, building rents are transfer payments; they are not signals that the buildings themselves are being consumed, but serve a rationing function to help the community minimize consumption of other resources—the general class of products which can be produced currently and among which the economic system must choose. With an adequate system of building rents, the economic system can choose less new housing expenditure and more of other things.

PROPINQUITY

It is an inherent and distinguishing characteristic of housing that one dwelling unit or structure influences the usefulness and desirability of those near it. If residential properties are relatively small, as in the single-family area where each house is owned by a different individual, this influence is in the nature of an "external effect," for the owner of house B is not compensated for any losses in its usefulness resulting from an action of the owner of house A. Nor can the owner of A expect to be paid by the owner of B if the action happens to be beneficial rather than harmful. The economic interaction of separately owned residential properties is not governed by a market process.

For example, if the man across the street lets his front lawn turn into an unsightly patch of brownish weeds, I will derive less enjoyment from living in my own house. Correctly or incorrectly, I may feel that the value of my own housing investment is impaired. On the other hand, if the homeowner across the street lavishes skill and money to create a tasteful garden and lawn, I may receive benefits both monetary and psychological. Money would not change hands as a result of either real change in the usefulness and value of resources. Such situations occur in great variety in the housing sector of a city's economic life and in different form, with perhaps greater intensity, in the nonresidential sector.

There are, of course, ways in which the community as a collection of individuals may take heed of propinquity, making up for what the marketplace is inherently incapable of providing. The moral pressure of "neighborliness" varies in effectiveness among population groups, sometimes producing rigid uniformity of external housekeeping practices, sometimes mere token efforts at mutual consideration. Larger units of ownership make it less likely that harmful effects will arise or that an opportunity for beneficial effects will be neglected. The community may impose legal restrictions upon the uses of individual property, such as zoning or building laws, or fire and health regulations which penalize those who create hazards.

It would be wrong to imagine that the competitive market simply ignores the external effects of propinquity (assuming a system of small ownerships). Indeed, some of the more serious economic effects of propinquity stem from the natural responses of entrepreneurs to this interesting characteristic of the housing market. Where specific public regulations permit, such as zoning and building laws, the entrepreneurial response to the problem of residential propinquity may take either of two forms. In subsequent residential construction activities it may either conform to the patterns indicated by the extent and quality of external relationships or it may abandon the district so affected.

Conformity means that new buildings do not change the character of the area. Thus, an entrepreneur—whether landowner, developer, lender, or whoever—who decides against putting a $50,000 new home on a lot available in a district of $15,000 homes is likely to be quite rational in his decision. From his point of view the same home could be sold more readily, and probably at a better profit, in a district of high-priced dwellings. The entrepreneur may then elect to build a less expensive home, say one which would sell for $18,000, in the original district, thus conforming with the prevailing land uses. He may, on the other hand, decide that the market does not justify new homes in the $18,000 price class and so abandon efforts to develop the lot in question.

In turn, these responses by entrepreneurs produce subsequent effects upon the housing economy of the city. The usefulness of existing districts is, to some extent, protected. At some point, however, the best use of the district might alter, so that new residential (or even nonresidential) construction of a different character would serve the interests of the community as a whole. Perhaps, to carry the above illustration a bit further, the community has a surplus of older homes in the $15,000 price class and the district in question would function adequately to serve a growing higher-priced market. The transition would be, we can assume, productive for the community when completely achieved.

The problem is that no individual entrepreneur, however astute he might be on the subject of market analysis, could be sure that his venture in transforming the area would bear fruit, for he could not be certain that enough other entrepreneurs would be in a position to imitate his behavior. Until a large portion of the district has already been transformed, the ordinary entrepreneur is not likely to proceed in a direction clearly desired by the market. The concept of propinquity discourages housing pioneers, however clairvoyant and sensitive.

There is a mirror image of this problem in a community

with a different set of entrepreneurial attitudes or business and social institutions. Instead of "conformity and abandonment" we may find "nonconformity and progress," to use some colorful but perhaps misleading characterizations. If intrusions of new residential types into an established district are tolerated, grudgingly or not, by all parties, then the transition of neighborhoods in the face of changes in community population, incomes, and housing preferences may be accomplished much more readily. However, the very tolerance supposed as a condition for transforming a district from one use to another is likely to produce a district of no particular character and a community without well defined districts. This is no problem so long as there are no real propinquity effects, but since there usually are, a proclivity to nonconformism and tolerance, however generous, may yield up a stock of housing with less inherent capacity to satisfy all the needs of the community's inhabitants than the resources thus employed would really permit.

Intermixture of use types may not be seriously detrimental to the physical functioning of the city so long as it does not reach the level of major use categories. That is, different house-price classes might coexist fairly well, but the interspersion of industrial or commercial uses in residential areas can be the source of some real disadvantages. The inclination toward conformity is probably much weaker when a major change is contemplated than when the change is confined to subcategories of residential use. Hence, often it seems more necessary for the community to control land-use mixture at a gross, major level, leaving the precise degree of intra-area conformity to the natural forces which are present in the market.

It is easier to discourage nonconformity, however, than to avoid the abandonment of sizable districts by entrepreneurial interests. The cities of an affluent United States have long been afflicted with the "gray area problem"—large inventories of dwellings which, all things considered, the market seems willing to replace but which, partly because of their very extent and the phenomenon of propinquity, discourage individual entrepreneurs.

Part of the problem of gray areas is the relation of public facilities to the opportunity for area-wide reconstruction. Obsolete street patterns and utility systems, and perhaps neglected public buildings as well, are beyond the power of the most adventurous individual entrepreneur to change. But should the public sector undertake direct reconstruction of gray areas, it encounters a social or political obstacle which is usually unimportant to private entrepreneurs, for a public agency has some responsibility for residents who would be displaced by a program of upgrading the community's housing stock. Gray areas represent a public–private dilemma in the field of urban housing economics. The problem involves other conceptual issues than that of propinquity, however, and we might continue our inventory of urban economic concepts by discussing one other aspect of housing replacement activity.

REPLACEMENT LAND

We have discussed some aspects of housing replacement activity in an earlier chapter. One of these is the requirement for a supply of "swing" land on which, directly or indirectly, the inhabitants of an area undergoing reconstruction may be settled during the process. This treatment of the subject takes an optimistic view of the readiness of entrepreneurs and landowners to collaborate in transforming a no-longer-needed portion of the housing stock into a frontier of housing progress.

The fact is that however deteriorated and outmoded older dwellings may be, their existence obstructs reuse of the land on which they rest so long as these structures have significant capital value. They retain capital value and real economic value so long as some segment of community housing demand has no superior housing alternatives. Alternatives cannot be supplied without land and so, in the absence of effective "swing" developments beyond the present area of the city, a kind of vicious circle is created.

The condition should be noted with care. We might suppose that a smoothly dynamic and relatively responsive market would meet replacement demand by creating a supply slightly in excess of numerical housing needs. By thus depriving owners of some obsolete buildings of reasonable expectation of capital value, some previously used land would come back upon the market.

This would encourage further building, further loss of capital value in some other obsolete property, and so on. The renovation and improvement of the housing stock would be accomplished in a continuous and spontaneous fashion. The "urban land ratchet" would not operate.

Let the demand for housing improvement be suppressed for some time, however, creating a large backlog of improvement need, and the problem of diminishing capital values sufficiently to permit the reuse of land for replacement construction becomes very serious. The "ratchet" effect appears. The effect of delay in meeting improvement demand is an inflation in "land" prices in this entrepreneurial sense. It will diminish the entrepreneur's opportunity for successful new development and thus compound the problem of insufficient construction even when the barriers which initially obstructed housing improvement are removed. Land prices in a community may thus reflect the ghost of long-past housing shortages, as well as such immediate and useful things as advantageous location.

STRATEGIC USES

It is perhaps obvious that most cities have geographic features which depart from the featureless, flat plain of elementary theory. There are rivers, lakes, ravines, marshes, hills, and other features which bend the pattern of land uses, including residential, away from the tidy, concentric rings around which most theorizing revolves. Sometimes the natural qualities of the land may impart subjective overtones to residential value, if a hillside commands a pleasant view of the city's harbor, for example, or if hard soil interferes with drainage and gardening. As natural features which cannot be removed or created, we can only expect that the pattern of residential uses would adapt to them. Whether this adaptation is purely private and individual or publicly supervised, and whether it is likely to be effective or self-defeating are matters too dependent on individual circumstances to warrant useful generalizations in our present study.

There are many man-made features of the urban landscape which also have significant influence upon patterns of residential development within cities. The location and characteristics of roads, schools, parks, and other public facilities affect the usefulness of residential land and buildings; the nature of this influence may be a part of the decision to create these facilities. Whereas land use may adapt passively to natural features, the design of public facilities which have a strategic influence on private, urban development actively shapes the residential inventory.

The impact of public improvements upon private development is quite inescapable and so it makes the intellectual problem of creating public facilities extraordinarily complex. De novo planning of a city's street pattern or schools, for example, will have complex and massive effects upon existing and future residential development throughout the city. The welfare of every household, present or future, and the wealth position of every property owner or investor will be materially affected by the design of public facilities. It is a theoretical problem of the greatest magnitude simply to outline the main features of this interdependence. The further task of deciding which of many alternative systems, together with their respective repercussions, best serves the public interest is many times more complex. Within the limited purposes of this book, only a few aspects of the public planning and decision problems can be considered.

One is the fact that much public urban investment, like private housing development, is such a small increment in the total that the broad pattern of existing uses can be taken as permanent. Street improvements in district X will leave other districts unchanged. The impact upon residences in district X and the implied impacts on other districts are thus foreseeable and concrete, at least in their major outlines. The smaller the scale of public undertakings, the more rationally can they be designed. Community-wide programs of street improvement, school development, rezoning, etc. will produce effects which are much more difficult to anticipate simply because they leave less unchanged. One hole in a large ship can be patched while at sea, but the ship itself cannot be reconstructed. Conscientious city planners, whose schoolbook maxim warned them to "make no small plans" find that the intellectual resources of the urban professions do not yet support the making of large plans.[9]

The political manner in which strategic public land uses are proposed and designed may materially assist the planner. If he does not have a massive computer to tell him what changes in the residential economy and other land-using activities of the city will result from a specific proposal for public action, he may get similar signals from the expressions of private interest. The market, after all, is the original economic planning computer, letting all voices be heard, assigning weights and striking a balance consistent with the residual impact of prior decisions. The political process of urban planning may, in effect, be a market for complex public goods. This is not an inevitable characteristic of urban planning, merely a possibility. More authoritarian systems are known and these, whether by exceptional, intellectual prowess or by intuition and luck, might produce programs as much in the public interest as the most enlightened and efficient "public goods market."

The "payoff" of public activity, the criterion for selection of programs, need not be thought of in terms of commerical coin. The satisfaction derived by citizens from a good school, an attractive park, or modern fire-protection equipment is not necessarily measured by increases in property values. This is not a sentiment but an aspect of ordinary price systems. Many civic improvements are in the nature of transfers, gifts of resources from one part of the society which may benefit the giver as well as the recipient without causing the giver's money income or wealth to increase.

MOBILITY AND LIQUIDITY

The "competitive market process" which appears in many of the above-discussed concepts of urban residential activity assumes very substantial mobility on the part of households, entrepreneurs, and investors. Families move when better housing is available, entrepreneurs adjust the inventory when an opportunity for individual gain appears, and investors (including property owners) can and do liquidate one holding when there is a net advantage in shifting to another.

This is a larger assumption than it may seem. It is not only a question of attitudes, but also one of market organization and business institutions. Residential real estate has legal, social, psychological and financial dimensions as well as physical form —all of which can be so complex as to tax the understanding. To overcome these problems and to set the stage for mobile responses to changes in demand or supply factors, a set of specialized functions must be performed as supplementary to the market of exchanges. Just as the purchase of a refrigerator is dependent to some extent upon the arrangements for installing it, and perhaps for disposing of an older model, the transfer of an interest in residential property is dependent upon facilities for legally accomplishing the transfer, for insuring that the physical and legal characteristics of the property are as the buyer believes them to be, and for bringing other parties into the financial arrangements to the best mutual advantage. A mere "meeting of the minds" is not enough. Adjustments in the supply and use of residential property which are of mutual, private benefit and serve the clearest interests of the public at large as well may be frustrated by the absence or imperfection of mediating devices.

Consider, for example, a situation in which the market is so large that specialized residential brokers are an indispensable means of communication between prospective sellers and buyers, but that the ethical standards of brokers are generally believed to be very poor, and that there is no escrow system for the protection of funds deposited before completion of the sale. Both buyers and sellers will be reluctant to approach the market in the first place, for fear of substantial harm at the hands of a dishonest broker. If they do meet, the buyer and seller will be tempted to bypass the broker and conclude a transaction on their own. The seller may feel that a prospective buyer who is compliant in this respect is preferable to one who will offer a higher price for the property but who needs the technical assistance of a broker. The volume and effectiveness of market transfers suffer.

Or, imagine that legal institutions offer such protection to housing occupants that the foreclosure of owner-occupied homes is not realistically possible. Loans for the acquisition of homes would then be based primarily on the personal credit and other wealth of the buyer, and the opportunity for home purchase and for exchanges of owned dwellings would be narrow. Such dwellings would be relatively illiquid investments so that the real economic cost of housing would be so much higher. Without an effective, widespread, and realistic system of appraisal, lenders, investors, and developers cannot consider their properties to be liquid and so would favor options which did not depend on liquidity for their worth.

Liquidity and mobility are attributes which enhance the social value of residential resources, not because it is inherently undesirable for households and businessmen to form attachments to property, but for the simple reason that the needs and capacities of people and firms with respect to such property are subject to unexpected change. However deep the association of a household with its home or neighborhood, an illiquid dwelling investment is a grave disadvantage if the breadwinner should find his employment relocated to a different city, for example. The investor who finds an unexpected opportunity in some industrial stocks, but whose wealth is tied up in illiquid real estate, pays an opportunity cost for his earlier investment. Institutions which enhance liquidity do not beguile people into unproductive mobility; they simply facilitate desirable adaptations.

The creation of a set of institutions to make residential property liquid is a joint responsibility of public and private business. This subject will be explored at length in the following chapter, but we can say at this point that the legal environment and the varieties of financial institutions which best serve the dynamic needs of the residential market cannot spring spontaneously from the private sector. Just as a city of private ownerships cannot function without public streets, a market of private transactions cannot operate with full effectiveness without public encouragement and regulation of business practices which are indispensable to the essential but complex allocation functions of the market.

SPECIALIZED BUILDING TYPES

The greatest degree of mobility and liquidity in residential property would be permitted by a stock of structures which was as nearly uniform in their physical, financial, and legal particulars as the inevitable dimensions of time and location would permit. An inventory of this type would faciliate adjustments of locational needs and the desire for new as opposed to deteriorated dwellings. Unless households were quite uniform with respect to other aspects of their housing requirements, however, this inventory would achieve mobility and liquidity at the expense of convenience for atypical households.

Specialized building types and arrangements of tenure and financing thus illustrate an economic value which is counter to the benefits of mobility. We can say that market institutions which improve the liquidity of the residential inventory are an unambiguous advantage to the housing economy of the community. But we cannot say that limitations on the variability of housing units or on legal and financial attributes of possession are an unmixed blessing, though these attributes would also improve liquidity.

Households do differ as to family size, access to credit, tastes concerning interior arrangement of dwellings, and tenure preferences, to mention only a few significant characteristics. In principle, we might say that each household is unique, so that a supply of residential units which suited individual tastes as nearly as residential resources would permit might be "perfectly differentiated," with no two units just alike.

Such a community would be afflicted by perfect immobility in its housing arrangements. To meet any change in the housing needs of any household would require the creation of a new unit, with all the attendant sacrifice of current resources which that implies. The failure of the housing sector to provide such "perfect differentiation" has the effect of conserving resources. There is a resource cost of differentiation because of the illiquidity which results from it.

This illiquidity is part of the rational decision framework of the housing entrepreneur, owner, or investor. On the private side, however, illiquidity only appears as a cost to the extent that it affects the property immediately in question. The impact of innovation in housing styles upon the liquidity of existing "standard" types of dwellings is not relevant to the atomistic decision. For example, it was common, for a long period of time in American cities, that older homes were divided up into rooming units and rented to young, single adults. In recent years specialized apartment buildings, inherently better suited to the housing needs of these people, have been constructed in large numbers. The developer of such new buildings is aware that his financial success depends on trends within a narrow segment of the population, and this fact may temper his enthusiasm. He is able to ignore the fact that owners of the older buildings, which in a prior state of affairs could be converted into rooming units, suffer a distinct loss in the liquidity of their possessions when the new apartment units appear in quantity. The market opportunities for the older dwellings are narrowed, and housing adjustments by owner-occupants of those buildings are rendered more difficult. The community may judge the net effect to be beneficial but it must, in principle, consider all the effects of differentiation, not just the marketability of the new housing design concept.

It is clear that differentiation is a separate dimension of the conservation of housing resources. The loss of market liquidity by the housing stock depends on the degree to which the housing inventory is differentiated. Some degree of differentiation is worth the sacrifice of inventory-wide liquidity, so that a "trade-off" decision is required.

We can conjecture that the loss of liquidity through differentiation is, in part, a function of the size of the community. A town of twenty or thirty dwellings would probably experience a perceptible loss of liquidity through any deviation of building types from a single standard. A city of a hundred thousand dwellings can, in the same social and economic context, afford many distinct dwelling types. Indeed, this is one of the more concrete examples of the external economies of urban growth. In any community, though, the loss of market liquidity is a relevant consideration in the introduction of new dwelling types.

We can also conjecture that the sacrifice of liquidity which can be accepted in return for specialized housing is, in part, a function of the wealth or income of the community. As real incomes rise, it may be expected that the residential market would become increasingly responsive to the special requirements of subcategories among the population. The nature of the cost associated with this income effect upon housing is not immediately obvious, however, for it is an external cost of relatively abstruse character. It is a real and significant phenomenon which is likely to escape the most sophisticated, private calculus.

SOCIAL POLICY

In an earlier chapter we have discussed the relationship between the physical form of housing and the sense of "community." (See Chapter 2.) In the United States during the 1930's, much federal activity in the housing field was designed and defended in part because of the effect it would produce upon the attitudes of people toward themselves and their communities. Homeownership was furthered through the FHA (and later the VA), and public housing projects were offered to transform the environment of slum dwellers, always with a public eye toward a change in personal and social values. In the Soviet Union, the officials in charge of housing and city planning have interpreted communist principles to the effect that certain housing types— i.e. single-family homes—foster individualism which is detrimental to the purposes of the state.

There is enough evidence to believe that social values can indeed be influenced by the immediate housing environment, perhaps not always in the patterns which social planners consciously envisage, but at least in some fairly objective way. There is some causal interrelation. Given that fact, we can derive the important corollary that no society is without at least an implicit social policy with respect to housing development. Any set of market and public institutions, from complete laissez-faire to absolute central control, interacting with the already present proclivities of the citizenry, will produce some pattern of social values related to the housing environment.

Once we become aware of a causal relationship between the activities of the housing sector and the emerging social values of the population, we cannot help considering the latter when we make decisions about the former. The entrepreneurs in the housing sector or the public agencies which operate in that sector cannot provide housing without doing something to the development of social attitudes, to the manner in which members of the community think about and conduct their lives.

Now certainly the choice of an optimum set of social values

for the emerging population is not the responsibility of "housing economics," and we shall leave the subject without doing more than acknowledging its existence and its relevance. The important reason for acknowledging it is that we may clearly understand that the subject of economic behavior, however we may narrow it down to sectors or subsectors, is neither neutral nor sterile, for economics is a social science, not merely an exercise in arithmetic.

The Optimization Decision

A community's housing stock is a system of compromises. The concepts identified and examined in the preceding pages point to the several dimensions of that compromise arising from entrepreneurial decisions, from the determination of community housing policy or from a combination of these factors. Three explicitly "economic" dimensions were identified at the outset —namely, the level and distribution of residential density with its correlative in the real cost of housing-related transportation, the level of differentiation in the housing stock and its correlative in market liquidity, and the general level of housing quality with its correlative desire to minimize the use of new community capital for housing.

This gives us six fundamental, economic criteria with which to describe and ultimately to evaluate the community's stock of housing and increments to that stock. The six criteria are "paired off" in the sense that if we move in a positive direction with respect to one, we may cause an opposite or negative effect upon its correlative. We cannot lower aggregate transportation costs and lower residential densities at the same time. It may be possible to lower total transportation costs while leaving the overall density unchanged—for example, by switching apartment dwellers to the center of the city and single-family home occupants to the fringe—but there is always some density effect of transport-minimizing efforts. The same principle applies to the other two paired sets of criteria.

Each criterion in this group of six may also interact with any of the four others outside its own pair. Thus, substantial rebuilding of a community's housing stock for the purpose of reducing transportation costs may require scrapping of substantial amounts of inherently usable housing already in existence, without necessarily raising the level of housing quality.

To illustrate the usefulness of these criteria, we may write them in the form of "objectives," or desirable direction of change in the housing stock, and consider the way in which a hypothetical housing program could be evaluated. The following outline table is a useful format. To improve upon its usefulness, we can add some of the criteria which we have had occasion to discuss in the preceding pages, but which are less readily described as "economic."

10 ALTERNATIVE HOUSING PROGRAMS

Objectives	A	B	C, D, . . .
⌠ Reduce total transport cost	—	+	
⌡ Lower residential density	+	—	
⌠ Increase stock differentiation	0	+	
⌡ Improve stock liquidity	0	—	
⌠ Raise general stock quality	+	0	
⌡ Reduce consumption of new capital	—	0	
Pursue social policy	x	+	
Pursue esthetic policy	x	x	
"Score"	xx	xx	

Program A might be, for example, the housing activity expected through private market efforts during the coming year, without any alteration in market environment stemming from public actions in the community. In physical terms this might mean constructing replacement housing at a high-quality level in the previously undeveloped fringe area. This would raise aggregate transportation costs (beyond any increase required by growth in the city's population) and lower residential densities. Levels of differentiation and liquidity, as we have used the terms, would be unchanged. The quality of the stock would be raised at the expense of some new housing resources. Effects on social and esthetic aims would, obviously, depend on what those aims were.

Program B might represent a policy of encouraging the

construction of centrally located apartments for elderly households. In itself this effort could be expected to lower transport costs for the community, increase densities, further differentiate the stock, reduce the liquidity of the stock, and move in the direction of a social goal. It might have no net effect upon the overall quality of the stock or the "normal" consumption of new capital, and its esthetic effect would depend on the nature of this goal and the degree to which the social goal was coordinated with it.

Programs C, D, etc. could be other programs representing several elements of private market activity or variations of private activity if certain new controls or aids were provided by the community, or efforts of public entrepreneurship. Each alternative program might be thought of as a whole complex of public and private activities, or as one element in the complex. In either situation, the sum of the level of all alternative activities must be not greater or less than the expected total level of housing activities (measured in units built, capital created, land developed, or some other binding dimension).

The above illustration implies that criteria for judging the optimality of the housing stock of a community can be applied incrementally. That is, we take the view that we cannot decide what kind of stock we would like and then create it in entirety, but rather that we must seek to control the increment so that the stock changes in directions which improve its usefulness to the community.

This does not leave us without guidance as to what the optimal characteristics of the stock as a whole must be, even though these characteristics must be set down in the form of limits rather than exact prescriptions. The economic relationships which we have discussed are interrelated in such a way that we can make the following statements about the characteristics of an optimal housing stock:

1. Transportation costs are not literally minimized, for this would require intolerable densities whereas low density is an economic value in itself for which it is valid to expend resources. To minimize transportation resources through otherwise unnecessary reconstruction of the residential inventory will waste existing capital stock.

2. The housing stock of the community will be partially differentiated, for if it were carried to an extreme, the convenience immediately enjoyed by the varied households would be offset by major loss of liquidity, leading to excessive future consumption of new capital. Households less ideally served by the semi-standardized stock will be forced to "make do" in the interest of the community at large.

3. Substantial portions of the stock will be obsolescent and deteriorated, again "making do" with a legacy of capital not ideally suited to today's needs and purchasing power, for the sake of reducing the claim of the housing sector upon the current investment capacities of the community.

Taking a fairly typical view of a private housing sector we can say that private motivations are likely to move in directions opposed to the broad community interest in the following ways:

1. Inability to coordinate use of "gray areas" will tend to produce unwarranted outward movement for meeting replacement demand. Use of transportation resources would be raised. If there is a social disutility to income transfers resulting from higher site rents, then private efforts to accommodate a growing population will be unaware of this external effect and, by moving in the direction of lower density will boost the community-wide structure of site rents.

2. The community's need for differentiation of the housing stock may be misjudged. On one hand, the illiquidity effect of differentiation is an external cost of an attractive private opportunity, so there is some incentive for excessive differentiation. On the other, the poor state of market understanding among housing entrepreneurs, particularly lenders, seems to create a "myth of illiquidity" such that innovations which are warranted both socially and privately may be discouraged. The net effect is likely to be erratic and often unsuccessful differentiation, with valid opportunities neglected.

3. Competition for the improvement market may lead to excessive consumption of new capital, and the destruction of property values based on still useful structures. That is, the improvement in housing standards may not be worth scrapping substantial existing improvements.

The private sector can be encouraged to move in the direction of social and esthetic policies, but not very much by simple exhortation. Specific restrictions, information, and assistance will lead to entrepreneurial behavior which in principle can be anticipated.

The public sector is most likely to err in the pursuit of its aims or preferences by failing to see that the many possible objectives which might be pursued publicly or privately are interdependent in complex ways. That is, the "price" of a public policy in terms of the other latent objectives which must be sacrificed to achieve it is obscure because policy-makers work in an environment which does not produce prices. The public sector is likely also to see only the direct and not the indirect means to achieve a particular goal, though the indirect approach may often be more efficient in terms of resources used. An example is the debate about direct construction and management of housing for low-income groups versus a stimulus to market replacement and "filtering." The public sector may also find itself directed toward spurious purposes, such as the desire to increase property tax revenues, aspects of urban living which in themselves have no resource consequences.

7 · ▞

ADMINISTRATION OF

THE HOUSING SECTOR

In the preceding chapters we have offered a systematic comparison between the direction which a market economy in housing would take and that which would be "ideal" when all of the community's aims were taken into account. There is almost certain to be some kind of "gap" between the two, because market institutions in housing tend to contain substantial imperfections (in the economist's sense of the word) and because the use of urban housing resources creates significant externalities—i.e., inadvertent effects on third parties. The existence of a gap does not necessarily imply, however, that the market system should be replaced by a system of government production and distribution. The choice of systems for administering the housing sector of the economy is much more complex than that, with complexities arising from the nature of the commodity itself rather than from moralistic squabbles about "socialism versus free enterprise." *

---

* The subject of this chapter is, in effect, the strategy of public control of economic processes. The relevant literature is immense, but the concept which emerges here may best be placed in ideological perspective by referring to *A Strategy of Decision,* by David Braybrooke and Charles E. Lindblom (New York: The Free Press, 1963). On a somewhat different plane, the distinction between impersonal business relationships and unbounded personal responsibilities which are implied in a nonbusiness system is practically the same as the distinction between "Gemeinschaft" and "Gesellschaft" which the sociologist F. Toennies introduced in *Fundamental Concepts of Sociology,* New York, American Book Co., 1940,

Alternative Roles of Government

We might begin by identifying the major alternatives for public control of the housing sector. Figure 43 depicts four different schemes for meeting the housing needs of the public. Fig 43A is the "laissez-faire," or simple, market economy in which effective demand for housing is directed to the market— i.e., to private enterprises—and the market responds with a supply of dwellings. The dashed line, P, reaching up to Government, represents such things as complaints from those who need housing but lack the effective demand to purchase it, observations about inefficient behavior of housing entrepreneurs, and controversies among housing users themselves (about neighbors who leave garbage in their yards, for example). This line is labeled "political data" because it serves only to judge the viability of the laissez-faire system rather than as a channel leading to a series of limited, compensatory actions by government.

Fig. 43B describes a socialized housing sector. Private entrepreneurs are replaced by public entrepreneurs. Information flowing from the public now consists largely of specific data on needs—family sizes, location of employment, and so on, plus data on resources available to satisfy these needs. In addition, the same sorts of complaints which might have been directed against the market system—about bungling or discriminatory performance by the entrepreneurs and about incompatible neighbors—flow toward government in this socialized scheme. In this instance, though, complaints may result in limited adjustments in the performance of public entrepreneurs rather than a scrapping of the whole system. The supply activity is "administered" by more-or-less conscious decisions in this system.

Fig. 43C describes a system called *Public Governorship*. Here the market responds to effective demand for housing, subject to regulations (such as zoning, tenant rights, etc.) and assistance (such as favorable tax treatment or insurance for investments). Government is not unresponsive to housing needs and complaints which escape consideration by the marketplace itself. The response takes the form of specific curbs or incentives

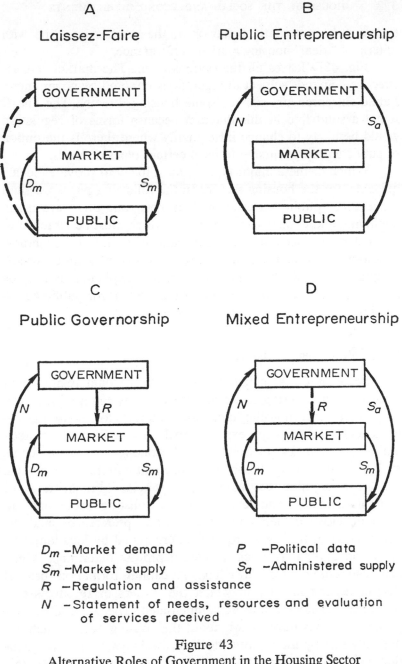

A
Laissez-Faire

B
Public Entrepreneurship

C
Public Governorship

D
Mixed Entrepreneurship

D_m –Market demand
S_m –Market supply
R –Regulation and assistance
N –Statement of needs, resources and evaluation of services received

P –Political data
S_a –Administered supply

Figure 43
Alternative Roles of Government in the Housing Sector

to bring the automatic behavior of the market into line with criteria of "ideal" housing market performance.

Fig. 43D leaves all the options open. The market satisfies effective demands subject to regulations imposed by government. Public entrepreneurs provide some housing directly. The line R is not a solid line in this diagram because forms of regulation would be likely to change infrequently where there is the option of public entrepreneurship to meet certain types of needs.

Which of these major types is most likely to provide "ideal" guidance for the housing sector? In the following pages we shall argue that "public governorship" is best, but there are many qualifying and explanatory conditions which must be attached to this judgment. Because the background of social and economic conditions in which a housing economy operates differ widely around the world, these qualifications and explanations may be more important than the thrust of the argument for public governorship.

Social Processes in the Housing Sector

Some of the principal types of interpersonal relationships created by the housing sector are suggested by Figure 44. In this diagram several housing users—i.e. families or households—contend for units in the existing stock of dwellings. This stock embodies resources provided by the economic system at large, such as finance, land, labor, materials, and entrepreneurship (in the sense of resource management whether bureaucratic or profit-motivated). The several users are distinct from one another in terms of their housing needs and preferences, and the components of the stock are also differentiated by location, size, type, and quality. A stock allocation process determines which user can enjoy which dwelling. A capital formation process determines the manner in which the owners of resources embodied in the stock are to be compensated. The stock allocation process provides information about the housing needs which are not fully met by the existing stock of dwellings, and in conjunction with further operation of the capital formation process, this information leads to the creation of new dwellings.

Housing users thus contend among themselves and with a

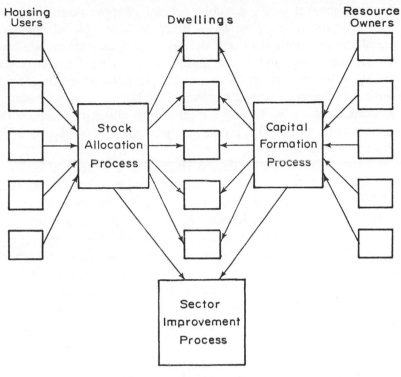

Figure 44
Housing Sector Processes

collection of resource suppliers for control of the existing stock. This contention carries over to the further development of the stock. The fact that dwellings are durable goods lends some vigor to this competition, for resources are committed to the stock in advance of payment by users, and once distributed to users are difficult to redistribute, with the probable result that windfall gains and losses will occur among housing users and resource suppliers. Durability means that there is some uncertainty in the "quid pro quo" of housing economics, uncertainty which breeds many-sided reluctance and inflexibility.

THE STOCK ALLOCATION PROCESS

The stock allocation process involves four distinct functions. The first of these is a matter of communication. However the allocation procedure is to be carried out—whether by an impersonal market or by a public official charged with administration of the housing stock—it must be based on information about the characteristics and desires of the several households, on the one hand, and the attributes of the several dwellings in the stock, on the other. In earlier chapters we have considered the complexities of these characteristics, but it is now necessary to examine the administrative mechanisms which can cope with these complexities. The process of allocation must begin with collection of information.

Much information relevant to the stock allocation process is "objective." That is, it is concerned with concrete realities, such as the number of children in a family and the number of rooms in a house. In addition, there is general agreement that only a finite number of objective circumstances are of real significance in housing allocation, so that it is reasonable to group households together (such as "all four-person families in which the breadwinner works in the central business district") and to group dwellings (such as "all three-bedroom homes in the suburbs") before we begin the process of allocation. So long as objective matters only are involved, the allocation process need not be very complicated.

If we consider certain subjective matters to be important in deciding who lives in which house, however, then the stock allocation process takes on subtleties. Does it matter, for example, that Household A has a particular liking for Victorian architecture or that Household B does not want to live near a cemetery? There may also be individual, subjective responses to features of particular dwellings which are intangible or imperceptible to a third party, for a family may feel that "there is something about this house" which it either likes or dislikes. If subjective aspects are to be considered in the process of allocating the stock of dwellings among potential users, the opportunity to simplify the task of matching groups of households with groups of dwellings must be forsaken. It is also impossible to evoke subjective responses without exposing individual households to at least representative segments of the inventory. To find out how suitable each dwelling is to each potential user is a major task of information-gathering. However, it is only the first step in the housing stock-allocation process.

The second step is criteria selection. Out of the many possible ways in which a given number of households and a number (not necessarily the same) of dwellings are to be matched, one pattern must eventually be chosen. Five households and five dwellings can be matched in 120 ways, for example. If the choice is not to be random, there must be a "theory" or a rule, or set of rules, for making this choice. We could develop a formula for attaching a desirability score to each possible matching—ten points for each household which has at least one room per family member, seven points for each breadwinner located not more than five miles from his place of work, and so on. The matching with the highest score would be the "optimum" arrangement. Clearly subjective preferences on the part of households could be represented in such a formula only with great difficulty, while subjective weighting of the formula's elements by some responsible person would be inescapable.

Alternatively, we could establish priorities for individual choice. Households having certain characteristics—those with longest residence in the community, for example—could be given first choice of the inventory, after which the second priority group would have its choice, and so on. As a variation on this we could limit the range of choices permitted to any priority group, saying, for example, that a large family may not choose a small dwelling unit or vice versa. Another variant would be to establish priorities, but to leave the choices of dwellings for members of a priority group to an administrator rather than to the households themselves. In short, there are many possible systems, not excluding some limited element which is random, such as a lottery for new dwellings, by means of which the plan for distribution of available housing may be designed.

A third element in the stock allocation process (which may be implicit in the second) is the compromising of individual and community housing objectives to fit the dimensions of characteristics of the inventory. Many, or even most, of the households will find that their dwellings fall short of their needs in some respects. Perhaps there will be too few really large houses for the number of very large families, and some of the latter may feel compensated if homes which are somewhat too small are well soundproofed or have extra large yards, for example. Some dwellings near good schools may be too small for families with school-age children. Some dwellings which are internally well suited to the needs of elderly people may be too far from the kinds of medical and recreation facilities which such people require. For bachelors or bachelor girls who do not wish to do their own housekeeping there may be insufficient dormitorylike dwellings with dining facilities attached. Thus, a set of compromises and compensations must arise in even the best of circumstances and there is a related set of questions concerning who must compromise the most and in which housing dimensions, and which forms of compensation will be allowed and to whom.

A fourth aspect of stock allocation is effectuation of the optimal matching pattern. It is all very well on paper, as the saying goes, to decide where each household in the community should live, but it is something else again to make them live there. More important, perhaps, is the establishment and enforcement of a system of charges for the use of the housing inventory. Whether these charges are called rents, prices, amortization and interest payments, or taxes, it is nearly inevitable that households will be required to part with some income or wealth in exchange for housing, primarily to reimburse the suppliers of housing resources. If there were no housing charges, then households might comply with a scheme of allocation which corresponded only roughly to their housing desires, but when they must pay for their dwellings, housing users take a more active interest in the correspondence of their desires to what they receive. How shall each household be persuaded to accept the dwelling designated for it at the designated price? How shall households once assigned to dwellings in conformity with a general plan be kept from exchanging dwellings and perhaps confounding the plan? Shall any unplanned variations be permitted at all, or should a system of charges be used to discourage but not to outlaw such variations?

The means of effectuating the allocation plan range from crude compulsion at one extreme to a system of rewards on the other, with moralistic persuasion in between. The rewards need not be actual gifts, since households generally expect to pay out of income or wealth for housing services, but they can simply be expressed as particularly favorable housing charges—i.e. virtual subsidies. Whatever the system, a concrete effort is required to effect the allocation of the housing stock and this effort is a separate problem in social and economic design.

The fifth and most challenging aspect of housing stock allocation is provision for changes in the allocation to meet changes in relevant characteristics of housing users, such as changes in family size or job locations, and changes in the nature of the dwelling stock due to deterioration, obsolescence, new transportation developments, changes in neighboring nonresidential land uses, and so on. Even the crudest concept of an efficient housing economy must acknowledge almost continuous background motion in household and dwelling characteristics which are relevant to the allocation process. Hence, virtually continuous reallocation must be a part of the community's housing system. This fact produces a set of questions in the dynamic dimension, symmetrical to the "static" allocation issues previously discussed. Which households should be entitled to change their dwellings when certain circumstances occur? Should their next choices be limited to dwellings coincidentally vacated by other households or should some households whose circumstances have not changed be reassigned to make room for those requiring immediate change? What tolerances in the compromise of individual housing requirements should be permitted under various conditions of background change? How is each household to be persuaded to change its residence at the required time?

Allocation of the housing stock is not a simple matter of visualizing the kind of dwelling which each type of household should enjoy, or the kind of occupants best suited to each available type of dwelling. It is a problem of compromising intricate needs with inexact resources, measuring out housing benefits and charges in different amounts to different people, settling people physically and resettling them at dissimilar intervals, all in accordance with principles which at least have general consent.

THE CAPITAL FORMATION PROCESS

The second process in the diagram, Figure 44, is labeled *Capital Formation*. This refers to a set of activities linking the owners of resources of various kinds with the stock of dwellings.

If housing were not a durable good, this process might simply be called "production," for one aspect of it is the bringing together of resources into a product which serves a consumer need. The durability of the housing commodity, however, does provide this process with a special aspect which complicates the interpersonal relationships involved.

Durability means that a large portion of the housing inventory at any one time has been carried over from a previous production period. In effect, much of the housing commodity is produced well in advance of its use; this element of time means that the task of coordinating the resources used to produce housing includes a specialized function of "holding inventory"—akin to the inventory aspects of retail trade but of much greater significance. The necessity of a holding period means that resources will be committed irrevocably to the product long before the use anticipated for the product will materialize. During its period of usefulness, the housing commodity may prove to meet needs quite different from those originally foreseen, so that risks of gains and losses in the capital value of the housing inventory, and in individual components of that inventory, are necessary conditions on the decision to produce.

The diagram shows five types of resources. These are finance, land, labor, materials, and entrepreneurship. It would be easy to subdivide this brief list to recognize subcategories of resources which are sometimes of great significance, such as the distinction between land currently in nonurban use and land which has an existing urban improvement upon it. For our present purpose the short list of resources will do. In fact, our main point concerns only a three-way distinction among housing resources. It is helpful to group land, labor, and materials into a single category which can be called "quick resources," for we commonly think about the economic process of creating housing as one in which the physical inputs are acquired on terms which are independent of the long life expectancy of the product which they help to create. In a market system, the suppliers of these resources are "paid off" before the housing product which they collaborate to produce is actually offered for its first use. The other resources —finance and entrepreneurship—are involved in the production of housing very largely and quite explicitly because of the element of durability. Thus, as we usually think about the creation of a residential inventory, the process involves a distinct "division of labor" or the separation of specialized functions.

The waiting aspects of housing creation need not give rise to specialization, and it is useful to imagine a situation in which this specialization is absent. Suppose a landowner decided to build a house to rent out, using only materials which he already possessed (such as lumber from trees growing on his land) and his own labor and tools. This person would be able to make all the decisions about producing the dwelling, since he controlled all the resources. Here there is no separation of functions—nor of rewards and risks—among persons. This "unitary decision" might seem attractive on grounds of simplicity, but, in fact, it confronts the decision-maker with some serious limitations and reduces the likelihood that what he produces will represent an efficient use of economic resources from the community's point of view.

For one thing, the kind of dwelling he produces will be limited to the combination of resources at his disposal. That particular land with its locational and physical characteristics, that particular type of lumber, his own skills in carpentry and design can be combined to produce only a limited number of alternative dwelling types. The single decision-maker must rely on his own understanding of the needs of housing users and must be governed by his own system of time preference in deciding how durable a structure he will create. Again, a single individual possesses all these characteristics and resources only in a fixed combination, and if the thing to be produced is limited to the compass of that input combination, the chance to use resources in ways most agreeable to the ultimate housing user is diminished.

In other respects the "costs" of nonspecialization in the housing capital formation process are substantial. The single decision-maker's labor and skill might be better suited to the production of some other commodity than dwellings, his entrepreneurial ability better employed in some other enterprise, and the land and timber put to uses more meaningful to the community. The artificial conjunction of a set of particular resources limits the usefulness of their joint product.

So it is almost universally customary that most of the physical resources used in the production of housing are acquired from separate suppliers, paid for on the spot, and assembled under the direction of a specialized housing entrepreneur. There would be little housing built if only that labor could be used for housing which was willing to wait twenty years or so to be paid, and if only those materials could be used which were supplied by people skilled in the architecture and marketing of dwellings, some odd forms of shelter might appear. The advance of housing comfort and quantity is much dependent upon a complex form of specialization which the diagram calls the capital formation process.

It is relatively common for the functions of supplying land and entrepreneurial direction to be combined in the development of housing. The incentive lies in that not only is urban land usually expected to increase in value as time goes by, but also that current uses will pay the owner an income on his wealth. Thus, urban landowners commonly do take an interest in entrepreneurial techniques, including the ability to make effective judgments about the state of housing demand. Nevertheless, entrepreneurship is conceptually distinct from land ownership, and it is useful to think of the housing development process as one in which the initial landowner, like the laborer and the materials supplier, sells his resource for a "quick" cash price to an entrepreneur.

It is also common to think of the functions of finance and entrepreneurial direction at least in part, as being combined in one person. Indeed, many discussions of housing business and housing policy refer to the developer or entrepreneur as an "investor" and vice versa. The idea that housing entrepreneurs must commit some of their own cash to the undertaking, as equity investment, is very widely held, both as a presumption of what actually happens and as an opinion of what should happen. Again, however, it is both possible and instructive to make a distinction between the two functions and to realize that they may be performed by completely separate persons. In countries with well developed capital markets the resource costs of housing development can be borrowed so effectively that little in the way of cash is actually required by entrepreneurs. Since housing is a necessity which enjoys an inelastic demand in the aggregate, long-term risks are viewed as relatively modest.

We are left, then, with three resource types, representing specialized functions in the creation of housing capital. These are the physical inputs which are acquired and paid for concurrently with the decision to produce housing, financing, and entrepreneurship. Financing is the ability, plus the willingness, to make long-term investments which will be subject to the inherent risks and opportunities of the housing market. Entrepreneurship is skill in coordination of physical resources, plus the willingness to venture on the outcome.

The capital formation process thus brings together basic types of economic behavior on the resource side, and links these with the multitude of housing users on the demand side of the long-term housing market. Several principal sets of questions arise from this complex of interpersonal relationships, the first of which may be referred to as the "partnership problem," or the task of deciding how the rewards and risks of housing development are to be shared among the suppliers of the three main resource types. We have already suggested that the owners of physical resources customarily demand payment without waiting for the usefulness of their joint product to be exhausted. It is also possible to make a fair case that such transactions enhance the social usefulness of all the resources involved. If labor must be acquired for the construction of housing at a price which measures its best current alternative use, that labor is less likely to be used extravagantly, inefficiently, or to poor economic effect. The same is generally true of the materials involved, which usually have alternative uses in some other sector of the economy and which are to be rationed among sectors by the mechanism of current prices.

The price of land as housing input is a more difficult matter. The alternative uses of urban land are relatively limited, and the conditions of supply often make it possible for landowners to exact at least a portion of the anticipated entrepreneurial return or even consumers' surplus. Thus, a problem arises in determining the share of land suppliers in the market proceeds of housing development—a problem which is persistent, difficult, and very nearly universal. Even if land is publicly owned, there is no small problem in seeing to it that investment returns, physical input prices, or consumer utility are not overstated because the value of land is not appreciated. It is so difficult to judge the resource value of land that it may be either under- or over-valued with the result of inefficient use of other resources involved in housing.

The terms of the continuing partnership between finance and entrepreneurship also present puzzles in economic logic and, if we like, in equity or justice. An arrangement which leaves the entrepreneur with any eventual profit, but the supplier of finance with any eventual loss, would really suit neither party, for the entrepreneur would have little chance to practice his skills. The problem is to evaluate the probabilities of gain and loss and to relate them to the functions actually performed. Suppliers of finance and of entrepreneurship are both paid in the coin of probability, but they supply very different things.

Another question in the capital formation process is concerned with "motivation." The process links the suppliers of housing with the users of housing, and so must translate housing satisfactions received by users into income received by suppliers. Because a stock of housing once produced is "sunk capital," it is perfectly possible to arrange a set of housing prices which denies the suppliers of finance and entrepreneurship the returns for which they entered upon their long-term partnership. Imposition of rent control is an example. When (and in what detailed manner) this might be done without harm, at least to the continuing economic function of capital formation in housing, is a problem which every society faces. One very narrow issue is whether the prices of housing to users should be fixed in relationship to historic cost. If this is done, the suppliers of housing resources will not receive direct information about the success of what they have created. They will not know that one type of housing in the inventory was not worth the resources used or that another type caused an improvement in consumer welfare. Resource suppliers would thus be rewarded on bases other than the desirability of what they produced, those who judged housing needs well getting the same as those who judged poorly.

A further aspect of capital formation is "liquidity." The

long-term partners of finance and entrepreneurship may hesitate to enter into an arrangement from which the individuals involved cannot withdraw so long as the housing which they helped to create continues to be of value. Financial and ownership interests serve their economic purposes best if they can be liquidated—transferred to others—without excessive loss, uncertainty, or delay. Thus, a subprocess is implicitly required within the task of capital formation. The process of transferring interests involves the establishment of prices, excepting the prices of the original physical inputs, just as in the original definition of the development venture. The persons who supplied financing or entrepreneurship, moreover, may find it desirable to liquidate only parts of their original interests, so that the subsequent pricing problem can be more complex than the original.

The final kind of issue embodied within the capital formation process is the "administration of windfalls." As the housing stock moves on through the years of its economic life, events which were only probabilities at the outset become certainties. Some dwellings, or the land they occupy, acquire enhanced values and others become less desirable, for reasons perhaps entirely exogenous to the decision framework of original development. A public decision may change the transportation system in such a way, for example, that some residential districts are benefitted while others decline. Or the purchasing power of households with respect to housing may be redistributed, enhancing the demand for some housing while diminishing it for others. Upon whom are such windfalls to descend? Whether the basic cause is a public decision, a change in technology or tastes, or a natural phenomenon such as an earthquake, the incidence of gains and losses is a public question. Again, of course, the resource suppliers who were paid off at the time that the affected inventory was created are usually assumed to be exempt from benefit or loss from windfalls.

The capital formation process thus requires decisions about the sharing of housing benefits and costs among users or categories of users and suppliers of resources. The issues in this sharing process are varied and the resolution necessarily complex. Housing is not developed merely by spending one's own money on lumber and nails, but by a many-sided process which extends into the future. Diverse interests and contingencies of various kinds must be weighed in the process of creating an inventory of housing.

THE SECTOR IMPROVEMENT PROCESS

The diagram shows a third function of the housing sector which is identified as the *sector improvement process*. Capital formation occurs in anticipation of needs, and the stock allocation process attempts to satisfy those needs out of the stock which has been created. Inevitably the stock will fall short of being the ideal resource combination for the needs which do appear because of unanticipated shifts in those needs and perhaps because of inefficiency in the complex process of capital formation itself. We can therefore expect that at any moment of time there is a latent opportunity to use new capital resources to good effect in amending the available stock. To use an analogy, a tailor who is making a coat may err in his measurement and make the sleeves too long, or the purchaser may change his mind about how long the sleeves should be while the coat is being made, so that some correction undertaken after the original work is complete may be worth additional expense. The correction process in the housing sector is a substantial aspect of the whole performance of the sector.

Correction of the capital stock involves recognition of defects, decision about the form of the corrective action, and decision about the incidence of the cost of correction or, alternatively, the incidence of the cost of leaving the error uncorrected. All of these elements touch upon many individuals, giving rise to issues of equity and resource conservation. Suppose, for example, that a number of new houses are constructed in anticipation of a new industrial plant which eventually is constructed in a fairly remote area. Should special new transportation facilities be provided so that the new housing can be used as anticipated? Or should the new houses be made available to replace older dwellings in the community sooner than might have occurred otherwise, causing capital losses to owners of those older dwellings but permitting more new dwellings to be constructed nearer the actual location of the new industrial plant? There are several other alternatives which might be worthy of consideration, but any form of correction will be costly of resources of some type. Should the proprietors of the new plant be required to bear these costs, perhaps passing along part of the burden to their customers? Should investors in the original new dwellings bear the entire cost, perhaps by demolishing their new dwellings to protect the values of buildings already in the community? Should local, state, or national governments levy taxes to make up for the additional resource expenditure? Again, many alternatives are possible and each involves a decision which is at once economic and social.

The distinction between capital formation and a correction, or improvement, process is one of causation rather than one of technique. Whenever new housing capital is to be created, whether to serve an anticipated demand or to amend the stock when the demand has actually made itself felt, physical resources must be acquired and financed, and the process must be directed by an entrepreneurial agent sensitive to the costs of resources, on the one hand, and the intensity of needs, on the other. The improvement process might be called a "feedback" from the fundamental conjunction of demand and supply which has already occurred, giving rise to signals for marginal adjustments. These signals and these adjustments do, in the long run, amount to information for the development of capital formation decisions, in a kind of learning process which improves the performance of housing development. But the improvement or corrective process is never obviated until demand characteristics, and housing resource technology and cost, are all in a static mold, an unlikely situation whatever our views of the social and economic process, for the ultimate characteristics of facilities for human habitation are not yet in sight. One function of any economic sector is improvement in the pattern of its performance.

The improvement process has two aspects. One is the performance of ad hoc adjustments in the inventory, and the other is a more fundamental correction of the stock allocation and/or capital formation processes. Ad hoc adjustments require as inputs sensitive knowledge about the needs unsatisfied by the compromises of stock allocation. They also require techniques including the ability to search for indirect as well as direct means of making the adjustments. For example, if the number of single-family dwellings which has been produced falls short of the need, the deficit may be supplied either by producing additional single-family dwellings or by creating incentives for some of the less urgent present users of single-family dwellings (such as elderly couples or young couples without children) to occupy multiple-dwelling structures instead. If the number of low-income dwellings is inadequate, the need may be supplied via the "filtering" process and construction of additional units for other groups. That is, the improvement process can maximize present satisfactions by considering individual needs in the broadest possible perspective.

Changes in the other two housing sector processes require conceptual understanding of the source of past housing sector diseconomies—essentially a matter of exercising the intellect—and implementation of reforms in operating process. For example, it may be learned that lack of skill or ethics on the part of housing brokers has produced unnecessary dissatisfactions to buyers and sellers of dwellings. The corrective action may be public regulation or the design and adoption of more sophisticated practices by a trade association of brokers. Traditional self-limitations by mortgage lenders may prove, upon study, to be harmful to the economic use of housing resources, suggesting public guarantees to encourage sound but unfamiliar practices.

This discussion of housing sector processes indicates that the satisfaction of housing needs is dependent upon not just one set of decisions but upon a complex of interdependent decision situations. It is not housing need alone which determines what the housing sector shall do, nor housing resources alone, nor the structure of decision-making institutions. All three of these interact upon each other.

The housing sector's involved and integrated activity compels us to recognize at point after point that the desires of one participant cannot be met without sacrificing the desires of others. Households compete among each other and with resource suppliers as a group for the stock; resource suppliers compete for the benefits extracted from housing users; and all the agencies involved in carrying out the functions of the housing sector are subject to obsolescence of their skills and positions.

The housing sector as a whole requires a set of rules and institutions adapted to the special characteristics of the housing commodity. Our next task is to describe the common forms of business institutions associated with the housing sector, to show that these institutions have evolved in recognition of the complexity and interpersonal nature of housing processes. The evolution has produced, in apparent paradox, a set of simple, impersonal institutions. We must see how this paradox is resolved.

Business Service Functions in the Housing Sector

A business system organizes itself in a very distinct fashion in order to carry out the three processes—stock allocation, capital formation, and sector improvement—described in the preceding section. There is a set of functions to be performed and it is natural that functional specialization would appear. Some functions are "tangible"—construction, development, and investment. Others are "intangible"—valuation, brokerage, and management. Each function has skill and organizational requirements peculiar to itself.

The "tangible" functions have been described in Chapter 6. These are functions which change the physical housing inventory, by construction, alteration, maintenance, and demolition. To an important degree these physical activities "look" the same whether the housing economy is socialized or private. In both systems there are carpenters, architects, plumbers, etc., and land-use decision-makers. Public and private housing economies are distinguished more by the *in*tangible functions or services which each requires as inputs to physical activity planning. Our description of a market economy in housing thus concentrates on the nature of these intangible or "service" functions.

VALUATION

The individual with a home to sell or in search of a home to buy must decide what a particular dwelling is "worth." Philosophers have long argued about the meaning of "value" and social scientists recognize that one dwelling or all dwellings together can have elastic and obscure value to the community, but the buyer or seller of a dwelling must put a price on it. The business decision will not answer the questions of philosophers or social scientists, but it can be made in a manner which serves the purposes of housing users, investors, and arbitragers.

The "traditional" tools of valuation (though they are not in universal use nor of any considerable antiquity) are three "approaches to value" which are generally presumed likely to coincide. These three methods correspond roughly to the three types of markets which we have identified, though it is customary to use all three methods regardless of the nature of the immediate business decision.

One method may be referred to as a "marketing" concept. What a particular dwelling is "worth" in this approach is what is being paid currently for similar dwellings. No two housing units are exactly alike, but the experienced valuation expert has enough information about recent transactions to bracket the peculiar characteristics of the property in question at the moment. There may be no recent sales information for a particular seven-year-old dwelling, but an educated guess can be made from data on otherwise similar dwellings which are five or six years old, and eight or nine years old.

The valuation expert or appraiser does not explain *why* a particular dwelling is likely to sell for about $18,000, and in plain fact he would not be able to, because the fundamental reasons for economic behavior are unfathomable and the complex interactions of the market are nowhere reduced to intellectually satisfying formulae. He can simply form an opinion that the house in question probably will not bring a much higher price and would be an unnecessary gift to the purchaser if sold for less. The seller is protected by this information, or opinion, from asking less than buyers have recently paid for similar dwellings (after adjustment for minor points of difference) and the buyer is protected from offering more. The appraiser's estimate of value facilitates the business decision of buyer and seller though it skirts all the issues of causation.

The probability of the appraiser's being correct depends, in part, on the relative insignificance of the transaction at hand. He does not really "make" the price, but merely "reads" it from the recent behavior of the market, as one reads stock quotations on a ticker or in the financial pages. Since his estimates are based on past data, however recent, he will err in respect to changes in market conditions (unless the "feedback" process has led him to introduce trends or other explicit adjustment elements in his calculations). But if market transactions are numerous, small, and nearly continuous, his error will remain small.

The "investment approach" to valuation identifies the net income which the property is capable of producing and converts this into a present capital value. The net income may be estimated from the actual experience of the property or, as in the marketing approach, by weighing the income experience of similar properties. The conversion factor involves a capitalization rate or rate of required return on investment which is obtained from observation of current investment practices. Both the income data and the conversion factor are thus based on the assumption that what households have been paying for rent, what expenses income properties have been incurring, and what rates of returns investors have been realizing, will not change materially. Again, changes in market conditions will mean that invalid income, expense, or rate of return information may be introduced into the appraisal, but the experienced and informed appraiser may perhaps sense such changes and allow for them, more or less intuitively. Here also, the fact that transactions occur frequently operates to keep the valuation error small.

The third appraisal method may be called the "hypothetical construction approach." If the dwelling under consideration were not available to the inventory, it could be replaced by employing resources presently available at market prices. Land could be acquired, labor and materials obtained, and the services of finance and entrepreneurship employed to make a hypothetical substitute. The sum of the resource prices thus incurred provides another widely used indication of the value of the property in question. It may be noted that this concept assumes that the subject dwelling is replaced "directly" rather than "indirectly." The possibility that resources might be used to produce a different type of new dwelling which would indirectly cause some existing house like the subject dwelling to become available on the market is not made use of by any of the common appraisal methods.

Whichever method we are considering, the techniques of housing valuation are most effective and useful when the process is applied to voluntary transactions involving one unit at a time. The appraiser is not in search of "truth," but simply wants to predict what a given individual will voluntarily do in a particular situation. This is what his information consists of; he adds nothing more than perceptive measurement. He cannot say what housing is worth to a society, what the possession of property is worth to a human spirit, nor how the pattern of voluntary housing transactions will be affected by a major reconstruction of the housing stock or a recomposition of population. These are at least too complex for the appraiser's tools and they may be insoluble. Appraisers are often called upon to answer questions like these (as in eminent domain and public redevelopment undertakings), and not every practicing appraiser is aware of limitations inherent in his profession. Valuation facilitates business decisions and it often seems required for public enterprise as well, but in the latter, the developed and practiced tools of valuation do not really apply.

BROKERAGE

The essence of a market is exchange, but exchanges do not arrange themselves spontaneously even when they are advantageous to both parties. We might say that the test of adequate performance of the brokerage function is that the use of a dwelling or the enjoyment of any of the financial or business rights associated with it is not transferred unless mutual benefit is possible; that of all possible purchasers the person who will benefit most becomes the buyer; and, that the exchange itself is consummated without unnecessary expense which diminishes the inherent productivity of the sale. For example, A would consider selling a house if the price could be greater than $15,000, B would be willing to pay $14,000, C to pay $16,000, and D to pay $17,000. Letting these amounts represent real economic satisfaction, for the moment, we can say that D should become the buyer. If the costs of transfer amount to $1,000, the outcome will not be changed, but if the cost is $2,000 or more, no net economic advantage is secured by the transfer. Supposing that the $2,000 cost includes some activities which are unnecessary or inefficient, due to a remediable lack of skill on the part of the intermediaries to the sale, then an inherently productive exchange which could improve the usefulness of the housing stock or some interest in it will be thwarted.

The brokerage function has three essential elements. It includes first, a search among holders of interests in residential property, whether these be the rights to use dwellings, rights to receive income, debt repayment or increases in capital value, and a corresponding search among potential purchasers of these interests. In principle, each potential purchaser is exposed to each existing right. The second element is negotiation, which on the surface is the resolution of complex, technical matters, but which is at root a device to screen out nonoptimal purchasers. The third function is to pay heed to the resource costs of performing the other two.

A business system of housing brokerage simplifies an inherently complex problem by using the device of "particular prices." Looking at a stock of dwellings, on the one hand—each with its unique physical features and atmosphere—and at the population of households, on the other—each with some distinct housing needs and preferences—it might seem nearly impossible for a responsible intermediary to decide which household should live in which dwelling. The same difficulties arise in different form in the allocation of other interests in housing, such as the ownership of the equity or the size, origin, and conditions of a mortgage. Business brokerage resolves this by developing prices which facilitate decisions, not by the broker but by the sellers and buyers individually. The prospective seller is asked, for example, whether his continued ownership and use of the dwelling is worth $17,000. This seller knows his present dwelling in all its complexity, and its suitability to his present needs. He understands that part or all of the $17,000 may be used to acquire another dwelling from a stock with which he is less familiar. All the tangible and intangible aspects on both sides of his prospective sale are to be summed up in a "yes or no" answer to the question posed above. This is not an easy decision, but it is substantially easier than one which extends his responsibility to include the welfare of the prospective buyer. He does not have to decide whether Buyer B, C, or D would benefit more from the possession of the house than he, himself, or than one another. The seller sells to a market, not to a person. Only his own welfare need enter into his acceptance or rejection of a particular price.

The potential buyer's decision problem is the mirror image of the seller's problem. The buyer does not know intimately the tangible and intangible aspects of the dwelling (or other property interest). He does appreciate the sacrifice represented by a payment of $17,000, perhaps including the sale of his present dwelling. He does not need to consider whether the seller, A, may be making a disadvantageous bargain or, perhaps, realizing a substantial windfall profit. The needs of the seller, whether physical or moral, are not an element in the buyer's decision about price. The house will be purchased, if the sale is completed, from an impersonal "market" and not from a personality. The buyer has only to survey his own feelings (and the dwelling in question) to decide "yes or no," whether possession of that dwelling promises to be worth more than $17,000. If the buyer's answer is "yes" and the seller's answer to his own question is "no" (that is, continued ownership is not worth $17,000), then a transaction is possible. The price is not important in itself but rather for what it accomplishes in administering the use of housing resources.

By extension, different prices arise from the confrontation of other prospective buyers with the seller, A, and this seller is faced with a decision of a different kind. Of those buyers offering an acceptable price, which one is preferable? This is a relatively simple problem so long as the transaction is regarded as impersonal, for there are no housing intangibles to be weighed. The "rational" seller would merely select the highest money offer. Units of money are homogeneous, and the other elements of the transaction are constant among alternative buyers. An actual price emerges from the second decision, for identification of the optimal buyer is the sufficient condition for a transaction. Still, the figures written on the sales contract are of importance primarily for the effect they have on the use of housing resources. Prices are means to an end, not ends in themselves. The nature of the housing market makes "particular prices" both valuable and, in a business system, necessary, because housing is heterogeneous. The "market price" for housing may exist as an index number of some social interest, but it is not an operating parameter in housing market equilibrium.

Clearly, the great advantage of a system of brokerage involving particular prices depends upon its simplicity. Decisions involve weighing money against money, or money against a narrow set of intangibles. This raises a question of considerable social interest—namely, whether the money prices which an individual can "afford" for housing measure the social advantage of his use of parts of the housing inventory (or possession of some other interest). Families with low income will inevitably be screened out of portions of the market, for example, under a system of particular prices. We must defer this point briefly, though it is close to the essence of our problem. First, we must complete the description of the business system and then consider alternatives to this system as a whole. An answer to this important question will arise at that point.

The term "brokerage" is not being used in this context in its literal meaning. The function to be performed is communication rather than some intermediate ownership and risk-taking. Sellers want to know who would be interested in buying a specific housing interest, while buyers want to know about the range of their choices among dwellings, equities, and other transferable interests. The "search" function does not always require a third party, but it ordinarily does require specialized facilities. Buyers and sellers must literally "find" each other and jointly examine the property to be transferred. Many housing interests, such as mortgages, are in a form which allows them to be traded in a central place akin to a stock exchange. Other interests, such as possession and ownership, cannot be traded without visits to fixed locations, and the nature of housing means that such visits will cover a wide geographic area. There are many more or less mechanical ways in which the mutual identification of buyers and sellers can be assisted, such as the publication of lists, the adoption of a standardized format for preliminary description, and a screening technique which limits the area of direct contact for both buyers and sellers to situations with significant probability for mutually advantageous transactions. Where there is a personal intermediary (such as the ordinary housing broker), there are major, potential sources of inefficient communication in limitations on that intermediary's access to the entire range of buyers and sellers, so that a seller may never be put in contact with the optimal among all potential buyers, and the buyer may never see the property best suited to his needs. Since personal intermediation involves judgment, the breadth of the intermediary's knowledge and, perhaps more significantly, his trustworthiness are further limitations on his ability to perform effectively. By developing community-wide organizations of cooperation among brokers to share information, and by improving both the competence and the professionalism of the intermediary, these potential diseconomies in the market process can be minimized. These observations imply that there must be a system for the continuous improvement of professional skills and standards as well as structural forms for sharing information about the market. It does not suffice simply to call into being a number of brokerage offices.

Real estate markets, including the residential sector, are both primary and secondary. This distinction refers to the newness of the interest in question; the market for newly constructed houses as opposed to that for exchanges of the existing inventory, for example; or the creation of a new mortgage as opposed to exchanges of existing mortgages. Secondary markets provide liquidity which enhances the usefulness of the existing inventory, by permitting smooth adaptation in the face of changing individual circumstances. A householder whose job location has changed or a mortgage lender whose current obligations are rising will be at a disadvantage if he is "locked in" by the lack of a secondary market for the real estate interest which he owns. Neither the housing stock nor the savings resources of the community will be used to their best advantage unless liquidity is created by secondary markets.

The nature and organization of secondary markets differ

somewhat from those of primary markets. Physically, an older dwelling has attributes which cannot be readily ascertained from blueprints or lists of material components. Less is known about some aspects of serviceability, though the fact that a building has stood the test of time and usage provides information about older dwellings not available for new dwellings. Financially, a mortgage which has been extant for a few years enjoys the advantage of having tested the credit of the borrower, but a disadvantage in some uncertainty about the change in value of the security. Equities in new properties are subject to far greater uncertainty and risk than equities in established properties. Thus, the type of information required for a meeting of minds on the part of buyers and sellers differs as between primary and secondary markets. The individuals or firms likely to be in these two types of markets may be quite different too, for certain types of households may seldom be in the market for new dwellings, and some types of lenders and equity investors have strong preferences for frequent turning over of their residential portfolios. The market for junior liens is notoriously thin, so that the establishment of an effective market in this form of interest is definitely a specialized function.

Negotiation is another basic function of market intermediaries. This can be understood to include a process of bargaining, but in housing market transactions, there is usually much more to completing a transaction than agreement on price. The commodity is such that various assurances must be sought that the sale will have the legal effect intended by the buyer and the seller. Real estate cannot be delivered physically, nor can a mortgage instrument simply be handed from one individual to another. A series of steps must be taken first to ascertain the extent of the rights which the seller is entitled to offer and to make the sale binding. The man who purchases a deed to a house and then finds he does not have the right to occupy it (because of a leasehold, perhaps) or the investor who purchases a mortgage but is unable to recover prepayments of which he was not aware would not be well served by the market process. In fact, the "detail" of residential real estate transactions is cumbersome and complex, requiring the services of competent and trustworthy specialists to uncover circumstances which require special consideration and to clear away doubts that other difficulties may have been overlooked. Only when the buyer and seller know as exactly as possible what they are transferring can the discussion turn to price.

The magnitude of the value in most real estate transactions makes the specific financial arrangements a matter of basic importance. A household with good income and excellent credit will seldom have funds in cash for the purchase of a home, and the developer intent upon acquiring land will usually prefer to use credit facilities. Part of the negotiation process is, therefore, a supplementary negotiation with sources of finance. Indeed, it is not misleading to think of the whole residential mortgage system as a brokerage arrangement for joining the housing sector to the capital market, adapting the instruments of housing finance to the preferences and understanding of the nation's savers and financial institutions. This may take the form of specialized thrift institutions such as savings and loan associations which tap primary sources of savings and make investments almost exclusively in the housing sector. It may, on the other hand, involve generalized credit institutions, such as commercial banks, for whom residential finance is only one aspect of their lending program so that the ebb and flow of industrial credit requirements impinges directly on the supply of residential credit. It may involve also the securities markets directly, as equity or debt instruments of residential development or management firms are offered in competition with industrial and other securities for purchase by individuals or institutions. There may be intermediate agencies in the financial area, such as mortgage brokers and mortgage bankers, to perform specialized communication and service functions which will make lenders the more ready to invest in even distant residential real estate. In short, there is a network of specialization on the financial side alone which acts in a supplementary role to the process of carrying out basic housing market exchanges.

The sale of equities, particularly of income properties, involves considerations on both sides which may be more complex than the household's desire for a home or the lender's desire for a stream of net income. Factors such as the capital gains tax position of the exchanging parties are relevant. The form of an estate, or the liquidation of community or jointly held property may be of great importance in an individual case. To ascertain that Buyer X is going to benefit more than any other from the purchase of Y's equity calls for sophisticated knowledge of the large business environment as well as realistic understanding of the particulars of the housing commodity and housing finance. The personality and situation of the owner is likely to have important consequences for the property's management and for its economic life, so that the trading of equities affects the usefulness of housing resources. Lack of skill or market organization in this respect must raise the probability that housing resources will be wasted, at least in a market sense.

Brokerage, or more broadly the whole process of putting transactions together, is the business system's way of deciding who shall enjoy specific interests in the stock of housing resources and for what period. It is a set of specialized functions, linked together by business articulation rather than by bureaucratic protocol. Apart from its dispersion of responsibility, it has two characteristics of broad importance. Its decisions are based on benefits measured in money rather than in considerations of welfare (which money is, nevertheless, thought to approximate). And it determines what shall be done to house people and compensate factors of production by disposing of one piece of the inventory or property interest at a time, solving each problem by considering only the positions of the parties directly involved. The system ignores aspects of any transaction which cannot be related to monetary terms by the parties immediately involved. Specifically, it ignores the "external" effects of a transaction, the consequences of any transaction in housing upon people who are excluded from that transaction. These simplifications in what is to be considered makes it possible for the business system to function, to dispose of a massive responsibility in apportioning resources which always count very heavily in a community's total economic wealth.

MANAGEMENT

A third element in the business system may be called management. Valuation and brokerage are services which facilitate the actions of principals, but the responsibility for action lies with the proprietors of individual interests. In a previous chapter most of these proprietary situations have been discussed and analyzed so the present review can be brief.

There can, of course, be specialized managers of any type of residential property interest. Hired managers look after apartments, collecting rents, handling turnover, arranging for repairs, keeping financial records, and so on. Specialized firms or departments within large financial institutions manage mortgage portfolios, receiving and recording payments, following up on delinquency, taking action in the event of foreclosure, and even processing sale of portions of the portfolio. Trust companies, attorneys, or other agencies may administer equity interests on behalf of beneficial owners. These important and technical functions are one aspect of what we mean to convey by the term "management." They are performed following the business ground rules which appear in the present chapter—treatment of one case at a time, and the elimination of "external effects" from the decision. Only the direct benefit of the owner is considered by these administrative decisions, but with regard, of course, to limitations and obligations imposed by law. The decision framework is narrow and choices are usually free of ambiguity.

Taking "management" to mean the whole burden upon entrepreneurs, we can appreciate that the decision to incur risks is a part of this function. No residential transaction is completely free of risk or, at least, of contingencies. The owner of a residential interest is subject to risks which may be not only very substantial, but which can and do change. An apartment project may operate satisfactorily for many years in a thriving community, producing mortgage yields for lenders, capital appreciation for owners and housing services for occupants; a change in the economic base of the community, however, or a deterioration of the immediate neighborhood, or any of numerous other types of events may put the property in a much poorer competitive position.

Opportunities for additional capital improvements may occur during the period of ownership, creating decision situations for equity owners and for lenders as well, and the holder of any interest may find it wise, at some point, to liquidate his interest. These decisions are problems of information, timing, and judgment, all of which must be supplied by the entrepreneur (which we take to include the holder of any interest). This is a residential function, more or less, so the kinds of problems which arise for the entrepreneur are likely to be varied. The entrepreneur is, thus, a generalist with respect to the form of interest he holds, though that may be a specialized type of interest. He is the man at the wheel, and while the range of probable decisions is limited by the nature of the vehicle—like the operator of a bus, an airliner, or a speedboat—he must handle whatever situations arise.

The manager or entrepreneur, broadly understood, makes decisions which are in his own interest and makes decisions only for the property which he himself controls. In the housing market it is relatively rare for an entrepreneur's decision respecting one interest to react upon some other interest which he holds. It can happen, however, as, for example, to a mortgage lender who holds a significant fraction of the total residential debt of a community so that a loan for new construction can weaken the value of existing properties. However such situations are resolved, it would be expected of a business system that the resolution would be based on the entrepreneur's best interests alone. This kind of problem does suggest, however, how the simplicity of an atomistic market process may become a morass of complex interactions in a centrally directed housing economy.

STRUCTURAL DEVELOPMENT

Business "systems" such as we have described do not arise spontaneously, nor do they adapt themselves without conscious direction to changes in the nature of using housing resources to meet housing demands. To create and to modify the structure of business practices in the housing sector requires collective action on the part of the enterprises themselves, public direction and control, or some combination of the two.

In appraising, the three structural requirements are reasonable uniformity of method, ethical business relationships, and a system of education by which appraisers may be trained. Changes in the structure of appraising practices require, in addition, research into emerging problems of appraisal practice as social, economic, and technological changes occur which affect housing. Structural changes may also require modification of procedures for entering into and practicing the appraisal profession. Appraising is a "professional service" in the sense that practitioners dispense advice based on theories and information to which the clients of appraisal services do not have access. Hence, these clients must be able to trust the appraiser's ability and objectivity. Where this trust is not preserved, the community is not well served in its need for judgments of residential real estate value, and the business system of the housing market functions inefficiently.

Uniformity of method means that estimates of value provided by different appraisers for different properties are comparable. If estimates of the value of interests in residential property are not comparable, then the likelihood of a prudent choice by householder, lender, entrepreneur, or developer is very much diminished. Indeed, it can be said with justification that the appraiser's method is more important than his estimate of value. Like paper money, its value is derived from its general acceptability, so that a home owner who secures an appraisal based on standard methods can be assured that mortgage lenders and subsequent buyers of the same properties will receive comparable information and hence will look upon the value of the dwelling in much the same light as the home owner's appraiser did.

Standardized methods may be achieved by public licensing and supervision, or by the discipline of a professional trade organization. The latter may be institutionalized in the form of a trademarked designation for members in good standing—i.e., for those whose methods conform to the society's standard. Either method requires a form of "entrance examination" which unavoidably dwells on rote, and on a system of penalizing those who do not qualify or who do not conform. Public education is also a part of this system, so that potential users of appraisal services are forewarned about the significance and desirability of standardized methods.

Valuation practice, particularly in the more popular forms of the residential market, is difficult to police in detail, for much of the thought process may not be reduced to writing. Confidence in the appraiser's ethical standards is important for this reason. Ethical behavior is even more significant in situations where parties to a real estate transaction would benefit from influencing the estimate of value. The seller who wishes to realize an extravagant price or loan for his property might induce an unethical appraiser to provide a substantiating estimate of value. Such is the nature of the housing market that such an "unstandard" valuation might soon prove to be a good approximation to market value. Still it would represent deception, for until the new market circumstances are realized, the prospective buyer or lender who was influenced by this procured valuation would be in danger of financial loss.

Ethical behavior can be encouraged in several ways, none of them foolproof. Entry requirements, whether public or private, may be set in such a manner that only responsible individuals are likely to qualify, for example, by disqualifying persons previously convicted of some criminal practice involving business ethics. Endorsements by persons already in the profession, or in other responsible real estate activities, may also be required. Sample "audits" of current appraisals, using standardized techniques and well-organized market information as measuring rods of performance will establish a climate of discipline. Obviously, these efforts require a continuing supervisory effort and some expenditure of resources, the cost of which may be borne by the general public—for the benefit of a competent appraisal corps is very widespread—or by the clients of appraisers. The ultimate incidence of the cost would be about the same in either case, though higher appraisal fees may discourage the use of this important service by some decision-makers. If the cost of supervision is borne by appraisal clients, there is some possibility also that appraisers will develop a proprietary attitude toward this system and employ it to further their own interests rather than those of their clients, by setting high minimum fees, for example.

Recruits to the appraisal profession might be expected to educate themselves to the point of qualifying for the right to practice or use a distinguishing trademark. This might be considered a desirable proof of earnestness. However, little can be learned until teaching materials have been created and a corps of teachers established. The curriculum must include the rote material of currently accepted valuation methods, of course, but the evolutionary nature of valuation problems and methods argues for a theoretical and analytical component of this education as well. Moreover, the nature of the economic system and the housing sector differs among nations, at least, making some aspects of valuation more important in some areas than in others. The practice of ground-leasing is a case in point, as is the institution of cooperative housing. There is no universal system of appraising or of valuation analysis; thus, training materials developed in one context cannot serve the whole need of the profession elsewhere.

It is natural that emerging problems in valuation be studied as a part of this system of training, and that modifications in standard appraisal methods be developed concomitantly. Further, the need to change the system of appraisal supervision ought to appear in the course of such studies, though the actual adoption of changes, say in required qualifications for new appraisers, must rest with administrators, whether public or private, rather than with educators or researchers. The burden of the educational system is nevertheless substantial.

The structural aspects of brokerage bear much similarity to those of valuation. Standardized methods must be developed, the use of improper methods discouraged, an educational program carried out, and the system itself subjected to continuing review. Brokerage differs from appraising in being more concrete and in involving less dependence upon unquestioning trust by the client. The types of information which a broker must convey to his principal or to the other party, and the things he must not say, can be spelled out with relative clarity. What a broker has actually done in a particular case can be revealed without much difficulty where it concerns the handling of documents or money. His service is not so much a matter of rendering a judgment as is true in appraising. It is more in the nature of communicating specific facts and performing specific acts. The broker may provide varying amounts of interpretation and "salesmanship" in addition to his more mechanical functions, but once more the boundaries of what is in the interests of the community as a whole in these regards are relatively discernible. Customary forms of selling effort are generally understood by people in the marketplace and, indeed, expected, though abuses are always possible.

One of the principal areas of concern about the brokerage function is the handling of money, such as earnest money, and of valuable documents, such as deeds and mortgages. For this reason a partial separation of functions between the sales agent and an escrow agent, with the latter subject to strict regulation and supervision, is a practice which recommends itself. It is to the interest of brokers as a group that the public be assured of scrupulous handling of such valuables and the establishment of escrow regulations is not a reflection upon the integrity of people who act as brokers.

The broker is most nearly in an advisory capacity to the buyer of property when he describes the extent of the interest in property which is being offered. How can a prospective buyer know, for example, whether the broker's principal is the legal owner of the property being offered, or that liens against the property do not exist? Supplementary to this brokerage function, or, indeed, to the whole business system of real estate—both residential and other—is a publicly established system of determining property interests. The clearer and more available are the legal records of property interests, the easier is the broker's task and the more secure the prospective purchaser can feel. Title registration, competent and honest title transfer machinery, and some form of title insurance reduce the opportunity for fraud or dissatisfaction in the transaction, to the benefit of the broker as well as buyers and sellers. The object of this supplementary system, as in escrow regulations, is a reduction of risk and uncertainty for those who engage in real estate transactions. Less uncertainty means more opportunity for economically productive transfers of property and, hence, better use of housing resources.

Among the more mechanical aspects of brokerage as a system is communitywide communication of the fact that certain properties or interests are for sale or that certain households, investors, or entrepreneurs are in the market for specific types of property rights. The device to facilitate this communication may be a single exchange, literally a specially equipped building where all transactions are developed, or a communications service which is in touch with all the independent offices of brokers who deal in residential property interests. Mortgage interests seem more likely to go through central exchange facilities while possessory interests and equities generally are handled by large numbers of independent agents linked together in some way for exchange of offers. One reason for this may be that possessory interests and equities depend very much for their value on unique aspects of individual properties and location in particular, so that geographical specialization by brokers is generally advantageous. Whatever the structure, each type of interest requires some kind of intercommunication system to make the market as broad as possible.

Mortgage interests enjoy markets which, in principle, are nationwide. The sale or origination of mortgages of any priority involving lenders outside the region in which the security is located represents a geographical flow of funds. Net inflows to a particular region may be necessary for the efficient use of the nation's capital resources if the region in question enjoys relative economic advantages for growth. Yet interregional mortgage flows require a network of sensitive and skilled traders, linked with each other and confident in each other's ability to create sound mortgages. Standardized terminology, to say nothing of mortgage terms, with a background of standardized appraising, and possibly a program of insurance against loss in the value of the mortgage, assist in the development of useful interregional flows. Common and reasonable legal definitions of property rights and of procedures in case of loan default, plus some efficient system for administering loans (e.g. collecting payments, handling delinquencies) held on distant properties are also necessary if the flow of mortgage funds is to accord with the implicit requirements of the national capital market.

Education and research needs in the field of brokerage— we have used the term here to include financial intermediaries— are no less important or far-reaching than for appraising. Entering practitioners should be expected to know the principal legal, financial, and physical aspects of the property interest in which they will deal, and the organization of the market. They must be prepared also for the inevitable modification of these things as changing economic and technological circumstances make modifications necessary, so the education should be, in part, analytical. This education cannot take place unless there is a body of learning, both descriptive and theoretical, to be acquired and an educational institution to impart it.

Lastly, there must be a superstructure of some kind—a public or trade association, or some combination of the two—to oversee the application of general standards and to take action when structural changes become desirable. This superstructure can easily supplant the business system it sets out to rationalize if its supervision is too close, or it can become an agency of self-protection against the interests of the community at large if it is directed by brokers alone, some of whom may not be conscious of that larger interest. Thus, the form of this controlling device and the nature of its evolutionary changes in the system it controls are matters of genuine public concern.

Housing entrepreneurship is not a "profession" in the sense that is accepted in appraising and brokerage. Personal consultation is not involved. The entrepreneur produces a physical product, a dwelling, or a change in the use of dwellings. He does not advise others to do it, but does it himself. There are some points, however, at which entrepreneurship calls for some coordination and standards.

One of these, but a matter generally beyond the subject of this book, is contracting. Building firms produce complex products which may conceal fraudulent or careless materials or workmanship for which the housing consumer and society at large ultimately will pay. It is a general practice to provide public regulations for contracting firms and for some ancillary activities such as architectural services. Though construction firms very often act as housing entrepreneurs, it is not our intention to broaden our discussion to these other large matters. We are concerned with entrepreneurship as the decision about what kinds of uses shall be made of housing resources, rather than with the exact manner in which those decisions are carried out.

A more precise instance of public concern with entrepreneurial behavior is illustrated by the common practice of urban land zoning. Urban land uses interact spatially as well as in terms of competition for the market. There is, moreover, adequate experience and reason to suppose that a collection of completely isolated decisions about the uses of individual parcels of land within a city will not produce a pattern of uses satisfactory to the decision-makers themselves. Intermixture of land uses—factories, stores, and houses indiscriminately adjoining one another—is a pattern less useful in many practical ways to all the members of the community than is a pattern showing some separation of uses. Entrepreneurs themselves derive substantial benefit from zoning of this nature, though every set of land-use regulations confers windfall gains upon some entrepreneurs and windfall losses upon others. The net effect of some separation of uses over none is almost certain to be large and positive. The choice of land-use plans for a community includes one which has the greatest net benefit, though the degree of superiority and the terms in which this benefit is to be measured are imponderables. In this instance, any plan tends to be better than none, and the choice of a specific plan is an issue in totally different dimensions.

A community whose land uses are in the hands of entrepreneurs thus has some tendency toward voluntary coordination, though carrying out this coordination in fact requires public power. Zoning is, in a way, a microcosm of the public aspects of a business system for the housing sector. Private individuals acknowledge a desire for a rule-creating public agency. Once created, the public agency becomes conscious of interests which are broader than those of the business community itself. The manner of public supervision can decompose the business system, or it can support that system in the face of discomfort on the part of other individuals—abolishing or refusing to adopt rent controls, for example. In the latter situation, the public functionaries can adopt rules which preserve the competence of the business system but point it in new directions so that the complaint which is external to that system is assuaged.

Rather like the issue of zoning or separation of land uses is the matter of providing "public services" to a residential area.

Streets, utilities, schools, fire and police protection, and other aspects of community life are necessary if residential development is to succeed in either the narrow terms of entrepreneurial gain or in broad economic terms of effective resource use. Yet these things cannot usually be supplied in toto by the entrepreneur. He builds upon a system of existing community services; normally he does not build those services himself. Even if he should undertake to install them in a large, new, residential development, he must perforce surrender control of them to the community, else they are no longer public services. So, once more the entrepreneur is dependent upon and eager for active participation by the public sector in order to carry out his own specialized tasks. And once again, by putting himself into partnership with the community, he may seem to embroil the community in the external aspects of what he is doing, and to enlarge his own frame of reference to that of public administrators. Should he construct a readily marketable luxury-housing development with substantial public cooperation, when low-income families are living in unsafe dwellings? Should the community exact an unprofitable development as the price for extending the indispensable public services to this entrepreneur's undertaking? Leaving these questions for later discussion, we must note that housing entrepreneurs are not able to make fully independent decisions about resources which they "own." The public has a stake, and it is a stake conceded in the first instance by the entrepreneur himself.

The requirements for entry into the field of residential development or administration seldom (if ever) include examination and licensing. Anyone who owns property has some concurrent rights to determine how it shall be used. Limitations on willful destruction, on specific uses deemed to be unsafe or immoral, and on the physical form of the improvement usually exist. But the owner is, almost by definition, an entrepreneur, free to make major decisions about the use of property, including the decision to dispose of it or of some separable interest in it.

This implies public confidence that ownership carries with it "rational self-interest," so that uses of properties resulting from the exercise of this right will tend to produce a coherent and broadly efficient use of housing resources, noting, of course, the proclivities for specific types of coordination just described. In turn, this implies that the owner is informed about the several markets in which his property belongs—the market for housing services, the market for residential equities, and the market for residential mortgages—and that he is able to analyze the facts emerging from those markets. He is assumed to be a competent judge of what is in his own interest, even in such a complex domain as housing economics.

In fact, perhaps, we might well ask—who knows more about the position of a given residential property interest in the market than the person who owns it? For the very complexity of the subject has left the housing sector largely without abstruse theoretical constructs to which only a professional elite can be privy. The inherent uniqueness of each urban property is additional reason to suppose that if the owner is not as competent as he might be concerning his own property, there is no official or bureau or computer who is more so.

That would be a poor place to let matters stand. If entrepreneurial decisions require knowledge about the housing market, there are two ways in which this knowledge can be improved —both involving the public in some way. On one side of the coin, market data—population, family formation, income trends, housing preferences, mortgage terms, volume of transactions, and so on—can be compiled efficiently if this is done centrally and the results communicated effectively to entrepreneurs. The supplying of local housing-market data, interpreted as carefully as analytical techniques allow, is a centralized if not necessarily public function quite advantageous to the self-interest of housing entrepreneurs and perhaps to the community at large.

The other side of the coin is the education of the entrepreneur in his specialized functions. A person who buys residential property is not immediately endowed with appreciation of all the multidimensional opportunities and dangers before him. If he were, the chances of his making a prudent decision in the first place, and optimal decisions thereafter, would be improved. So it is reasonable to inquire how urban property owners learn about urban property and whether this knowledge can be improved by programs emerging from an organization of these entrepreneurs or from public agencies. Thus, the entrepreneur has a need beyond himself for information related to his ownership and for concepts necessary to an understanding of it.

Characteristics of a Business Decision

A business decision in the housing sector involves only a few variables. While there are many factors which influence the desirability, the value, profitability or rate of investment return which can be realized from a transaction in the housing market, most of these factors are constant or "given" when the decision problem arises. The number of choice variables—things which the entrepreneur must decide on, such as the rent to be asked for a particular dwelling—is limited; and the dependent variable— the amount of income the property will produce, for example— is a relatively simple kind of information which the decision-maker can assess without much difficulty.

Some general and simplified expressions will reveal the form of the business decision and, at the same time, suggest the complex nature of decisions which face the alternative, centrally administered housing sector. Three entrepreneurial situations can be distinguished on the "supply" side, along with one "demand" situation. Let us say that the developer (or use-changer) is interested in securing profit (P), the landowner wants to create value (V), and the lender measures his success by his rate of return (R). Employing a few additional symbols to convey the flavor of entrepreneurial decisions, we can see that these "payoffs" are determined as follows:

$$P_1 = f_D(C, L, U_1, U_2, \ldots U_n)$$

that is, the profit for developing Property No. 1 is a function of the developer's costs for land, materials, and labor (C), the size and terms of the available mortgage loan (L), the use to which Property No. 1 will be put (U_1), and the uses of all other residential (and perhaps some nonresidential) properties in the community, $(U_{2...n})$,

$$V_1 = f_o(U_1, U_2, \ldots U_n),$$

and

$$R_1 = f_L(L_1, U_1, U_2, \ldots U_n)$$

where L_1 is the amount to be lent on Property No. 1 and the terms of the loan.

In simple business situations the developer cannot change the prices of things he will buy nor the loan terms available to him; neither developer, landowner, nor lender can affect the uses of properties other than the one in question; and the lender may not be able to determine what use is to be made even of Property No. 1. Changing these influential but uncontrolled variables into constants (K), the profit, value, and return functions become:

$$P_1 = f_D(U_1, K_D)$$
$$V_1 = f_o(U_1, K_o)$$
$$R_1 = f_L(L_1, K_L)$$

The decision problems then have only two dimensions. The amount of profit which the developer will realize depends on how he uses this one piece of property, the form of the relationship being determined by forces over which he has no control, for which he has no responsibility, and which will not vary regardless of his decision about the use of Property No. 1. The owner can influence the value of his property only by changing its use, and the lender can determine his rate of return only within the bounds of his decision to make a loan against Property No. 1.

For the housing sector as a whole, or for an economic system, the variables summed up by the K terms, above, are, of course, not constant. A central administrator of the housing sector or of the economic system must not only determine U_1 and L_1 but all the U's and, perhaps, the components of C (land, labor, and materials prices) as well. The choices cannot be arbitrary, for the uses are interdependent and may also depend on the level and pattern of input prices. The business system, on the contrary, is a system of simplified decision-making.

The "payoff" of an entrepreneurial decision is limited to the effects on the entrepreneur himself, but there are effects on other people in the community which flow from every entrepreneurial decision. The developer's decision to erect a medium-rent apartment on a given site, for example, may produce a profit for him which he anticipates in making his decision, and a loss for owners of existing apartments—due to the expansion of the inventory—which this developer is free to ignore. If he were not free to ignore these externalities, his decision would require information of a far-reaching and perhaps subtle character. His decision would be difficult and ambiguous and his motivation would be reduced.

The following verbal scheme will help to visualize how a business system permits housing users and entrepreneurs to make simple, clear decisions:

Total Effects:
(gain to public + gain to individual) > (loss to individual + loss to public)
Market Equilibrium Effects:
gain to individual > loss to individual
Basis of Business Decision:
price received > loss to individual
or
gain to individual > price paid

An optimal decision, if total effects are to be considered, requires that the sum of gains to the public and to the individual concerned in the particular instance (i.e., a household or entrepreneur) exceed the sum of losses to that individual, plus losses to the public. The gains and losses all include a variety of tangible and intangible effects, such as the enjoyment a family will derive from living in a particular dwelling.

A market equilibrium decision ignores the external effects, letting the individual concerned decide whether the gains to him exceed the losses. Still, intangibles are present in principle, for if he buys a house (or sells one) many unique satisfactions are acquired (or lost) as well as mere shelter and location. The business decision transforms the intangible element on one side of the expression into a measure of money. Since the tangibles are also measurable in money, one side of the expression is a price, a simple number. The other side involves both tangibles and intangibles, so that the decision is whether a particular bundle of goods and satisfactions is worth more or less than the market price. The business system simplifies decision problems but at the expense of ignoring external effects on both sides of the exchange.

Turning to the demand side, the problem of the household in search of a dwelling can be represented by the following expression:

$$\text{Maximize } U = \Sigma c_1 X_1 + c_2 X_2 + \ldots c_n X_n$$
$$\text{subject to} \quad c_i = 0, 1, \text{ and}$$
$$\sum_{i=1}^{n} c_i = 1$$

This means that the household has a choice among n dwelling units, each one of which will provide some net advantage (utility less the price paid) represented by X, but that the choice (c) is limited to "yes or no" for each, and one—but only one—dwelling can be selected. The task is simply to say "yes" $(c = 1)$ for the dwelling providing the greatest utility $(X$ and $U)$. Prices which the household would have to pay for each available dwelling are market-determined, limited, that is, to the maximum which any other household would offer. Thus, in principle, every dwelling in the inventory is available to the highest bidder. The individual household is not obliged to consider what becomes of unsuccessful bidders for the dwelling he obtains by this process (people whose opportunity for net advantage is low because the housing prices asked would require a sacrifice of other necessities). The household can also ignore the significance of the price to the seller, whether it is a source of great profit or a heartbreaking sacrifice.

If we examine the assignment of dwellings to households in a broader context—i.e., as a problem in social administration— the characteristics of the problem change in important ways. The assignment of one dwelling to one household has implications for other households which cannot be ignored. The prices paid become transfer payments and economic rent, not necessary in themselves except as a form of taxation and income redistribution. That is, the welfare and deserts of all other households and the system of compensation to property owners (including lenders, prior landowners, construction workers, etc.) are relevant to the decision about where each household should live.

One side of the centralized decision-process for meeting housing demands out of a given stock can be expressed as follows, using the symbol u_{ij} to indicate the amount of total benefit or utility created when Household i occupies Dwelling j:

$$\text{Maximize} \quad \sum_{i=1}^{n} \sum_{j=1}^{n} c_{ij} u_{ij}$$

subject to: $\qquad c_{ij} = 0, 1$

$$\sum_{j=1}^{n} c_i = 1, \quad \text{for any } i$$

$$\sum_{i=1}^{n} c_j = 1, \quad \text{for any } j$$

Total rather than net benefit is relevant because optimum use of a fixed stock does not depend on the rents which users are charged so that, in effect, the stock is distributed free of charge to users. The symbol c_{ij} means the choice of Household i to occupy Dwelling j, and, of course, this is limited to a "yes or no" (0, 1) decision in every case. The other conditions say that Household i can be assigned to one and only one dwelling unit and that Dwelling Unit j can be allocated to one and only one household. The problem is to pick a permutation C matrix (with one and only one nonzero element in each row and column) which maximizes total utility from the use of the housing stock. There are, in principle, $n!$ $(n \times (n-1) \times (n-2) \times \ldots (n-n+1))$ such permutations. There are more than 3.6 million ways in which ten households may be matched with ten dwellings, for example.

This elaborate problem is made substantially more difficult by the fact that the utility matrix, U, is not a set of market bids for the use of dwellings in the inventory, but rather a compilation of the objective needs, transportation costs, and subjective enjoyment associated with the alternative occupancy of each dwelling by each household. All this information needs to be created and integrated before the computational steps can be taken. Each change in the relevant characteristics of households or of housing units creates the possibility of improvement by reassignment, but costs of excessive mobility have to be taken into account as limitations on the frequency and completeness of any such reassignment.

The other side of the problem of central administration of the housing inventory is the compensation of factors of production responsible for creating the inventory in the first place. The simple position may be taken that as all costs represented by the inventory are "sunk costs," no problem of motivation arises. That is, the inventory might be confiscated and handed out free of charge, the whole burden falling upon owners at the time of expropriation, including the owners of partial interests such as mortgages. In the interest of future motivation to suppliers of housing resources, or perhaps for reasons of "fairness," some positive payments may be made, but then the relationship between charges for specific dwellings and payments to specific factors of production arises as a new, and multidimensional problem. Finally, the charges to housing users under a system of central administration may be considered a form of tax, or forced saving for the economy as a whole, producing revenue for general community purposes.

Benefits derived from the use of one dwelling unit by a particular household need not be seen only from the viewpoint of that household. We might say that an "optimal" distribution of the housing stock locates that household in a dwelling unit which results in the greatest benefit for the community as a whole. Something in the nature of "social zoning" can at least be imagined, in which certain districts are reserved for certain groups within the population—suburban areas for child-raising families, central apartments for people without automobiles, etc. An obverse policy, specifying that some of each type of family must reside in each neighborhood, for example, is also conceivable. That is, there may be considerations going beyond the household itself which helps to assign housing users to portions of the inventory. The U term in the preceding formulation might be expanded to include matters of interest to the community, or the same effect might be achieved by adding some constraints to the maximization problem.

The Efficiency of Indirect Business Solutions

One of the practical implications of a business system for housing sector decisions is that responses to changes in the conditions of demand or supply may take an indirect form which is superior in several respects to direct response. This aspect of the system is somewhat obscure but very significant. It it also surprising to learn about, perhaps, because in the main there is no central, conscious direction of a business system. Yet it is in the nature of such a system to sense and respond to complex problems of economic efficiency which public administrators have difficulty grasping.

A simple numerical illustration will make the point. Suppose that there is a microscopic community consisting of just two households having different preferences for housing (by virtue of different incomes or tastes), that each inhabits one of only two houses in the community, and that a third family moves into this community. The problem is, which kind of house should be constructed to accommodate the new member of the community?

Call the initial households No. 1, with lesser housing demand, and No. 2, with more housing demand, and let the newcomer household be similar in housing demand to Household No. 1. Call the initial dwellings A and B, being the less desirable and more desirable dwellings, respectively, and designate as C a superior type of dwelling which it has become technically possible to build but which does not yet exist in this community. (This concept was discussed also in the preceding chapter.) We begin by specifying a matrix of housing utility, money measures of the satisfactions which each household would derive from living in each dwelling:

UTILITY MATRIX

		Dwellings		
		A	B	C
	1	40	50	60
Households				
	2	45	60	80

Initially, the utility provided by the stock of two dwellings is maximized if Household 1 occupies Dwelling A and Household 2 occupies Dwelling B, the total utility being 100 money units. Next, we need to know the cost of producing one dwelling of each type. Though the existing dwellings, A and B, have accumulated some deterioration and obsolescence, there will be some form of newly constructed house which will represent the same amounts of housing satisfaction, and the cost of these equivalents and of the new type, C, may be:

	Dwelling Types		
	A	B	C
Cost of new unit	40	50	60

Whichever type of dwelling is built to accommodate the expanded community, an increment will occur in the aggregate of housing utility and there will be an incremental cost as well. If the new dwelling is of Type A, the new household will be accommodated directly, so that the increment in total housing utility will be 40, achieved at a marginal cost of 40. If Type B is built, the new dwelling will be occupied by the newcomer or by initial Household 1, but the total housing utility will rise by 50, and the marginal cost will also be 50. If Type C is constructed, it will be occupied by Household 2, Dwelling B will be occupied by the newcomer or Household 1, total housing utility will rise by 70, and the marginal cost will be 60, resulting in a net gain of 10. These possibilities are summarized as follows:

ALTERNATIVE HOUSING CONSTRUCTION PROGRAMS

Type Dwelling Constructed	Total Utility	Marginal Utility	Marginal Cost	Surplus Utility
A	140	40	40	0
B	150	50	50	0
C	170	70	60	10

There is an economic opportunity for net economic gain by constructing Dwelling C, not for the newcomer, but for Household 2. The newcomer is accommodated, and it is his arrival which creates the opportunity for a profitable transaction, yet the form of the transaction is only indirectly related to meeting this newcomer's needs. Supposing that each household owns its dwelling and that there are no other entrepreneurs, we can perceive a motivation to supply the new household arising from the nature of a business system. Household 2 finds that its original dwelling, B, can be sold for a price of 50 to the "market"—no matter to whom. This is a loss of 10 in its value to Household 2, but if this loss is accepted, it can acquire satisfactions of 80 from Dwelling C which will cost only 60. So, Dwelling B is put on the market, and a demand is created for one unit of the new house type, C, as an indirect result of the appearance of more demand in another portion of the market.

This result obviously depends upon the particular numbers used to construct the illustration. Other numbers might indicate a preference for the construction of dwelling type A or B. The principles remain, however, that a chain of transfer opportunities and the elasticity of demand for housing of various types presents some "optimal" response to a change in demand, that this response may be indirect, and that in any event the optimal response will be encouraged by a business system. Profit-motivated entrepreneurs and absentee owners of rental dwellings could be introduced into this picture, and the chain of housing market business interrelationships could be expanded to the size of a more realistic community without changing these principles.

The optimality of such indirect results has several aspects.

An opportunity for a net improvement in the use of resources can be realized when indirect as well as direct responses are permitted in the housing sector. More concretely, the level of housing quality in the community rises, the introduction of improved housing design or technology is fostered, and several households have an opportunity to raise their housing standards. The direct response, producing a new dwelling at a cost of 40 and with a value of 40 in our illustration, would be a false economy. One of the most important characteristics of a business system in the housing sector is that false but superficially attractive economies are avoided. The impersonal and decentralized nature of business decision-making does not prevent it from sensing its way through an intricate pattern of pressures and opportunities to produce a socially beneficial result. Unfortunately, the business system is sometimes criticized for "blindness" and inefficiency for not responding in the direct pattern which the general public seems to consider self-evidently proper.

Public Entrepreneurship

The simplicity of business decision-making is achieved at the expense of external considerations. The welfare of parties not involved in a housing transaction, but certainly, and sometimes greatly, affected by it, does not sway the decision-maker in a business system. Thus, a landlord may decide to raise rents in response to an increase in demand, despite the obvious loss to his tenants. A landowner may decide to demolish or sell a building, at substantial inconvenience to the occupants. A developer may elect in his own interest to extend the urban fringes, disregarding the upward shift in location rents and the concomitant transfer of income from housing users to landowners which results from extensive development. These and other situations can arise, and, indeed, may be expected to arise in a business system. They give rise to appeals for controls over business processes in the housing sector, in effect, transforming external consequences into internal decision-making considerations.

One general category of community response to these appeals is the substitution of public entrepreneurship—i.e., public decision-making—for private entrepreneurship in matters of housing. Several practical difficulties in public entrepreneurship have been suggested in the preceding pages, but it is useful to consider this alternative method of guiding the use of housing resources in a direct and organized fashion.

The main argument for public entrepreneurship is "equity" or fairness to a broader segment of the community than has a voice in individual business transactions. Balanced against this potential gain, sometimes directly confounding it, are several disadvantages inherent in detailed community decision-making for the housing sector. In general, the problem is that public entrepreneurship, replacing market-determined behavior, deprives itself of information which the market and a business system necessarily create, while at the same time creating a need for other types of information which is very complex in character, difficult to amass, and even theoretically troublesome to interpret. The results are that imperfect information can lead to resource-wasting decisions; disagreements within the public decision-making body can lead to lags in entrepreneurial behavior at a loss in utility to housing users; and flaws in interpretation or analysis of economic information can produce inequities (even by the community's own standards) and misdirection of the use of resources, both existing and new. It is necessary to develop these contentions with some care lest the ultimate concept of integrating public responsibility with business decision-making not be appreciated.

Three types of decision problems may be considered—allocation of the existing stock of housing, replacement of the stock, and location decisions associated with expansion or replacement construction. Public entrepreneurship faces problems with each which are different in nature from those faced by a business system, and inherently more complex.

The problem of allocation is one of deciding which of the many households in the community, each with varied characteristics and deserts, shall occupy which dwelling unit, each of which differs in physical characteristics, location, and qualitative detail from every other. Where the business system awards dwelling units on the basis of individual, competitive bids, public entrepreneurship is constrained to award them on the basis of collective, competitive merit. Merit must be collectively determined because the ultimate allocation must be endorsed by the collective community. It may seem sound in a physical sense that larger families should occupy larger dwelling units, but persons with prestigious occupations may be deemed to be more entitled to them. If there are fewer suburban single-family homes than families desiring to have such dwellings, a community consensus must be reached on which families shall be obliged to make do with something else, such as a centrally located apartment. If no one wants to live in the dwellings which happen to be near a factory or railroad yard, the community must designate some households to make the sacrifice. If the housing stock becomes absolutely insufficient because of a disastrous fire or a sudden influx of the population, the community must decide, in a non-business system, who shall double up with whom. Indeed, it must settle every neighborhood relationship, establish the personal composition of every school district, and virtually determine the clientele of every shopping facility and medical clinic. Depending on the way in which community decisions are reached, this allocation may be governed mainly by the desires of individual households, weighed against each other by some system of priorities, or reflect a traditional view as to what population patterns and distribution of housing standards are in the interest of the community as a whole. Shall child-raising families be allowed to live in ramshackle houses with large yards or should they be brought together in tidy, compact apartments where collective child-care facilities can be more easily provided?

No matter where along this spectrum a particular community's decision system lies, types of information are required beyond the simple amount of money which each household is willing and able to pay for each unit of the housing stock. The family may have more intense desires or needs than it is able to pay for, or needs which it does not itself recognize. Beyond that, the reactions of other members of the community to the housing situation of each household are relevant, and these cannot be expressed directly by monetary offers.

Unlike the individual decisions of the business system, the

allocation decisions of public entrepreneurship must be made simultaneously. The allocation decision for one household is not complete until the allocation plan for all households has been determined. No part of the preexisting pattern, which is assumed by the business system to remain unchanged for any single decision, is necessarily constant. Equity in sharing of the housing stock is, in part, a matter of relative justice; thus, the wisdom of a given assignment depends on what each and every other household will receive. Each decision problem, though it initially concerns just one household, requires, in principle, a reexamination of the entire program of administering the housing stock. Hesitancy in making large-scale changes because of the emergence of a small imbalance in the use of the stock is a sacrifice of the very principle of equity which argues for public entrepreneurship in the first place.

Allocation of housing stock is ordinarily associated with the imposition of user charges. That is, households are required to pay for the housing they receive. Apart from the fact that housing allocation may be considered a form of income redistribution— that is, some families receiving more housing than they themselves can afford—there is a substantial issue in deciding how far the community should go in requiring families to pay for housing which they occupy against their own individual preferences but in conformity with the public plan. Should a family whose income has risen be required to give up its earlier home to some family less affluent, to pay a higher price for a more expensive dwelling? The system of charges used in conjunction with the allocation of the housing stock can be a means of motivating individual households to "prefer" dwellings which the community wants them to occupy for the broader good, but here the community's housing sector accounts are unlikely to be balanced. How much subsidy should be employed to achieve these housing sector goals, and what should be the incidence of the subsidy cost? These are questions of great scale and intricate reasoning which cannot be avoided in a system of public entrepreneurship.

The system of charges, whatever it may be, is likely to create a dilemma unique to public entrepreneurship. Housing costs rise over time, so that new buildings are more expensive than those constructed before. Should occupants of older buildings benefit by cost-related rents? If they are allowed to remain in dwellings with low historical cost bases, and if rents are based, however approximately, upon such costs, then a set of "housing privileges" is created, the incidence of which and the effects upon relative housing standards will be very largely accidental. Older households might experience rising incomes but enjoy continued low rents in older dwellings, while younger households, whose income has not yet reached its lifetime peak must pay high rents governed by the cost of current construction. These housing privileges in turn enter into the balance sheet of equity, for subsequent housing allocation plans for the community must consider the removal of these privileges. Thus, a form of allocation inflexibility is installed in a system which depends very much upon great flexibility to make housing resources meet housing needs. In the end, such privileges may bring about a substantial reduction in overall housing standards, for new housing construction will be limited by the budgets of the newly formed households. In the face of rising housing costs, this new construction will have to be intrinsically inferior to the older stock.

Decisions about the replacement of housing stock encounter a barrier in a system of public entrepreneurship which exists in much less aggravated dimensions in a business system. If the community as a whole "owns" the existing stock of housing, it finds itself in the position of an absolute monopolist. It has real incentive to curtail any forms of new enterprise which would reduce what amounts to sunk capital values. Supposing that households in the community were already being charged as much as they "should" pay for housing, then any expenditure on new housing to replace parts of the existing stock would bring in no additional revenue to the publicly administered housing sector. Replacement would have to be directly and explicitly subsidized. In a business system, replacement destroys capital values adhering to the most vulnerable properties, so that the incidence of this cost is "external" to the individual development decision. But public entrepreneurs must be aware of the fact that any replacement construction diminishes the usefulness of some of the collective capital stock. Thus, if replacement is not to be seriously inhibited under a system of public entrepreneurship, it must be mapped out with elaborate logic and justification, so that the bulk of the households in the community may feel that their share of the benefit of replacement construction is worth their share of the necessary public subsidy occasioned by the destruction of accumulated capital value. A nonbusiness system tends to provide itself with the least amenable sort of "capitalist" mentality, for it must defend its own investment at the cost of its own collective progress.

Decisions related to the location of new housing construction under public entrepreneurship take a form which differs fundamentally from those under a business system. Site rents which emerge in business-system land-markets ration land to developers according to the locational functions to be served by the new developments. In a system of public entrepreneurship there is, in principle, no land market and, hence, there are no site rents to serve as rationing devices for the location of new developments. Instead, the things which supposedly underlie the site rents of a business system—the real savings of transportation resources, plus special amenity values of particular locations—must be considered directly in each individual case. Where there are no site rents, the question of where to locate a planned new apartment structure requires that the real effect on community-wide transportation resources and upon any other tangible or intangible components of the community's economic life be examined ad hoc, for each proposed development and for each potential site. Market-determined site rents ignore many external effects of location, but they do reflect the interaction of a multitude of different locational interests—the several locational pulls acting upon each of the many land users of the community. To reduce the transportation elements of this problem to a form suitable for conscious decision-making is a large, theoretical undertaking to say the least. To add inevitable social judgments about the propriety in respects other than transportation of each location decision makes the problem still less manageable.

It is not difficult to show that decision problems in the housing sector are more difficult for public entrepreneurs than for a business system. Perhaps the greater complexity is nearly self-evident. There is a further problem for public entrepreneurship, however, that the main, advisory elements or "tools" of business decision-making in the housing sector are not available to public entrepreneurs. Appraising is vitally important to business decisions, but it is possible because it forecasts approximately what will happen to a specific property on the assumption that no other land uses change substantially. It may forecast properly, but it never "explains" the result—that is, it does not probe into the "whys" of values. Public entrepreneurship starts with the assumption that the entire pattern of uses may and perhaps should be changed. Hence, the basic premise of valuation in a business system is lacking in a nonbusiness system. The public entrepreneur must base his judgments upon "value" in a far more fundamental sense than that which appears in appraisal reports. Value—to the mind of the public housing-sector administration—must include the human benefits of shelter, comfort, convenient location, and the concern of each citizen of the community for the welfare of each other. The value of an elderly widow's house in the marketplace is one thing, but in the eye of the community it is inevitably something very different. The value of a deteriorated tenement filled with hard-pressed families is measured in one way in a business system, but in a much larger context in a system of public entrepreneurship. Every resource-using decision requires estimates of value as inputs and outputs; these estimates are produced by a market system through the medium of appraising services, but the estimates and the methods which suffice for business decisions are inadequate for public decisions. The question about a parcel of land or a dwelling, new or old, is not what it will sell for, but what good or harm it can do to the community— and what forms of good or harm. Land prices and the economic rents of buildings emerge from a market system and are taken at face value by the appraising process in a business system, but as these payments represent transfers of income, or "unearned income" arising out of the ownership of property, they will either not exist in a nonbusiness system or will be subject to interpretations involving the equity of income distribution.

The brokerage function of a business system is really a communications device which links independent decision-makers to the "external" economic forces of the community. In a system of public entrepreneurship the need is for internal, rather than external, communication. Within the public agency responsible for the housing sector, a great volume of information must be generated and delivered. Such a communications system is, perforce, separated from the people in the community who are directly affected by housing decisions. Somewhere within the public agency there must be a spokesman for the housing preferences of each and every household who, in principle, should have some contact with the people he represents. There must be a spokesman for the forces of technological change, urging specific forms of new land development or house construction, and this person should be linked with the industries involved, both as a collector of information and a source of feedback about the response and needs of the housing sector. There must be a spokesman for the conservation of existing housing and related urban resources, resisting too much scrapping of useful wealth or the wrong kinds of demolition, but yielding just enough and in just the right places. He should be realistically apprised of the condition and usefulness of each item of existing capital. This would be the public-entrepreneurship equivalent of brokerage activities in the business system. It is clear that the form of the communications problem is very different, though the degree of difficulty in creating and organizing such a system is probably not so great as it is in substituting for business valuation.

It is not impossible to imagine a system of public entrepreneurship which makes decisions as expeditiously and with as much attention to individual preferences as an ideal business system, improving the actual outcome by taking into account at least the major externalities of business solutions. In truth, however, such a system would be marvelously complex, resting on theories and procedures not yet envisaged. It is more common to associate public entrepreneurship in the housing sector at present with a variety of special issues and dilemmas which, taken together seem to reveal grave weaknesses in the measurement of housing demand. The numbers of households, their sizes, and incomes may be readily recognized, and their locational characteristics sometimes roughly approximated, but housing preference, or what economists refer to as a "utility function" cannot be said to exist in operational form.

Certain types of evidently inefficient behavior arise out of the imperfect information usually available to public housing entrepreneurs. One of these is a point of view which can be called "land conservation." In many communities public agencies show a marked preference for multistory dwellings, even when household attitudes strongly favor single-family homes at low densities and a practical willingness to bear the cost of low density is in evidence. The resource argument for multistory dwellings is that there is a saving of transportation costs which, for some households, is more important than the loss of comfort and privacy which high-density living normally implies. Sometimes we find public agencies developing high-rise structures in outlying areas, where no transportation saving is possible, so that the net result is a sacrifice of significant housing amenities. Furthermore, publicly developed, multistory dwellings are often reserved for just those household types—families with school-age children—which exhibit the strongest preference for single-family homes.

"Land conservation" seems to arise out of a failure to appreciate the shape of the "transport cost–low density trade-off" of individual housing utility functions. There is also a tendency to misread land price information in a system of mixed public and private entrepreneurship. Thus, the public agency may acquire "inexpensive" land in suburban areas, thinking to economize on housing costs thereby, but failing to realize that low land prices in such areas are the result of high transportation costs. Further, land prices are transfer payments about which it is essentially pointless for a public agency to be concerned, while transportation costs occasioned by suburban location are real resource sacrifices. If their purpose is to save economic resources, suburban multifamily dwellings are gravely inefficient, yet we do find public entrepreneurs frequently persuaded that the opposite is true. Their economic information and their interpretation of that information are faulty. High-density dwellings conserve resources when they are centrally located, but the sacrifice of household amenities which is bound up with such housing forms is sometimes, and for some households, simply not worth the transportation resources saved.

Another frequent error of public entrepreneurs is a negative reaction to gain. In Figure 45 the marginal cost of housing is below the price which has emerged in a business system, because the short-run supply of housing is inelastic and the demand is high (perhaps due to an influx of population or an increase in household income). Private developers will make profits on new

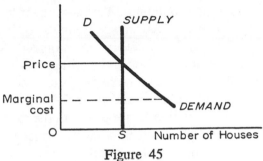

Figure 45

housing and owners of existing dwellings will receive windfall gains (i.e. economic rent). This is a simplified picture of a typical "housing shortage" situation. The business response is to increase the supply, because profits can be made in doing so; the capital losses which occur when prices gradually fall are absorbed unwillingly by landowners who, in a competitive market, are unable to prevent additional construction. The end result would be an expanded supply and a return of housing prices to the level of costs.

Public agencies sometimes take the point of view that profits or windfall gains in the housing sector, such as the diagram illustrates, are an unambiguous social loss, a business "tax" against households encumbered by a housing shortage. Through rent controls or similar devices, the inflation of housing prices is stopped. This removes windfall gains, but it also removes the business incentive to produce additional housing. The public agency is often prone to respond to a housing shortage with measures which—in the name of "equity"—prevent the supply of dwellings from increasing and may actually cause it to decrease.

By removing the symptom of a housing shortage, the public agencies deprive themselves of a very convenient measure of its strength. When popular complaints about the persistent shortage are heard in terms other than prices (i.e., progressive deterioration of the stock), the public agency is unable to tell how much additional housing is required or, perhaps more important, what kinds of new housing are needed. It is common in a mixed system of public and private housing entrepreneurship that a period of strict rent controls will give way to a period in which the prices or rents of newly constructed dwellings are not controlled, while controls remain on older buildings. This is thought to be a blend of equity and motivation, securing households against exploitation while stimulating private housing development to make up the shortage. The results are generally disappointing, however, for the very simple reason that a large gap is created between the controlled rents of old buildings and the prices of new buildings, so that the qualitative differential is not worth the extra cost (i.e., rent) to most households. Many households prefer to gamble on the chance of securing a rent-controlled dwelling rather than enter into the very much more costly new housing market. Demand for new dwellings is thus much weaker than the underlying shortage conditions really indicate.

As an extension of this last point, it may be said that public entrepreneurs often adopt decision rules for the allocation of housing which have the effect of weakening the "real" demand for housing in the sense of consumer willingness to sacrifice resources. When housing is distributed on the basis of "merit" or by lottery, or when prior distributions give rise to the kinds of privileged housing positions previously discussed, households have less opportunity to secure improved housing by paying for it. They are encouraged by such procedures to strive for better housing in very indirect and essentially unproductive ways so that the resources needed to produce better housing are not created in exchange for it. Households are encouraged to lobby for recognition of greater relative "merit" for themselves or their indentification group, to derive satisfactions from what is, in fact, gambling as a substitute for immediate housing amenities, and to spend what they save on privileged rents for nonhousing commodities as a substitute for improved housing. Housing demand per se becomes submerged under these administrative rules and public entrepreneurs may then be greatly misled about the intensity and the directions of actual consumer desire to give up some resources in exchange for housing. When a game becomes very complicated, there are fewer players.

Finally, we may note the tendency for public housing entrepreneurs to be overly concerned with physical characteristics of the inventory—with deteriorated dwellings and rundown sections of the city—rather than with the question of using resources to meet human needs. This concern takes two forms—actions to remove deteriorated portions of the inventory, and actions to diminish the rate of housing obsolescence. The first imposes a virtual tax upon those households unlucky enough to need the "socially undesirable" dwellings. The second inhibits the community's striving for gradual improvement in individual housing conditions. Both sacrifice individual housing preferences—the one for more of "other goods," and the other for more "housing" in the familiar indifference curve concept—in favor of community objectives which boil down to a confusion of physical appearance for economic function.

Public entrepreneurship, in short, has objectives which generally far outreach its tools. The criticisms of housing resource administration under a business system which serve as the rationale for a system of public entrepreneurship are valid in many respects, but the act of substituting public for private decision-making in the detailed administration of the housing sector is scarcely public wisdom if the necessary and sophisticated elements of a public system are not available. The troublesome performance of many programs of public entrepreneurship is evidence that the substitution has often been made carelessly.

Public Governorship

A business system for the housing sector does not come into being, nor does it flourish, without important assistance from the community. The very concept of property rights, which are the stock in trade of a business system, is a legalistic creation of the community mind. Financial instruments cannot be created or used without the establishment of an effective monetary system. The quality and reliability of business practices cannot be assured without public attention, and the needs of individual business practitioners in the field of urban housing for specific coordination and public facilities are nearly self-evident. Only with this active public support and partial guidance can a business system operate effectively in the pursuit of individual business interests.

On the other hand, business decisions tend to overlook certain external costs and benefits which may be harmful to the community's overall interest in economic resources or to the community's sense of equity. In return for necessary and extensive public support, the business system makes expeditious and sensitive decisions, but it is not a docile servant of the broad public interest.

This discrepancy suggests that the role of the public in the operation of the housing sector be more direct and positive than merely an agent of the business system. At one extreme this concern gives rise to the substitution of public for business entrepreneurship, in the hope that decision-makers with a broader frame of reference than business represents can produce housing resource uses more in harmony with broad public interests, not only of efficiency in the use of resources, but with the aim of satisfying the public conscience. We have, however, outlined difficulties which must be encountered by public entrepreneurship, and the question arises whether there may not be some blend of business performance with the pursuit of public goals.

Such a blend may be called "public governorship." The community can set in motion a vehicle for making housing resource decisions (i.e. a business system) keep watch over the broad pattern of land uses and welfare effects produced by this impersonal decision-making system, and introduce corrective pressures where necessary. These corrective steps alter the substance of business decision but do not impede the process. A subsidy is the simplest example. If competition for housing resources leaves some households with dwellings which fall below the community concept of minimum housing, a subsidy to these households to be used in competing for better housing, and further subsidies if necessary to promote expansion of the inventory of standard dwellings, uses the business mechanism to achieve a community purpose. Whether the additional construction resulting from the subsidy serves the affected households directly or indirectly can be left within the province of business decision-making, for this system is sensitive to opportunities for meeting needs indirectly when better use of resources results. Simply removing these households from the concern of a business-directed housing sector, installing them in publicly owned buildings, does no necessary harm to the business mechanism but creates a segment of public entrepreneurship where decisions are much more difficult to come by and may ultimately lack both the equity and the progress which were initial purposes.

To set a system of business entrepreneurship in motion, a distinct and relatively complex type of infrastructure is required. That is, a set of institutions must be created, all of them with some assistance or guidance from the public, and some of them remaining as continuing public functions. The principal elements of this urban business infrastructure are described below:

Legal systems

Housing interests must be defined clearly and recorded in an accessible manner so that ownership can be determined readily. The division of interests in housing property should be limited so as to facilitate individual transfers but not so limited that the scale of transfer opportunities is narrowed.

Adequate reservation must be made in the definition of these interests for the exercise of public responsibilities.

Valuation

Standardized business appraisal methods should be recognized and provision made for gradual improvement in these methods.

Ample systems of data collection concerning housing demand, transactions, building and land development costs, operating costs, neighborhood trends, and housing finance terms should be established and maintained.

Methods of assuring the quality of appraisal practices must be adopted.

A separate methodology for evaluation of land and building for public purposes should be developed and implemented, so that community actions in response to some externalities of business behavior do not produce unanticipated external effects of their own.

Brokerage involving equity and possessory interests

Clear and comprehensive disclosure requirements should be promulgated so as to reduce the uncertainty and risk of the potential transaction, with public inspection to develop or support such disclosure items wherever appropriate. Establishment of an escrow system to assure against error or mishandling of funds in housing market transactions is strongly recommended.

A cooperative or public system of publicizing offerings and bids should be created so that maximum exposure of properties and households to the market can be effected.

Methods of assuring the quality of brokerage services should also be adopted.

Brokerage involving intangible interests

Standardized loan terms should be adopted with provision for change, and with emphasis upon minimizing equity requirements.

Systems of mortgage and/or value insurance should be instituted to the maximum, feasible extent.

Credit institutions should be assisted and guided in the development of residential mortgages, and secondary mortgage credit institutions brought into being to improve the liquidity of mortgage investments.

Guidance of development

Clear and effective environmental controls—zoning, traffic systems, etc.—should be instituted.

The program of developing urban facilities related to housing should be set forth in long-term and realistic fashion.

Research and development of housing technology should be encouraged.

Housing market research and research into opportunities for innovations in housing types should be encouraged.

Education for housing business

There must be public as well as business support for training of entrants into housing sector business and related public agencies, and for analytical research on housing economics.

Pattern guidance

Public agencies must make continuing reviews and forecasts of housing needs and housing circumstances as they are actually emerging from the business systems.

There must be continuing study into the usefulness of instrumental variables—such as taxes, subsidies, land-use regulations—which the community may use to influence business decisions and, through these, the pattern of housing resource development and use in the community.

Selected instrumental variables must be applied toward specified public purposes and their effects evaluated.

Principles of Public Control of the Housing Sector

A community with such a complex of public and private institutions is well prepared to manage its housing resources with prudence and equity. This list does not provide the community with a set of housing goals toward which the activities of the sector should be directed. Nor does it define and limit the public role except by inference. We can move some distance in these directions by describing the manner in which a community should approach its housing issues.

First, it would be appropriate to encourage the creation of a set of business institutions such as were described. Many of these institutions serve urban real-estate markets generally, not merely the needs of the housing sector, and most of them draw upon the basic resources of entrepreneurship, public order, and relatively stable economic systems which are necessary and useful for much larger purposes. It is likely that if these background conditions do not exist for the community or nation as a whole, they cannot be created de novo just for the convenience of operating the housing sector.

An interesting fact about the housing sector is its lack of dependence on more complex "social overhead" resources such as the sophisticated industrial processes or massive transportation systems. So elementary is the ordinary housing product that the community's concept of "standard housing" can be fabricated of simple resources and, of course, land is a simple endowed resource. So localized is the production and market for housing that bulky resources need not be transported interregionally. The inputs into housing itself which are ordinarily most critical are financial and, broadly, legal. These are inherently mobile resources whose movement is slowed only by poor public administration. Public facilities within the urban area, such as utility systems and transportation may require fairly complex inputs, but the physical form of any urban community can be adapted to the kinds of such public resources which are available.

Thus, the housing sector cannot be said to be a prisoner of industrial backwardness, and it is rare that technological research is the key to effective urban housing development. The stumbling block to the achievement of realistic community housing goals is most likely to be a badly contrived or poorly understood set of housing sector institutions. To avoid or to remedy this fault is the first charge for a public agency entrusted with housing welfare.

In carrying out this charge, five major themes are best borne in mind regarding the private or business elements within this institutional framework. One of these is simplicity. Housing is large, expensive, complex in nontechnological ways, and universally necessary. A market can function well only if the people in it—sellers and buyers alike—understand what it is they are trading. Legal definition of property can be too simple to permit the application of diverse interests and resources to housing needs, for example, by failing to clarify the rights of mortgage lenders. It may also be too complex, by creating separable interests which need to be brought together before a transaction in one of the three basic housing markets—use, equity, and lien—can be accomplished. The systems of property definitions should be geared to the general level of comprehension so that unambiguous discussion can occur and so that buyers and sellers can deal in confidence. An example of aversion to complexity is the "condominium" concept which in the United States has enjoyed very little success despite significant business and government interest, because it does not define overlapping rights and responsibilities with acceptable clarity.

Confidence is the second theme. It applies not only to the legal form of property interests, but to the ethics of business and public intermediaries upon whom some reliance must be placed in almost any housing market transaction. It applies to the physical product itself, to the extent of liability for public charges associated with ownership of a housing interest, and to the future value of the property. Insurance is one means of providing confidence—title insurance, mortgage insurance, bonded or otherwise responsible brokers, all the various forms of casualty insurance related to housing, and to the concept of value insurance for equity interests. Effective regulation of business standards in the housing sector is another means of sustaining confidence. Measures to improve the liquidity of housing interests fall under this general heading, as does the principle of public respect for permissible interests in property and the recommendation that community actions immediately affecting residential districts be proposed and carried out in a manner least likely to create uncertainty among people having interests in those areas.

The third theme is competence. Business operators and public administrators alike should bring to their functions as much basic education about the housing sector as is feasible, plus attitudes conducive to good service to households in search of housing in its broadest sense. Households themselves should be encouraged to inform themselves about this complex commodity.

Communication is theme number four. The housing sector in all its parts has particular need for quick, accurate, and large-scale information handling by virtually all the means known to society from face-to-face conversation to television advertising. Inaccessible information or incomplete and distorted information can be very expensive of community housing resources and harmful to actual housing welfare.

Competition is the final theme. In some ways it is the central element, for one might presume that effective competition in the business activities of the housing sector—both demand and supply—would produce the environment described by the other four attributes. The housing sector is distinguished by strong tendencies toward competition in the sense of very widespread control and interaction. There is often complaint that business operators, and real estate brokers in particular, are overly competitive with the result that the individual client receives inadequate exposure to the market or is served by a person who knows too little about the broader dimensions of housing economy, who is marginal in his share of the market and his earnings, so that he may be overeager and inclined to short cuts in his performance. Yet, if the level of competence among housing market operators and the network of communications are adequate, this kind of marginal performance will be minimized. Competition is too vital to a more basic type of communication—transmitting the reactions of people to the quality of the housing interests they have or aspire to have—to be dispensed with because of marginal misbehavior. Better to secure against that misbehavior and maintain the fundamentally competitive nature of the sector.

These themes relate basically to sound performance by business decision-makers. There are three additional themes which tell more specifically how the responsible public agencies should conduct themselves toward the housing sector. The first is the principle of indirectness. It was noted in a preceding section that a change in the composition of housing needs sometimes requires an indirect rather than a direct response, in the interest of best using housing resources, and that business decisions in the housing sector tend to follow these indirect lines. Public agencies should learn to appreciate the value of accomplishing their housing sector aims by indirect means. In the first place, this requires a careful evaluation of what effects are really to be achieved and of the catalog of public instruments which will cause private business decisions to produce this effect. Low-income housing is a common example. If the desire is to raise the standard of housing for low-income households, then this will be accomplished when these households are as well accommodated as households currently just above the margin of concern. Whether this goal can be reached with least use of resources by construction of new dwellings for the low-income group or indirectly by accelerating replacement activities throughout the housing inventory depends on a variety of economic and technical matters, all of which are capably handled by a proper set of business institutions. The public responsibility is to select the most effective lever affecting business behavior so that the desired result—not something qualitatively different—will be produced.

Indirectness as used by the public agencies thus has two dimensions. It means accepting housing sector behavior which conserves resources by meeting the direct need in an indirect fashion. It means working through the business system rather than directly as a partial substitute for that system, so as to conserve the basic resource of economic management.

Direct participation by public agencies in housing sector activities creates a decision-making environment far less conducive to orderly processing of demand-and-supply data than the impersonal business system. A public agency has heterogeneous and total responsibility. A publicly owned housing complex becomes responsible not just for the housing enjoyed by its occupants, but for their health, social interaction, morality, and industry. If the housing is subsidized, the public agency must judge who is to be favored by the subsidy and to what extent.

The second theme for public administration in the housing sector is a specific application of the first. The community helps to determine the parameters of business response to conditions of supply and demand, so by intentionally altering these parameters, the community can make the inherent directions of business enterprise coincide with public interests. For example, the volume and direction of private mortgage lending is governed, in part, by lenders' perceptions of risk and illiquidity. Government-sponsored mortgage insurance and secondary markets can reduce these elements materially, as experience in the United States has shown. Private lenders continue to make decisions based upon their own best interests but, because of some changes in external factors affecting the calculation of return, these private interests tend to produce a result desired by public agencies. It might be, of course, that factors other than lenders' attitudes had been depressing the rate of housing development or that some other aspects of lenders' investment decision processes were of relatively greater significance than risk and illiquidity, with the result that these particular types of government programs would be abortive. Not just any public program will accomplish its stated goals. The method must be carefully selected to fit the nature of the public objective and the parameters of business decisions. So closely is business decision-making in the housing sector related to the environment of public administration that it can be said with safety that there is probably always in the hands of the community an appropriate and efficient instrument for achieving its housing goals via the business system—provided, of course, that there is a functioning business system.

The final theme must be the selection of community housing goals. The dimensions of this subject were examined in previous chapters relating to optimality in the housing sector. There are issues relating to the aggregate scale of residential resources development and to the spatial extent of the urban area. There are issues dealing with the composition of the inventory and relative locations of different housing types. Alternate chapters have described the elements of "equilibrium" answers to these questions—that is, the answers which a business system could be expected to provide. Some "external" consequences of the pattern of business decisions were also identified, and it is these externalities which ordinarily provide the rationale for public intervention in the housing sector.

Goals for the housing sector may be absolute or relative, a distinction which does not coincide with our convenient division of this general subject into "aggregative" and "distributional" compartments. Absolute goals include the desire to conserve resources, both transportation and housing capital, so that both the total scale of residential development and its composition are relevant. The relative goals have largely to do with equity, such as the degree of dispersion in the quality of the inventory, the degree of separation of residential types and the incidence of economic rents. Esthetic goals may call for the sacrifice of resource conservation in favor of equity, the reverse, or the sacrifice of both in favor of an independent goal.

The community must, of course, select its own goals. Our work has been to indicate the diversity of problems on which the public conscience or pride may work and to suggest the complex though useful means by which personal and community aspirations about housing can be approached.

Mixed Entrepreneurship

Figure 43D at the beginning of this chapter represents a system of decision-making in the housing sector which includes both private and public entrepreneurs. There is also a line, *R*, which symbolizes regulatory devices by which government influences market behavior. This is a broken line because, given the option of public entrepreneurship to satisfy unmet needs for housing, the regulatory powers of government may lie dormant. Property taxes, for example, always influence private housing-market decisions but may not be formulated intentionally to make the market serve some public purposes.

This system of mixed entrepreneurship provides three ways of closing the gap between unchecked market behavior and the "ideal" pattern of housing sector performance. First, of course, market behavior may be regulated or assisted so that social goals are met directly through the marketplace, as in housing allowances given to low-income families. Second, public entrepreneurs may compete with private entrepreneurs, as in American public housing, giving the recipients the option of "buying" from either type of supplier. Third, regulatory powers may be exercised against consumers, prohibiting market operations in housing of special types and driving these consumers into publicly supplied dwellings. Welfare recipients, for example, might be required to live in public accommodations. Another example would be the socialization of apartment buildings, leaving single-family homes in the private sector.

The natural response to the range of alternatives represented in the whole of Figure 43 is probably to prefer that which provides the greatest number of options, which surely is the mixed entrepreneurship alternative. There is also something vaguely inevitable about a system in which the government has got a little of everything on the books, perhaps by a process of political evolution. Yet it is our duty to show that excessive options may prevent the taking of effective action.

Recall the fable about the donkey between two bales of hay, starving because he was unable to choose between them: There is a closely parallel situation which appears very often in matters concerned with housing. We might all see that poor people are badly housed; but private entrepreneurs, for example, will resist regulatory efforts by blaming bungling public entrepreneurs, while public entrepreneurs lay the problem at the door of the marketplace and call for more regulation. Alternatively, private entrepreneurs may see the plight of the poor as a good argument for a program of subsidies, as empire-building public entrepreneurs try to claim the poorly housed population as clients for the socialized sector. While the argument about who is to blame and who should get the subsidies goes on, the poor remain in unsatisfactory housing.

A dual system of correcting problems in the housing sector means that there is no way to evaluate the performance of either part. Each has a tendency to bury the other's mistakes, and each can evade criticism for unsatisfactory conditions that persist. In such an uncertain science as housing economics, options are dilemmas.

This peculiar disadvantage of the mixed entrepreneurship system in housing exists in addition to the serious problems of public entrepreneurship already described. Administering a public supply of dwellings is, in principle, as complex in a mixed system as in a system of complete public entrepreneurship. Harnessing a regulated market system in tandem with a socialized system merely buys a new kind of trouble—deciding which has been unresponsive to obvious and perhaps critical needs. Since this mixed system can be seen in effect almost everywhere we look, the extent and persistence of "housing problems" in the world's cities is that much easier to understand.

8 · ▦

URBAN U.S.A.—WHEN

IS A HOUSING PROBLEM

NOT A HOUSING

PROBLEM?

The Housing and Urban Development Act of 1968 is generally regarded as the most ambitious and comprehensive legislation in the history of Federal involvement in American cities. Through the involvement of large and small private businesses, nonprofit associations, and all levels of government it seeks to redirect the physical evolution of cities and suburbs. It contemplates a wide range of subsidies, some deep and some shallow; the creation of new institutions to foster urban development and redevelopment; and coordination of programs for massive healing of personal and social ills with programs for physical reconstruction.

Congress conducted extensive hearings on the legislation before it was passed into law.[1] Numerous organizations and knowledgeable individuals representing the deprived, the concerned, and the responsible were consulted. But the vast majority of the nation's city dwellers were not heard from; they simply stayed away. The National Association of Real Estate Boards, an organization which usually seems to take the side of the employed, property-owning, urban middle class, confined its participation in the hearing almost entirely to the relatively minor matter of Federally assisted fire protection for riot-threatened areas.

Why this indifference? Surely everyone has heard of the "urban crisis," the problems of segregation, property taxes, congestion, crime, pollution, rising land prices, welfare scandals, blight, and strikes by sanitation workers. How can the majority of the population be unconcerned about the nature of Federal plans to deal with all these matters that affect daily life in the cities for all of us?

It may be, of course, that most citizens do not really feel touched by the "urban crisis." Perhaps it seems to be a set of familiar issues which has been exaggerated by alarmists. Professional worriers, after all, have to be inventive to get much attention in an affluent, science-wise, and generally "cool" society.

On the other hand, perhaps the great bulk of the urban population recognizes that although problems do exist in city life, the Federal Government is incapable of dealing effectively with them. For one thing, of course, no "housing act" in the United States deals with law enforcement or garbage strikes or rising assessments. Responsibility for what are probably the urban issues of widest concern lies outside the Department of Housing and Urban Development. For another thing, "massive housing programs" such as public housing, urban renewal, or moderate-income housing have proved to be neither massive nor meaningful. The people they seem directed to serve get pushed aside, and the programs drown in their own directives. There is no identifiable cadre of professional housing-program administrators to make the results look something like what was intended.*

Housing is part of the urban problem in the United States, but it is inseparable from other aspects. In war-torn countries after World War II the "housing problem" was one of replacing

---

* For a recent, semi-official evaluation of Federal programs in housing see The National Commission on Urban Problems, *Housing America's Low- and Moderate-Income Families,* Research Report No. 7, U.S. Government Printing Office, Washington, D.C., 1968.

buildings which had been destroyed. In the United States today the "housing problem" is more correctly described as the result of inadequate economic institutions and uneasy social relationships. The job is to wrestle with fundamental social and economic issues; in many ways that is more difficult than simply creating buildings.

What Are the Problems?

Two major study commissions at the Federal level have very recently produced quantitative estimates of the housing problem—the National Commission on Urban Problems, headed by former Senator Paul Douglas, and the President's Commission on Urban Housing. They generally agree that six million or more housing units are substandard and should be replaced. To eliminate substandard housing conditions in one decade would mean doubling the level of housing output approximately from the present rate of about 1.3 million per year to 2.6 million per year. In effect these estimates define the housing problem by saying that the rate of housing replacement is too low. Table 11 shows ten-year needs as estimated by the Department of Housing and Urban Development, substantially similar in magnitude to estimates by special study commissions.

The study commissions do tell us a little more, namely that many households are unable to afford standard housing, either because their incomes are too low to let them pay the economic cost of good (not necessarily new) housing, or because discrimination shuts them out of the market for standard housing. They flesh out the complaints, reciting restrictions imposed on builders by building codes across the country and by building trade unions, the moral being that because new housing costs more than it should, low-income people remain trapped in substandard dwellings.

None of these detailed points is new and none is without its documented counter-argument. Supposing them to be incontrovertible, however, they still provide less than the insight we really need into the nature of our urban housing ills. The reasons are simple: housing subsidies and antidiscrimination

11 ESTIMATED HOUSING CONSTRUCTION AND REHABILITATION
NEEDS TO ELIMINATE SUBSTANDARD HOUSING CONDITIONS
OVER A TEN-YEAR PERIOD (1967–1977)

	millions of units
For net additional household formation	13.1
To permit an increase in vacant and seasonal units	4.4
To compensate for units abandoned because of population shifts	1.0
To compensate for demolition, casualty and other losses of non-dilapidated units	2.0
To permit the removal of all existing dilapidated units	2.0
To permit the removal of all units becoming dilapidated over the decade	2.0
Rehabilitation of nondilapidated, substandard units with public assistance	1.7
subtotal: new units and unassisted rehabilitation	26.2
Rehabilitation of nondilapidated, substandard units with public assistance	2.0
total need including publicly assisted rehabilitation	28.2

Source: Committee on Banking and Currency, Hearing on Housing and
Urban Development Legislation of 1968, March 21 and 22, 1968,
U.S. Government Printing Office, Washington, D.C., 1968, p.
1344.

Note: a housing unit may be classified "substandard" for either of two
reasons: it is dilapidated; or it is not dilapidated but it lacks private plumbing facilities.

measures have been tried and found wanting; the most extreme
reforms in building codes and building union practices would
barely dent the cost of new or rehabilitated housing, and would
not at all affect the price of good, existing housing. These points
are also so well known that the publication of recent commission
studies has failed to excite optimism that housing problems are
about to be solved. In fact, the studies were published well after
the 1968 Housing Act became law—that Act which was designed to correct conditions identified by the subsequent studies.
Our Federal housing "doctors" do their surgery before the
X-rays come back from the lab.

Thus we lack a useful public statement of what is really
wrong with urban housing in the United States. This is a little
puzzling, because the problems are fairly easy to see if we look
at the city without preconceptions about what needs to be done.

Four interdependent problems—perhaps we should regard them as constraints in the application of our abundant economic resources to the task of raising the minimum standard of urban housing—deserve to be spelled out and thought about.

12 PROJECTED GROWTH OF UNITED STATES POPULATION 1960 TO 1985 (population in 000s')

	1960	1985	change
United States total	179,323	252,185	72,862
in SMSA's *	112,884	178,138	65,254
in central cities	58,208	65,581	7,373
outside central cities	54,676	112,557	57,881
outside SMSA's	66,439	74,047	7,608
total white population	158,832	217,714	58,882
total nonwhite population	20,491	34,471	13,980
US SMSA population			
white	99,692	151,164	51,472
in central cities	47,852	45,435	−2,417
outside central cities	51,840	105,730	53,890
nonwhite	13,192	26,974	13,782
in central cities	10,356	20,146	9,790
outside central cities	2,836	6,827	3,991

* Standard Metropolitan Statistical Areas.
Source: The National Commission on Urban Problems, *The Challenge of America's Metropolitan Population Outlook—1960 to 1985,* Research Report No. 3, U.S. Government Printing Office, Washington, D.C., 1968, various tables.

The first of these constraints is the fact that ethnic minority populations will continue to concentrate in the older central cities of our metropolitan areas, whether or not their housing problems are solved. Table 12 shows a recent projection of this growing racial imbalance. If their housing is to be improved it will have to come about through substantial reconstruction of central cities. This segregated pattern will reflect common consent—ideally satisfactory to no one, but acceptable to most. Blacks and other minority people will be kept within the city as much by emergent ties of identity as by fear of isolation or hostility in the suburbs. The white majority has been abandoning the obsolete physical plant of the central city for decades and will have progressively less incentive to return. This forecast is entirely consistent with a substantial softening of barriers to integration, and it can be expected that many or most suburban areas will become color-blind. Still, the central city will be predominantly nonwhite. Several generations will pass before ethnic minorities are actually dispersed through the American metropolis. Their present housing problems are central-city problems. The extent of these problems is suggested by Table 13; nonwhites in central cities had more than double the ratios for whites of substandard housing and overcrowding in 1960.

The second constraint is that better housing for these central-city people must be new, for the most part, and it must be developed and designed for levels of purchasing power which are substantially higher than these people have now, because their incomes are going to rise sharply. Moreover, the new housing will not be "project housing" because those who live in it will not consent to be wards of the Federal government nor anyone else. These conditions follow from an optimistic view of employment and business opportunities which are opening up for ethnic minorities. At the moment the prevailing mood is probably one of pessimism, with slow, ineffective, or token efforts going into the areas of job training and small-business development. But housing that is about to be built in the central cities is going to be around for a long time; during the economic life of that housing it is inconceivable that American society will not stop wasting the skills and talents of people now confined to menial work or handouts. There is a huge job to be done, but it is an investment with gigantic benefits for American society as a whole, and it is hard to find anyone opposed to doing it. So, without making this employment problem part of the housing problem we face, it is reasonable to assume that it will be solved. Its solution, though, raises a very interesting obstacle to the development of housing, in that the new housing should cost more than the people who are going to use it can presently afford. The development must be premised on anticipated financial capacity, not on documented present or past credit-worthiness. At the same time the arrangements must not have an eleemosynary taint.

13 SELECTED HOUSING DATA FOR STANDARD METROPOLITAN STATISTICAL AREAS OF OVER 250,000 POPULATION, IN 1960

	SMSA Total	Central City	Outside Central City
Housing units per square mile	153	2,150	75
Percent owner-occupied of all occupied	58.2	45.4	72.7
Percent nonwhite of all occupied units	10.4	16.2	3.8
Percent of units substandard	9.7	10.8	8.4
Percent substandard of nonwhite-occupied units	25.1	22.7	37.0
Percent of units overcrowded *	10.0	10.6	9.4
Percent overcrowded of nonwhite-occupied units	23.9	23.0	28.0
Percent of units in multi-family structures	34.3	50.3	16.3

* more than one person per room.
Source: The National Commission on Urban Problems, *Housing Conditions in Urban Poverty Areas,* Research Report No. 9, U.S. Government Printing Office, Washington, D.C., 1968, p. 12.

Third, land is expensive in the central cities. There are several reasons why this is so—the impersonal advantage of central location, the intensity of uses permitted, the reflected exploitation of minority-groups' housing needs, the difficulty of assembling sites suitable for building, the scarcity of undeveloped sites, and so on. It is not necessarily "uneconomical" to build housing on such high-priced land because land generally increases in value rather than wasting away as do buildings. But such construction requires a larger initial cash investment than does suburban housebuilding. Thus it seems that the people who possess least in the way of liquid assets and who generally have least access to credit institutions have to buy up much of the most expensive land in the nation before they can begin to satisfy their need for better housing.

Fourth among the constraints is the fact that before new housing can be built in the central city some existing housing must be destroyed to make room for it, and there is not much relocation housing for people who will be displaced in the process. This is like the relocation problem which already plagues urban renewal in this country, but it is aggravated by two special factors. Urban vacancy-rates fell sharply after the credit crunch of 1966, as the level of house-building generally declined; the effects of this credit situation promise to be around for a long time. Then, too, minority people have not been able to expand readily into neighborhoods where there might be some slack in the housing supply. Minority demands are bottled up and, given increases in the number of households along with significant demolition of housing in minority areas for various public works, there is not much room to get an effective house-building program going in the central cities. People can't stand in the streets while houses are being built for them.

These are the real problems. Not much is lost by boiling them down into one statement: a large volume of new housing must be built where it is least practical to build, and must be financed by institutions which have not yet been invented.

One "solution" to the composite problem has been available for some time. The housing problem might solve itself when the income and employment problems of the depressed central-city population have been solved. The reasoning goes that education, family stability, job training, and much improved employment prospects will bring most minority households into the mainstream of the housing market, with sufficient credit to borrow and money enough each month to pay the mortgage or rent for sound, desirable housing provided by ordinary, profit-motivated housing entrepreneurs.

Cynics might say that the low-income housing efforts of this nation have been so unsuccessful that this "wait 'til it all blows over" approach is the only real policy we have. In fact, there are groups which evidently think so poorly of urban renewal and other Federal programs that they would rather hang on to the slums they live in, while building up economic strength, than let some bureaucratic bulldozer grind their nascent communities into dust.

Clearly, this "solution" might not work at all. Higher incomes through improved education and employment might well be drained off in part by increased land values in the central city, garnered largely by absentee land owners. For the rest there is no guarantee that present business and credit institutions would know how to assimilate the recent poor who differ so much in their concepts of financial business from the middle-class community. Minorities in American cities have gotten much less than others for their housing dollars in the past, and there is no special reason to believe that they will do much better in that respect when they have more to spend.

This warning does not say the cynics will be proved wrong. Perhaps, in fact, nothing will be done which substantially overcomes the several obstacles mentioned above. But something could be done. Listed below are the essentially feasible elements which seem implied by these obstacles.

Some Answers

1. A deferred-interest plan is the simplest means of bridging the financial gap between immediate housing needs and the expectation of significantly higher ability to pay for housing some years hence. That is, payments on the mortgages to finance new housing construction could begin five years or so after completion, or payment schedules could at least be calculated to allow much lower payments in the early years, picking up in later years in one large step or several smaller steps. The deferred interest could be added to the principal, though someone is bound to suggest that at least part of it should be paid by government grant. In a modest way mortgage lenders and merchants do defer payments, allowing home-buyers one or two months to get settled, or allowing Christmas shoppers to start payments on their big-ticket purchases sometime in February or March. The principle is not new. The scale of a meaningful deferred-interest program for building new houses in the central city would have to be massive, and special kinds of guarantees would be necessary to protect thrift institutions from loss. In effect these guarantees would pool the credit—or the expected improvement in credit—of large groups of the present "urban poor." Liens running with the property would be secured in effect by the near certainty of growing, real aggregate incomes among the central-city population, but the certainty would be much less for an individual property.

There are other schemes which might get housing built now to standards which future incomes must justify. Outright public construction, or institutional construction with disguised subsidies from land write-downs or tax privileges might be equally effective in the physical sense. Perhaps the American political process will prefer them. The principle of deferred interest, however, is superior on two points which deserve to be better understood. Simplicity encourages speed; a building program which relies primarily on the ordinary institutions of a business-oriented society will change the urban skyline faster than a program that requires the creation of pristine intermediaries—i.e., non-profit sponsors, who supposedly do not profit from a public program to help the poor but who in fact come out of the woodwork only when the after-tax yield exceeds 20 percent. The other point is that public construction or institutional development (by a church group, or a business consortium monitored by government bureaucrats) is "anti-soul." It solidifies dependency at the very time when the dependents are trying so hard to become their own men. To be beholden to a bank for one's new home is the American way; to be beholden to a Federal agency or to members of the white, liberal elite who have elected themselves to positions of guardianship over "lovable unfortunates" is really something else. A deferred-interest scheme—even if some of the interest is eventually written off by the larger society—is by comparison a relatively clean approach to improving the effective demand for housing among the urban underhoused, today.

2. While simple, direct financial arrangements for the new housing seem quite desirable, the high level of central-city land prices creates an inescapable complexity. What needs to be done, in essence, is to save households in the urban core from the grave financial burden of individual land ownership while preserving or invigorating the principle of community control of land uses. This means that new-housing enterprises should have the option of leasing land rather than acquiring it outright, and that ground rents should be based in fact upon user cost—i.e., the cost of supplying residential properties with public services and private management—rather than on opportunity cost. Dick Netzer has done an interesting discussion of user charges as an alternative to

local property taxes.² There are several potential advantages of aggregating land ownership into large holdings under public control, such as the ease of implementing future land-use plans. Properly conceived, ground leasing need not remove the ordinary "speculative" incentive for developing dwellings or other buildings.

To achieve this attractive result—land at low rentals rather than very high capital costs—requires only a certain amount of paper work. Transfers of title to land do not result in a "real" economic cost to the society, and the pains of redistribution will be slight because ownership of the land in question is already in process of change. The hard job is to create an institution to hold land as that land is acquired for reconstruction of the central-city housing stock. The good old nostrum of the nineteenth century, socialism or "public ownership" of capital or land, flounders on the modern urban fact that government ownership is not the same thing as community control, not by a very long shot. The proper device for holding the necessary land is something in the nature of a neighborhood trust having direct, legal, and specific obligations to a community of persons who themselves possess a kind of moral nearness.

3. "Swing land" to permit reconstruction of the crowded urban core must be found primarily in the suburbs. Thus, before the rehousing of central-city households can be started there must be a burst of suburban building based upon intensified replacement-demand. At the same time there must be significant dispersion of some central-city population into the suburban ring.

This sounds like an impossible program—to recommend new homes for the rich as an indirect way of getting low-income housing programs off the ground, plus a quantum jump in the level of suburban integration. Yet the mischievous genius of the American political system is likely to bring it off, in part by the hypocrisy called "new communities." Large-scale suburban developments will probably be undertaken within the coming ten years or so, subsidized and supervised in a variety of ways, pretending to be havens for the oppressed but becoming in reality the domain of smug prosperity. The political process, goaded by our liberal-intellectual elite, will declare the new communities to be society's gift to the unfortunate; then the elite will move in. These are the people who will fancy the plans of the "planned community"—having had much to do with the planning of them —and they are the people who can and will pay exorbitant prices for arty townhouses seventy miles from town.

Here and there some new communities will be racially integrated. A few may turn out to be predominantly nonwhite. The chances are that black or other minority households who do leave the central city will end up mostly in older suburban areas, either integrated among not-so-affluent younger whites of liberal persuasion, or concentrated in tract-type ghettos. By and large the situations or attitudes of minority households who move out from the core of the city will be distinguishable from the characteristics of the households which remain in the core. Somebody will call the movers "Uncle Toms" and the integrated new communities "Uncle Tomsvilles." But there seem to be Negroes in American cities who don't think too much of Black Power, "natural" hair styles, or soul food; they have been called names all their lives and a little more won't stop them from seeking out homes with picket fences around them and thirty-year mortgages inside. The more unpleasant aspects of minority militancy will help bring black and brown faces of the "acceptable" type to suburban real-estate offices. There will be enough integration in the suburbs to provide slack in the housing supply of the central city, and this integration—where it occurs—will be painless, or even fun.

The "relocation" problem of rebuilding the central city's housing stock will thus be solved by forces at work and not by design of thinking men. There will be a "pull" from the new communities, about which we shall have to lie to ourselves. There will be a "push" from the fractious stirrings of the ghetto, about which we shall try to maintain a knowing silence. If this is cynical it is also optimistic, two casts of mind which mark the urban man.

4. The ethnic communities of central cities will need new or much invigorated institutions to manage their housing and other affairs. To say that deferred-interest financing may be made available for the building of these new homes is not to guarantee

that people who incur this financial obligation will honor it. To imagine that a neighborhood corporation could make land available for housing for a minimal ground rent is not to create the consensus which must precede the legal establishment of such a corporation.

In short, people who would move upward from a marginal economic existence to economic self-determination need both opportunity and discipline. They need jobs and a will to work, political forms and articulate citizenship, business credit and business ability. A black bank will need black depositors, black loan officers and appraisers, black auditors and black bill collectors. To get housing built and to keep on building it there must be black developers, black lawyers and black escrow agents as well as black carpenters. Someone—a black someone—will have to see to it that there are black janitors and garbage collectors.

What makes these activities and talents appear are "institutions" in the sociological sense. These institutions can emerge only from the kind of cohesion that common cultural or religious background provides. For many immigrant groups arriving in the United States this cohesion was strong enough to ride out a generation or more of overt discrimination, the Jewish community being perhaps the outstanding example. Other minorities, such as the Chinese, are well endowed with the cultural legacy to foster institutions as they are needed to cope with the challenges of urban existence here.

The American Negro is enormously handicapped by the lack of such cohesion. Blacks as a group do not have the sharply defined loyalty to a creed or code of behavior that other minority groups have or had, which tells them what to do or whom to obey. While new ethical systems have been created in modern times—Mao's Red Guards, for example—the process is unpleasant at best, and halting. Smashing old precepts is more nearly a science than is discovering and inculcating new precepts that make life both technically feasible and worth living.

Some comfort can be drawn in the midst of violent malaise in the American city today by imagining that it represents the birth of the necessary black ethic. Indeed, the very specific credo of Black Muslims, Black Panthers, and other groups would seem to point in this direction, or at least toward the intention to fill an important gap in American urban institutions. A person or a collection of persons does not automatically know how to order life within the framework of economic limitation and desire. Self-government does not appear smoothly upon the removal of external governance. One can hope, and even expect, that black America is in the process of forging a cluster of institutions suited to the purpose of functioning effectively as an equal rather than a dependent component of American society. It is a terribly difficult thing to do, and it is urgent, but nobody else can do it.

This makes the "good" solution to the urban housing problem depend in part on something vastly more intangible than housing or land. If we were as a nation more resolute, selfless and insensitive, some direct, physical but "less good" solution to the physical decay of the older city's stock of dwellings could be made to work. But we are not like that, and reconstruction of the city, if and when it gets done, will mean a great deal more because of this.

Beyond the Ghetto

Problems associated with the ghetto are, in a manner of speaking, the "dessert" on the housing economist's menu. These are the popular, spectacular issues on which distinctive pronouncements are de rigeur. But there is a main course—basic but less exciting fare, consisting of the issues apart from race, the questions about housing which arise in the ordinary, nonminority household and in community discussions across the board. Since housing policy must be for all the people, we have to consider now what is done and what might be done by public efforts for housing in general in America's urban areas. Like a child, we have had our dessert first, and must now settle down to plainer but more extensive concerns.

FORMS OF GOVERNMENT PARTICIPATION IN THE HOUSING SECTOR

Despite the often-repeated pledge of the federal government to assure "a decent home and a suitable living environment" to every American family, housing programs of the United States government have been, and continue to be, selective and limited.* The great mass of the population is affected by housing programs only indirectly if at all. The following is a set of descriptions and comments on each of the major types of housing programs undertaken at the Federal level since the New Deal days of the 1930's. The list identifies major categories of programs instead of specific measures because the specifics are in fact so profuse as to be unwieldy. Specific programs are frequently changed, renamed, buried, or dissected. And though programs of more recent vintage might be said to be more intricate and specialized than earlier measures, the chronology of developments is really not worth disentangling either.

Improving the liquidity of mortgage investments.—The Federal Housing Administration operates a mortgage-insurance program. Private lenders, such as banks, may be reimbursed for losses suffered when mortgages they hold have to be foreclosed, the funds for reimbursement coming from accumulated premiums charged to home-buyers. A large element of risk is thus removed from investment in residential mortgages and, other things being equal, institutional lenders are more willing to finance housing at the expense of other investment opportunities such as industrial plant-expansion. The FHA screens applications for loan insurance very carefully, in effect taking the burden of risk-evaluation from the lending institutions. The methods employed by the FHA for screening applications, while subject to criticism on various moral or economic grounds, have had the effect of standardizing mortgage quality, so that FHA-insured mortgages can be sold by one lending institution to some other institution without the necessity of reinspecting the property in question or the credit worthiness of the borrower. Further liquidity is provided by the Federal National Mortgage Association, which stands ready to buy (at market-determined discounts) insured mortgages held by private financial institutions and subsequently to resell these mortgages to other private financial institutions. The existence of FNMA further encourages banks,

---

* This phrase appears in the Declaration of National Housing Policy which was incorporated into the Housing Act of 1949.

insurance companies, and other institutions to lend money for housing development or purchase, and may equalize the availability of housing credit among the several regions of the country as well as over the course of a business cycle.[3]

The Veterans Administration provides a guarantee for mortgage loans to qualified former servicemen, as a kind of welfare benefit. The VA loan guarantee differs from the FHA insurance in some important technical ways (less equity is required for VA loans, for example) but the principal effect on the availability of mortgage funds for housing is the same. VA loans also are traded by FNMA.

At one time the majority of residential mortgages being made in the United States were either FHA or VA loans. More recently the proportion has fallen below one-fifth, primarily because the maximum interest rates allowed under these programs lagged behind rising market rates for long-term loans. One of the most interesting aspects of the FHA-VA experience, however, is the fact that uninsured or "conventional" loans have shown a marked evolution toward the standardized characteristics of government-assisted mortgages, except for interest rates. FHA appraisal methods have had great influence over residential appraisal practice in general; the term of a conventional loan is likely to be almost as long as that of an FHA or VA loan; and the ratio of loan to value for conventional loans is not much below that of FHA or VA loans for moderately priced properties. In effect, the FHA-VA concept has had an "educational" effect upon mortgage lending in general, persuading financial institutions that loan terms which are relatively generous to borrowers with modest incomes nevertheless can be sound investments. The supplementary support of FNMA is not available for conventional loans, however; home financing in the United States thus continues to suffer from illiquidity of the mortgage investment.

FHA and VA programs have been oriented primarily to the task of financing the construction and purchase of single-family homes for owner occupancy. Efforts to extend the mortgage-insurance principal to rental housing have come a cropper on misunderstandings concerning the role and requirements of equity investors.[4] A mild but significant form of rent control is required by FHA on multifamily projects. Complex rules intended to limit the return on equity to some "fair" level have also discouraged developers. Though demographic shifts in recent years have required a great expansion of the inventory of rental housing, there is no Federal program which explicitly assists the housing industry in meeting this need. Indeed, for about twenty years there has been no significant proposal for Federal encouragement of market-rate (i.e. unsubsidized) rental housing development.

Subsidized low-income housing.—Approximately one percent of the housing inventory in the United States consists of "public-housing units which are owned and operated by local housing authorities (see Table 14). These units—subsidized to the extent of debt service by the Federal government and, further, by exemption from local property taxes—are made available to households which are too poor to afford adequate housing in the private market. In more than thirty years of operation the public-housing program has gradually alienated most of its clientele and its early supporters without winning any new friends among its traditional opponents (such as real-estate interests, and middle-class homeowner or taxpayer groups). At the present time the public-housing program is undergoing metamorphosis into a set of variants which seem to have general support. Since the butterfly in this particular cocoon was created by committees of several past Congresses it may be less than graceful when it emerges, but it is almost bound to be an improvement.

The defects of traditional public housing in the United States are numerous. Projects often look like prisons instead of homes. They have become "government ghettos" because it is mostly nonwhites who have been too poor to obtain decent private housing. They have become charity wards, since a large proportion of the occupants derive their limited incomes from welfare allowances. They are sometimes islands of criminality, particularly among juveniles who are pent up in the despondent climate of dependency and harried supervision. They pay no property taxes (though in-lieu payments tend to weaken this criticism). They tend to be located in undesirable corners of land within the city. Projects evict people who are too poor to pay the minimum rent (in principle, the pro rata operating costs of the project). And, paradoxically, there are not nearly enough such dwellings to meet the shelter needs of badly under-housed

14 UNITED STATES FEDERAL HOUSING PROGRAMS: CUMULA-TIVE PERFORMANCE THROUGH 1968

	units (000)
FHA mortgage insurance	
single family home sales (sec. 203)	8,020
rental housing projects (sec. 207)	229
cooperative housing (sec. 213)	153
urban renewal housing (sec. 220)	64
moderate income housing (sec. 221)	332
below market interest, moderate income (sec. 221 d3)	127
homes for families of military personnel (sec. 222)	212
homes in declining areas (sec. 223 e)	9
housing for elderly people (sec. 231 and sec. 207 elderly)	43
FHA home improvement loans	29,190
Rent supplement units	59
Low-rent public housing units	744

Source: Department of Housing and Urban Development, *Monthly Fact Sheet* (January, 1969).

families who meet income and other requirements. This scarcity results in part from very high construction costs, about one-third higher than privately constructed multifamily units (see Table 15).

For each of these and other criticisms there is a counter-argument, which dedicated project managers and some others express with force and skill whenever their good intentions are questioned. Indeed, the public-housing bureaucracy stands head and shoulders above other housing agencies—such as redevelopment or code enforcement officers—as defenders of the welfare and integrity of the urban poor. At least they put roofs over people's heads instead of tearing roofs away; but their knightly armor is pretty rusty and unwieldy. Traditional public housing is an archaic enterprise.

There are several recent innovations in housing assistance to low-income families, some administered by local housing authorities and some by other agencies. Instead of massive projects isolated from other residential neighborhoods, some public hous-

15 UNITED STATES HOUSING CONSTRUCTION, 1959–1968

year	number of units started (000) total	privately owned total	privately owned 1 unit	publicly owned	construction cost ($ bil.) total	privately owned total	privately owned 1 unit	publicly owned	average cost per unit ($000) total	privately owned total	privately owned 1 unit	publicly owned
1968	1,547	1,507	899	40	23.2	22.6	16.7	.6	15.0	15.0	18.5	14.0
1967	1,322	1,292	844	30	19.1	18.7	14.6	.4	14.4	14.5	17.3	13.1
1966	1,196	1,165	779	31	17.0	16.6	13.0	.4	14.2	14.2	16.8	12.6
1965	1,510	1,473	964	37	20.5	20.0	15.6	.5	13.6	13.6	16.2	12.6
1964	1,591	1,557	972	33	20.8	20.4	15.0	.4	13.1	13.1	15.4	12.4
1963	1,641	1,609	1,021	32	20.7	20.3	15.1	.4	12.6	12.7	14.9	11.9
1962	1,492	1,463	992	30	18.7	18.4	14.2	.3	12.6	12.6	14.3	11.7
1961	1,365	1,313	975	52	17.1	16.5	13.5	.6	12.5	12.6	13.8	11.7
1960	1,296	1,252	995	44	16.4	15.8	13.6	.5	12.6	12.7	13.7	12.0
1959	1,554	1,517	1,234	37	19.2	18.8	16.5	.4	12.4	12.4	13.4	11.8
10-year total	14,514	14,148	9,675	366	192.7	188.1	147.8	4.5	13.7	13.3	15.3	12.3

Sources: 1959 to 1964, U.S. Bureau of the Census, *Housing Construction Statistics: 1889 to 1964*, U.S. Government Printing Office, Washington, D.C., 1966. Table A-5.
1965 to 1968, U.S. Bureau of the Census, *Housing Starts*, C 20-69-1, January, 1969, U.S. Government Printing Office, Washington, D.C., 1969, Appendix A.

Note: totals may not add, due to rounding.

ing has been built on scattered sites to blend in with those neighborhoods. Instead of cumbersome and costly public-construction projects, some public housing is put up by private builders and offered on a "turnkey" basis (i.e., ready for occupancy) to the housing authority. Low-income families have been placed in leased units in privately owned and operated apartment buildings, the difference between the market-determined rent and the amount the family can afford to pay being provided by subsidy. This leasing program has several advantages for private landlords (secure leases) and the city (payment of property taxes) but does not directly increase the housing stock. Low-income households can be placed in public projects intended for households of somewhat higher income, with subsidies to cover the difference in rent. Public housing projects designed exclusively for low-income elderly people take on the appearance of retirement communities, free of many of the negative aspects of all-purpose, low-income projects.

In effect, American public housing may be "spinning off" a number of its functions to more viable entities. An interesting question which does not seem to have been aired publicly is whether there will be any role at all for low-income housing programs when and if "guaranteed incomes," "guaranteed employment," or really effective results of the "war on poverty" are realized.

Slum clearance.—Although the proportion of housing units which are "sound, with all plumbing facilities" is not much lower in central cities (79.6 per cent in 1960) than in suburban areas (84.4 per cent; see Table 16), substandard housing in the central areas is usually bunched together in old, decaying slums. Since 1949 Federal funds have enabled local Urban Redevelopment Agencies to buy slum properties at "fair value," demolish the buildings, and sell the land for some new use at a price usually well below the acquisition price. This is the central concept of "urban renewal," easy enough to perceive in the initial laws and in the scattering of ultimate results, but now encrusted with gimmickry that lets it appear to be all things to all people, or whatever the local political situation requires.

Although it might seem nothing more than simple civic prudence to sweep away unsightly hovels and let the land of

16 SELECTED CHARACTERISTICS OF THE UNITED STATES HOUSING INVENTORY IN 1960

| | All housing units | | | | | Occupied housing units | | | | | | | | | Vacancy rate | |
| | | Percent— | | | | | Percent— | | | | | | Owner | Renter | | |
Area	Total number	Median number of rooms	In one-house-unit structures	In structures built 1950–1960	Sound, with all plumbing facilities	Total number	Median number of persons	With 1.01 or more persons per room	Moved in during 1958–1960	Occupied by nonwhite	Owner occupied	Renter occupied	Median value (dollars)	Median gross rent (dollars)	Homeowner	Rental
Total	58,326,357	4.9	76.3	27.5	74.0	53,023,875	3.0	11.5	31.9	9.7	61.9	38.1	11,900	71	1.6	6.7
Inside SMSA's	36,386,215	4.8	67.6	29.8	81.8	34,000,044	2.9	10.4	33.0	10.3	58.9	41.1	13,500	75	1.7	6.4
In central cities	19,622,145	4.6	53.1	19.8	79.6	18,505,949	2.6	10.7	33.5	15.4	47.4	52.6	12,300	72	1.5	6.2
Not in central cities	16,764,070	5.1	84.7	41.5	84.4	15,494,095	3.2	9.9	32.4	4.1	72.7	27.3	14,400	81	1.9	7.0
Outside SMSA's	21,940,142	4.9	90.8	23.7	60.9	19,023,831	3.0	13.6	29.9	8.7	67.1	32.9	8,600	58	1.3	7.3
Urban	40,763,865	4.8	67.8	27.7	81.4	38,320,370	2.9	10.2	33.2	10.4	58.3	41.7	12,900	73	1.6	6.6
Rural	17,562,492	5.0	96.2	27.2	56.7	14,703,505	3.2	15.1	28.5	7.9	71.2	28.8	8,300	55	1.5	6.9
Nonfarm	13,996,171	4.8	95.5	31.0	58.2	11,137,184	3.2	15.4	32.6	7.8	70.3	29.7	8,300	55	2.1	8.7
Occupied farm	3,566,321	5.8	98.9	12.2	50.9	3,566,321	3.4	14.4	15.7	8.4	73.8	26.2	—	—	—	—

Source: U.S. Census of Housing: 1960, United States Summary, Final Report HC(1) No. 1, U.S. Government Printing Office, Washington, D.C., 1963, p. 1–2.

Note: some data based on sample.

the affluent city be covered with good buildings, urban renewal has itself turned out to be a civic carbuncle. It has been very harmful and unfair to people dislodged from the slums; it has resulted in substantial benefits to families or businesses which hardly require subsidies; and it appears to create new slums where there were none before.* This dubious bounty is obtained at prodigious expense, making the whole enterprise a kind of sequel to Alice in Wonderland. There must be a rational way to achieve slumless cities, but urban renewal is not it. Buildings should be torn down when we have something better to do with the land, not just because someone is angry with the buildings.

There are two embarrassing facts among whatever good intentions the framers of the American urban-renewal scheme possessed. Urban renewal does not provide housing assistance for the displaced (any housing help they get is provided under other programs), so that these people have come to resist being "bulldozed." It does not have a ready market for the land which is cleared of slums, because almost all varieties of urban land-use in the United States are moving away from the high-density pattern which redevelopment plans generally imply. A third fact, which in effect links the other two, is the reluctance of many parties to see dwellings demolished which might be repaired at some lesser cost. These three points add up to a large public doubt about the wisdom of redevelopment efforts generally. Instead of portraying itself as the answer to the "urban problem," urban renewal tends now to be seen as a contributing factor— a curious fate for a civic housekeeper.

Gradually, and defensively, urban redevelopment people began to refer to what they were doing as "human renewal" instead of "urban renewal." The implication is that people who live in slums can be raised permanently from squalor by giving attention to their problems of health, alienation, education, social organization, and employment. Cure such problems, the reasoning goes, by grafting generous welfare casework efforts onto the crude business of getting people to move, and the city's slum clientele would be permanently diminished. The relocatees could

---

* For a skillfully compiled review of literature relating to urban redevelopment in the United States see James Q. Wilson, ed., *Urban Renewal— The Record and the Controversy* (Cambridge: M.I.T. Press, 1966).

"make it" in the private housing market as well as in the job market and the other businesses of living.

"Human renewal" is at best too late to win necessary support for urban redevelopment programs, because the client population has come up with some significant ideas of its own about what these programs should do. At worst, "human renewal" is just window dressing for an unreconstructed demolition program. Finally, the concept of "human renewal" has been snatched away by a popular, but still inoperative, new Federal effort called the "Model Cities" program which simply writes these appealing precepts in very large type.

The brief era of urban renewal and model cities has also been the era of emergent militancy and community organization among urban minority and low-income groups. These groups have the numbers and the strategy to secure political control over federally sponsored programs, though they have not as yet brought this off. Their aims with respect to housing, employment, education, and other matters are generally very clear. They are not immediately concerned with fixing up buildings or fixing up people. They want to fix up the system which crippled the people and which let the buildings rot. This rather fundamental approach has the ring of truth. It means revising the rules of the urban game—the ownership of property and business, the governing of the streets and schools and professions. It is not what the framers of urban-renewal legislation had in mind, but it is what they have helped to evoke. That may finally turn out to be the best thing to be said about urban renewal in the United States.

Sponsored middle-income housing.—Housing commentators in the United States are fond of producing data which show that new housing is priced beyond the means of most of the middle-income population as well as the low-income group. It is a non sequitur to conclude that middle-income households require housing subsidies, because this group finds its housing primarily in the existing stock of dwellings. Indeed, the ordinary home builder's reason for not trying to build homes for the lower-middle income group is that he cannot compete with the used housing market where such families get substantially more for their housing dollar.

Urban policy-making seems to thrive on non sequiturs,

however. The United States has a number of subsidy programs for middle-income housing, leaving aside the original FHA, single-family home mortgage-insurance program—which may not be a subsidy at all—and the Veterans loan guarantee which is a subsidy but not along income-class lines. The most important of these is undoubtedly the "221 d3" program, which provides FHA mortgage insurance and FNMA support for a mortgage covering as much as 100 per cent of the cost of a housing project which will be available only to families falling between prescribed income limits, in effect, between the maximum income limit for public housing and a figure 35 per cent higher. In its most important variant, the "d3" program limits the interest rate of the mortgage to as little as 3 per cent, well below market interest rates which now approach 8 per cent, for the purpose of keeping rents low. Despite time-consuming procedural routine, more than 125,000 units had been built under this program through 1968.

This program illustrates a number of major problems in the development of an effective housing program in the United States. In the first place it is probably based on a misconception about the nature of the housing market. The subsidy employed would probably expand the housing inventory more rapidly and more meaningfully if it were put more or less directly into the hands of the households it is supposed to benefit, letting them enter the regular housing market with substantially enhanced purchasing power in the form of low-interest financing. The program errs also in encouraging moderate-income households to accept rental, multifamily housing in spite of clearly expressed preferences for single-family homeownership.

The "d3" program uses the FHA mortgage insurance principle simply as a vehicle for creating a financial instrument; loan insurance is not intended as a subsidy nor could it actually provide the subsidy. FNMA really picks up the tab along with the newly written mortgage.

Cost ceilings written into the "d3" program, to assure that rents would be within the ability of moderate-income families to pay, have fallen behind rapidly rising construction costs. In city after city it has become unfeasible to build within the cost ceilings.

The fear of public officials that private builders or developers might derive some profit from a subsidized project intended to house needy people has led to a standardized requirement that many housing programs, including the "d3" below-market-interest-rate program, should be carried on by "sponsors" who appear unmotivated by the desire for profit. The "ideal" sponsor, perhaps, is an affluent church bent on doing good, but the typical sponsor, in reality, is probably a trust fund looking for an attractive investment and guided by people (often paid consultants) who know a few angles. There are some money-making angles in the "d3" program, or at least a number of professionals concerned with it so believe. The public phobia about the appearance of profit, however, cuts the program off from almost the entire market for residential mortgage funds in the United States. It makes a well intended program take the dimensions of a token effort.

The "d3" program actually is being phased out. A new scheme brings the mortgage-interest cost down to one per cent by a subsidy device which allows the mortgage itself to bear a market rate. FNMA has given up its "d3" responsibilities to a new agency called GNMA (Government National Mortgage Association). A companion program allows one per cent loans to low-income home purchasers, presumably removing them from the clientele of the "d3" program and its successor. In several ways, the demise of the "d3" program comes from the built-in defects mentioned above, particularly the dilemma of getting lower-income households into newly constructed buildings when the cost of construction rises so rapidly. The Congressional answer has been to provide more subsidy. The "sponsorship-FHA" vehicle continues in use unquestioned, however.

As an historical note, the profit phobia of American housing legislators dates primarily from a generous multi-family FHA program which operated from 1948 through 1950. Though very successful in generating a large volume of new rental housing in a short span of time, the program brought windfall profits to a number of developers and indignation to government leaders.*

It is not inconceivable that FHA-endorsed "sponsors" may also come under a cloud someday, because many things done in

* See citation 4, above. The program was known as "Sec. 608."

the name of simon-pure housing welfare by sponsors are promising grist for the mills of scandal. Not least is "elderly housing," which turns out often to be a luxurious and elaborate set of facilities for well-heeled and able-bodied senior executives or their widows. Sponsorship does not in fact correlate with low-income occupancy, nor with economy in construction or management, nor with absence of interest in gain. In general, the requirement of sponsorship is probably the most effective way that could be devised to keep the nation's specialized housing efforts from getting off the ground.

The lissome logic that leads to subsidized new housing for the middle-income as well as the low-income population is, in principle, a much larger threat to a sensible housing program than the fetish about sponsors. We cannot rebuild our entire stock of housing every year, so someone—chiefly middle-income households—must put up with "yesterday's" houses, or else we are in serious trouble. The notion that government has a duty to assist the downtrodden middle class to get new housing is likely to linger for generations. That the duty will be honored mainly in the breach, we can be very sure.

For all its conceptual faults, the "sponsorship" requirement in much housing legislation may serve to reveal the implicit strategy of the Federal government. There is a quantitative limit to the amount of housing help which is to be offered, a limit which would be quickly surpassed if all inadequately housed families were deemed to have a "right" to better housing. Instead of setting an effective floor beneath housing standards for all households and letting the chips fall where they may with regard to the number and costs of new buildings, the Federal strategy appears to be one of allocating funds for a specific number of units of "better" housing which are to be rationed by sponsors among inadequately housed families. The sponsors' responsibilities are limited, quantitatively, without any embarrassment, and the Federal government is also let off the hook when criticism about insufficient low-income housing arises by pointing to the dearth of sponsors.

Ending housing discrimination.—Before 1948 it was accepted as true that the incursion of minority races into a neighborhood would lead to its decline in value and condition. Hence Negroes, Orientals, and anyone else who fell into the category of "undesirability" were unable to buy or rent dwellings in all but narrowly restricted portions of most American cities. It was a legal disability in many cases, being based on provisions in deeds to property, but it was backed up and extended by informal sanctions. Consequently, racial segregation was open and obvious, as indeed it remains.*

During World War II a large migration of Negroes from the rural South began. It has continued to the present time and, together with other minority population shifts such as the arrival of many Puerto Ricans in New York, has required that increasing amounts of housing in cities of the North and West be occupied by people against whom the white majority generally discriminated, in housing as in other matters. The problem was resolved by transfer of whole neighborhoods, often rather suddenly, from white to nonwhite occupancy. There is this peculiar dynamic aspect to housing segregation in the United States which casual commentators seem to miss. The "ghetto" of American cities has flexible, if impenetrable, walls.

Neighborhood transitions have taken place selectively, however, and often against stiff opposition. It was the low-income, working-class, white population—frequently with a precarious but precious stake in a mortgaged home—who felt the threat and had to move. But these people did not move away so rapidly that demand pressures in the existing ghetto could not build up. Within minority areas the very intense demand helped property owners to exploit householders through undermaintenance. This factor plus the low-income, poor-credit situation of most minority households led to rapid deterioration of nonwhite neighborhoods. The prophesy of declining physical standards of the neighborhood through nonwhite incursion fulfilled itself.

In 1948 the Supreme Court ruled that segregation by provisions in property deeds was illegal. It remained possible for landlords, homebuilders, home owners and real estate agents to

---

* A basic source on segregated housing patterns in the United States is Davis McEntire, *Residence and Race* (Berkeley: University of California Press, 1960).

refuse to sell or rent specific dwellings to nonwhites, but these forms of housing discrimination came under attack increasingly. Local "open housing" laws were passed in some communities (and failed to pass in others). Congress hemmed and hawed about the matter until 1968, when it passed some potentially far-reaching laws against housing discrimination. Before that, the Executive branch had made a fairly meaningful gesture toward denying "government assistance" (mostly FHA mortgage insurance) to developers who were not pledged to "open occupancy." The Supreme Court, more recently, has decided that a law passed some one hundred years ago really outlawed most forms of discrimination in housing anyway. So the legal position is now about 180 degrees away from what it was in 1947.

The real situation, though, is that there is now at least as much racial segregation as before in American cities. By measures recently devised but widely accepted, the proportion of urban nonwhites living in predominantly nonwhite areas appears to have increased over the period.[5] In part, government housing programs have been responsible for this, since public housing projects in most cities have had an increasing proportion of nonwhites, as economic progress lifted more and more white families out of the low-income category.

It may seem a little strange, but militant liberal or minority cries for "open housing" have subsided with the passage of Federal laws, even though it is manifest that legislation has not and will not bring about housing integration. There are several aspects of this situation which help to explain it, including the recognition that in passing laws the Federal government has gone about as far as it can go. There is also some feeling that the existence of laws, even though weakly enforced, will have a long-term leavening effect on the attitudes of people with middle-class morals—the kind of people who stop at stop signs even when there is no other traffic and no police car in sight.

Stronger factors seem to be that minority families themselves are reluctant to integrate with white families, and that income differences continue to draw a fairly sharp line between white and nonwhite households. Even when he has the money and the mortgage credit to buy in a white area, a nonwhite householder has to reckon with the large possibility that his wife and children will be exposed to insults, and perhaps worse. The militant integrationists are a minority of the minority, despite their ability to appear otherwise. It is also very important to realize that militant separatists have been stealing the show in recent years, and that their aims run directly counter to the literal intention of most recent "civil rights" laws.

Improving existing dwellings.—The FHA's first charge, when it was established in 1934, was to encourage home owners to fix up their properties, thus creating jobs in the home-improvement business and raising the quality of the housing stock. From that day to this, successive Housing Acts have piled "rehabilitation" section on "rehabilitation" section. The purpose has shifted somewhat over the years, and it can now be said that this kind of effort aims to reduce the relocation burden attendant upon full-scale urban renewal efforts and also to minimize the increase in housing costs which slum dwellers are likely to face when their housing circumstances are improved. That is, rehabilitation is an alternative to redevelopment.

At first FHA could offer loan insurance for only a fairly small ($3,500), short term (five years), high interest rate (about 10 per cent) home improvement loan. At latest count, a home owner wishing to fix up his property may receive $3,000 as an outright grant or a long term, low interest loan up to $14,500. There is also a way to rehabilitate a home and refinance the entire property with an interest cost of only one per cent to the owner.*

Despite the growing generosity of property-improvement assistance, it has not been nearly so effective as was hoped, particularly as an adjunct to, or substitute for, urban renewal. Code enforcement programs by local agencies, in which property owners are supposed to be encouraged or even forced to seek property improvement loans tend to be frustrated by the unwillingness of lenders and FHA alike to see the efforts as "financially sound"—i.e., productive of increased value. Estimates of rehabilitation costs for buildings in redevelopment areas have

---

* FHA Sec. 221 h, as revised in the Housing Act of 1968.

been so high that demolition and new construction is cheaper. The truth in this matter is perhaps hopelessly lost behind a thicket of subsidy provisions and accounting practices. Perhaps more significant, rehabilitation is unpopular with many urban-redevelopment officials because it tends to vitiate their large-scale area improvement plans.

Rehabilitation occupies a particularly dark corner in the gloomy library of housing policy. Between 1950 and 1960 there seems to have been a major wave of property improvement in American cities, converting as many as four million substandard dwellings to standard condition, but the causes for this and the means employed are unknown.[6] The change occurred primarily through the installation of plumbing, a factor which is sufficiently concrete to make the census reports credible. There does not seem to be any particular connection between Federal rehabilitation aids and this massive upgrading of the stock of dwellings leading one to conclude that it was just a response to better purchasing power and the transition, in that decade, from a seller's market to a buyer's market in housing. If matters continue, the United States may run out of dwellings which need and deserve fixing up before it has a program designed to do the job. As Table 17 shows, lack of plumbing facilities is a significant, but not major, complaint about U.S. housing.

New communities.—The Housing Act of 1968 provided, among other things, for Federal guarantee of debentures used to secure funds for developing entire new communities. Such efforts, falling far short of the scale and functions of British "New Towns" or similar programs abroad, have done very poorly in the United States, primarily because of adverse cash-flow characteristics. That is, really big land development schemes, involving thousands of housing units together with public facilities intended to serve them, require that a lot of money be laid out before any money starts coming in. The 1968 Act provides potential assistance in bridging that gap, since it will give people who lend money to cover this gap the protection of a government guarantee. In return for its assistance the government will get to decide whether the plan for development meets criteria which have yet to be spelled out.

17 EQUIPMENT OF HOUSING UNITS IN THE UNITED STATES
HOUSING INVENTORY, 1960

	number of units
Total number of housing units	58,326,357
Water supply	
Hot and cold piped water inside structure	50,869,876
Only cold piped water inside structure	3,320,754
Piped water outside structure	600,762
No piped water	3,526,905
Toilet facilities	
Flush toilet, exclusive use	50,608,544
Flush toilet, shared use	1,731,492
Other toilet facilities or none	5,978,261
Bathing facilities	
Bathtub or shower, exclusive use	49,706,246
Bathtub or shower, shared	1,690,412
No bathtub or shower	6,921,639

Source: U.S. Bureau of the Census, U.S. *Census of Housing: 1960,* Vol.
I, States and Small Areas, United States Summary. Final Report
HC(1) –1, U.S. Government Printing Office, Washington, D.C.,
1963, Table 3.

American housing developers are not likely to drag their
feet on physical planning standards, having learned that such
planning is a powerful marketing tool. The government, for its
part, is not likely to insist on incorporating basic employment-
giving activities into the plan, since industry itself is not interested in playing the city-planning game or getting enmeshed in
the woes of a "company town." There is likely to be some
friction about the matter of getting "socioeconomic balance"—
i.e., a mixture including some poor people and some minority
households. This is a matter of economics, in some part at least,
because low- or middle-income housing has been hard to market
in such communities as have already been developed, and the
existence of such housing threatens the marketability of higher-
priced housing.[7] In the end, the "new communities" provision of
the 1968 Act will probably just help more suburbs get built.

Fiscal and monetary measures aimed at housing.—Home
ownership in the United States is favored by the exemption from

income taxation of the value of housing services received, even though the imputed income thus received is entered into the National Income accounts. This benefit might be equivalent to roughly 5 per cent of the home owner's cash income. Investors in rental property can benefit from accelerated depreciation provisions (not limited to housing, however), and the strength of this provision in stimulating apartment construction has been made very clear in recent years.

General monetary policies, such as the purchase or sale of government securities by the Federal Reserve system, have a pronounced and relatively predictable effect upon the availability of credit for the housing sector. Operations of FNMA, as discussed earlier, can reinforce or offset the effects on housing of the Federal Reserve system, though perhaps not very much. The Home Loan Bank system extends short-term credit to member savings and loan associations when they are caught, individually or collectively, in a credit pinch.

It is revealing that the most significant and certain levers which the Federal government has on the operation of the housing sector are these gross and indirect tools. By and large, they are beyond the purview of the Department of Housing and Urban Development, which is nominally responsible for the health of the housing economy. But every one knows that if there is a real housing problem, the Federal Reserve system and the Secretary of the Treasury, not HUD, will have to solve it. Even if HUD knew what it wanted to do and how to go about it, in its limited domain of some particular housing problems, its work could be undone or rendered unnecessary by relatively minor shifts of fiscal or monetary policy. If credit is tight, urban vacancy rates fall and relocation from urban renewal areas becomes impossible. If a negative income tax is instituted, who will live in all the low-rent public housing? If new communities can tap a very large pool of capital in a relaxed money market, why renew the old communities?

There is, indeed, a much larger dimension to the issue. Urban housing issues are inextricably bound up with local school problems, urban transportation problems, crime, job training, pollution, and aid to mothers with dependent children, to mention just some of the broad categories. Vandalism, for example, is an enormously powerful deterrent to housing investment. New communities will almost certainly sell "law and order" and ready access to metropolitan centers as much as they sell houses or lots. Our urban problems are beyond the reach of one per cent mortgages, even with FNMA to back them up.

The American housing program has strong fingers and weak eyes. It has unquestioned impact on small areas but seems to be unaware of, or unable to control, the total effect of what it is doing. It is not an injustice to the thousands of people who have devoted their lives to defining and implementing a housing program for this country to wonder whether we might conceivably be better off, collectively and individually, without any program at all. There is enough reality behind that question that it at least deserves to be asked, and to be faced.

SOME POLICY GUIDELINES

Of course, it is a little unfair to imply that housing administrators or policy-makers must assume responsibility for the totality of urban behavior. There must be some set of principles which would guide housing efforts in the most constructive direction, whatever helpful or disruptive things are happening in the wider environment. The elements of a "best effort" housing program must differ from nation to nation and from era to era. In the United States today the nature of housing issues and the context in which the housing sector works suggest the following few points:

1. We must make effective use of the whole housing inventory, not relying automatically on specially organized construction programs to meet newly defined needs. Construction programs take years to "tool up," during which time the needs either evaporate or change. They probably waste resources, and they certainly invite bungling. The housing inventory is not a static mass, but a growing and changing thing, which at any one time offers many alternative ways of meeting specific public goals.

2. In a market economy the essential economic functions of government are the removal of market imperfections (e.g.,

noncompetitive practices) and the offsetting of externalities (e.g., the investment risk in fixing up just *one* building in a dense slum).

3. Significant imperfections exist in the supply of credit for housing, both in the aggregate (i.e., housing's share in total national investment) and in the particular (i.e., whether a particular family can qualify for a mortgage loan).

4. The amount of credit available to the housing sector as a whole should always be sufficient for the growth component of demand (i.e., for expanding the inventory as the total number of households expands).

5. Above this level, variations in the amount of credit

18 COMPONENTS OF CHANGE IN THE UNITED STATES HOUSING INVENTORY, 1950–1959

	number of units *
dwelling units, April, 1950	46,137,000
net change, 1950 to 1959	+12,331,000
units added through:	
conversion (net)	807,000
new construction	15,003,000
other sources	1,050,000
units lost through:	
merger (net)	815,000
demolition	1,933,000
other means	1,783,000
dwelling units, December, 1959	58,468,000

Source: U.S. Bureau of the Census, *United States Census of Housing: 1960*, Vol. IV, Components of Inventory Change, Part I-A.

Notes: the definition of "dwelling unit" differs from that of "housing unit" employed in the 1960 Census.

"conversion" means dividing one existing unit into two or more units.

"other sources" of additions include adapting non-dwelling structures to dwelling purposes.

"merger" means combining two or more adjacent units into one.

"other means" of housing loss includes fire, flood, earthquake damage sufficient to cause removal of structure.

* based on sample

available to the housing sector should be determined on the basis of the comparative merits of raising the rate of housing-stock replacement versus raising the rate of other forms of net investment such as additions to industrial equipment. This is inescapably a matter for central economic policy-making, not a decision which the marketplace will make, or one which housing administrators can or should make. Over the period 1950 through 1959 about 4.5 million units were removed (not all of them substandard), which is roughly 10 per cent of the beginning inventory, implying an average economic life of 100 years (see Table 18).

6. On the individual level, credit should be available for housing purchase without discrimination. People who are old enough to constitute a household or raise children should have access to adequate single-family housing in the traditional way (i.e., ownership financed by a mortgage) without regard to employment, marital status, or assets. Such dwellings are clearly the "normal" type of American housing, as Table 19 shows. In effect, this calls for a "national patrimony," translating the whole society's accumulation of wealth into a limited but meaningful line of credit for new adults.

7. A system of value insurance should replace the mortgage-insurance program. Mortgage lenders must be assured unequivocally that the physical property is all the collateral they need, and borrowers should be protected against loss of equity due to unanticipated events—such as a slump in the market when the home is being sold.

8. Housing policy-makers and administrators should be continuously concerned about the possibility of substantial imperfections in the supply of other factors—labor, materials, land and information—to the housing sector. These imperfections are likely to call for ad hoc, technical measures in wide variety rather than sweeping once-and-for-all reforms. Again, referring back to point 1, the management of the entire housing inventory, not just the housebuilding industry, must be scrutinized for imperfections. For example, there may be abuse or waste in title and escrow systems in some places.

9. The principal technological problem of housebuilding is

not to make dwellings cheaper but to make them better. This is the way, in an economy of rising real incomes, to get the maximum benefit from our housebuilding dollar. If policy-makers are to be concerned about housing technology they should be concerned in the right direction.

19 NUMBER OF UNITS IN STRUCTURE, IN UNITED STATES HOUSING INVENTORY IN 1960

number of units in structure	*number of units*
total, all structure types	58,314,784
one-family units, detached	40,103,346
one-family units, attached	3,655,210
two-unit structures	4,464,216
three and four-unit structures	3,087,649
five or more unit structures	6,237,798
trailers	766,565

Source: U.S. Bureau of the Census, *U.S. Census of Housing: 1960,* Vol. I, States and Small Areas, United States Summary, Final Report HC(1)–1, U.S. Government Printing Office, Washington, D.C., 1963, Table 5.

Note: total number of units varies among tables because data is partly based on different samples.

10. One kind of externality which troubles the housing sector is that the submarginal incomes among a part of the urban population lead to housing-management decisions which result in submarginal dwellings—slums—and whole neighborhoods of them. The long-run remedy is perfectly clear: there should not be submarginal incomes or at least submarginal housing budgets. Quick application of income or housing supplements may require special measures to assure that these supplements don't just cause the price of slum housing to rise, but these special measures must be self-liquidating.

11. Another externality is the discouraging effect of deteriorated neighborhoods on individual efforts to restore or replace buildings within them. This is a phenomenon vastly too widespread to be dealt with by the lumbering juggernaut of urban redevelopment. It is also a problem which raises deep issues of policy, since the dynamics of future metropolitan development may not require the rebuilding of urban gray areas,

or at least not in the form that present investors might have in mind. This problem aside, there need only be a system of bonuses—such as depreciation allowances, low-interest financing, or assured "take out" of equity—for developers who try to brighten up a blotch of gray. Greater bonuses might be given for early developers than for those who come later, and greater bonuses might be given for large-scale undertakings than for individual-parcel redevelopment.

12. There is a large set of externalities related to residential land use but going beyond the bounds of housing per se. New housing developments cause congestion on existing roads, deprive the community of "open space," and create a potential for certain kinds of pollution. Some of these problems can be cured with money, some with local regulation, and some with both. Realistically, though, these problems are caused not so much by housing as by a serious and worsening "hang-up" in local government. The politics of urban planning is a crisis area today, and it does indeed involve the performance of the local housing economy. But it is just not within the realm of "housing policy." It is an interesting problem, but it is another story.

NOTES

Notes for Chapter One

1. Charles Abrams, *Man's Struggle for Shelter in an Urbanizing World* (Cambridge: M.I.T. Press, 1964).
2. Frederick E. Case, *Real Estate* (Boston: Allyn and Bacon, 1962), Chapters 12 and 13.
3. Richard B. Andrews, *Urban Growth and Development* (New York: Simmons-Boardman, 1962), p. 255 ff.
4. Paul A. Samuelson, *Economics* (New York: McGraw-Hill, 1967), p. 530 ff.
5. Henry George, *Progress and Poverty* (New York: Garden City Publishing Co., 1926), and various earlier editions.

Notes for Chapter Two

1. Richard F. Muth, "The Demand for Non-Farm Housing," in *The Demand for Durable Goods*, A.C. Harberger, ed. (Chicago: University of Chicago Press, 1960); Sherman J. Maisel, "Nonbusiness Construction," in *The Brookings Quarterly Econometric Model of the United States*, J.S. Duesenberry, et al., eds. (Chicago: Rand McNally, 1965).
2. American Public Health Association, Committee on the Hygiene of Housing, *An Appraisal Method for Measuring the Quality of Housing* (New York, 1945); see especially Part III.
3. Chester Rapkin, Louis Winnick, and David Blank, *Housing Market Analysis, A Study of Theory and Methods* (Washington: Housing and Home Finance Agency, 1953).
4. Muth, *ibid.*
5. Glenn H. Beyer, *Housing and Society* (New York: Macmillan, 1965), Ch. 14.
6. Wallace F. Smith, "Urban Land Prices and Public Policy," a paper presented at the Meetings of the Japan Section of the Regional Science Association, Tokyo, 1967.
7. Ronald P. Dore, *City Life in Japan* (Berkeley: University of California Press, 1958).

498

8. Peter Hall, *The World Cities* (London: World University Library, 1966), p. 171.

9. Roland Artle, "On Some Methods and Problems in the Study of Metropolitan Economies," *Regional Science Association Papers,* Vol. VIII, 1962, pp. 71–92.

10. Wilbur R. Thompson, *A Preface to Urban Economics* (Baltimore: Johns Hopkins Press, 1965), p. 141 ff.

11. Julius Margolis, "Metropolitan Finance Problems: Territories, Functions, and Growth," in *Public Finances: Needs, Sources and Utilization* (Princeton, Bureau of Economic Research, Princeton University Press, 1961).

12. Kevin Lynch, "The City as Environment," *Scientific American* (September 1965), 209–219.

13. Thompson, *Urban Economics,* Ch. 1.

14. Kingsley Davis, "The Urbanization of the Human Population," *Scientific American* (September 1965), 41–53; and Gideon Sjoberg, "The Origin and the Evolution of Cities," *ibid.,* 55–62.

15. I. M. Robinson, H. B. Wolfe, and R. L. Barringer, "A Simulation Model for Renewal Programming," *Journal of the American Institute of Planners* (May 1965), 126–133.

Notes for Chapter Three

1. Samuelson, *Economics,* Ch. 4.

2. Wallace F. Smith, *Aspects of Housing Demand,* Research Report No. 29 (Berkeley: Center for Real Estate and Urban Economics, University of California, 1966), Ch. III.

3. Sherman J. Maisel, "A Theory of Fluctuations in Residential Construction Starts," *American Economic Review* (June 1963), 359–383.

4. Rapkin, Winnick, and Blank, *Housing Market Analysis,* p. 22 ff.

5. Smith, *Aspects of Housing Demand,* Ch. II.

6. *Ibid.,* Ch. V.

7. Sherman J. Maisel, "Changes in the Rate and Components of Household Formation," *Journal of the American Statistical Association* (June 1960).

8. Ralph W. Pfouts (ed.), *The Techniques of Urban Economic Analysis* (West Trenton, N.J.: Chandler-Davis, 1960).

9. Artle, "Methods and Problems in Metropolitan Economies."

10. *Medium-Term Economic Plan* (Tokyo: Economic Planning Agency, Government of Japan, 1965), pp. 70–72.

11. Samuelson, *Economics,* Ch. 4.

12. Sherman J. Maisel, *Financing Real Estate* (New York: McGraw-Hill, 1965), especially Chapter 2.

13. Frederick E. Case, *Real Estate* (Boston: Allyn and Bacon, 1962), p. 212.

14. Wallace F. Smith, *The Low-Rise Speculative Apartment,* Research Report No. 25 (Berkeley: Center for Real Estate and Urban Economics, University of California, 1964), Ch. VI.

15. Samuelson, *Economics,* p. 710 ff.

16. *National Report of Japan,* 28th World Congress of the International Federation for Housing and Planning (1966), p. 58.

17. Abrams, *Struggle for Shelter*, Ch. 2.

18. Hans Blumenfeld, "The Modern Metropolis," *Scientific American* (September 1965), 70–71.

19. Abrams, *Struggle for Shelter*, Ch. 3.

20. Beyer, *Housing and Society*, pp. 201–202.

21. Smith, *Low-Rise Speculative Apartment*, Ch. VI.

Notes for Chapter Four

1. Samuelson, *Economics*, p. 429 ff.

2. Karl Sax, *Standing Room Only: The World's Exploding Population* (Boston: Beacon Press, 1960).

3. Abrams, *Struggle for Shelter*, Ch. 1.

4. Walter Isard, *Location and Space Economy* (Cambridge: Technology Press, 1956), Ch. 8.

5. Jean Gottmann, *Megalopolis* (Cambridge, Mass.: M.I.T. Press, 1961).

6. Peter Self, *Cities in Flood* (London: Faber and Faber, 1957).

7. Walter K. Vivrette, "Housing and Community Settings for Older People," in Clark Tibbitts, ed., *Handbook of Social Gerontology* (Chicago: University of Chicago Press, 1960).

8. Margaret G. Reid, *Housing and Income* (Chicago: University of Chicago Press, 1962), Ch. 1.

9. Sherman J. Maisel and Louis Winnick, "Family Housing Expenditures: Elusive Laws and Intrusive Variances," *Proceedings of the Conference on Consumption and Saving*, Vol. I (Philadelphia: University of Pennsylvania, 1960), pp. 359–435; and Margaret G. Reid, *ibid*.

10. A. H. Schaaf, *Economic Aspects of Urban Renewal: Theory, Policy and Area Analysis*, Research Report No. 14 (Berkeley: Center for Real Estate and Urban Economics, University of California, 1960).

11. Sherman J. Maisel, *Housebuilding in Transition* (Berkeley: University of California Press, 1953), p. 17 ff.

12. Louis Winnick, *Rental Housing: Opportunities for Private Investment* (New York: McGraw-Hill, 1958), p. 195 ff.

13. Abrams, *Struggle for Shelter*, p. 106 ff.

14. Charles P. Kindleberger, *Economic Development* (New York: McGraw-Hill, 1965), p. 87 ff.

15. Abrams, *Struggle for Shelter*.

16. Leland S. Burns, "Housing as Social Overhead Capital," in *Essays in Urban Land Economics*, James Gillies, ed. (Los Angeles: University of California Press, 1966), pp. 3–30.

17. Jane Jacobs, *The Death and Life of Great American Cities* (New York: Random House, 1961), esp. Ch. 4.

Notes for Chapter Five

1. Maisel and Winnick, "Family Housing Expenditures; Elusive Laws and Intrusive Variances," in *Urban Land Economics*.

2. Frederick E. Case, *The Costs of Home Ownership,* Real Estate Research Program, University of California, Los Angeles, 1956.

3. George Sternlieb, *The Tenement Landlord* (New Brunswick, N.J.: Urban Studies Center, Rutgers University, 1966).

4. Paul F. Wendt, "Large-Scale Community Development," *Journal of Finance* (May 1967), 220–239.

5. Wendt,"Large-Scale Community Development."

6. Miles Colean, "The Realities of Today's Real Estate Investment," Parts I, II, III, and IV, *Architectural Forum* (April, May, and June 1955), and Winnick, *Rental Housing.*

7. William Grigsby, *Housing Markets and Public Policy* (Philadelphia: University of Pennsylvania Press, 1963).

8. Maisel, *Housebuilding in Transition,* pp. 58–61.

9. Sherman J. Maisel, *Financing Real Estate* (New York: McGraw-Hill, 1965), Ch. 3.

10. Larry S. Bourne, *Private Redevelopment of the Central City,* Research Paper No. 112 (Chicago: Department of Geography, Chicago University, 1967).

Notes for Chapter Six

1. Richard U. Ratcliff, *Urban Land Economics* (New York: McGraw-Hill, 1949), p. 371.

2. See, for example, William Alonso, *Location and Land Use* (Cambridge: Harvard University Press, 1964).

3. Robert M. Haig, "Toward an Understanding of the Metropolis," *Quarterly Journal of Economics* (May 1926).

4. I. M. Robinson, H. B. Wolfe, and R. L. Barringer, "A Simulation Model for Renewal Programming," *Journal of the American Institute of Planners* (May 1965), 126–134.

5. Homer Hoyt, *One Hundred Years of Land Values in Chicago* (Chicago: University of Chicago Press, 1933).

6. Ernest W. Burgess, "The Growth of the City," in Robert E. Park, *et al., The City* (Chicago: University of Chicago Press, 1925).

7. Sherman J. Maisel, "Background Information on Costs of Land for Single-Family Housing," *Housing in California, Appendix to the Report,* Governor's Advisory Commission on Housing Problems, Sacramento (1963), pp. 235–241.

8. This is the basis of Henry George's famous proposal for a "single tax" in *Progress and Poverty.*

9. Richard S. Bolen, "Emerging Views of City Planning," *Journal of the American Institute of Planners* (July 1967), 233–245.

Notes for Chapter Eight

1. U.S. Senate, Committee on Banking and Currency, *Housing and Urban Development Legislation of 1968—Hearings,* Parts 1 and 2 (Washington: U.S. Government Printing Office, 1968).

2. Dick Netzer, *Economics of the Property Tax* (Washington, D.C.: The Brookings Institution, 1966), pp. 214–217.

3. Sherman J. Maisel, *Financing Real Estate* (New York: McGraw-Hill, 1965), Chapters 4 and 5.

4. Miles Colean, "The Realities of Today's Real Estate Investment," *Architectural Forum* (April, May, and June 1955).

5. *Report of the National Advisory Commission on Civil Disorders* (New York: Bantam Books, 1968), p. 236 ff.

6. Bernard J. Frieden, *The Future of Old Neighborhoods* (Cambridge; M.I.T. Press, 1964), p. 23.

7. Edward P. Eichler and Marshall Kaplan, *The Community Builders* (Berkeley: University of California Press, 1967), especially Chapter 6.

SELECTED REFERENCES

Land Economics

Alonso, William. *Location and Land Use.* Cambridge: Harvard University Press, 1964.

Andrews, Richard B. *Urban Growth and Development.* New York: Simmons-Boardman, 1962.

Bourne, Larry S. *Private Redevelopment of the Central City.* Chicago: University of Chicago, Department of Geography, Research Paper #112, 1967.

Gillies, James, ed. *Essays in Urban Land Economics.* Los Angeles: Real Estate Research Program, University of California at Los Angeles, 1966.

Gottman, Jean. *Megalopolis.* Cambridge: The M.I.T. Press, 1961.

Hoyt, Homer. *The Structure and Growth of Residential Neighborhoods in American Cities.* Washington, D.C.: Federal Housing Administration, 1939.

Nourse, Hugh O. *Regional Economics.* New York: McGraw-Hill, 1968.

Perloff, Harvey S. and Lowden Wingo, Jr., eds. *Issues in Urban Economics.* Baltimore: The Johns Hopkins Press, 1968.

Ratcliff, Richard U. *Urban Land Economics.* New York: McGraw-Hill, 1949.

Scientific American. *Cities.* New York: Alfred A. Knopf, 1966.

Thompson, Wilbur R. *A Preface to Urban Economics.* Baltimore: Johns Hopkins Press, 1965.

Turvey, Ralph. *The Economics of Real Property.* London: George Allen & Unwin, 1957.

Housing Problems and Policies

Abrams, Charles. *Man's Struggle for Shelter in an Urbanizing World.* Cambridge: M.I.T. Press, 1964.

Anderson, Martin. *The Federal Bulldozer.* Cambridge: M.I.T. Press, 1966.

Beyer, Glenn H. *Housing and Society.* New York: Macmillan, 1965.

Colean, Miles L. *American Housing.* New York: The Twentieth Century Fund, 1944.

Fisher, Robert M. *Twenty Years of Public Housing.* New York: Harper, 1959.

Grebler, Leo, Blank, D. M., and Winnick, L. *Capital Formation in Residential Real Estate.* Princeton: Princeton University Press, 1956.

Grebler, Leo. *Housing Issues in Economic Stabilization Policy*. New York: National Bureau of Economic Research, 1960.

Grigsby, William G. *Housing Markets and Public Policy*. Philadelphia: University of Pennsylvania Press, 1963.

Twenty-Eighth World Congress of the International Federation for Housing and Planning. *Procedures and Reports*. Tokyo: 1966.

Laurenti, Luigi. *Property Values and Race*. Berkeley: University of California Press, 1961.

Meyerson, Martin *et al. Housing, People and Cities*. New York: McGraw-Hill, 1962.

Needleman, Lionel. *The Economics of Housing*. London: Staples Press, 1965.

Nevitt, Adela A., ed. *The Economic Problems of Housing*. New York: Macmillan, 1967.

Reid, Margaret G. *Housing and Income*. Chicago: University of Chicago Press, 1962.

Rossi, Peter H. *Why Families Move*. New York: The Free Press, 1955.

United Nations. *Methods for Establishing Targets and Standards for Housing*. Bureau of Social Affairs. 1968. New York.

Wendt, Paul F. *Housing Policy—The Search for Solutions*. Berkeley: University of California Press, 1962.

Wheaton, William L. C., *et al.*, ed. *Urban Housing*. New York: The Free Press, 1966.

Winnick, Louis. *American Housing and Its Use*. New York: Wiley, 1957.

Finance and Construction

Eichler, Edward P., and Kaplan, Marshall. *The Community Builders*. Berkeley: University of California Press, 1967.

Gillies, James, and Mittelbach, Frank. *Management in the Light Construction Industry*. Los Angeles: University of California, 1962.

Jones, Oliver, and Grebler, Leo. *The Secondary Mortgage Market*. Los Angeles: Real Estate Research Program, University of California, 1961.

Klaman, Saul B. *The Postwar Residential Mortgage Market*. Princeton: Princeton University Press, 1961.

Maisel, Sherman J. *Financing Real Estate*. New York: McGraw-Hill, 1965.

Maisel, Sherman J. *Housebuilding in Transition*. Berkeley: University of California Press, 1961.

Sternlieb, George. *The Tenement Landlord*. New Brunswick: Rutgers State University, Urban Studies Center, 1966.

United Nations. *Financing of Housing and Community Improvement Programs*. Bureau of Social Affairs. 1957. New York.

United Nations. *Technical Co-operation Activities of the UN in the Field of Housing, Building, and Planning*. 1962. New York.

Winnick, Louis. *Rental Housing*. New York: McGraw-Hill, 1958.

Social Aspects of Housing

Duhl, Leonard J., ed. *The Urban Condition*. New York: Basic Books, 1963.

Foote, Nelson *et al. Housing Choices and Housing Constraints*. New York: McGraw-Hill, 1960.

Frieden, Bernard J. and Morris, R., eds. *Urban Planning and Social Policy*. New York: Basic Books, 1968.

Gans, Herbert. *The Urban Villagers*. New York: The Free Press, 1962.
McEntire, Davis. *Residence and Race*. Berkeley: University of California Press, 1958.
Morris, R. N. and Mogey, John. *The Sociology of Housing*. London: Routledge and Kegan Paul, 1965.
The National Advisory Commission on Civil Disorders. *Report*. New York: Bantam Books, 1968.
United Nations. *Social Aspects of Housing and Urban Development*. Economic and Social Council: Pub. No. E/c. 6/35, 1965. New York.
Wilson, James Q., ed. *The Metropolitan Enigma*. Cambridge: Harvard University Press, 1968.

Urban Planning

Braybrooke, David, and Lindblom, Charles E. *A Strategy of Decision*. New York: The Free Press, 1963.
Frieden, Bernard J. *The Future of Old Neighborhoods*. Cambridge: M.I.T. Press, 1964.
Lichfield, Nathaniel. *Cost-Benefit Analysis in Urban Redevelopment*. Berkeley: University of California, Center for Real Estate and Urban Economics, 1962.
Meyerson, Martin and Banfield, E. *Politics, Planning and the Public Interest*. New York: The Free Press, 1955.
Stone, P. A. *Housing, Town Development, Land and Costs*. London: Estates Gazette, 1963.
United Nations. *Report of the Third Session*, Committee on Housing, Building and Planning, 1965. New York.
Wilson, James Q., ed. *Urban Renewal—The Record and the Controversy*. Cambridge: M.I.T. Press, 1965.
Wingo, Lowden Jr. (ed.). *Cities and Space*. Baltimore: Johns Hopkins Press, 1963.

City Studies

Hall, Peter. *The World Cities*. New York: McGraw-Hill, 1966.
Green, Constance M. *American Cities*. New York: Harper, 1957.
Jacobs, Jane. *The Death and Life of Great American Cities*. New York: Random House, 1961.

INDEX

American Public Health Association, 47

Appraisal: in investment, 241–242, 380; methods, 244–246, 407–410, 476; institutional requirements, 419–422; and economic system, 444, 451

Brokers: ethics, 12; functions, 55, 174–175, 379, 410–417; institutional requirements, 422–425; and economic system, 444–445, 452

Budget ratio, 179–183, 233

Builders: ethics, 12, 425; equipment, 135–136. *See also* Construction

Building materials: scarcity, 132–133; social cost, 197–198; in Japan, 197; and safety, 197; innovations, 197–198; capital requirements, 198. *See also* Construction

Capital-output ratio. *See* Economic development

Capitalization: and durability, 15; method, 244–246; rate, 245–246, 409; reversionary value, 243; and land use succession, 247, 249. *See also* Appraisal; Equity Investment

City size: spatial extent, 114; economies of scale, 159–167. *See also* Density; Land; Migration; New communities; Population; Transportation

Collectivism, 83–85

Congestion, 158

Construction: statistics, 46; forecasts, 98–110, 140–141; prefabrication, 115, 134, 496; and labor supply, 135; scale economies, 188–189, 213; "gestation period," 194; temporary dwellings, 217–218; planning, 286–288, 291–292; contracting, 286, 425; financing, 296; and building codes, 464; rehabilitation, 489. *See also* Builders; Econometrics; Housing inputs

Density: definition, 46; and building materials, 132; optimum, 156, 161–167, 345–350, 386; and transport cost, 162, 346–347, 446; and capital markets, 163; and durability, 165; and speculation, 165; and replacement, 193; and location, 316; and redevelopment, 482. *See also* City size; Population; Transportation

Depreciation: and replacement, 108; in capitalization rate, 246; tax incentive, 258, 492, 496–497

Developer. *See* Entrepreneur

Durability. *See* Economic life

Ecology, 89–92

Econometrics, 51, 108, 140–141. *See also* Construction

Economic analysis, 48–53, 98, 138–140. *See also* Entrepreneur

Economic base, 110–115, 168, 278, 491

Economic development: and housing sector, 200, 205–223; capital-output ratio, 205–223 *passim;* and migration, 208; forced saving, 209–212;

Sunk cost, 19–20, 37, 248, 325, 358, 365–371, 402, 434. *See also* Filtering; Housing inputs; Housing inventory
"Swing land." *See* Land

Tenant rights, 9, 130, 204
Tokyo, 359
Transportation: cost and housing location, 7, 97, 127–128, 133, 156–158, 162, 324, 330, 341–345, 365, 386; system, 11, 187, 191, 284; density trade-off, 346–347, 446. *See also* Density; Land; Land use patterns
Turnover, 146–148

Urban economics, 88–89
Urban redevelopment, 467–483 *pas-*

sim. See also Government role in housing sector; Replacement
Utility systems, 8, 26, 47, 116, 128. *See also* Government role in housing sector; Neighborhood; Transportation

Vacancy: concept, 99, 145–146; types, 100, 145, 175, 251; and turnover, 146–148; optimum level, 173–176; in operating plan, 239–241; in United States, 468. *See also* Housing demand
Veterans Administration, 476
Von Thuenen, Heinrich, 329–334, 351, 353, 364

Zoning. *See* Government role in housing sector